LAW AND ECONOMICS OF POSSESSION

Possession is a key concept in both the common and civil law, but it has hitherto received little scrutiny. *Law and Economics of Possession* uses insights from economics, psychology, and history to analyze possession in law, compare and contrast possession with ownership, break down the elements of possession as a fact and as a right, challenge the adage that "possession is nine-tenths of the law," examine possession as notice, explain the heuristics of possession, debunk the behavioral studies that confuse possession with ownership, and explore the LightSquared dispute from the perspective of "possession" of spectrum frequency. The book also provides new insights into old doctrines, such as first possession, adverse possession, and property jurisdiction. The authors include leading property scholars, who examine possession laws in, among others, the USA, UK, China, Taiwan, Japan, Germany, France, Israel, the Netherlands, Spain, Portugal, Italy, and Austria.

YUN-CHIEN CHANG is Associate Research Professor at Institutum Iurisprudentiae, Academia Sinica, Taiwan, where he also serves as the Co-Director of its Empirical Legal Studies Center.

LAW AND ECONOMICS OF POSSESSION

Edited by
YUN-CHIEN CHANG

CAMBRIDGE
UNIVERSITY PRESS

University Printing House, Cambridge CB2 8BS, United Kingdom

Cambridge University Press is part of the University of Cambridge.

It furthers the University's mission by disseminating knowledge in the pursuit of education, learning and research at the highest international levels of excellence.

www.cambridge.org
Information on this title: www.cambridge.org/9781107083547

© Cambridge University Press 2015

This publication is in copyright. Subject to statutory exception and to the provisions of relevant collective licensing agreements, no reproduction of any part may take place without the written permission of Cambridge University Press.

First published 2015

A catalogue record for this publication is available from the British Library

Library of Congress Cataloguing in Publication data
Law and economics of possession / edited by Yun-chien Chang.
pages cm
ISBN 978-1-107-08354-7 (Hardback)
1. Possession (Law) I. Chang, Yun-chien, editor.
K726.L39 2015
346.04–dc23   2014039860

ISBN 978-1-107-08354-7 Hardback

Cambridge University Press has no responsibility for the persistence or accuracy of URLs for external or third-party internet websites referred to in this publication, and does not guarantee that any content on such websites is, or will remain, accurate or appropriate.

To Vera and Phil, who motivate and inspire me

CONTENTS

List of figures   xi
List of contributors   xii

Introduction   1
YUN-CHIEN CHANG

I   **Foundation**   7

1 **Ownership and possession**   9
THOMAS W. MERRILL
1. Introduction   9
2. How possession differs from ownership   11
3. The law protects possession independently of ownership   18
4. Previous explanations for legal protection of possession   20
5. Possession in the material world   24
6. Possession, ownership, and information costs   27
7. The interaction of ownership and possession   34
Conclusion   37

2 **The law is nine-tenths of possession: an adage turned on its head**   40
CAROL M. ROSE
1. Introduction   40
2. Theorists and jurists   41
3. Possession as a legal concept   49
4. The independent normative claims of acting like an owner   55
5. Adverse possession revisited: the claim of right   57
Conclusion   60

3 **The elements of possession**   65
HENRY E. SMITH
1. Introduction   65

2. Possession and the basic conventions of property   69
3. The generalization of possession   80
4. The persistence of possession   88
Conclusion   96

4 The economy of concept and possession   103
YUN-CHIEN CHANG
1. Introduction   103
2. The nature of possessory rights   108
3. Possession as a basis for acquiring or relinquishing titles   113
4. Possession as a fact   117
Conclusion   124

5 What behavioral studies can teach jurists about possession and vice versa   128
DAPHNA LEWINSOHN-ZAMIR
1. Introduction   128
2. Nonphysical possession   130
3. Possession versus ownership   136
Conclusion   142

6 The possession heuristic   149
JAMES KRIER AND CHRISTOPHER SERKIN
1. Introduction   149
2. Evolution and the possession heuristic   150
3. Possession, priority, and ownership   152
4. Applications, problems, and fixes   154
5. Possession and property   168

7 Dividing possessory rights   175
DANIEL B. KELLY
1. Introduction   175
2. Types of division   179
3. Private incentive to divide may be suboptimal   182
4. Private incentive to divide may be excessive   186
5. Theories justifying restrictions on division   191
6. Applications   198
Conclusion   201

8 The titling role of possession   207

BENITO ARRUÑADA

1. A general theory of impersonal exchange   207
2. Hypotheses on reliance on possession as evidence for titling   212
3. The informational value of physical possession in commercial exchange   216
4. The informational value of possession in real property exchange   220
5. The informational value of documentary possession   226

II Specific issues   235

9 Possession and licenses: the FCC, weak spectrum rights, and the LightSquared debacle   237

RICHARD A. EPSTEIN

1. Introduction: possession and ownership, then and now   237
2. Ownership and possession of land and chattels   238
3. Spectrum rights: property or license   246
4. The LightSquared debacle   254

10 Jurisdiction, choice of law, and property   266

DANIEL KLERMAN

1. Introduction   266
2. Choice of law   269
3. Jurisdiction   281
Conclusion   287

11 Small property, adverse possession, and optional law   290

SHITONG QIAO

1. Introduction   290
2. Challenging property law through small property   291
3. Framing the question: adverse possession in Ayres' cathedral   296
4. Structuring legal entitlements for small property   302
Conclusion: an optional law approach to informal property rights   315

12 Title in the shadow of possession   320

ABRAHAM BELL

1. Introduction   320
2. Justifying the importance of possession   321
3. Possession as a valuable attribute   324
4. Different kinds of property rights   325
5. Lawful and unlawful possession   328

6. Black markets   329
7. Preventing black markets in possessory assets   331
8. Custom as an analogue   332
9. Salvage as an alternative   333
Conclusion   334

Index   338

FIGURES

9.1 Normal distribution of frequencies   252
9.2 Distribution of spectrum   255

CONTRIBUTORS

BENITO ARRUÑADA, Professor of Business Organization, Pompeu Fabra University and Barcelona Graduate School of Economics.

ABRAHAM BELL, Professor of Law, Bar Ilan University Faculty of Law and University of San Diego School of Law.

YUN-CHIEN CHANG, Associate Research Professor, Institutum Iurisprudentiae, Academia Sinica.

RICHARD EPSTEIN, Laurence A. Tisch Professor of Law, New York University School of Law; the Peter and Kirsten Bedford Senior Fellow at Stanford University's Hoover Institution; James Parker Hall Distinguished Service Professor of Law Emeritus and Senior Lecturer, the University of Chicago Law School.

DANIEL KELLY, Professor of Law, University of Notre Dame Law School.

DANIEL KLERMAN, Charles L. and Ramona I. Hilliard Professor of Law and History, Gould School of Law, University of Southern California.

JAMES KRIER, Earl Warren DeLano Professor of Law, University of Michigan Law School.

DAPHNA LEWINSOHN-ZAMIR, Louis Marshall Professor of Environmental Law, Hebrew University of Jerusalem.

THOMAS MERRILL, Charles Evans Hughes Professor of Law, Columbia Law School.

SHITONG QIAO, Assistant Professor, Hong Kong University Faculty of Law.

CAROL ROSE, Gordon Bradford Tweedy Professor Emeritus of Law and Organization and Professorial Lecturer in Law, Yale Law School; Lohse Chair in Water and Natural Resources, University of Arizona College of Law.

CHRISTOPHER SERKIN, Professor of Law, Vanderbilt Law School.

HENRY SMITH, Fessenden Professor of Law, Harvard Law School.

Introduction

YUN-CHIEN CHANG

Possession is a two-thousand-year-old institution, and scholars have debated the concept of possession since the mid-nineteenth century, but modern scholars lack consensus on the definition of possession. Although common-law countries appear to avoid exactly defining possession, civil codes in the European Continent and East Asia take on the challenge. They differ, however, over how possession is and should be delineated. Some countries, such as France and the Netherlands, distinguish possession from detention, whereas others, for example Germany and Taiwan, use the terms "possessors" and "agents in possession." A few jurisdictions, such as Japan and Korea, consider possession to be a right while others, for instance China, treat it as a fact. Some civil codes, such as those of Germany and Taiwan, simply define possession as actual control, but others, for instance France's and the Netherlands', also require specific intents. In short, the concept of possession is either ambiguous or messy.

Law and economics has been the dominant legal analytical approach for the past half-century, yet rarely have scholars applied economic analysis to various possession issues. This timely book fills the gap. Leading economic lawyers from both common law and civil law jurisdictions offer their insightful treatment of possession, some at the abstract level, and others toward a specific issue.

The book begins with Thomas Merrill's "Ownership and Possession." Merrill analyzes the concepts and relations of possession and ownership from the perspective of information costs. Possession imposes low information costs in the world of "strangers," whereas ownership, harder to prove, requires more information costs in order to conduct impersonal exchange. In the modern world where recording or registration of titles is cheaply available, the reason to continue protecting possession independently of ownership is to expand access to law as a means to enforce property rights.

Carol Rose, in Chapter 2, analyzes the proverb "possession is nine-tenths of the law," inquiring what the other point of the law is (one regular candidate being provenance) and whether this proverb is an accurate description of the world. Rose argues that possession is not just about physical control (compare Chapter 4), or the right to exclude, but about acting like an owner. Generally, using makes one act like an owner. She finds support for such a claim from the case law of first possession and adverse possession. Rose also emphasizes the importance of community support and recognition of possession. Her takeaway point is that when the law is weak, possession is nine-tenths of the law. By contrast, when the law is settled, the law is nine-tenths of possession.

Henry Smith offers a modular theory of possession. Like Rose, Smith emphasizes salience in identifying and delineating possession. For Smith, along the same lines with longtime coauthor Merrill, possession is very much based on social norms and is the default in property law because it is low-cost and intuitive for the public. More formalized legal tools, such as ownership, will be used only when stakes become high. Note that possession itself is a formalized version of the possessory custom, the ultimate default regime for assigning things to persons. Possession thus exhibits what Smith calls the "elsewhere pattern," meaning that "possession is defined by not being anything else." More specifically, possession is the most basic rule in many scenarios, and possession applies when nothing else does. Smith also observes that although civil law treats property as the law of things, common law eschews this notion. However, the function that the concept of things served in civil law is captured by the concept of possession in the common law. Possession (with close ties to customs and informal norms) and accession work in tandem to determine thinghood.

In a sense, my chapter, "The Economy of Concept and Possession," serves as the book's point of departure. Drawing on Henry Smith's economy of concept theory, Chapter 4 argues that a simpler concept of possession (with actual control as the necessary and sufficient condition) economizes on information costs and makes the possession law much more comprehensive. The confusion in the civil codes and the scholarly literature arises from conflation of three different concepts: possession as a fact; possession as a (subsidiary) right that is one stick in the ownership bundle; and possession as a basis for acquiring and relinquishing titles, as in adverse possession, first possession, and abandonment. Actual control is the least common denominator in all possession-related issues; thus, possession qua actual control is a fact. The subsidiary possessory right is implied in the property structure, but it is never spelled out. It can be transferred from owners to, for example, holders of *usufruct*. Finally, intents only matter when possessors gain or lose titles, and the required intents differ across contexts; thus, a specific intent should not be embedded in the baseline definition of possession, but left to specific doctrines.

Several chapters in this volume contrast, if not challenge, my simplified definition of possession with their own. For example, Merrill argues that actual control carries more weight than intent to possess, though the latter alone might be honored, at least in the "social possession" context. My chapter, which is concerned more with "legal possession," dismisses the role of intent to possess when no title change is involved. In addition, Daphna Lewinsohn-Zamir makes a case for "the new possession," that is, broadening the domain of possession to intangible entitlements, while Chapter 4 argues that the concept of possession, at least in the civil law system, should be simplified. These two views are not in direct conflict with each other, as I prefer not to describe "holding intangible entitlements" as possession – otherwise the concept of possession becomes overly complex again. In Chapter 9, Richard Epstein contends that actual control, the critical element in my concept, is not always easy to ascertain.

Lewinsohn-Zamir, in Chapter 5, draws on the findings of behavioral-law-and-economists. She takes these researchers to task for failing to distinguish possession from ownership (not to mention lawful from unlawful possession), but notes that the few studies that attend to the difference suggest that possession itself looms large in creating the "endowment effect."

Like Lewinsohn-Zamir, James Krier and Christopher Serkin, in Chapter 6, draw on the psychological literature, most notably the System 1 versus System 2 theory popularized by Daniel Kahnemann. Krier and Serkin point out that the scholarship of Thomas Merrill and Henry Smith (both contributors to this volume) focuses on information costs and the right to exclude; thus, their views can be characterized as emphasizing the quick but error-prone role of System 1. Other scholars, by contrast, stress the importance of making complex arrangements in property law to promote normative goals, such as human flourishing. It takes the sharp but energy-consuming System 2 to perform this trick. As their chapter title suggests, Krier and Serkin focus on possession as a heuristic, echoing Merrill, in Chapter 1. They powerfully apply their possession heuristics thesis to criticize the theoretical literature and court decisions in the realm of relativity of title, first possession (capture) of wild and domesticated animals and natural resources, finders of lost versus mislaid movables, shared possession in concurrent ownership, and adverse possession, several of which are also discussed in other chapters of this book.

Daniel Kelly, in Chapter 7, critically reviews the (scant) literature on whether an owner's private incentive to divide possessory rights will exceed the socially optimal level. Kelly contends that most costs and benefits of such division are internalized, and thus fragmentation is unlikely, particularly for tangible objects. As in the two preceding chapters, Kelly draws on the psychology literature, observing that individuals are inclined to hold full rights (rather than partial rights) in a resource. Contributing to the debate on the efficiency of the *numerus clausus* principle, Kelly points out that property forms, as compared to contracts, better deter strategic behaviors, implying that in areas where owners' incentives to divide possessory rights are suboptimal, adding new property forms could improve efficiency, as new property forms facilitate division.

Focusing on information costs, as the Merrill, Smith, and Chang chapters do, Benito Arruñada, in Chapter 8, examines how possession gives notice to facilitate impersonal exchange. Drawing examples from the Roman law and medieval English law to modern German and US law, Arruñada demonstrates that "exercise" of possession is effective as a titling mechanism when it is observable by third parties and "delivery" of possession (for example, livery of seisin) is public knowledge. In addition, as possession is only effective to inform one single in rem right, relying on possession for titling requires that all other rights be either reduced to in personam status or be burdened by the possessory in rem right. Arruñada also analyzes documentary possession (such as possession of negotiable instruments), and argues that documentary possession is effective as a titling mechanism only in the absence of multiple in rem rights.

Part II of this volume comprises four chapters that deal with more specific possession issues. Richard Epstein, in Chapter 9, focuses on spectrum rights, particularly the so-called LightSquared Debacle. He begins with a restatement of possession versus ownership law in Roman and English law (also discussed in Chapter 8), tracing the concept of possession. After a detailed description of the LightSquared controversy, Epstein points out that the weak property rights given to spectrum licensees are due to the FCC's ill-advised regulatory policy. He argues that the same system of possession and property rights used in the common law is also applicable to spectrum, which more resembles trade names and trademarks than copyrights and patents. The nuisance law, in particular, can be carried over to protect holders of broadband interests.

Daniel Klerman, in Chapter 10, analyzes choice of law and jurisdiction issues in property, with appropriation of water, adverse possession of stolen arts, and first possession of wild animals as the prominent examples. Klerman argues that the situs rule is mostly correct, in terms of giving individuals, legislators, and judges the right incentives to behave efficiently (such as making efficient laws or making best use of the land and attendant water). In the context of adverse possession of stolen arts, however, a choice of law rule that applies the law of the last place of undisputed ownership gives the relevant parties the best incentives. Regarding jurisdictional issues, although Klerman points out that there is no clear-cut best rule in stolen arts issues, he contends that the courts of the place where the art was last undisputedly owned are good candidates.

Shitong Qiao, in Chapter 11, focuses on a unique adverse possession problem: "small property" in Shenzhen, the fourth largest city in China. In China, rural land is collectively owned, whereas urban land is state-owned. Only urban land can be commercially developed, and the only way to convert rural land to urban land is through eminent domain. The economic development in Shenzhen in the past few decades was faster than the pace of providing enough (affordable) housing by the government. As a result, farmers/villagers in Shenzhen started to build illegal houses and condominiums despite the legal ban. That is, they adversely possessed and developed public land. Without an adverse possession law, developers could not acquire formal title to the buildings and only had "small property rights." Using the optional law framework that Calabresi and Melamed initiated in 1972 and Ian Ayres systematized in recent years, Qiao demonstrates that Rules 1, 2, 3, 4, and 6 have all been used by the Shenzhen government to deal with the illegal buildings that fly in the face of land use regulations. With first-hand materials (such as interviews with government officials, developers, and villagers and on-site observations) from his yearlong fieldwork in Shenzhen, Qiao argues that Rule 2 (a call-option liability rule) is the most efficient in dealing with the small-property conundrum, because of information asymmetry between the government and the numerous holders of small-property rights.

In the final chapter, Abraham Bell leads us to one of the most famous possession doctrines, the first possession rule, and reexamines the normative impulse for property law's use of possession as a key to acquiring greater property rights. Bell challenges Richard Epstein's classic view in his seminal article, "Possession as the Root of Title." Epstein posits that first possession is an essential rule in property law primarily because it long has been used, and it provides for rapid dissemination of private property rights. Bell argues that in some cases property law recognizes first possession as a source of title for an entirely different reason: it is essential to recognize rights *de jure* that already exist *de facto*, lest the legal system of property lose its salience. Put differently, if the law did not recognize legal rights as a result of possession, many first possessors would find it advantageous to eschew legal rights and protect their possessory rights extra legally. Indeed, in cases where the law denies property rights notwithstanding possession, robust extralegal asset markets have developed, undermining the goals that led lawmakers to split property rights from possession. Examples of this phenomenon can be found, for instance, in the markets for illegal antiquities and natural resources. However, first possession is often a problematic way to allocate title; salvage rules can often provide an alternative that both rewards *de facto* possession and reduces wasteful overexploitation.

This book grows out of the 5th Law and Economic Analysis conference held in Institutum Iurisprudentiae, Academia Sinica, Taiwan, organized by the editor Yun-chien Chang. Several contributors presented their draft chapters at the conference. More chapters were solicited after the conference. I deeply appreciate the financial support of my home institution. Chiehhan Wang, Han-shin Lin, Apple Ching-fang Hsu, Ivan Chiang, and many others helped at the conference. Charline Jao and Christine Yuan provided valuable research assistance as I compiled this volume.

I

Foundation

1

Ownership and possession

THOMAS W. MERRILL

1. Introduction

One of the enduring mysteries about property is why the law protects both ownership and possession. In a pre-modern world, with low rates of literacy and no formal method of registering titles, one can understand why the law would protect possession. In such a world, there may be no concept of property beyond the understanding that persons should respect possessory rights established by others. It is less clear why possession should be protected once property comes to be understood as ownership. Ownership and possession will commonly overlap, and protecting ownership will protect possession. Nevertheless, even in the most sophisticated legal systems, where digital records and title registries protect ownership, possession continues to be legally protected independently of ownership. The objective of this chapter is to explain the persistence of this dual nature of property law, whereby the law protects both ownership and possession.

The thesis advanced is that information costs explain why possession persists as a distinct subject of legal protection in a world that has otherwise fully embraced the concept of ownership. The great advantage of possession is low information costs. The cultural knowledge that communicates when others possess tangible objects is easily assimilated without formal instruction by virtually everyone in the relevant community. Armed with this knowledge, individuals can tell at a glance based on physical cues what things others possess, and their ability to draw these rapid inferences makes possession a low-cost tool well suited to processing information about large numbers of persons and objects. Respect for possession established by others is also a nearly universally shared norm – one

---

Charles Evans Hughes Professor, Columbia Law School. An earlier version of this chapter was given as the keynote address at the 5th Law and Economic Analysis Conference at the Institutum Iurisprudentiae, Academic Sinica, Taiwan. I thank the conference participants and especially Yun-chien Chang for their many helpful responses and suggestions.

that operates both in informal social settings and with respect to conduct regulated by law. Not surprisingly then, possession continues to be relied upon in a wide range of activities in establishing who is entitled to what, ranging from assignment of work stations in offices, to retrieval of suitcases from luggage carrousels, to low-valued commercial transactions.

Ownership is a more secure basis for determining rights to things, in the sense that it identifies those who have a legally enforceable right to things to the exclusion of all other potential claimants. Establishing ownership entails an investigation into the history of the object in question in order to ascertain whether those who purport to have legally enforceable rights came to acquire those rights in a legitimate fashion. Ordinarily, this means that the rights must have been acquired through a series of consensual transfers, although occasionally questions of original acquisition arise. Although establishing ownership provides much greater security of rights than establishing possession, it is clearly much more information-intensive. It entails investigating the chain of title or provenance of the object, which entails consulting deeds, previous contracts of sale, or registries of rights.

The information-cost differential between establishing possession and ownership explains why the concept of possession continues to perform critical functions even in a society that has a legal system that protects ownership. Establishing ownership is cost-effective for the relatively small audience of persons interested in engaging in exchange of particular high valued rights to things. Establishing ownership is much too costly, however, for everyday purposes of determining who is entitled to what. For those whose interest in valuable things is simply to avoid interfering with the rights of others, ascertaining possession and respecting possession established by others is far cheaper, indeed, it operates virtually automatically without conscious thought. Possession also works well in numerous settings where ownership is legally relevant, but making a formal determination of ownership would represent an excessive information-cost burden. Possession in these contexts serves as a low-cost proxy for ownership.

The information-cost differential explains why possession performs critical functions in society, but it does not explain why the law continues to protect possession as opposed to relying solely on the social norm of respect for possession established by others. Part of the answer is that the law itself seeks in many ways to capitalize on the information-cost conserving features of possession. The classic example is conferring standing on persons in possession to bring actions against those who interfere with property rights. Since proving possession is much cheaper in information-cost terms than proving ownership, this greatly expands access to law as a means of enforcing property rights. More generally, given the widespread social norm of respect for possession established by others, it makes sense for the law to draw upon and integrate the concept of possession into the law of property. By harmonizing legal protection of ownership with protection of possession, the law of property enjoys greater public support and legitimacy than it would if law protected ownership alone.

2. How possession differs from ownership

Before trying to explain why the law protects both ownership and possession, it is important to clarify what these concepts mean. Skepticism about whether either term has a common core of meaning dominates the Anglo-American literature.[1] I think this skepticism is overdrawn. Both concepts do far too much work in ordinary discourse as well as law to be empty placeholders for some kind of situation-specific balancing exercise. It is of course true that there will be disputes over which of two persons has a better claim to be "in possession" in some contexts. It also is true that the prerogatives of "ownership" will differ from one society to another and even from one type of asset to another (Merrill 2012). However, disagreements about application of a concept do not mean that the concept is itself empty. Nor do differences in the full specification of rights associated with a concept mean that the concept lacks a core of meaning common to all variations.

2.1. *Possession*

If we look back to earlier scholarship, roughly speaking before the rise of Legal Realism, we find broad agreement about the meaning of possession. Here the seminal thinkers were Oliver Wendell Holmes and Frederick Pollock, both of whom relied on German legal scholars like von Savigny, who sought to explicate the meaning of possession in Roman Law (Pollock and Wright 1888: 1–42; Holmes 1881: 130–94; von Savigny 1848: 1–112; see Gordley and Mattei 1996: 294; Posner 2000: 536–51). For these nineteenth-century commentators, possession refers to a particular relationship between a person and a thing. That relationship consists of the person establishing control over the thing, and behaving in such a way that others recognize that he or she intends to maintain control over the thing. Control here means the ability to exclude others

---

[1] Skepticism about any common core of meaning of possession can be found among both English (Harris 1961) and American (Reisman 1939; Shartel 1932) authors. Americans also tend to be skeptical about ownership (Grey 1980).

from the thing. To be in possession of a thing is to acquire enough control to exclude others, and thereafter to signal to others an intention to continue excluding others from the thing (Bingham 1915: 549; Hickey 2010: 97).[2]

In the civil law tradition, as Yun-chien Chang documents (Chapter 4), there is significant disagreement about which aspect of possession properly deserves emphasis. Civil law codes and commentators sometimes describe possession as a fact, and sometimes regard it as a right. They also disagree about whether the critical attribute of possession is actual control of a thing, or intention to control a thing. As he further observes, common law systems are much more casual about identifying the precise features that define possession, and exhibit a tendency to treat possession and ownership at least implicitly as interchangeable concepts.

Without purporting to offer any definitive resolution of these issues, it may be useful to consider how possession operates in various social settings where law does not directly enter the picture. Lawyers and judges tend to focus on possession in circumstances where it intersects with legal doctrine, for example under the rule of first possession or the doctrine of adverse possession. But possession often operates as a purely social norm to organize relationships between persons and valued objects. Considering how possession functions in these nonlegal contexts may help us identify some salient features of possession, without worrying that they have been introduced because of their significance in the law of property.[3] I will describe two examples where possession operates as a social norm, although there are many more as to which the same or similar points could be made.[4]

---

[2] Thus, for example, the Restatement (First) of Property defines "possessory interest in land" to mean "a physical relation to the land of a kind which gives a certain degree of physical control over the land, and an intent so to exercise such control as to exclude other members of society in general from any present occupation of the land" (American Law Institute § 7).

[3] Anglo-American scholars, following the lead of Pollock, often distinguish between "de facto possession" and "legal possession" (Pollock and Wright 1888: 11–20). I tend to agree with Salmond, who commented, "There are not two ideas of possession – a legal and a natural ... There is only one idea, to which the actual rules of law do more or less imperfectly conform"(Salmond 1924: 295).

[4] Other examples might include claiming spots on a beach, parking places in a lot, or carrels in a library; waiting in queues, the assignment of rooms within a home, the allocation of fishing spots in open access waters, and so forth. American professors who teach property are particularly fond of using the example of possessory rights in parking places shoveled out after heavy snowstorms, perhaps because of its Lockean overtones (Epstein 2002).

The first example concerns the allocation of seats in a movie theater. Here, the common practice is to allocate seats on a first come, first-served basis; that is, by first possession. The first persons to enter the theater choose which seats they wish to occupy, and sit down in those seats. Presumably, these are relatively desirable seats, or at least ones that the initial patrons find desirable. Later arrivals select unoccupied seats, which they occupy. The process continues, with seats becoming progressively less desirable, until all the seats in the theater are full. The use of possession as a principle of allocation here is entirely a matter of owner discretion; law does not require it. The theater owner owns all the seats, and could choose another method of allocation, such as selling only reserved seats, but tacitly allows patrons to select their own seats using the concept of possession.

One important thing to notice about allocating theater seats by possession is that no one requires instruction in the operation of the system. Perhaps young children, when they first attend a theater, require some explanation from their parents, or perhaps they simply sense how the system works by observation. But a primary reason theaters use this method of seat allocation is that it is self-executing; it operates without any need to hire ushers or otherwise expend resources matching patrons with seats. A second important point about the possession system is that it is almost unheard of for someone to use force or threats of force to take a seat that already is occupied. Polite requests to move down or consolidate a row are not uncommon, but there are no forcible ejections. Once a seat is possessed, there is universal respect for possession previously established by others.

There are some interesting details in the way in which the system of theater seat allocation operates. Often a patron will arrive, claim a seat, and will then make a quick trip to the lobby to use the restroom or buy concessions. The patron will mark his seat with a coat or other article of clothing, or perhaps will ask a neighboring patron to "save" his seat. These symbolic markings (or appointments of gratuitous agents) signify an existing claim of possession that other patrons usually honor. In other words, continuous "actual" control of the seat is not required, but merely a communication showing that control has been established and that the patron intends to resume control. The exact form of the communication will presumably vary from one culture to another, but it does not appear that any formal instruction is required to teach patrons about this. Sometimes a group of friends will decide to attend the theater together, and one member of the group will enter the theater before the others arrive. Here, too, the early arriving patron will often attempt to claim multiple seats in a row by marking the seats in some fashion, perhaps with various articles of clothing. These claims of future intent to control may also be honored, although if the theater fills up and the friends do not arrive, it is likely that other patrons will challenge the legitimacy of the claimed multiple seats, and this challenge may force the early arriving patron to relinquish the seats. Evidently, signaling an intention to exercise future control over a seat carries some normative weight, but less so than actual control followed by a manifestation of an intention to remain in control.

The second example concerns the allocation of offices and workstations in a corporation or other organization. Here, a first-come, first-served system is not used. Instead, offices and workstations will be assigned to particular individuals by the head of the department or by some other system like seniority, with the understanding that the individual is entitled to exclusive use of his or her workspace. In organizations with a high degree of stability, like universities, the assignment of offices can persist for decades. In organizations with a short life span, or with high rates of turnover, the assignment of workspaces will change much more frequently. At any given time, however, everyone working in the organization will understand which employees are assigned to occupy which offices or work stations. Law compels none of this. The corporation (or organization) owns all the offices and workstations, and it could allocate them any way it wants without legal constraint. For example, it could allocate these spaces by lottery on a daily basis. Similarly, no employee has a legally enforceable right to any particular workspace. The system is governed entirely by rules or norms that have evolved within each organization.

Corporations and organizations give particular persons possession of particular offices and work stations because this is more efficient than other methods of allocating workspaces. Stability of possession allows individual workers to customize their space in order to facilitate their particular tasks and create a congenial work environment. For example, workers may install particular programs on their computer, may keep particular reference books in their space, or may decorate their space with family photographs. The degree to which each individual exercises exclusive control over an assigned workspace will vary from one organization to another and from one type of office or workspace to another. Senior employees with separate offices will typically be able to keep their office locked when they are away, although supervisors and security guards will likely be able to gain access if need be. Lower-level employees with workstations cannot exclude others from the space, but may be able to keep drawers with sensitive papers or special keepsakes locked. Likewise, the permissible degree of individual modification of workspaces varies considerably from one organization to another and one type of workspace to another. The information about the permissible degree of exclusivity and customization generally is not communicated in any formal fashion but is assimilated by observing what others do.

As in the case of theater seats, forcible evictions from offices or workstations are extremely rare. When employees die or quit, they (or their heirs) are usually given a grace period to clean out personal effects. When employees are fired, they may have to remove their personal property more quickly. Otherwise, employees and supervisors respect each employee's personal workspace. As with theater seats, continuous actual control is not required. If employees leave for vacation, and lock their office or their desk before they depart, everything will be the same when they return. A more prolonged absence, perhaps a sick leave or a temporary reassignment to another city, may result in another employee occupying the space on a temporary basis. However, the original occupant will generally regain possession when he or she returns. An interesting, but rare situation would be an employee being assigned an office but for some reason never showing up to claim it. My guess would be that this space, if not reassigned, eventually would be treated as a workroom or hideaway for other employees. In other words, a bare intention to claim possession without ever establishing actual control of the space will be regarded as weaker than a claim backed by actual control.

What generalizations can we draw from these examples of "social possession"? One is that both actual control and an intention to remain in control are important in establishing possession, as Holmes (1881) and Pollock and Wright (1888) asserted. Others may honor a manifest intention to control a resource without establishing actual control. But establishing actual control carries significantly more weight, whether it is control of a theater seat or space in an office. At the same time, once control is established, others will generally respect an intention to maintain control. Theater patrons can leave their seats temporarily and, if they have signaled an intention to return, that intention will be respected. The same holds for employees who leave their offices to go on vacation.

A second generalization is that establishing control and evincing an intention to maintain control entail communication. As Carol Rose (1994) puts it, possession "looks like a kind of speech, with the audience composed of all others who might be interested in claiming the object in question" (Rose 1994: 14; see also Smith 2003: 1117–22). In many cases, the relevant communicative act is self-evident. Sitting in a seat or at a workstation will be construed by all as a claim to control the relevant space, and hence to be "in possession" of it. When actual control is temporarily relinquished, however, it is necessary to perform a symbolic act that others will understand as evincing an intention to remain in control. Often this will be an act that easily is understood as such a signal, such as an employee locking the office door when leaving. Other symbolic acts, like draping a coat over the back of a seat in the theater, require some cultural knowledge. Consequently, the precise actions that signal an intention to establish or remain in possession will turn on local custom, at least to a degree. Perhaps the most famous illustration of this is the nineteenth-century whaling industry, where different whaling communities followed different conventions in determining when a particular whaling boat had secured possession over a particular whale (Ellickson 1989). Still, while the communicative acts may differ from one community to another, members of the community appear to assimilate the relevant communicative acts quite easily and without formal instruction.

A third generalization is that respect for possession established by others is a widespread norm in human societies. Whether or not possession is a fact (perhaps a "social fact?"), respect for possession obviously is a norm. I strongly suspect (although I cannot prove) that all or virtually all human groups recognize the norm of respecting possession established by others. Thus, one does not need to have a formal legal system to have possession. Respect for possession is especially prominent within "close-knit" communities like workers in an office or the members of a household (Ellickson 2008: 117–19). But it also emerges in gatherings of strangers, such as patrons waiting to see a movie in the theater. One could perhaps say that the moviegoers share a common purpose – to view the movie without undue disruptions such as conflicts over seats. This common purpose may suppress any impulse toward taking resources that others possess. Where there is no close-knit community and no common purpose, respect for possession established by others may break down. Especially under circumstances of war or ethnic strife, respect for possession may give way to looting. Still, it is remarkable that in a wide variety of settings, including both close-knit communities and gatherings of strangers, respect for possession appears to arise spontaneously, and provides a means of establishing an ordered relationship between persons and valued things.

2.2. Ownership

The meaning of ownership, like the meaning of possession, is contested. As in the case of possession, the disputes may have more to do with which features of the institution to emphasize, rather than offering up radically different conceptions. I have argued elsewhere that ownership always entails, as one of its constituent elements, the right to control a thing, or if you will, the legal right to exclude others from a thing (Merrill 1998; see also Penner 1997: 68–104; Chang and Smith 2012). This is not to deny that ownership may also entail other important elements, such as the right to use the thing, to consume it, to transfer it to others, and so forth. However, the right to exclude is an irreducible common denominator. Give people the right to exclude others from a thing and they have property; deny them the right to exclude others and they do not have property.

Superficially, this sounds a lot like possession. Both possession and ownership refer to control of things, in the sense of excluding others from things. But in fact, there are important differences. Possession requires that a person perform acts that are understood to constitute *actual* control over a thing. Ownership does not require actual control; one can own a thing without ever having been in actual control at all. Similarly, possession requires that a person communicate an *intention* to remain in control over a thing. Again, no such intention is required of an owner; one can own a thing and intend never to actually control it. In short, one can be a possessor without being an owner, and one can be an owner without being a possessor, although being an owner ordinarily entails the right to determine who will be the possessor. Indeed, owners of things will commonly designate themselves to be the possessor. To the extent they do, ownership and possession will coincide. However, this is not always true.

Two further generalizations about ownership and its relationship to possession seem clear. Possession, or respect for possession, as previously noted, often exists as a social norm without the explicit sanction in law. Ownership, in contrast, exists only within the context of a formal legal system. When ownership is contested, duly constituted authorities charged with the resolution of legal disputes must resolve the conflict. There may be a social norm of respecting ownership without regard to possession. If so, it is most likely an aspect of a more general social norm supporting respect for the law.

It is also clear that ownership, where it exists, trumps possession, even legally protected possession. Owners can oust possessors who do not have their permission to occupy or use a thing (although they may have to get a court order to do so). Owners can also transfer possession of things temporarily to others, as through bailment or lease, and then regain (or retransfer) possession of the thing later.

I will have more to say later about the ways in which possession differs from ownership – differences relevant to an information-cost explanation of why the law protects both ownership and possession. First, it is necessary to establish that the law does in fact protect possession, separately and independently of its protection of ownership.

3. The law protects possession independently of ownership

The examples reviewed earlier demonstrate that respect for possession often exists as a social norm without any direct sanction or compulsion in law. Does law also sometimes protect possession? In other words, can possession constitute a legally protected right, independent of legal protection of ownership? It is easy to show that possession plays an important role in property law. Whether or not it is more than "nine points in the law" (Chapter 2), possession is unquestionably important. It can lead to ownership, as in the rule of first possession or adverse possession. In addition, it is often used as a proxy for ownership, as in low-level commercial transactions or in determining who has standing to sue under torts like trespass and conversion. In each of these contexts, however, one can argue that possession is significant only as a means of acquiring ownership or as a proxy for ownership. In other words, one can argue that in each of these contexts ownership is the legally dispositive concept, and possession is relevant only as evidence of ownership.[5] This by itself may be enough to justify an inquiry into the differences between possession and ownership. But I would go further, and contend that modern legal systems also protect possession, at least in some circumstances, without regard to ownership or perhaps even in opposition to

---

[5] First possession applies in contexts where resources are unowned or abandoned; consequently, the first possessor becomes the owner once the resource is reduced to possession (Epstein 1979). In effect, we zip directly from possession to ownership; there is no need for an intermediate stop in the form of legally protected possession separate from ownership. Similarly, the role of possession in adverse possession is to establish ownership. One day before the statute of limitations expires, the owner can oust the adverse possessor; one day after, the possessor becomes the owner, and can oust the previous owner. Again, the law zips directly from possession to ownership, without pausing to recognize legally protected possession as such.

ownership. What follows is not intended to be an exhaustive treatment of the subject, but only to provide enough examples to demonstrate the point.

The law of finders provides a particularly striking illustration. The relevant cases involve an owner who inadvertently or accidentally has lost possession of an object. The object has not been stolen or procured by other illicit means; nor has the owner abandoned it. Someone else finds the object, and takes possession of it (Hickey 2010: 96). The finder is not regarded as the owner. Nevertheless, the law regards the finder-as-possessor as having significant rights independent of the owner. Legal systems differ in the details, especially with regard to the duties of the finder in seeking to locate the owner or protect the interest of the owner (West 2003). In general, however, the finder/possessor is deemed to have rights in the object superior to the entire world except the owner. The finder, for example, is protected by both criminal law and tort law against unwanted takings of the object by a third party (*Armory* v. *Delamirie* [1722] 1 Stra. 505). This is a clear instance of the law protecting possession independently of ownership.

The law of bailment provides another illustration. A bailment is a temporary transfer of possession of an object from an owner (the bailor) to another (the bailee), typically for a particular purpose. Bailments can be gratuitous or based on contractual consideration. Examples range from borrowing a bicycle from a friend to taking a computer to a shop for repairs. What is significant for present purposes is that the law gives the bailee, as the party in possession, rights against interference with the object by third parties, independent of the rights of the owner. Specifically, the bailee can use self-help to repel takings or damage to the object, and can sue in tort for conversion or damage to the object, holding any recoveries for the benefit of the owner (*The Winkfield* [1902–03] All E.R. 346). Here again we see an example of the law protecting possession independently of ownership.

A third example is the differential treatment of defense of possession versus recovery of possession. A person in possession of land or chattels may use self-help to defend possession against intrusions or takings by strangers, including the use of reasonable force. In contrast, an owner seeking to recover property that is in possession of another is much more constrained. In many states, owners of real property must obtain a judicial judgment in order to recover possession, giving the party in possession an opportunity to raise any defenses that may exist that would defeat the attempt to take possession (*Berg* v. *Wiley*, 264 N.W. 2d 145

[Minn. 1978]). Even where self-help repossession is permitted, as under the Uniform Commercial Code for recovery of personal property subject to a security interest, it is universally limited to "peaceable" methods (*Williams v. Ford Motor Credit Co.*, 674 F.2d 717 [8th Cir. 1982]). Force, reasonable or not, is forbidden. Here we see a systemic preference for possession, even when set in opposition to ownership.

A final example concerns the major forms of criminal and tort liability that protect interests in property. The law of larceny, for example, originally applied to unlawful takings of objects from the possession of another. Thus, for example, larceny applied to robbery and theft, but not to embezzlement or conversion by a bailee, because the object in these latter cases was in the possession of someone else when it was taken. It took many years, and many acts of legislation and creative judicial interpretation, to extend larceny to cover unlawful deprivations of ownership that did not entail direct takings from possession (Fletcher 1976). Similar stories can be told about the torts of trespass and conversion. Both torts originally applied to violations interfering with possession. Only over time were they gradually extended to apply also to ownership, often through the fiction that the owner is in "constructive possession" of the property subject to the intrusion. The point is that each of these forms of legal protection originally was linked to deprivation of possession, and still today, each is available to any party deprived of possession. Protection of ownership has been only gradually (and even today, incompletely) extended to owners not in possession. Insofar as there remains a gap, the law protects possession independently of ownership.

In sum, we see many examples where the law differentiates between possession and ownership, confirming that these concepts remain distinct and have continuing operational significance. We also see that the law not infrequently extends protection to possession independently of ownership, or extends greater protection to possession than ownership. This long has been regarded as a puzzle in need of explanation.

4. Previous explanations for legal protection of possession

Many esteemed commentators have remarked upon the mystery of what I have called the dual nature of property law – its protection of both ownership and possession. As Pollock and Maitland (1895: 40) put it, "Why should law, when it has on its hands the difficult work of protecting ownership and other rights in things, prepare puzzles for itself by undertaking to protect something that is not ownership, something that will from time to time come into sharp collision with ownership"? Various explanations have been offered for this puzzle. These explanations are not necessarily wrong. However, they are incomplete, and they make it difficult to account for the enduring protection of possession, especially in the face of significant reductions in the costs of protecting ownership associated with the digitalization of information and the proliferation of registries of rights.

The first explanation is that possession is valued for its own sake, whether or not it is conjoined with ownership. One could express this in terms of personhood.[6] Things that are possessed are often very close to the possessor, both physically and psychologically. People are wrapped up in the things they possess. Thus, an attack on possession is felt as an attack on the person. To deprive a person of possession is a kind of assault, and so the law protects possession just as it protects the person from assault. Modern psychological experiments involving the endowment effect suggest that persons place an independent value on possession (Korobkin 2003; see also Chapter 5). College students given physical possession of a coffee mug consistently demand more to give up the mug than they would offer to pay another to obtain ownership of the same mug. Biologists have suggested that this preference for possession may be a product of our evolutionary past, and now is hardwired in human psychology (Stake 2004: 1764–66; Jones and Brosnan 2008: 1953–63). Perhaps this is sufficient to explain why the law protects possession independently of ownership.

Clearly, there is something to the idea that people become attached to the things they possess. But people are also attached to what they own. Usually, ownership and possession coincide, so by protecting ownership the law will also protect possession. Indeed, since ownership includes the right to transfer possession, as by bailment or lease, protecting ownership covers a wider swathe of situations than protecting possession alone. In order to justify legal protection of possession independently of ownership, based on personhood or psychological attachment, it is necessary to show that there is a significant set of circumstances in which persons have possession to which they are strongly attached, but do not have ownership. There are unquestionably such cases – adverse possessors and

---

[6] Several nineteenth-century German scholars theorized that possession was protected because "the possessor's will was actualized or expressed in his dominion over an object" (Gordley and Mattei 1996: 297). For a modern version of personhood theory, see Radin (1982).

finders immediately come to mind. However, to provide legal protection to possession apart from ownership, we may also have to protect various bad faith possessors like squatters and thieves. It is not clear that the welfare tradeoff here – greater protection for good faith possessors who are not owners versus greater immunity for bad faith possessors who are not owners – is positive on net (Helmholz 1983). At the very least, the net gains seem too weak to justify a general and universal practice of protecting possession independently of ownership.

The second explanation, which is to some extent derivative of the first, is that the law protects possession "for the better maintenance of peace and quiet" (Pollock and Maitland 1895: 41).[7] If possession is valued for its own sake, as a kind of extension of the person, then an attack on possession will be perceived as an attack on the person. Thus, the argument runs, the law protects possession in order to deter these attacks (LaFave 2003: 919–20). For the same reason, an attack on possession will commonly elicit a defensive response, which may itself be violent. By protecting possession, the law discourages this kind of aggressive self-help. As one court put it, "Any other rule would lead to an endless series of unlawful seizures and reprisals in every case where property had once passed out of the possession of the rightful owner" (*Anderson v. Gouldberg*, 53 N.W. 636 [Minn. 1892]).

There is also something to this explanation. However, it is not clear why the deterrent effect of the law would not be nearly as great if the law protected only ownership. After all, most things worth invading or stealing are owned, and the subset that are currently in the possession of someone who is not an owner do not ordinarily advertise themselves as such. When a thief enters a car park, some of the cars will be owned, some rented, some leased, some borrowed from friends, and occasionally one or more may have been previously stolen. But the thief is not likely to differentiate among potential targets according to the ownership status of the vehicle (Penner 1997: 75–76). All are owned by somebody, and it will be a felony to steal any one of them. This will be true regardless whether the law protects only ownership, or also protects possession independently of ownership.

Probably the greatest protection against unwanted loss of possession is the privilege to engage in self-help, whether of the purely passive variety, such as installing locks or alarms, or the more aggressive form,

---

[7] This was Savigny's explanation for the Roman interdicts that protected possession independently of dominion (Gordley and Mattei 1996: 294–96).

such as using reasonable force to resist dispossession. Owners clearly have the privilege of exercising self-help to protect their property (Smith 2005: 84–86). The question, again, is whether it is also necessary to give those who have possession but not ownership the same privilege, in order to discourage disruptions of possession. Perhaps it is in some contexts. One can imagine that rates of theft at pawnshops or bank safe-deposit vaults might increase if mere possession of goods did not permit the proprietors of such venues to use self-help to deter takings. Outside these specialized contexts, however, thieves are not likely to differentiate between owners in possession and possessors without ownership. From a deterrence perspective, giving possessors the right to engage in self-help, independently of ownership, will not add greatly to the deterrent effect of allowing only owners to engage in self-help. In any event, even if there is a sound reason for allowing bailees to use self-help to protect possession, this takes us only part way toward giving full legal protection to possession. For that, we need a more robust explanation.

A third explanation is that the law protects possession as a kind of surrogate for the protection of ownership. "To prove ownership is difficult, to prove possession comparatively easy" (Pollock and Maitland 1895: 42). Thus, by protecting possession, the law reduces the costs of protecting ownership, and strengthens the rights of owners.[8] One consequence of this is that the law must occasionally protect wrongful possession, even at the expense of ownership. On balance, however, owners are better off with the law protecting possession. This explanation often is conjoined with an account of the English doctrine of relativity of title. Judicial disputes over rights to things take the form of a bilateral contest between two parties. The court will ask which of the two has the better claim; it will not inquire who has a right good against the world (*Parker v. British Airways Board* [1982] QB 1004, 1008). Thus, if A is an owner, A need only prove prior possession to defeat B. A need not prove ownership, which will be more difficult. This also means that B can defeat C, if C comes into possession after B; and C can defeat D who comes after C, and so forth. But, the argument goes, the As of the world are generally better off under this system than they would be if the law protected only ownership. After all, A can trump any of the subsequent possessors, B, C, or D, simply by showing that A was in possession before any of them.

---

[8] The nineteenth-century German scholar Ihering is often credited with this theory (Gordley and Mattei 1996: 294–98).

The surrogate protection explanation is, I think, largely persuasive on its own terms. The problem with the explanation is that it is incomplete. The explanation focuses narrowly on one aspect of the information-cost problem: the cost of assembling information about ownership to present to a court in a contest between an owner and a rival claimant. It is plausible that requiring proof of possession rather than ownership allows such disputes to be resolved at lower cost, especially in a world in which there is no registry of rights and proof of ownership requires the examination of multiple documents contained in diverse places. As I shall argue, however, the information-cost problem extends much further than judicial disputes. The disparity of information costs affects not just parties to lawsuits, but all persons as they attempt to navigate their way through the everyday world filled with objects claimed by others. As such, my main criticism of the surrogate protection explanation is that it does not go far enough.

5. Possession in the material world

As a prelude to developing a more general information-cost theory of why the law protects both possession and ownership, it is important to take note of some further differences between ownership and possession – differences that have not been widely recognized in the relevant literature.

One further and significant point of difference concerns the range of interests covered by ownership as opposed to possession. Ownership applies to a very broad range of things that have value. Ownership obviously applies to a variety of tangible rights, in including land and interests in land such as easements and leases, as well as to all kinds of personal property like cars, boats, and clothing. In addition, ownership extends to a variety of intangible rights, including future interests, security interests, beneficial interests in trust, intellectual property interests, choses in action,[9] bank accounts, and shares of stock in corporations. At the margins, there are debates about where ownership ends and promissory obligation begins (Merrill and Smith 2001). But in both ordinary discourse and law, it is common to speak of ownership of mortgages or patents or shares of stock.

---

[9] A chose in action is a right, typically created by contract or by an action for breach of contract, "which can only be claimed or enforced by action and not by taking physical possession" (*Torkington* v. *Magree* [1902] 2 K.B. p. 430).

Possession, in contrast, applies to a much narrower range of interests. Possession is limited to tangible objects, that is, things that have physical dimensions. One can possess real property like land and buildings, movable things like cars, clothing, and computers, and even wild animals that have been trapped or killed. One can also possess fugacious materials like water, oil, and gas, provided they have been captured and secured in some kind of containment. But one cannot possess intangible rights, such as future interests, security interests, intellectual property rights, bank account balances, or shares of stock in a corporation. I recognize that most of the intangible rights subject to ownership were originally (and sometimes still are today) embodied in some kind of deed, certificate, or passbook, and that it is possible to speak of someone being in possession of one of these pieces of paper. But this only proves the point. A piece of paper can be possessed; an intangible right, even one evidenced by a piece of paper, cannot.

The law of adverse possession reflects the limitation of possession to tangible objects. As one would expect of a doctrine grounded in possession, adverse possession applies only to interests in tangible property. One can obtain title by adverse possession to land or chattels, and one can obtain by prescription an affirmative easement in the land of another. It is even possible to obtain a prescriptive right to commit a nuisance on the land of another, at least one that entails the invasion of visible particles or sound waves. But one cannot adversely possess a future interest, security interest, intellectual property right, or share of stock in a corporation. The limitation of possession to tangible objects will play an important part in my information-cost explanation for the law protecting possession independent of ownership.

A second point of difference concerns the nature of the evidence relied upon in establishing ownership and possession. Claims of ownership are generally established by documentary and testamentary evidence about specific transactions involving things. (Gordley and Mattei 1996: 331). Deeds establish ownership of land and buildings. Bills of sale, wills, or oral testimony about gifts establish ownership of movables. Registries of patents maintained by the patent office establish ownership of intellectual property rights. Indeed, with the exception of certain important situations in which possession can ripen into ownership, such as the rule of first possession or adverse possession, evidence of transactions, whether private or with the state, establish all claims of ownership.

Claims of possession, in contrast, are established by engaging in physically observable acts. This is well known with respect to wild animals, where acts that qualify as "capture" of the animal establish possession (*Pierson* v. *Post*, 3 Cai. R. 175 [N.Y. Sup. Ct. 1805]). But possession of land is also established by engaging in physical acts – living on the land, cultivating it, or improving it – that are understood as reflecting a claim to be in control over access to and use of the land (Rose 1994: 19). The same holds with respect to possession of tangible personal property, where claims of possession are frequently established by affixing one's name to the object, or keeping the object in a place like one's home or office where it is understood that the possessor exercises control.

A third point of difference concerns the duration of interests. Rights of ownership typically have a substantial and often indefinite duration. In the case of absolute ownership or what the Anglo-Americans call the fee simple, ownership has a potentially infinite duration. Even in the case of time-limited ownership interests like easements or leases for a term of years, ownership rights can endure well beyond the lifetime of any given owner. This means, among other things, that rights of ownership can be inherited and, of course, can ordinarily be transferred by sale or gift.

Possession, in contrast, endures only as long as the person in possession maintains the relevant intention to control the resource. Thus, possession is lost by voluntary relinquishment or abandonment (Gordley and Mattei 1996: 333). Clearly, this is true with respect to social possession: if one gives up a theater seat without marking it in a way designed to signal an intention to return, the seat returns to the common pool subject to claiming by others. Pollack argued that possessory rights could be transferred (Pollock and Wright 1888: 23). But it appears he was referring to cases in which possession serves as a proxy for ownership, or (as in adverse possession) ripens into ownership. Perhaps for this reason possession in these contexts takes on some of the features of ownership in the eyes of the law.[10]

Finally, ownership is capable of many types of internal division. Multiple co-owners can own a single asset; it can be divided between present and future interests; it can be leased and subleased; it can have use rights hived off in the form of easements and profits; it can be subject

---

[10] It is instructive to note in this regard that in the law of adverse possession "tacking" the period of possession from one adverse possessor to another is permitted only if the possessors were in "privity of estate," meaning acting like owners in transferring rights from one to another (*Howard* v. *Kunto*, 477 P. 2d 210 [Ct. App. Wash. 1970]). A series of entries by successive possessors will not do.

to various liens and security interests. This capacity for fragmentation or "inclusion" is what gives ownership much of its value (Chapter 7). The potential for fragmented ownership also underscores the need for a potentially complex inquiry into transactional history before any particular right of ownership can be established.

Possession, in contrast, is "single and exclusive" (Pollock and Wright 1888: 20; Thayer 1907: 187). As Pollock and Wright (1888: 21) put it, "If two men have laid hands on the same horse or the same sheep, each meaning to use it for his own purposes and exclude the other, there is not any *de facto* possession until one of them has gotten the mastery." With an asset like land, it is possible to speak of a small number of closely related persons, such as a married couple or a family, being in possession. However, in order for this to make sense, it is necessary for all members of the unit to be actively engaged in exercising control over the land. If, for example, a brother and sister own land as tenants in common, but only the sister lives on and manages the land, one would say the sister is "in possession" of the land, but the brother is "out of possession."

In short, ownership exists in a world of lawyers, courthouses, legally significant documents, and title registries. Possession exists in a world of physical objects and of persons who are physically engaged with these physical objects. These important differences provide the material for a general explanation of why the law protects possession independently of ownership.

6. Possession, ownership, and information costs

We now see that there is a radical discontinuity in the information costs associated with possession compared to those associated with ownership. Possession is determined by observing the relationship between natural persons and tangible objects. In ascertaining whether some object is possessed, we rely on physical cues that tell us whether some person has brought the object under control and intends to maintain control to the exclusion of others. These cues are often rooted in functional logic, such that sitting in a seat in a theater, reeling in a fish on a line, or putting up a fence around a field is understood to signify being in control of the relevant object without any further form of communication. In terms of signaling an intention to remain in control, symbolic acts enter the picture, and decoding these acts requires some cultural knowledge. Thus, blazes on trees will signify an intention to remain in control of land in one culture, whereas cairns of rock will communicate such an intention in another. But these cultural signals appear to be ones that members of the community easily learn without any need for formal instruction. Information costs remain low because the relevant communication consists of visual observation of physical cues about objects, mediated by cultural knowledge that is easy for all members of the community to assimilate, typically simply by observing others.

Ownership can be determined only by engaging in a much more expensive process of gathering and processing information. The fundamental axiom of ownership is *nemo dat quod non habet* – one cannot convey that which one does not have. Thus, to establish ownership, we need to have information about the chain of title or provenance of the object. Undertaking these historical researches entails a much more complex and costly inquiry than that associated with ascertaining possession. In modern societies, this information is in documents – deeds, bills of sale, financing agreements, registration papers. In traditional societies, it may be based on symbolic markings or testimony of persons who have witnessed ceremonies in which the relevant rights have been exchanged (Ellickson and Thorland 1995). The concept of ownership thus requires, at a minimum, the ability to engage in symbolic manipulation, separate and apart from understanding the cues conveyed by the physical facts that communicate possession. This higher-order inquiry requires the assistance of persons with legal expertise, whether they are lawyers, notaries, title insurance companies, registrars of rights – or shamans.

The difference in the cognitive processes associated with ascertaining possession and establishing ownership is captured by the theory of Kahneman (2011) about two systems of judgment and choice he calls "System 1" and "System 2," or thinking fast and slow (Chapter 6). System 1 processes are rapid, automatic, and intuitive. They operate "with little or no effort, and no sense of voluntary control" (Kahneman 2011: 105). This appears to describe how individuals perceive if any given object they encounter is or is not "possessed" by someone else. System 2 processes require conscious attention and intellectual effort, such as gathering empirical information and assessing it according to the rules of logic or statistical inference. Only System 2 "can follow rules, compare objects on several attributes, and make deliberate choices between options" (Kahneman 2011: 36). This aptly describes how a legal expert establishes the "ownership" of an object.

6.1. Why we have two systems of property

Considering different audiences of property can illuminate the rationale for having two processes with radically different information costs for assigning rights to valued objects (Merrill 2011). In particular, it is instructive to compare two important audiences, which I will call the audience of strangers and the audience of potential transactors.

The audience of strangers consists of the large numbers of people who navigate daily among thousands of objects and who face the problem of differentiating their own objects from the ones that belong to others. By stranger, I mean any person who has no interest in particular objects of value other than to avoid interfering with those claimed by others. This is the attitude of most of us with regard to most of the things we encounter on a routine basis. Consider how most people respond to all the suitcases others wheel through an airport, or to the sea of cars parked in a public parking lot. Strangers in this specialized sense thus can include acquaintances and even friends, so long as we have no interest in their things other than avoiding a conflict over them.

As we navigate our way through life, we encounter vast numbers of things of value. The owners of these objects are strangers to us, in the relevant sense, and their identities and the circumstances of their ownership are irrelevant to our purposes (Penner 1997: 25–31). All we need to know about these things is "claimed by other" so we can avoid interfering with them. Similarly, the things we call our own are exposed on a daily basis to a variety of other persons, some closely related to us, but many of them also strangers in the relevant sense. These strangers likewise have no need to know who we are, or the circumstances of our holding these items. All they need to know is "claimed by other" so that they, too, can avoid interfering with our things. The basic objective of those in this audience – assuming they are well-socialized – is to avoid interfering with the rights of others.

Possession works well in this context because it employs a very low-cost informational rule that masses of people can easily learn and follow. Possession applies to tangible objects, and the fact of possession is communicated by physically observable facts about these objects. The significance of these facts usually can be inferred at a glance. To be sure, the observable acts that communicate possession will vary somewhat from one culture to another. However, this culturally specific knowledge is absorbed at an early age, requiring no special sophistication or study. As a rule, newcomers to any particular community can pick up these cues quickly.

If the audience of strangers had to rely on the concept of ownership in order to determine which things are "claimed by other" in everyday life, the informational burden would be overwhelming. Suppose we go on a one-day airplane trip to another city, and in the process cross paths with 10,000 different strangers, each of whom is accompanied by ten objects, subject to six different types of status in law (e.g., owner, co-owner, lessee, agent, bailee, trust beneficiary). Knowing the ownership of each thing would entail the need to call upon 600,000 separate bits of information. Perhaps in some futuristic world persons could be equipped with a new generation of Google glasses that automatically scan bar codes on objects, convey this information to a computer with massive data processing capacity, which in turn would respond with information about the ownership status of every object encountered. Even in such a world, it would be necessary to process and comprehend the information generated. Some shorthand surely would be developed, such as beeping a message to us equivalent to "claimed by other" so as to allow us to avoid interfering with the things to which we have no relationship or interest. We do not need to develop such a system, because we already have the concept of possession. The concept of possession allows us to navigate in a world filled with objects of value that belong to strangers without suffering from information overload.

The audience of potential transactors is much smaller, and consists of persons interested in engaging in exchange of rights to particular things having significant value and duration – things like land, buildings, machinery, boats, cars, airplanes, and artwork. By potential transactor, I mean anyone who has an interest in purchasing, selling, leasing, or borrowing against some object of significant value and duration. Thus, potential transactors are not just buyers and sellers, but include secured lenders, insurers, judgment creditors, asset securitization bundlers, and any others who have an interest in engaging in an exchange of rights with respect to valuable things, broadly conceived.

The audience of potential transactors is far more limited and has much more intensive interest in particular attributes of things. A core objective of the members of this audience is ensuring that they get what they have paid for, and that no third party will emerge to claim a superior right sometime after the exchange is complete (Arruñada 2012: 15–42). In order to communicate the information needed to sustain the social practice of engaging in exchange, we need a more refined concept than possession: we need ownership. Ownership means that the putative seller has the capacity to transfer to the putative buyer the legal right to control the object as against all other persons in the relevant community. This requires an investigation of the chain of title, a task to which ownership is devoted.

Suppose I have a late model BWM that I list for sale on craigslist.com. I am a potential transactor, as are any persons who are interested in buying a used BMW who happen to see the listing and are considering whether to contact me about a possible transaction. This audience of potential transactors will want to obtain much more information about the vehicle than would be of interest to a stranger. Potential transactors will want to know whether the listing party has good title to the car, whether there are co-owners who must agree to any transaction, whether the car is subject to a security interest, whether the registration and applicable tax obligations are up to date, and so forth. In short, the audience of potential transactors will want to obtain much more information than any stranger would care to gather.

Although the information about ownership is highly demanding relative to the information conveyed by physically observable facts, the burden of gathering and processing the additional information is not so great as to defeat all possibility of engaging in such transactions. For one thing, there are only a limited number of persons in the audience of potential transactors, each of whom has relatively high stakes in completing a transaction. Moreover, the forms of ownership are standardized, which reduces information costs (Merrill and Smith 2000). A registry of rights, if one exists, will further reduce information costs, allowing potential transactors to ascertain whether there are any outstanding security interests in the property. Experienced buyers will want to obtain this information for their own protection. If the purchase is to be financed, the lending agency will insist on this additional information for its protection.

Of course, if the value of the goods that are the subject of the proposed exchange is not high enough to justify the higher costs of establishing ownership, then these costs will not be incurred. With respect to low-valued exchange of rights, individuals routinely rely on possession as a proxy for ownership (Chapter 8). This is true not only in flea markets, but with respect to virtually all purchases of foodstuffs, clothing, and low-value personal property like computers. Evidence of ownership is demanded only with respect to objects of high value and durability, where the higher stakes justify greater investment in information gathering and processing (Baird and Jackson 1984). Possession stands-in for ownership in all other commercial transactions – precisely because of its lower information costs.

Once we understand that property has these two important audiences – the audience of strangers and the audience of potential transactors – we can see that possession and ownership constitute distinct rules operating in different social settings within the universe of property law. The concept of possession is a vital tool that allows people to navigate through the everyday world without interfering with the rights of others. Each person continually observes the objects around him or her and can tell at a glance based on physical cues whether they are possessed or not possessed. If moderately well socialized, these individuals will then conduct themselves in such a way as to avoid interfering with the objects that are possessed.[11]

The concept of ownership is a vital tool that allows people to engage in exchanges of rights to things of significant value and durability. Ownership signifies the legal right to control an asset against the entire world. To assure that the parties to an exchange have such rights, it will be necessary to conclude (to a satisfactory degree of confidence) that all relevant rights to a thing have been accounted for. This will entail at the very least rudimentary evidence of title (e.g., a bill of sale); with respect to the most valuable and durable assets like land, a more complete investigation of the chain of title or reference to a registry of rights will be undertaken.

6.2. Why social norms are not enough

This analysis of the functional significance of possession and ownership explains why the law protects possession independently of ownership. We can now see that possession is critical to social ordering. Possession allows us to avoid interfering with things belonging to others, and it serves as a proxy for ownership in low-valued commercial transactions, among other functions. However, recall that possession operates both as a social norm and as a legally protected right. Why not leave the enforcement of possession entirely to social norms, reserving the force of the law for the protection of ownership? After all, as previously observed, possession and ownership commonly coincide, and protecting ownership will, derivatively, protect possession to a significant degree.

---

[11] Even thieves seek to deprive other persons of their possessions selectively. In most encounters with most strangers most of the time, thieves respect the difference between objects that others possess and those that they themselves possess. Indeed, thieves would not be able to ply their trade if they did not understand this distinction.

We also have seen that strangers, in the specialized sense of the word, will commonly not be able to differentiate between things that are owned and things that are only possessed. So limiting the law to enforcement of ownership would go a significant way toward protecting possession.

The traditional explanations for the law's protection of possession independent of ownership provide part of the answer. Possession is valued for its own sake; failure to afford legal protection to possession might lead to breaches of the peace, at least in selective contexts such as bailments; and enforcing possession reduces the legal costs of proving ownership in court. The last point bears special emphasis. Because the information costs of identifying possession are much lower than the costs of establishing ownership, granting the protection of the criminal law and giving legal standing in tort to possessors greatly reduces the costs to owners – who are also typically possessors – of invoking the law for their protection. This significantly enhances the stability and security of ownership rights. We can now offer two, more general explanations.

First, even if a social norm protects possession, the law quite often and properly reinforces important social norms. By protecting possession independently of ownership, the law underscores the importance of respecting possession. Indeed, if the law were to ignore possession, and leave its enforcement solely to social norms, this might send the message that respect for possession is simply a matter of convention or courtesy, which might sap it of much of its strength as a norm (Merrill and Smith 2007).

Second, absent legal enforcement of possession, individuals would substitute away from the law toward other modes of protecting their things. One substitution would be to increase demand for records establishing ownership. When the law protects possession, documentation of ownership is unnecessary in cases involving strangers; one need only show possession. One can thus be casual about retaining receipts for bicycles and computers, safe in the knowledge that the law will protect possession of these items against third parties who steal or damage them. If the law protected only ownership, individuals would likely devote significantly more time and resources to retaining documentary evidence establishing ownership. Another substitution would be that individuals would invest more in self-help measures to protect possessions that lack documentary proof of ownership (Posner 2000: 558). Thus, the cost differential that favors possession over ownership would affect not only the cost of legal proceedings (the point previously found in the literature), but would also affect private behavior in ways that would at least partially nullify the cost advantages of possession.

An analogy, admittedly imperfect, would be a proposal to limit legal enforcement of contracts to those embodied in writing, leaving social norms to enforce oral contracts. Over time, failure to provide legal redress for breach of oral contracts could lead to a more opportunistic view of oral obligations. It might even erode the social norm that one should perform contracts more generally. It is also plausible that failure to enforce oral contracts would lead people to insist on written contracts in circumstances where they would previously have been content with an oral agreement. This would entail an increase in transaction costs in many circumstances and would constitute a deadweight loss for society. Similarly, failure to offer legal protection for possession could erode the social norm favoring possession, and could lead to increased social expenditures documenting ownership, another a deadweight loss.

7. The interaction of ownership and possession

Because ownership and possession often coincide, and because the law protects both ownership and possession, the concepts of possession and ownership will often interact. At least some of these interactions reinforce the information-cost explanation for why the law protects both ownership and possession.

7.1. The delivery requirement

The procedure for completing a valid exchange of property rights offers one interesting form of interaction. Historically, in order to consummate a sale of land, one had to engage in a ceremony called livery of seisin. This entailed having the buyer and seller appear together on the land and, in the presence of witnesses, having the seller hand a clod of dirt or a twig to the buyer. The ceremony was obviously a symbolic enactment of the transfer of possession. This made sense at a time when people living in the community were mostly illiterate and documentary evidence of transfers was privately held. Members of the community could readily comprehend the idea of possession being transferred from one party to another; the idea of a transfer of ownership may have been harder to grasp. By combining a symbolic transfer of possession with the transfer of ownership, the security of the exchange was significantly enhanced (Chapter 8).

Today, the necessity of conjoining transfer of ownership with transfer of possession lives on in the form of the requirement that a valid transfer of property requires delivery, either of the thing itself or of a deed that memorializes the exchange. The delivery requirement is enforced most strongly in the law of gifts. A valid gift, either *inter vivos* or *causa mortis*, requires both an intention to make a gift and delivery of the item by the donor to the recipient, literally or in some symbolic form (such as handing over the keys to a car). In effect, the law requires that there be a transfer of possession in order to establish a valid transfer of ownership. Commentators have been puzzled by this, although in family settings where documentary formalities are not routinely observed, the transfer of possession may provide vital evidence that gift was in fact intended (*Irons v. Smallpiece* [1819] 106 Eng. Rep. 467). Even in a transfer of property by deed, the law requires that the deed be delivered in order to establish a valid exchange of rights. Here the evidentiary value is more dubious. There are, however, not a few cases in which deeds are made out, signed, and then left in a desk drawer, which makes the transfer revocable at the option of the transferor. The delivery requirement – requiring a transfer of possession of the deed – reduces the potential for future dispute in these circumstances.

We can now see that there is an information-cost explanation for the vestigial requirement of delivery of possession in conjunction with a transfer of ownership. The transfer of possession supplements or acts as a substitute for the documentary record otherwise needed to memorialize a transfer of ownership, and does so in a low cost way designed to communicate information to participants and observers who may not be willing or able to assimilate the information reflected in a documentary record. Transfer of possession is in this sense a backstopping mechanism, and helps reduce the incidence of error or misunderstanding at low cost.

7.2. Security interests

Another interaction is found in the law of security interests, where it has long been understood that one way to memorialize a security interest is to transfer possession of the collateral to the creditor (Baird and Jackson 1984). This was originally called a "gage," hence the origins of the term mortgage. The borrower would transfer possession of property to the lender. If the loan was repaid the property would be returned; if not, the lender would seize and keep the collateral. The practice lives on in pawnshops, and the UCC still recognizes transfer of possession as a valid method of establishing a security interest in personal property.

Security interests are invisible. In a world without recording acts or title registration, transfer of possession, which is very visible, is a logical way of memorializing the fact that the property is being used as collateral for a loan. The transfer of possession also solves the problem of ostensible ownership, which arises when someone holds property subject to one or more undisclosed liens. This can act as a deceit on third parties, who advance credit to the owner on the assumption that the property is unencumbered.

Again, we see the informational function of possession. Possession serves as a substitute for title recordation or registration, and continues to perform this function in contexts where systems of recordation or registration do not exist or are incomplete.

7.3. *Adverse possession*

A third important interaction is the law of adverse possession. As previously noted, adverse possession does not protect possession as such. Instead, it reverses ownership from the titleholder to the possessor once the statute of limitations on an action to recover possession of the property runs and other conditions (open and notorious, continuous, under a claim of right, and so forth) are met. As a result, ownership always dominates possession in the law of adverse possession, but the running of the statute causes the identity of the owner to flip. Still, adverse possession is a striking example of the interaction between ownership and possession, and one that underscores the continuing importance of possession in property law.

Adverse possession furthers a number of functions (Merrill 1985), but one rationale for the doctrine is that it allows for corrections of mistakes in the paper record that defines ownership. If the title papers describe an ownership that does not conform to actual possession as it exists on the ground, adverse possession allows the title papers to be reformed by judicial judgment to reflect the actual practice and expectations of the parties. It is noteworthy that adverse possession operates outside of, and trumps, title as established by the recording act or system of title registration. The most meticulous examination of title cannot correct deviations between the paper record and facts on the ground (*Mugaas* v. *Smith*, 206 P.2d 332 [Wash. 1949]). Thus, purchasers must always do a physical inspection of the property – looking for possession not sanctioned by the state of the title – in addition to searching the title.

The rectification role of adverse possession again reinforces the information-cost explanation for the persistence of legal protection of possession. Adverse possession is not cheap; it usually requires a judicial judgment, which means litigation, and the doctrine itself imposes a number of conditions such as the passage of significant time, which must be satisfied in addition to showing possession. Nevertheless, by drawing on the concept of possession, the doctrine reduces the costs of correcting mistakes in the documentary record, in a way that conforms to the perceptions about ownership in the everyday world. Observed physical facts provide the basis for the correction of title, which allows errors to be corrected at lower cost than virtually any other approach that could be imagined.

Conclusion

We started with a puzzle: why does the law of property protect possession independently of ownership? The explanation offered here is that the concept of possession communicates information at a lower cost than does the concept of ownership. Possession is established by observed facts in the physical world, which conveys information at low cost. Ownership requires an investigation of the chain of title, which is significantly more costly. The lower information-cost burden associated with possession performs a vital role in allowing the mass of persons to navigate in the everyday world of property without interfering with the rights of others. It also performs a number of important supplemental roles in communicating information about ownership itself. Once again, we see the value of the information-cost perspective in understanding the structure of property law.

References

American Law Institute 1936. *Restatement (First) of Property*. St. Paul, Minn.: American Law Institute Publishers.
Arrunada, Benito 2012. *Institutional Foundations of Impersonal Exchange*. The University of Chicago Press.
Baird, Douglas and Jackson, Thomas 1984. "Information, Uncertainty, and the Transfer of Property," *Journal of Legal Studies* 13:299–320.
Bingham, Joseph W. 1915. "The Nature and Importance of Legal Possession," *Michigan Law Review* 13:535–65.
Chang, Yun-chien and Smith, Henry E. 2012. "An Economic Analysis of Common versus Civil Law Property," *Notre Dame Law Review* 88(1):1–55.

Ellickson, Robert C. 1989. "A Hypothesis of Wealth–Maximizing Norms: Evidence from the Whaling Industry," *Journal of Law, Economics and Organization* 5:83–97.
  1991. *Order Without Law: How Neighbors Settle Disputes.* Cambridge, MA: Harvard University Press.
  2008. *The Household: Informal Order around the Hearth.* Princeton University Press.
Ellickson, Robert C. and Thorland, Charles Dia. 1995. "Ancient Land Law: Mesopotamia, Egypt, Israel," *Chicago-Kent Law Review* 71:321–411.
Epstein, Richard A. 1979. "Possession as the Root of Title," *Georgia Law Review* 13: 1221–43.
  2002. "The Allocation of the Commons: Parking on Public Roads," *Journal of Legal Studies* 31:S515–44.
Fletcher, George 1976. "The Metamorphosis of the Larceny," *Harvard Law Review* 89: 469–530.
Gordley, James and Mattei, Ugo 1996. "Protecting Possession," *American Journal of Comparative Law* 44:293–334.
Grey, Tom 1980. "The Disintegration of Property," in *NOMOS XXII: Property* (J. Pennock and J. Chapman (eds.)). New York University Press.
Harris, D.R. 1961. "The Concept of Possession in English Law," in *Oxford Essays in Jurisprudence* (A.G. Guest (ed.)). Oxford University Press.
Helmholz, Richard 1983. "Adverse Possession and Subjective Intent," *Washington University Law Quarterly* 61:331–58.
Hickey, Robin 2010. *Property and the Law of Finders.* Oxford and Portland, Oregon: Hart Publishing.
Holmes, Oliver Wendell 1881. *The Common Law.* Mark DeWolf Howe (ed.) Boston: Little Brown.
Jones, Owen D. and Brosnan, Sarah F. 2008. "Law, Biology and Property: A New Theory of the Endowment Effect," *William and Mary Law Review* 49:1935–90.
Kahneman, Daniel 2011. *Thinking, Fast and Slow.* New York: Farrar, Straus and Giroux.
Korobkin, Russell 2003. "The Endowment Effect and Legal Analysis," *Northwestern University Law Review* 97:1227–93.
LaFave, Wayne R. 2003. *Criminal Law.* 4th edn. St. Paul Minn.: West Publishing Co.
Merrill, Thomas W. 1985. "Property Rules, Liability Rules, and Adverse Possession," *Northwestern University Law Review* 79:1122–54.
  1998. "Property and the Right to Exclude," *Nebraska Law Review* 77:730–55.
  2011. "The Property Prism," *Econ Journal Watch* 8:247–53.
  2012. "The Property Strategy," *University of Pennsylvania Law Review* 160: 2061–95.

Merrill, Thomas W. and Smith, Henry E. 2000. "Optimal Standardization in the Law of Property: The *Numerus Clausus* Principle," *Yale Law Journal* 110:1–70.
   2001. "The Property/Contract Interface," *Columbia Law Review* 101:773–852.
   2007. "The Morality of Property," *William and Mary Law Review* 48:1849–95.
Penner, J.E. 1997. *The Idea of Property in Law.* Oxford University Press.
Pollock, Frederick, and Maitland, Frederick William 1895. *The History of English Law*, vol. 2. Cambridge University Press.
Pollock, Frederick, and Wright, Robert Samuel 1888. *An Essay on Possession in the Common Law.* Oxford: Clarendon Press.
Posner, Richard A. 2000. "Savigny, Holmes, and the Law and Economics of Possession," *Virginia Law Review* 86:535–67.
Radin, Margaret Jane 1982. "Property and Personhood," *Stanford Law Review* 34:957–1015.
Reisman, David, Jr. 1939. "Possession and the Law of Finders," *Harvard Law Review* 52:1105–34.
Rose, Carol M. 1994. *Property and Persuasion.* Boulder, Co: Westview Press.
Salmond, John W. 1924. *Jurisprudence.* 7th edn. London: Sweet and Maxwell.
Savigny, Freidrich Carol von 1848. *Von Savigny's Treatise on Possession.* Translated by Sir Erskine Perry. 6th edn. London: S. Sweet.
Shartel, Burke 1932. "Meanings of Possession," *Minnesota Law Review* 16:611–37.
Smith, Henry E. 2003. "The Language of Property: Form, Context, and Audience," *Stanford Law Review* 55:1105–91.
   2005. "Self-Help and the Nature of Property," *Journal of Law, Economics & Policy* 1:69–107.
Stake, Jeffrey Evans 2004. "The Property Instinct," *Philosophical Transactions of the Royal Society* 359:1763–74.
Thayer, Albert S. 1907. "Possession and Ownership," 23 *Law Quarterly Review* 175–93.
West, Mark D. 2003. "Losers: Recovering Lost Property in Japan and the United States," *Law & Society Review* 37:369–423.

2

The law is nine-tenths of possession: an adage turned on its head

CAROL M. ROSE

1. Introduction

"Possession is nine-tenths of the law." So says the proverb. But is it so? The saying seems to mean that a possessor has an advantageous legal position in claiming property, but it has a distinctly uncertain pedigree. Its origin sometimes is attributed to sixteenth- and seventeenth-century essayists and commentators, but it is not entirely certain how the phrase was parsed in those early days (Erickson 2007: 370). The saying sometimes appears as possession is "nine points" of the law, leaving a question what the other point or points might be; or "eleven points" out of twelve, once again leaving open the question of the other point.[1] Aside from the issue of the missing point, in that early modern era of European history in which the saying seems to have arisen, "possession" included one particularly unattractive meaning: the takeover of the person by witchcraft, causing the satanically possessed individual to shriek and spin, speak in unfathomable languages, and in one litigated case, vomit pins (Levack 1995: 1618). If Satan had only nine-tenths of the soul, presumably it was because some glimmer of godliness remained to fight him off.

Lawyers, however, generally maintain that the phrase was inspired by a medieval English statute that long predated the usages that apparently began in the sixteenth century, namely the Forcible Entry and Detainer (FED) statute, which outlawed the forcible ejection of anyone who was in

---

Ashby Lohse Professor of Natural Resource Law, University of Arizona; and Gordon Bradford Tweedy Professor of Law and Organization, Yale Law School (Emer.). Thanks for many helpful comments go to the participants in faculty workshops at the Department of Philosophy, University of Arizona; School of Law, University of California, Davis; and Tulane University Law School.

[1] See www.answers.com/topic/possession-is-nine-points-of-the-law (giving several examples of different versions of the adage from late sixteenth through twentieth centuries) (last accessed October 17, 2013)

peaceable possession of a property.[2] But if the FED statute and its successors are the inspiration of the phrase, then the phrase has it wrong: possession should have been *all ten* points. The FED statute aimed entirely to protect a person who claimed to be the possessor in place, whether he was there by rightful title or not.[3] The statute did not aim at settling title at all but simply at keeping the peace until title could be determined by the courts, rather than by the owner's forcible self-help, which might well lead to protracted violence. Possession was not nine-tenths for the FED; it was the entire issue – but only until rightful title could be determined in a peaceful manner by ordinary legal institutions. Insofar as the nine points or nine-tenths phrase derives from FED statutes, the more modern meaning – that possession in practice establishes or almost establishes title – profoundly misunderstands the origin.

Nevertheless, the phrase lives on, with its own different twist, like a number of words and phrases that come to mean something quite different from their originals.[4] In the usages that appear to begin in the sixteenth century, the most obvious meaning of the nine-tenths phrase is what we might call the realist one: that possession represents facts on the ground, and that facts on the ground essentially direct ultimate legal decisions. Effectively, this interpretation would have it that what matters to the law is the literal strength of the possessor's holding – what Sir Frederick Pollock called *"de facto* possession" (Pollock and Wright 1888: 11). In this view, physical control comes first and the law follows, or at least nine-tenths of it follows; and for the most part, we could put aside other sources of legitimacy, whatever they might be.

2. Theorists and jurists

2.1. Hawks, doves, and coordination

The view outlined above – that the law largely acquiesces in the dominant position of the current holder – finds some support in a property theory that recently has gained some popularity. This is the theory that property basically is a game of "Hawk/Dove," a term borrowed from biology that

---

[2] *Beddell* v. *Maitland*, 17 Ch.D. 174, 188 (1881), citing 5 Rich. 2, stat. 1, ch. 8.
[3] See, e.g., *Paxton* v. *Fisher*, 45 P.2d 903, 909 (Utah 1935) (Wolfe, J., concurring) (explaining the saying as referring to the protection of a current occupant even against a rightful owner who would "take the law in his own hands").
[4] For example, the saying "the exception proves the rule" originally continued as "in cases not excepted," and the phrase in its entirety meant that the exception proved the *existence* of the rule. A more accurate reading of the original Latin verb (*probat*) was that the exception tests the rule. See (among others) Snopes.com/language/notthink/exception.asp.

now describes a set of moves in game theory jargon (Skyrms 1996: 76–79; Sugden 2004 [1986]: 61–74, 91–107; Krier 2009: 151–56). The underlying idea here is that property can be analyzed as a "game" that works only when the players hit upon opposite strategies: one party, the owner, takes the Hawk role to control a resource, while the other player, the nonowner, takes the role of Dove and defers to the Hawk. If it were not for the coordination of these opposing strategies, the resource might go unused (if both defer, that is, both play Dove) or it might be ruined and the players injured (if both play Hawk and insist on taking the resource and get into a fight over it).

The next question in this analysis is, who should play owner (the Hawk role) and who should remain the nonowner (taking the Dove role)? Australian political economist and philosopher Robert Sugden, along with others, have argued that possession plays a key role in this game: possession is a most salient focal point on which to coordinate the two players' strategies, with the possessor taking the Hawk position and the nonpossessor playing Dove. Interestingly enough, Sugden's discussion of this issue occurs in a chapter that begins with a section entitled "Nine Points of the Law" (Sugden 2004 [1986]: 91).

Then another question follows: why does possession act as a coordinating signal? One of Sugden's answers to the question, although certainly not his only one, comes back to the role of physical control. The possessor is generally in a better defensive position. Hence, the nonpossessor, assessing his or her underwhelming chances of success, will defer – at least when his or her damage from fighting outweighs the probable value of the resource. In other words, the possessor gets to keep the goods because the possessor is in a stronger position to hold them, while a rational fear of pointless loss keeps potential challengers at bay. (Sugden 2004 [1986]: 94–95; cf. Rose 2013).[5]

2.2. *The judges respond*

What do our legal institutions make of this realist understanding of the nine-tenths adage? The reception is decidedly mixed. In a number of cases, one or another party is reported to have stated, "possession is nine-tenths of the law;" the main object of those parties appears to be that of bolstering a doubtful claim to some object.[6] No one seems to pay a great

---

[5] Cf. Skyrms (1996: 76–79) citing similar advantages of possessors but stressing that very slight asymmetry can lead to correlated convention favoring possessors over nonpossessors.

[6] See, e.g., *Matter of Estate of Fiksdal*, 388 N.W.2d 133, 136 (S.D.,1986) (defendant cites adage, claiming jewelry of decedent was given to her and not part of estate); *State v. Boyles*,

deal of attention to these self-serving statements. In some other cases, judges themselves quote the saying, occasionally approvingly or more frequently neutrally, but sometimes distinctly disapprovingly. One sympathetic recital involved a couple of farmers who kept some farm equipment rather than turn it over to dealers who had been involved in defrauding them.[7] This case and a few others give some support to the Hawk/Dove view that a person in possession is better able to vindicate his rights than one not in possession, although what the judges seem to have in mind is that the fraudsters are likely to escape with the cash, never to be seen again.[8] Another sympathetic recitation occurred in a case that left an old collection of American Civil War era documents in an estate as an asset in bankruptcy, rather than give the documents to the state of South Carolina. Possession counted as presumptive ownership because no one had any record of the original ownership of the documents and South Carolina had no basis for an intervening claim.[9]

Many references to the nine-tenths phrase, however, include some distancing remark, referring to it as "the old adage" or "the old saw."[10] In recent years, one of the frequently cited precedents referring to the saying is *United States* v. *One 1985 Cadillac Seville* (1989)[11] where the judicial reaction was a stern rejection; the judge stated that the nine-tenths adage is nothing more than a reference to a "rule of force," and that the court would "prefer to apply the remaining one-tenth." Its disapproving attitude was reinforced in a couple of child custody cases in which the majority awarded custody to the adults with whom the children were living. The dissenting judges reproachfully accused the

---

unreported in P.3d; 2006 WL 2578289 (Wash. App. Div. 3, 2006) (dognapper cites adage, claiming dog was neglected).

[7] *Day* v. *Case Credit Co.* 2007 WL 604636 (E. D. Ark. 2007).

[8] See, for example, *Hoaas* v. *Griffin*, 714 N.W.2d 61, 68 (S.D. 2006); *Fletcher* v. *Rhode Island Hospital Trust Nat. Bank*, 496 F.2d 927, 930 (1st cir. 1974).

[9] *Wilcox* v. *Stroup*, 467 F.3d 409, 412–14 (4th Cir. 2006).

[10] See, e.g., *Optopics Laboratories Corp* v. *Nicholas*, 947 F. Supp. 817, 820, note 5 (D.N.J. 1996) ("old saw"); *Kyle* v. *Stewart*, 360 F.2d 753, 756 (5th cir. 1966) ("old saw"); *Matter of Swain* v. *Vogt*, 614 N.Y.S.2d 780, 784 (App. Div., 3rd Dept.1994)("old adage"); *Wofford* v. *Wiley*, 72 Ga. 863, 873 (Ga. 1884) ("old adage").

[11] 866 F.2d 1142, 1146 (9th Cir. 1989), cited in In re Forfeiture of Certain Personal Property 490 N.W.2d 322 (Mich. 1992); *Strange* v. *1997 Jeep Cherokee*, 597 N.W.2d 355, 359 (Minn App. 1999). The *Cadillac* case itself quoted *United States* v. *$79,123.49 in United States Cash & Currency*, 830 F.2d 94, 98 (7th Cir. 1987). The *Cadillac* case and others citing it concerned the question of which court should decide a criminal forfeiture matter, rather than the disposition of the forfeiture itself.

majorities of following the saying that "possession is nine-tenths of the law," a disposition that they clearly saw as improper.[12]

However well the nine-tenths saying may play out in theoretical games, then, judges are likely to look at matters in a different way, seeing the adage as a "rule of force" or rule of the stronger, to which law is the antidote. What, then, are these courts looking for? One regular candidate is what we might call *provenance* – where the claim came from. *De facto* possession without more says nothing about how the possessor got the property, whereas for legal title, that issue is exceedingly important if not essential. Does a property claim arise from some version of first or original possession, like discovery or invention? Or more likely for the vast majority of claims, does it derive from a voluntary transfer from the prior legitimate possessor, who herself received it from a prior legitimate possessor? Legal title reflects the principle – essential for the peaceful enjoyment of property – that with a handful of constrained exceptions, objects and resources normally cannot be transferred unless the prior rightful owner agrees. Moreover, behind that consensual transfer, there should lie another consensual transfer by a rightful owner, all the way down to the original possession.

Philosopher Robert Nozick famously argued that just entitlements are not "patterned," in the sense that we understand rights to be allocated on some principle of need, or deservingness, or equality. All those patterned distributions, said Nozick, would require constant and unacceptable interruptions and involuntary readjustments in order to recreate the chosen pattern. Instead, Nozick argued, legitimate claims are based on history, beginning with just first possession and succeeded by voluntary transactions from just claimant to just claimant all the way to the present (Nozick 1974: 150–64).

As others have noticed, Nozick's "all the way down" requirement is heroic – indeed, too heroic for a real world property regime to follow,[13] and herein lie the exceptions to the voluntariness principle. The supposedly initial claims may well be shrouded in time and possibly injustice. As thoroughgoing an advocate for property as William Blackstone

---

[12] *Chaddick v. Monopoli*, 714 So.2d 1007, 1017 (Fla. 1998) (Anstead, J., dissenting); Matter of Custody of C.C.R.S. 892 P.2d 246, 262 (Colo. 1995) (Scott, J., dissenting).

[13] See, e.g., Merrill (1989: 1129) citing the difficulties of tracking claims to remote sources; Ellickson, Rose, and Smith (2014: 74 fn. 4), suggesting that Nozick's theory of property is "too informationally demanding." Henry Smith, who has a particular interest in information theory in property, wrote this note. See, e.g., Smith (2003).

observed that questions about remote origins can be unsettling indeed – an observation that too few have noticed, given that it immediately qualifies his much more famous statement about the awe that is inspired by exclusive ownership (Blackstone 1979 [1766]: 2: 2*; Rose 1998: 604–06). Later claims of consensual transfer also may be fuzzy fictions. For all these reasons, property regimes in fact deviate from Nozickean principles, particularly for housekeeping purposes where claims are lost or grow stale.

Nevertheless, the issue of provenance is ordinarily joined for legal claims. Even where provenance is vague, as in the case of some long-standing variation on ordinary practice, the common law doctrine of prescription refers to the comforting fiction of a "lost grant":[14] a long-standing pathway across the neighboring property must have been agreed to sometime in the now forgotten past (Blackstone 1979 [1766]: 2: 265*). Thus, even if one were to suppose that possession might be nine points of the law, the missing tenth point is provenance – and it is a very powerful point indeed. Provenance lends a normative element to legal title – voluntary acquisition and transfer rather than force – that possession alone would not seem to include.

What, then, is the role for possession in a claim to ownership? Although they frequently reject the suggestion of force implicit in the nine-tenths adage, judges in a number of cases do maintain that possession counts for something in a claim to own something, but they treat possession only as evidence of the more important issue. That issue is title, and title, of course, refers back to provenance – where the claim came from. In the realist sense that the Hawk/Dove game suggests, possession is the *physical* ability to exclude others. But a chief hallmark of title, or even its central core, is the *legal* ability to exclude. Therein lies an all-important difference, one observed in the much-noted distinction between possession and property: the mere possessor must defend his own claim, whereas the property owner can safely leave the property unguarded, because others will respect his claim (Blackstone 1979 [1766]: 2: 2–9). This difference is enormously important for any modern economy, which could not function if people were required perpetually to stand guard over the things they claim. Instead, a modern economy can move forward because most nonowners respect what they regard as the

---

[14] See, e.g., *Graham* v. *Walker* Conn. 61 A. 98, 99 (Conn. 1905) (describing theory of "lost grant" in venerable common law doctrine of prescription, though rejecting it in the particular case).

legitimate claims of others, allowing owners in turn to proceed with their plans and investments.

Thus, the realist version of possession as Hawk/Dove rests ultimately on physical control by the holder, whereas property *title* depends on the willingness of others to recognize the holder as legitimate. How (and whether) possession might evolve into property – that is, claims recognized by others – is a topic of considerable debate, some of it referring back to David Hume's genial if sobering discussion. Hume postulated that property emerged from a kind of uneasy truce among *de facto* possessors, which then ripened into a convention recognizing a right of property in what previously had been held as mere possessions (Waldron 2013; cf. Rose 2013). Putting the pros and cons of the Humean truce to one side, the major relevant others who recognize property in the case of formal title are the institutions of the law; in the case of informal title, the relevant others are the surrounding community, though as we shall see, there is a considerable intertwining of formal and informal title.

2.3. Frail "possessors" and powerful neighbors

All this brings us to a point that Frederick Pollock observed well over a century ago in his treatise on "possession" with Robert Samuel Wright. In fact, the Hawk/Dove version of possession in itself is not very effective or even very realistic, because, as Pollock flatly stated, possession in the sense of a genuine power to exclude is "nowhere to be found." Pollock readily conceded that "it is worse to meddle with a strong man than a weak man or a child," but the strong possessor also can be overcome (Pollock and Wright 1888: 12).[15] Indeed, Pollock might have been thinking of the original medieval FED statutes, under which the person claiming current *possession* called on the law to protect him against violent ouster by another claimant – that is, the possessor was the weaker party, who feared ouster by a stronger nonpossessor.[16]

Pollock went on to make the very interesting observation that the real power of possession is the opinion of the "multitude" or the neighborhood – but what matters to the neighbors and others is the appearance of legality. Thus, "at least in a settled country," as he put it, physical

---

[15] Pollock wrote the first two parts of the book, including the pages in which this comment appeared, as well as all other references in this chapter.
[16] Sugden (2004 [1986]: 94) while expounding the Hawk/Dove explanation, acknowledges that the distinction advantaging the possessor may be very slight.

possession "readily follows the perception of title," but succeeds only with great difficulty in cases where the surrounding observers think that possession has been taken without the consent of the true owner (Pollock and Wright 1888: 14–15). Thus, it is legitimate title, or at least the perception of legitimate title, that determines possession, rather than the other way around.

We will return to Pollock's "settled" qualification later, but that qualification is an important one. It rules out polities in which law itself is contested, as in areas where implacably rivalrous groups compete to impose very different and partisan versions of what purports to be legal order, or where multiple layers of incompatible social and legal systems render legality itself uncertain.[17] As Henry Smith points out in Chapter 3, physical control is most significant where property conventions are least stable. But where the "settled" qualification can be met, Pollock's observations bear on a topic that has received some attention in the last generation: how legal norms interact with social norms. In a settled state, as Pollock asserted, the neighbors take their cue from their perceptions of legality. Conversely, legality may also take its cues from social norms – or fail to do so at the peril of loss of legitimacy (Tyler 2006: 178, 271). Whether as a matter of legal norms or social norms or both, however, Pollock reminds us that the chief factor that secures possession is the recognition and support of the surrounding community – the nonpossessors – rather than the strength of the possessor himself. The spectators dominate the possessors, rather than the other way around (Rose 2013).

Let us return to legal norms, where we have to deal with the stubborn point that even for judges, who generally reject the rule of the stronger, and who seek out provenance as a source of title, possession itself does give *evidence* of title. Indeed, it gives a quite powerful kind of evidence. Pollock noted that medieval law was organized around procedures for remedies, but there were no remedies for title as such – only for various kinds of damage to possession. Such was the power of possession, Pollock said, that the word had "usurped ... the name of property" itself (Pollock and Wright 1888: 5).

Where, then, does the salience of possession emerge even as evidence of title, supposing that title does not rest simply on the sheer force of the

---

[17] See, for example, Daniel Fitzpatrick (2006) (decrying "legal pluralism" and its disruption of ordered property arrangements); Alston, Leibcap and Mueller (1999) (describing unsettling effects of conflicting legal norms); see also Leif Wenar (2008) (denouncing capture of national natural resources by corrupt leaders).

occupant's position? Why would the neighborhood, or the public at large as represented by law, see possession as evidence that an occupant is something more than that – not merely an occupant, but also as one *entitled* to occupy?

2.4. Acting like an owner

One simple but centrally important reason is that "possession" itself does not mean exactly what we think it does, either for the neighbors or for the lawyers. Frederick Pollock observed that "[i]n common speech a man is said to possess or to be in possession of anything of which he has the apparent control, or from the use of which he has to the apparent power of excluding others" (Pollock and Wright 1888: 1). This is the view that I have called the realist conception. However, as was noted earlier, Pollock thought this conception was mistaken, and for a very good reason: that is not how we actually talk about possession. Consider the person whom the neighbors regard as a "possessor" of, say, a neighboring house. They would say that the possessor is someone who lives there and who is around the premises a good deal of the time. They are likely to surmise that this person is the legitimate owner, because homeowners generally do live in their houses; or if they do not, they license others to live there, notably renters. If someone moves in who is not the real owner, or whom the real owner apparently has not licensed, the neighbors (and the judges) would expect the true owner to object. Thus, what is called "possession" gives rise to a presumption of legitimate provenance and hence of title, simply because a true owner would not be expected to allow an interloper to take over.

But as observant readers will have noticed, a subtle shift comes into the meaning of "possession" when the term is used this way, as simply being around for a while with no obvious taint of illegality. The realist definition of possession would have it that the owner/possessor is one who is in a position to exclude all others by physical force. That is not what the neighbors see. The person who lives in the house is not there at all times. She goes to the grocery store. She goes to work. She takes the kids to school. She may lock the doors, but she may not. She is not even close to excluding others through personal strength, threat and intimidation. If she can exclude unwanted interlopers, it is because she can call neighbors and the police, and those third parties will help her to keep out intruders.

It is not unusual for scholarly commentators to discuss possession in its conventional realist meaning of *de facto* physical control,[18] but in this chapter, I hope to disrupt that conventional meaning. Pollock was right to point out that physical control itself depends heavily on the acquiescence of the surrounding community. For that reason, I argue that the meaning of the term "possession" itself largely is mediated by community conceptions and norms; in turn, those conceptions and norms reflect community perceptions of legality.

As we shall see, the legal understanding of possession does very largely overlap with an informal community understanding – and both add up to a far more relaxed view than the realist or *de facto* notion. In both formal and informal norms about the meaning of possession, the physical ability to exclude may play a role, but it is a decidedly minor one. The legal understanding of "possession" – and by extension, the informal understanding, too – is whatever set of acts people expect owners to take. Possession for the law means *acting like an owner*.

3. Possession as a legal concept

The most extensive discussions of the legal meaning of possession come in two kinds of cases: first possession on the one hand, and adverse possession on the other. Of the two, adverse possession is in some ways more interesting, both because there are so many more cases about adverse possession,[19] and more importantly, because in these cases, possession – as understood legally – can trump provenance as a basis for ownership. But we can start with first possession.

3.1. Possession in "first possession"

An opening approach to the legal understanding of possession comes with some cases about first possession,[20] which means a claim to ownership of something that was previously not owned; or if previously owned, already abandoned and hence returned to the "wild." In these cases, what

---

[18] See, for example, the essay by Thomas Merrill (Chapter 1), which argues that possession in the sense of physical control acts as a signal of ownership to nearby observers. See also the essay by Yun-chien Chang (Chapter 4), which discusses possession as physical control, to which civil law in particular adds the element of intent to own.

[19] See Kochevar (2013: 32 fn. 87), reporting that a Westlaw survey showed about 1,400 cases reported in the previous three years.

[20] For more discussion on first possession, see Chapters 10 and 12.

is called possession becomes the basis for a positive claim to property – that is, the legal entitlement that allows one to continue to claim an exclusive right even when one is not in possession, or not even in the vicinity. In such cases, the normative claim from provenance is most clear; at least in theory, the claimant is first in line, because there are no prior owners who are displaced.

What do these first possession cases tell us? The first thing that they teach is that legal possession consists of signals – signals that the claimant intends to do something (though it is not clear what) with the thing claimed. Harold Demsetz developed a well-known theory about the evolution of property rights, and his central example included a signal given by members of Native American tribal groups in northern Canada during the period of the great fur trade of the seventeenth and eighteenth centuries. After a disastrous run of overhunting on fur-bearing animals, family groups of these tribes began to establish their own hunting grounds, which they marked out by blazes on trees (Demsetz 1967: 352).

Somewhat similar to these tree blazes were the signaling behaviors in what Henry Smith (2003: 1122) described as "the famous case of Haslem v Lockwood." This 1871 case involved an ownership dispute over manure droppings that had fallen off a cart into the roadway, something that scarcely seems like the stuff of ownership disputes, except when we recall that manure was of considerable value to farmers at the time. The plaintiff had scraped the manure off the road and then arranged it into piles, but had then left the piles by the side of the road for later pickup. Meanwhile, the defendant made off with the piles. One might think that a pile alone was an ambiguous signal of ownership, but the court agreed that the manure belonged to the plaintiff, analogizing him to one who laboriously picked up grain that had slowly dropped from a wagon, and then left the grain in heaps while he went in search of an appropriate sack. Evidently, the piled-up status of the manure was supposed to be a sufficient signal of the plaintiff's claim. Similarly, in describing property conventions, Robert Sugden (2004 [1986]: 99) mentioned an old practice by which a person who gathered driftwood could mark the piles with two stones and then come back to claim them later.

We might pause here to note to the nonexistent role of physical exclusion in these instances, when the claimants were not on the scene at all. With respect to Demsetz' story, a blaze on a tree is not a very informative signal unless one is already aware of what it means. A stranger who viewed such a mark might find it vaguely menacing, without having a clue about what it signified about hunting in the area. In *Haslem*, not only was the plaintiff not present, his gestures did nothing to put the scraped-up manure in his physical control. One might say the same about people gathering driftwood and marking the piles with stones.

Somewhat more demanding about signals was the very famous case of *Pierson v. Post*, concerning a rather improbable dispute over a fox pelt: the fox had been hunted by the aggrieved party but was killed by an interloper when the hunting expedition ended.[21] Hunting and fishing are relatively rich sources of first possession issues. Although modern wildlife law has changed the picture, wild animals have long been considered to be unowned and thus available to first possession; and because many wild creatures are commercially valuable (for example, fish), there are in fact a number of examples of conflicting claims to ownership of animals taken from a wild state (Arnold 1921). But of all these, the *Pierson* case is undoubtedly among the best known. This is because the different opinions in the case offered competing views of the criteria for first possession, criteria that in turn would become the foundation for property rights in the dead animal. The majority opinion in the case took the conventional view that property rights would accrue at the point of killing or capturing the beast – that is, subjecting it to physical control – a view apparently supported by volumes of venerable legal treatises. The dissenting judge, on the other hand, would have left the determination of first possession and hence ownership to a less formal definition, relying on the community of hunters to decide.

The majority seemed to be saying that first possession required a clear and decisive signal that the hunter controlled the now-defunct animal. But one might notice that even with this strong requirement of physical control, capturing the beast is only actual physical possession vis-à-vis the beast itself, and not vis-à-vis *other people who might want it*. I might capture a wild rabbit and put it in a pen, but that capture says nothing about my ability to prevent someone else from coming along and taking the animal out of the pen, or indeed taking the pen itself, rabbit and all. In short, my legal possession of the animal does not hinge on my physical ability to exclude others from taking what I have captured. The captive animal may be under my control, but other human interlopers are not. As I have argued elsewhere, the legal definition of possession refers to the signal that I give to others that I intend to retain something for myself, and their acceptance of that signal (Rose 1985). The argument between

---

[21] 3 Cai. R. 175, 2 Am.Dec. 264 (N.Y. 1805). For some commentaries on the background to the case, see Berger (2006); McDowell (2007); and Fernandez (2009).

the majority and the dissent in *Pierson* was really about which set of other people should be the target audience for the signal.

Neither the majority nor the dissent appeared to see legal possession in anything like the terms suggested by the realist rule of the stronger, where the possessor is capable of excluding all others. The majority demanded a clear act that would convey an intent and ability to control, but other first possession cases make it clear that the signal not need be followed by current control, and much less by the ability to exclude others. Current control might well intimidate others, of course, but current control is not necessary to claim property in something once "possessed." A signal of past control will do, if it appears that it will be followed up. *Haslem* v. *Lackwood*, the case about manure, makes this point: the winning plaintiff simply piled up the manure and then went away, but he still could claim ownership as first possessor. Other wildlife cases illustrate that any element of control has been loosely interpreted in first possession cases: fish in nets are "possessed" even if they may swim away; bees in hives are similarly "possessed" although they may fly off at any time (Arnold 1921: 397). The *Haslem* court evidently thought the piles were a sufficient signal that the collector intended to return and take the manure, so that the piles themselves would count as legal "possession" that immediately ripened into property.

Another first possession case brings out a different but very important element in the legal understanding of possession, one that is if anything more legally significant than simply marking and that to some degree even qualifies the significance of marking. That element is *use*. In *Eads* v. *Brazelton* (1861),[22] the plaintiff Brazelton discovered and placed a flag above an abandoned vessel on the bottom of the Mississippi, thus marking its location. But he then delayed salvage operations for many months. In the meantime, another wrecking firm began work on salvaging the vessel's contents, and Brazelton sued to stop its work. Brazelton, however, lost to the other firm. The reason that he lost, according to the court, was that he had never truly possessed or "occupied" the vessel by beginning salvage work. Brazelton had his reasons for the delay, but as the court said, that was his choice, but he would have to abide by the consequences for failing to move forward with his claim. In other words, the court would not recognize his claim as possession at all, much less reward it with entitlement, unless he took some further steps toward use of the object.

---

[22] 22 Ark. 499, 79 Am.Dec. 88 (Ark. 1861).

In all these instances, we can see the unfolding of the legal meaning of possession as the set of actions that an owner is expected to take, even if only within a given community. Someone who is claiming ownership through first possession is expected to mark out the object so that the relevant others will know that he or she is claiming it as property. However, *Eads* teaches that one also is expected to go forward by actually doing something with it. If not, one will not be recognized in retrospect as ever having "possessed" the object in the first place. One who does not go forward with some action with respect to the claimed object is not behaving as owners normally do. People will not realize that he or she is continuing to claim ownership and hence they cannot be blamed for failing to credit the claims, or for thinking that perhaps he or she did not mean to claim the property in the first place.

The lesson of these cases is that property is a sociable institution, depending on the recognition and respect of others, and the minimum that a claimant has to do is to let others know what one is claiming, by acting the way an owner would normally act. If one does not behave in the way that owners normally do, and continue to act that way, one may not even be recognized as ever having been a possessor at all – once again, because in the law, "possession" means acting in the ways that others expect an owner to act.

3.2. *Possession in adverse possession*

Adverse possession is a doctrine that allows a person who is actually occupying and using a property to gain title over against a true title owner if certain criteria are met. The adverse possessor's acts must be sufficient to give notice to the true owner that someone is dealing with his property in a manner inconsistent with his claims; the adverse possessor must not have requested permission from the true owner; and the adverse possessor must be in "possession" for a statutorily defined period of time, often ten or fifteen years.

Even more strongly than first possession cases, the numerous cases of adverse possession reinforce the idea that for purposes of the law, "possession" does not mean the rule of the stronger, but rather simply acting like a legal owner. An early case in the USA's development of adverse possession law was *Lessee of Ewing* v. *Burnet* (1837),[23] arising

---

[23] 36 U.S. 41 (1837).

from the early settlement of Cincinnati, Ohio. Like many adverse possession cases in later years, the legal provenance of the property was somewhat confused. Here an earlier frontier speculator had kept only very loose records, and in some instances (like this one) had sold the property twice (Merrill and Smith 2007: 198). Moreover, the lot was not a conventional city lot, but rather was situated on a steep slope running down to the Ohio River. The defendant's deed was the later of the two and thus presumably invalid. Despite that fact, he won the case through proof of a variety of factors – digging for sand and gravel on the lot, authorizing others to do the same, and denying permission to still others. In short, he acted like an owner.[24]

A more modern case gives another interesting example. *Ray v. Beacon Hudson Mountain Corp.* (1996)[25] involved a man and his family who started to use a cabin that had long been the leased vacation property of a deceased elderly relative. The cabin stood in a summer recreational community that had been reclaimed by the original lessor company from all the renters, including the Rays' relative. But thereafter, the community had been allowed to run down, and ultimately it was sold to another corporation. Ray and his family, however, had been using the deceased relative's cabin, and he claimed that through adverse possession, he had come to own the cabin over against the title owner. Virtually the entire discussion of Ray's "possession" concerned the things that owners normally do with properties of this kind, all of which, the court concluded, the Rays had done. They had occupied the cabin, not during the entire year, but during a sufficient portion of the vacation season; they had repaired and improved the cabin in various ways; they had installed electric and telephone service; they had paid for insurance and taxes. They had even taken some measures to exclude others – that is, posting signs and putting locks on doors to keep out thieves, and prosecuting vandals who were not deterred by ordinary signals of ownership. The court treated the locks simply as part of the evidence of the ways in which the Rays were possessors in the sense of acting like owners – not so much excluding or threatening to exclude the neighbors, but rather giving off signals of their claim to ownership.

---

[24] Several neighbors testified quite emphatically (in what unfortunately looked somewhat like rehearsed declarations) that he had appeared to be "in possession" during the statutory length of time (21 years).
[25] 666 N.E. 2d 532, 535–36 (N.Y. 1996).

4. The independent normative claims of acting like an owner

Possession in the legal sense of "acting like an owner" means that people think the possessor is the legitimate owner. Legitimacy normally depends on provenance, which in itself has the normative weight given to a sequence of voluntary transactions. However, possession in the sense of acting like an owner also carries some independent normative freight that can be seen in two other elements: being there first, and using the object.

Coming first is obviously the hallmark of first possession rather than adverse possession. "Firstness" has sometimes been linked to the intensity of the possessor's valuation. Taking possession of an object first, before anyone else claims it, hints that the first possessor is the one who most hotly desires the object – the one who may well have taken preparatory steps to get it, and the one who has plans for its future. This was the clear tension represented by *Pierson* v. *Post*, where the hunter had done all the preparation to kill the fox, but the interloper had actually "possessed" it by shooting it. In the normal case, however, the hunter is the person most likely to take the prize; the *Pierson* conflict represented a quite odd case.[26]

First possession, of course, is not alone in suggesting intensity of desire. Possession by purchase also suggests intensity of desire. Economists often assert that markets allow goods to flow to those who have the highest valuation on them. More poignantly, as of this writing, a friend of the author's was undergoing chemotherapy for cancer, but she accompanied another friend to stand on line for several hours at the opera, before a set of tickets went on sale. There is something admirable about this level of desire, suggesting the high value that my friend placed on those opera tickets. Even after a person has taken possession of something, the fact in itself that she *retains* the object suggests that she desires the object more than others do; otherwise, she would sell it to another who wants it more.

Ownership through first possession thus suggests intensity of desire, but so does later acquisition. Neither is a perfect indicator of desire, of course, given that transactions costs indeed may impede the flow of

---

[26] The case was peculiar in other ways as well; Peterson (2009) argues that the fox pelt itself was probably worth very little, and that the underlying conflict was more likely to have been interference with the hunter's sport. Other legal conflicts over wildlife, however, like cases about whaling, have involved prizes of very high value. See, e.g., *Swift* v. *Gifford*, 23 F. Cas. 558 (D. Mass. 1872).

resources from one person to another. Even when transactions costs are minimal, the ability to pay for an object is itself only a crude indicator of the intensity of desire. I may want your clarinet more than you do, and I may have much better use for it because I can play it much better than you can, but I still may be too poor to buy it from you.

Despite these caveats, however, ownership based on first possession says *something* about the desire of the possessor for the object; first possession is one way to indicate intense desire. But there is a next step beyond desire: the desire is for some end. Desire says something about the *usefulness* of the object in the hands of the person whom we see as the possessor – the person who so desires it that others cannot offer enough for him or her to part with it. Desire indicates plans for use, and *use itself* constitutes a central implicit normative element to a claim of possession.

Someone who uses the thing that is claimed normally meets the approval of the surrounding community, whereas those who claim to own things without using them are suspect, and increasingly suspect as times go on. Examples of this attitude are rife in everyday life. Consider an example from common social norms: we enter a movie theater and notice that some seats are marked with an item of clothing or piece of paper. One might surmise that the rather anxious-looking nearby patron who is "holding" the places for some friends placed these items on seats. She is anxious because she knows that others suspect that the absent friends may never show up at all – they are merely asking her to hog the spots for them. Ultimately, the friend may not be able to hold the seats because other patrons will not respect the claim. No one will object much if the friends show up promptly and sit in the seats. But other patrons do mind if the seats go unused while they and others have to scour around for other less desirable seats. Unless the seats are assigned, none of the patrons has any legal claim to a particular seat. But the old *Eads* case described earlier, in which the salvage company lost its claim to a wreck on the Mississippi river bottom, illustrates the same attitude in law: a claim can be lost when the claimant fails to do something and actually use the claimed object.

Adverse possession cases focus even more centrally on use. Indeed, so powerful is *use* that a person's use of an object – or especially, use of land – can even overcome legitimate provenance and formal title. Thus, *Ewing* v. *Burnet* made much of the defendant's actual use of the vacant lot in frontier Cincinnati, contrasting his behavior with the other claimant's dilatory procrastination. Other cases go into detail about the types and degrees of uses that will establish a claim of adverse possession, for example mowing hay and cutting grass.[27] Thus in adverse possession cases generally, the claimants' uses of the claimed property make up a central element. Legal possession means acting like an owner, and what owners are supposed to do is use their properties.

Parenthetically, the concept of adverse possession itself has traditionally performed a kind of meta-use for the larger institutions that we have for safeguarding property and for allowing markets to function, by clearing away claims of the title owner who has allowed his ownership to fall into a state of uncertainty (Merrill 1984: 1129). Surrounding property owners presume that owners will actually occupy and use the land, or that they will authorize others to do so. When a title owner fails to act in that manner, other persons – including potential purchasers – can become confused about title, making the conventional assumption that the adverse possessor is actually the owner or one licensed by the owner. However awkward adverse possession may be as a doctrine (Fennell 2006: 1062; Stake 2001: 2442), by turning ordinary expectations into reality, the doctrine has its own use in allaying unfairness to third parties and in removing what Pollock's essay called "scrambled" confusions that could clog commercial circulation (Pollock and Wright 1888: 23).

5. Adverse possession revisited: the claim of right

Whatever its uses for the overall property regime, the law of adverse possession has some subtle limitations that echo Powell's comment that the perception of title will still trump possession – trumping even possession taken together with use, and trumping even possession that has been together with use over a long period of time. An important limitation on adverse possession is that the possessor's use must be "hostile" or genuinely "adverse" to the claim of the title owner. This does not mean that there is some enmity between the adverse possessor and the title owner, but at a minimum means that the adverse possessor cannot claim the property if she has asked the owner for permission to use it.

One very good reason to deny the claim of one who has asked permission is that granting her title would make title owners wary of ever permitting others to use their property. Such doctrines discourage simple neighborliness, not to speak of tenancy and the accompanying

---

[27] See, e.g., *Ramapo Mfg Co. v. Mapes*, 110 N.E. 772 (N.Y. 1915).

specialization in the uses of property. Alston, Libecap, and Mueller's (1999: 203) study of titling problems in the Brazilian Amazon, for example, observes that when land reforms have favored tenants in expropriations, they have discouraged large landowners from leasing portions of their property (see also Mitchell 2003: 559–60).

But aside from considerations about owner incentives, the adverse possessor who has asked permission has acknowledged the title of the owner, showing that the adverse possessor knew all along that the property belonged to another. Generally speaking, such a would-be adverse possessor – that is, the one who moves onto a property after making an unsuccessful offer to purchase – will lose vis-à-vis the title owner, no matter how much the former has used the property as if it were his or her own. An acknowledged title trumps merely acting like an owner.[28] In some jurisdictions, there is an even stronger version of this normative principle: the doctrine that the adverse possessor must have a "claim of right" or even "color of title," that is, some ground, even if a mistaken one, to think that one is the property's true owner. As one case put it, "to enter upon the land without any honest claim of right to do so is but a trespass and can never ripen into prescriptive title."[29] Good faith is not universally required as a formal matter in American property law. Judges and juries, however, are unwilling to give title to the adverse possessor who has no excuse for thinking that he or she was entitled to be on the property, and who has simply moved in, despite knowing that the property belongs to someone else (Helmholz 1983: 347). They generally regard such a person as dishonest, perhaps little more than a thief. And judges and juries do not like thieves (Helmholz 1983: 342, 358). Neither do legislators, to judge by some recent legislative expansions of the good faith requirements.[30]

---

[28] See, e.g., *Cahill v. Morrow*, 11 A.3d 82 (R.I. 2011) But see Fennell (2006), taking the unconventional view, on efficiency grounds, that adverse possession should only apply to willful trespassers, provided they have made an offer to purchase. Fennell's normal case, however, appears to be one in which there is some impediment to the transaction, for example when the true owner cannot be located.

[29] *Simmons v. Community Renewal and Redemption, LLC*, 685 S.E.2d 75, 77 (Ga. 2009), citing *Halpern v. The Lacy Corp*, 379 S.E.2d 519 (Ga. 1989); see also *Gorman v. City of Woodinville*, 283 P.2d 1082, 1088 (Wash. 2012) (Madson, J., concurring) (noting extension of good faith requirement in several states).

[30] See, e.g., 2008 Colo. Session Laws 688, codified at Colo. Rev. Stat. Sec. 38-41-101 (2010), requiring among other things a good faith belief in ownership for adverse possession; 1989 Or. Laws ch 1069, codified at Or. Rev. Stat. Sec. 105.620 (same); Morawetz (2011) (similar legislation in Alaska).

But even here, there are some equitable considerations under which long use trumps known or knowable provenance as a normative principle, particularly in cases of sympathetic occupants or unsympathetic title owners (Helmholz 1983: 347–48). In some cases, juries have more sympathy toward long-time users than to title owners (especially unpleasant title owners), even if judges overturn the juries' preferred outcomes. One well-known case is *Van Valkenberg* v. *Lutz* (1952).[31] Lutz owned a lot and house in a subdivision, and over a thirty-year period, he gradually took over a neighboring vacant lot to grow vegetables and to use for other purposes, including building a cottage for a disabled brother. When Lutz got into a heated dispute with another neighbor, the neighbor bought the lot at a tax sale and then brought a trespass action to evict Lutz. Lutz defended with an adverse possession claim, and the jury decision favored him. The jury verdict was overturned on appeal (with a spirited dissent), but one suspects that after Lutz had used the lot so long, the jurors regarded his casual attitude about title as less reprehensible than the neighbor's vindictiveness. Similarly, neighbors of a derelict property may well prefer a squatter who uses and cares for the property to the title-holding bank that simply boards it up and waits for prices to rise. There are other unusual circumstances in which willful trespass is regarded by many as a good thing, particularly for expressive purposes, as in the civil rights sit-ins of the early 1960s (Peñalver and Katyal 2007).

The courts favor provenance when provenance is available as a basis for title – and it should be increasingly available for all parties as land records improve with computerization – but some of these instances suggest that in the popular imagination, the use that goes with "acting like an owner" may normatively outweigh actual title ownership. A recent paper by Steven Kochevar (2013) argued persuasively that the law of adverse possession provides a safety valve for the expression of community values, even where the letter of the law would favor the title owner. It may well be that in cases where community preferences are manifest, official legal actors, whether consciously or inadvertently, preserve their own legitimacy by bending to social norms (Tyler 2006: 271). Thus, informal social norms strongly favor legality under normal circumstances, but under some conditions, legal norms also bend to consider social norms.

---

[31] 106 N.E.2d 28 (N.Y. 1952).

Conclusion

This chapter argues that when the law is in a state that Pollock called "settled," the adage that possession is nine-tenths of the law is profoundly misleading. The truth is that legal definitions of possession largely refer back to legality itself. Legality – or at least the appearance of legality – is the chief focal point around which social norms of property congeal. Moreover, social norms make possession possible. However much "possession" is equated with physical control of some resource, physical control alone is ineffective – indeed often impossible – unless the surrounding community supports the so-called possessor. And under normal circumstances, what sways the community is the appearance of legitimacy. In fact, the adage has it backward. The law is nine points of possession, rather than the other way around.

Possession in legal parlance does not mean the physical ability to exclude others, but simply a set of acts that look like those of a true owner, who can exclude others with the help of neighbors and legal officers, but who can do many other things as well. In particular, the actor uses the property, and use itself carries a certain modicum of normative weight.

Possession in the sense of acting like an owner is only evidence of true title; one who can prove provenance will normally win out over one who merely acts like an owner, both for social approbation and for legal norms. To be sure, as we have seen, there are occasional exceptions in which looking like an owner trumps an actual title; this occurs in successful claims of adverse possession and prescription. Even though the rationale for these exceptions often is to clear away stale claims, an important background reason for these unusual doctrines is normative: the person who acts like an owner is likely to be making use of the property, and use generally meets the approval of the surrounding community, and the law as well.

Having said this, there are circumstances under which acting like an owner is problematic, for a variety of reasons, but they add up to one big reason. The law may be nine points of possession, since legal possession means acting like an owner, but for most ordinary language usages, the tenth point of possession includes some visible or otherwise perceptible element, and this normally implies some physical characteristic. One can "possess" a car, a book, or a house, even if one is not present – that is to say, the element of tangibility is not hard to satisfy as long as there is some physical thing to which "possession" can refer. But in the case of

THE LAW IS NINE-TENTHS OF POSSESSION 61

abstract financial instruments, there is little to create any such physical association. For that reason, as James Krier (2009: 156) has observed, the idea of possession carries little sway in the most important segments of a modern economy, and has no role as evidence of ownership in connection with banking, stock options, insurance, and so on. Even if the embezzler "acts like an owner" and cashes checks on an account that does not belong to him, those acts count for nothing against provenance as a claim to title.

Somewhat similar is the idea of possession in connection with intellectual property. Here, too, the legal property right is abstract. For the holder of intellectual property, the distinctive signals of "acting like an owner" generally mean little more than the holder's effort to keep others from using this very abstract right. However, use, not exclusion, lends normative weight to acting like an owner, whereas the intellectual property claimant's perceived assertions of ownership consist largely of excluding use by others, even when their use damages no resource. We should not be surprised that respect for intellectual property is correspondingly somewhat diminished; people who would not dream of stealing an unlocked bicycle will gleefully hack away at the applications on a game console.

Finally, "acting like an owner" in connection with physical resources can be damaging to certain uses of those resources, notably passive ones. Possession in the sense of acting like an owner generally means doing something that can be seen or at least perceived, but doing nothing is hard to see. You may "use" a mountain landscape for the beautiful view, but your view is hard for others to perceive. You may "use" a grove of trees for bird and butterfly habitat, but others may think that you are not using it at all (Sprankling 1994; Stake 2001: 2423; Fennell 2006: 1077–80). The failure to consider such unintrusive uses often is a manifestation of cultural parochialism: one social group does not notice or sufficiently appreciate how another uses things. This was the case, for example, with Native American management of forest growth through fires (Cronon 1983: 56–58, Pyne 2001: 46–64), and even more tellingly, with Aboriginal Australian place-specific ceremonies, tales, and songs (Meyers and Raine 2001: 123–25; Grossfeld and Hiller 2008: 1173–74).

Some legal institutions may now be taking steps to address the problems presented by unintrusive or passive uses of property, such as efforts to protect conservation lands from would-be occupants (Klass 2006: 309–15). But in other contexts, that is not the case. Even today, wildcat land claimants in the Brazilian Amazon, knowing what counts as "acting like an owner" to other wildcatters as well as land titling officials, have ignored environmental uses and cut down trees to create borders around their claims. At the same time, they have created fake title documents, and allowed crickets to munch on them to make them look authentically old (Campbell 2014).

And so, just as that tenth point of the law, provenance, looms very large over against what seem to be the nine points of "possession," so do tangible elements sometimes loom large over the heavy dose of legality that goes into our ordinary understanding of what it means to possess something. Indeed, as the law changes to protect wild areas against occupying claimants, we may expect that popular conceptions of what it means to act like an owner will change as well on those lands. Perceptions can change, and given any set of newly perceptible signals for any claimed object, the legal understanding of possession, and the social understanding that incorporates legality, will look elsewhere than to simple physical control.

Let us come back then, to the old adage itself, "possession is nine-tenths of the law." Where might possession – *de facto*, realist possession – count as nine-tenths of the law? The most likely place is where the law is weak, conflicted, or widely regarded as ineffective – in areas where the law is not "settled," in Pollock's term. That is to say, if *de facto* possession is nine-tenths of the law, we know that in effect, there is no law. There are probably not even social norms that would define property informally.

But where law is "settled," the community looks to the law; the law looks to the community; and in defining possession, both look to the normal practices of legitimate owners. It is not force, it is not exclusion, and it is not guarding or any of those things that define possession. Instead, whatever owners normally do – that is to say, whatever *lawful* owners do – sets the benchmark by which we ascribe meaning to "possession."

References

Alston, Lee J., Libecap, Gary D. and Mueller, Bernardo 1999. *Titles, Conflict and Land Use: The Development of Property Rights on the Brazilian Amazon Frontier*. Ann Arbor, Michigan: University of Michigan Press.

Arnold, Earl C. 1921. "The Law of Possession Governing *Ferae Naturae*," *American Law Review* 55:393–404.

Berger, Bethany R. 2006. "It's Not About the Fox: The Untold History of *Pierson* v. *Post*," *Duke Law Journal* 55:1089–1143.

Blackstone, William 1979 [1766]. *Commentaries on the Laws of England*, volume 2. University of Chicago Press.
Campbell, Jeremy M. 2014 "Speculative Accumulation: Property-Making in the Brazilian Amazon," *Journal of Latin American and Caribbean Anthropology* 19:237–59.
Cronon, William 1983. *Changes in the Land: Indians, Colonists, and the Ecology of New England*. New York: Hill and Wang.
Demsetz, Harold 1967. "Toward a Theory of Property Rights," *American Economic Review Papers and Proceedings* 57:347–59.
Ellickson, Robert C., Rose, Carol M. and Smith, Henry C. 2014. *Perspectives on Property Law*. 4th edn. New York: Aspen.
Erickson, Amy Louise 2007. "Possession—And the Other One-Tenth of the Law: Assessing Women's Ownership and Economic Roles in Early Modern England," *Women's History Review* 16:369–85.
Fennell, Lee Anne 2006. "Efficient Trespass: The Case for Bad Faith Adverse Possession," *Northwestern University Law Review* 100:1037–96.
Fernandez, Angela 2009. "*Pierson v. Post*: A Great Debate, James Kent, and the Project of Building a Learned Law for New York State," *Law and Social Inquiry* 34:301–31.
Fitzpatrick, Daniel 2006. "Evolution and Chaos in Property Rights Systems: The Third World Tragedy of Contested Access," *Yale Law Journal* 115:996–1048.
Grossfeld, Bernhard and Hiller, Jack A. 2008. "Music and Law," *International Lawyer* 42: 1147–80.
Helmholz, Richard 1983. "Adverse Possession and Subjective Intent," *Washington University Law Quarterly* 61:331–58.
Klass, Alexandra B. 2006. "Adverse Possession and Conservation: Expanding Traditional Notions of Use and Possession," *University of Colorado Law Review* 77:283–333.
Kochevar, Steven 2013. "Adverse Possession as a Means of Assessing Community Approval," Unpublished paper, on file with the author.
Krier, James E. 2009. "Evolutionary Theory and the Origins of Property Rights," *Cornell Law Review* 95:139–59.
Levack, Brian P. 1995. "Possession, Witchcraft, and the Law in Elizabethan England," *Washington and Lee Law Review* 52:1613–40.
McDowell, Andrea 2007. "Legal Fictions in *Pierson v. Post*," *Michigan Law Review* 105:735–77.
Merrill, Thomas W. 1984. "Property Rules, Liability Rules and Adverse Possession," *Northwestern University Law Review* 79:1122–54.
Merrill, Thomas W. and Smith, Henry E. 2007. *Property: Principles and Policies*. New York: Foundation Press.
Meyers, Gary D. and Raine, Sally, "Australian Aboriginal Land Rights in Transition (Part II): The Legislative Response to the High Court's Native Title

Decisions in *Mabo v. Queensland* and *Wik v. Queensland*," *Tulsa Journal of Comparative and International Law* 9:95–167.

Mitchell, Kristen 2003. "Market-assisted Land Reform in Brazil: A New Approach to Address an Old Problem," *New York University Law School Journal of International and Comparative Law* 22:557–83.

Morawetz, Jennie 2011. "No Room for Squatters: Alaska's Adverse Possession Law," *Alaska Law Review* 28:341–70.

Peñalver, Eduardo Moisés and Katyal, Sonia K. 2007, "Property Outlaws," *University of Pennsylvania Law Review* 155:1095–1186.

Pollock, Frederick and Wright, Robert Samuel 1888. *An Essay on Possession in the Common Law*. Oxford: Clarendon Press.

Nozick, Robert 1974. *Anarchy, State and Utopia*. New York: Basic Books.

Pyne, Stephen J. 2001. *Fire: A Brief History*. Seattle, Washington: University of Washington Press.

Rose, Carol M. 1985. "Possession as the Origin of Property," *University of Chicago Law Review* 52:73–88.

   1998. "Canons of Property Talk, or, Blackstone's Anxiety," *Yale Law Journal* 108: 601–32.

   2013. "Psychologies of Property (and Why Property is Not a Hawk-Dove Game)," in Penner, J. E., and Smith, H.E. (eds), *The Philosophical Foundations of Property Law*. Oxford University Press.

Skyrms, Brian. 1996. *Evolution of the Social Contract*. Cambridge University Press.

Smith, Henry E. 2003. "The Language of Property: Form, Context and Audience," *Stanford Law Review* 55:1105–91.

Sprankling, John E. 1994. "An Environmental Critique of Adverse Possession," *Cornell Law Review* 79:816–84.

Stake, Jeffrey Evans 2001. "The Uneasy Case for Adverse Possession," *Georgetown Law Journal* 89:2419–73.

Sugden, Robert 2004 [1986] *The Economics of Rights, Cooperation and Welfare*. Houndmills, Basingstoke, Hampshire; New York: Palgrave Macmillan.

Tyler, Tom R. 2006 *Why People Obey the Law*. Princeton University Press.

Waldron, Jeremy 2013. "'To Bestow Stability Upon Possession': Hume's Alternative to Locke," in Penner, J.E., and Smith, H.E., (eds.) *The Philosophical Foundations of Property Law*. Oxford University Press.

Wenar, Leif 2008. "Property Rights and the Resource Curse," *Philosophy and Public Affairs* 36:2–32.

3

The elements of possession

HENRY E. SMITH

1. Introduction

Possession is both mundane and mysterious. The notion of possession governs most people's relation to most things most of the time. From seats at a theater to the clothes on one's back, possession and its stability are a basic fact of life – or one of the most sorely missed aspects of social order. Yet the role possession plays – or should play – in the law has puzzled people for centuries. Philosophers controversially invoke some notion of possession in justifying property in the first place. Modern legal systems assign an important role for possession, but the variety of manifestations of possession within and across legal systems makes it seem unpromising to search for a unified explanation of possession. The reasons for protecting possession today and for preferring it sometimes to related notions like ownership have tied jurists and commentators in knots.

Nevertheless, there is a common set of elements to possession. In this chapter, I will show that a well-designed theory can capture not only these elements but also how they combine to produce the details and differences that come under the heading of "possession."

I argue that possession serves as a first cut at legal ontology in an overall modular architecture of property. Without needing to be deeply metaphysical, a theory of a legal system must define its elements and their relations: what are legal actors, legal things, legal relations, and the like? This basic furniture matters greatly to how and whether law serves its purposes. Any system of legal relations, informal or formal, must manage

---

Fessenden Professor of Law and Director, Program on the Foundations of Private Law, Harvard Law School. For helpful comments, I would like to thank Benito Arruñada, Yun-chien Chang, Eric Claeys, James Penner, Carol Rose, Koen Swinnen, and participants at the 2014 meeting of the Private Law Consortium at the University of Pennsylvania Law School, the American Law and Economics 2014 Annual Meeting at the University of Chicago, and the 2014 Colloquium on Property Law and Theory at the George Mason University School of Law. Any errors are solely mine.

the set of possible actions that people might take with respect to resources, because those actions will often come into conflict. To capture the benefits of coordinating patterns of use, the world needs to be divided into persons and things, and associations between persons and things need to be established. These associations will be in the interest of use, and so possession usually will require duties of abstention by other potential users. Depending on the nature of the group, the resources, and the universe of possible uses, this abstention can be implemented though norms of exclusion or of governance over particular uses.

Basic possession involves persons, things, and a connection between the former and the latter that gives the possessor rights against a group of others. Norms of possession emerge from a combination of psychological salience and economic function. "Salience" refers to anything that makes a feature of a situation prominent and attention grabbing. The notion of salience has been developed as a basis for selecting among possible strategies in a game, leading to conventions, including those of possession (Sugden 1986; see also Schelling 1960; Sugden 2011; Alberti, Sugden, and Tsutsui 2012). Salience makes certain choices focal, as in an experiment in which participants, when asked how they would try to meet in New York City with another with whom no communication is possible, chose the information booth in Grand Central Station at noon (Schelling 1960: 55 n. 1, 56). With possession, basic notions of control and nearness, as well as more artificial markings, all break the symmetry of claimants to a thing, making one person a good candidate for possessor. As I will argue, notions of control and nearness have efficiency implications: as Barzel 1997 has shown, with all else being equal we should expect actors maximizing the returns from assets to recognize greater residual claims in those who have the ability to affect the mean return from the asset. In the simple situations governed by basic possession, such persons are likely to be those near to and in "control" of the things in question. Rules of possession themselves can also be evaluated for their efficiency (see, e.g., Lueck 1995; Posner 2000).

When it comes to basic *de facto* possession especially – our starting point in the following discussion – salience and economic function reinforce each other. Which attributes are bundled together and count as a thing is a matter of salience and background knowledge, which responds, in part, to what is useful. Defining thinghood is the task of the principle of accession and its associated doctrines. For example, fixtures like buildings are deemed part of the real estate they stand on. The legs of a chair are part of the chair – so uncontroversially, that it rarely is mentioned as a matter of the accession principle. Further, salience and economic usefulness also determine who should be deemed in control of this collection. Sometimes the two questions, thinghood and possessory claims, are determined at the same time, most prominently in first possession. Possession and the principle of accession are closely related, and they work in tandem.

Possession thus occupies a unique place in property law. Concepts reflect considerations of informational economy and for this reason tend to be modular: they are made of components that interact as wholes with each other in stylized ways. A legal system is easier to use and to modify if its basic constituents are modular, thus making possible a system of great complexity and usefulness. (Smith 2012a; see also Simon 1981; Baldwin and Clark 2000; Langlois 2002). In property law, this modularity of concepts comes in partly through the *things* that are the subject of property (Smith 2012b). What counts as a thing emerges from a combination of possession and accession and makes these aspects of property a basic module, which serves as a default regime that can be displaced by more refined rules of title and governance. From this architecture, many of the puzzling features of possession receive an explanation.

Possession links to other concepts in formal property law in a process of formalization and accretion of new rules. First, general norms of possession are in rem. They avail against others generally. The definition of a thing helps in this respect. The more the thing is depersonalized, the easier it is for impersonal duty-bearers to process the duty. The more impersonal a thing is, the easier it is to alienate, which brings the thing more into the prototypical status of owned thing. Perhaps the biggest difference between possession and ownership is the protection of the one without the other – protecting nonowner possessors or owners not in possession – and the greater durability of ownership claims. Here, too, the formalized thing tends to make the shift from possession to ownership easier.

Nevertheless, possession is a cheap way to get us most of what we want from ownership. Thus, possession is not merely an artifact of the process of full-blown ownership. Possession can be a quick and rough way to establish ownership. Possession of a good like a pen is usually a good signal of ownership, for example, when someone is purchasing a pen from a shop. It also governs everyday life, where custom retains its importance, and law can benefit greatly by piggybacking on widespread custom, and if necessary, raw notions of salience themselves. Moreover, possession retains its character as the general rule, so possession is the solution whenever it is not worthwhile to add a more specific formal rule on top of it. Thus, possession tends to be important when the individual stakes are low and the situation is repeated. For this reason, possession retains its close association with customs and informal norms as well as the notions of salience that they rest upon. The system of property concepts achieves coordination of use while responding to constraints of information cost, and possessory notions serve as the low-cost general default.

This chapter begins with an account of possession as a social norm. As developed by Hume (1739–40), Sugden (1986), and Friedman (1994), conventions of possession emerge based on salience and focal points, which rest in turn on a combination of hard-wired perception and practical reasoning. I extend this salience-based account by breaking the possessed thing down into valued attributes as in Barzel's 1997 theory of property rights in the New Institutional Economics. Possession both secures use and announces rights to others by defining things in such a way that those who can most affect the mean return from a collection of valued attributes – the emergent thing – are assigned possessory rights. Possession is a social fact, but it is well suited to becoming the basic module of the system of property law. As possession becomes more legal, it tends to become more formal because it has to reach a more widespread and impersonal audience. True to its origins, this aspect of possession is in rem. Customs like the *pedis possessio* in mining illustrate this development from custom to law. Section 3 shows how the law builds upon *de facto* possession. The modular theory captures the relation of possession to ownership. I hypothesize that common law emphasizes possession more than civil law does because possession is a stand-in for the thing. Common law did not delineate things with as great a precision as did civil law, and more recently, the notion of property as a law of things has fallen even further out of favor. Talk of possession, and more recently the great emphasis in some quarters on the right to exclude, are not wrong. But they are incomplete. Possessory notions are partial substitutes for directly specifying things in property law. Section 4 shows how possession fits in the modular architecture of property. As the most general default regime, it is easily displaced by more refined rules based on title. Possession is also closely associated with exclusion regimes, which likewise give way to governance strategies in certain high-stakes contexts. The hierarchy of defaults (also known as the specific-over-general principle) and the consequent layering of legal regimes capture the fact that possession applies in a disparate set of circumstances without a unifying thread (it applies "otherwise" or "elsewhere").

Possession remains the cheap and rough way to deal with objects in everyday life, with a characteristic gravitational pull. In this, it is like the principle of *nemo dat quod non habet* ("one cannot give that which one does not have"), which likewise is displaced over much of its original domain by good faith purchaser rules. Like the competition between *nemo dat* and good faith purchaser rules, we expect the specific rules based on title and governance of use to be close cases at the margin, in comparison to the general default of possession. Finally, the chapter draws some conclusions about the place of possession in property.

2. Possession and the basic conventions of property

Possession is a *de facto* relation between persons by way of things, or put differently, it is a relation of a person to a thing communicating a priority of use-decisions by that person to other persons with a duty to respect those choices. In this section, I offer an economic account of *de facto* possession that serves as a plug-in concept that the law employs with modification in more rarefied contexts. I concentrate on common law for now, but will offer some comparisons to civil law.[1] I will draw on several strands of property theory that take *de facto* possession seriously, including those of Hume, Sugden, and Barzel. What emerges is a modular theory of *de facto*, and eventually *de jure*, property.

The basic relationship between persons and things is *de facto* possession, which is captured in Hume's and Sugden's accounts of how possessory conventions are rooted in salience. Hume (1739–40: 484–501) offers a theory of property that is meant as a thin justification, in that it justifies the overall practice of property without making strong moral claims for the justice of individual acts of acquisition. He notes that without some version of mutual respect for possession there would be social chaos. Without any top-down direction, people could see from experience that allowing current possessors to remain undisturbed in their possession would help prevent this chaos. For Hume, a convention is a regularity of behavior

---

[1] Chapter 4 adopts the modular framework to offer an insightful treatment of civil law based on a minimal module for possession – actual physical control – which then allows the rest of civil law to be captured simply by adding on other elements for adverse possession, leases, and so forth. The account here is within the same framework and relies on salience and Barzel-style grouping of attributes to do the basic work. It is an empirical question whether this always dovetails with what one would call physical control, and I will take up some examples in the literature (such as North Sea oil and pocketbooks on sidewalks) in which physical control plays an attenuated role.

that people generally expect and prefer to see respected, compared to the alternatives (see also Lewis 1969). And implicit in Hume's account is the idea that no other convention would have the salience needed to align people's expectations in the needed fashion. Further, he gives a more micro version of how salience and conventions establish who possesses what, which draw on widespread notions about nearness and control.

Sugden (2004 [1986]) gives this Humean account a modern interpretation in terms of game theory. The interaction in possession often is seen, especially in evolutionary accounts, as a repeated Hawk/Dove game, in which for each player it is best to fight when the other yields but worst when both fight. Under plausible circumstances, the equilibrium chosen because of salience and long-term convenience involves widespread adoption of the "bourgeois" strategy, in which nonpossessors defer to possessors (Maynard Smith 1982: 95–105; Krier 2009: 154). Whether Hawk/Dove is the best model and what degree of conflict and coordination characterize the problem (for criticisms, see Chapter 2) are matters we need not decide here. In general, with multiple equilibria, salience can help people converge on matching strategies. (This is true for pure coordination, such as which side of the road to drive on, and for games with some degree of conflict, as long as the benefits of coordination outweigh the distributional issues.) Thus, if someone is on a plot of land, that is a close connection, closer than anyone else's. Sugden shows that nearness plays a large role in salience and the formation of conventions. (Most dramatically, he illustrates a pure coordination game in which subjects are asked to join a black circle to one of a group of dispersed white circles, and are told they will receive a monetary reward for converging on the same white circle as a partner. In Humean fashion, the nearest circle is the most salient) (Sugden 2004 [1986]: 98). To be salient, the piece of information should be easily accessible and not subject to multiple interpretations. "To each according to one's need" would not work so well on this score. More recently, Sugden and others have elaborated on the sources of salience, and have shown how mutual advantage can be a source of salience (Sugden 2011). This more recent work draws on evolutionary game theory and models of similarity-based learning, which in turn build on Hume's theory of induction (Alberti, Sugden, and Tsutsui 2012).

Locke's theory of property is often regarded as more ambitious, especially on the interpretation that his account grounds claims of property in desert for labor (Locke 1689: 287–302). Nevertheless, as Rose (1985: 78–80) argues, the type of labor involved should announce itself to others in a clear fashion. At this point one is inevitably reminded of Robert

Nozick's famous (and supposedly) devastating hypothetical about mixing a can of tomato juice in the ocean: why doesn't this establish my claim over the ocean rather than constitute an abandonment of my tomato juice (Nozick 1974: 174–75; see also Waldron 1983: 43)? What if I include in the can a radioactive tracer element to track the mixing of the tomato juice with the ocean's waters? As Eric Claeys (2013) and others have recently argued, Locke is not best interpreted as saying that any labor will do. Only productive labor can ground an original claim to property (see also Mossoff 2002), and the mixing of the tomato juice contributes to no one's self-preservation or advantage of life, in their reconstruction of Locke's objective standard. Nevertheless, why does productively laboring on something not give one a mere lien on the resource (Epstein 1979: 1222–23), or the limited right to trace the value of one's contribution? Why do we recognize rights to exclude from things?

Possession and thinghood are closely related. In the emerging convention, we have to decide exactly what chunk of stuff constitutes the thing over which the person has possession. From the point of view of salience, this has to rely on widely shared background knowledge and a shared tendency to see certain associations as prominent. When I take a fish from the ocean I get possession (and ownership) of the fish, not of the entire stock of fish, not of the ocean, the planet, or the universe. Why?

The simplest answer may be that the practical proto-legal ontology here largely tracks general, everyday ontology. We know what a fish and a chair are. Everyday ontology gets us quite far in the case of tangible personal property, and less so in the case of land, which requires demarcating boundaries. (Everyday ontology and possession are even more attenuated in the case of intangibles, especially intellectual property, which requires more effort at delineation. See Smith 2007). Even in the case of tangibles, everyday ontology does not get us all the way, particularly when we can conceive of a part of something as a thing and things as parts of larger things.[2] Savigny (1848: 192) gives an example of the arm

---

[2] German law is very detailed on the question both of how to define a legal things and their components (see Rixecker and Säcker 2012: § 90 (*Begriff der Sache*, "concept of a thing"), § 93 (*Wesentliche Bestandteile einer Sache*, "integral components of a thing," setting forth which components of a thing are not separable enough to be the subject of legal rights), § 95 *Wesentliche Bestandteile eines Grundstücks oder Gebäudes*, "integral components of a parcel of land or a building"), § 96 (*Rechte als Bestandteile eines Grundstücks*, "rights as components of a parcel of land"), § 97 (*Zubehör*, "accessories)). On accessories in European law, see Swinnen (2012).

of a statue. Unless it is detached, we do not think of the arm as a separate object of possession or ownership (see also Penner 1997).

Here it may be impossible to completely separate salience from utility. Thus, what is a thing depends in part on the problem one is solving. With plots of land, a close-knit community may have common knowledge of how much land each person can work without overall damage to the resource. (I will return to one such example from mining.) What strikes a typical member of a group as salient sometimes may relate to effective use.

Consider how first possession would work if it responded primarily to economic considerations. Yoram Barzel (1997) hypothesizes that transacting parties will arrange things so that a person will have more control over a collection of attributes, the more that person can affect the mean return from the asset. In Barzel's theory, economic resources are analyzed into valued attributes over which people transact. For example, size, taste, color, and texture characterize an apple; land includes soil nutrients, support for buildings, terrain, and so on. When it is not cost-effective to capture value through property rights, actors will leave an attribute in the "public domain." Barzel gives the example of parking lots in suburban shopping malls and salt in restaurants as resources that are not metered separately and which people can, within a certain range, appropriate for themselves. It is not worth it to the owner of the mall or the restaurant to charge separately for the parking spot or the salt. Moreover, consumption of the parking spot or the salt is, again within a certain range, complementary to shopping and eating at the restaurant, thus providing a benefit to the owner.

Barzel's theory is about transacting over property rights and, on a more macro scale, about transitions between one set or regime of property rights to another. Barzel disclaims any attempt at accounting for the start of a system. He likens the beginning of property to a Big Bang, and his theory is about developments from then on. This is understable because for Barzel and for New Institutional Economics, "property rights" are very general. Barzel (1997: 3) defines a "property right" as "the individual's ability, in expected terms, to consume the good (or the services of the asset) directly or to consume it indirectly through exchange." This is consistent with other well-known definitions.[3] Nevertheless, using this very capacious definition, we can adapt his theory to possession, and even first possession.

---

[3] For an especially influential definition among economists, see Alchian (1965: 818) ("By a system of property rights I mean a method of assigning to particular individuals the 'authority' to select, for specific goods, any use from a nonprohibited class of uses."). See

Consider what the Hume/Sugden theory of (first) possession and accession would look like, if, along with Barzel, we break resources into their valued attributes. Now the question is, what collection of attributes should a person be deemed to have a right to use without interference, or, more robustly, to control by excluding others? The theory of possession based on salience has been worked out in detail elsewhere, especially in Sugden (2004 [1986]), but let me add some amendments that make it compatible with theories of possession that are more oriented to the law of possession. If we stick to possession as a pre-legal or extra-legal fact, the phenomenon is not a simple one, but it is much more tractable than the notion of possession writ large, especially as expressed in the law of possession. I will argue later that the law takes basic *de facto* possessory concepts and adds to them, formalizing them in a process of further modularization. If, for now, we stick to basic possession, as most clearly demonstrated in custom and among children, we can see some patterns emerge. Salience in this context relates to the desire to maintain mutual respect for possession, in Humean fashion. The signals have to be clear, but they also have to be useful. Thus, Barzel's notion of choosing the person who has the most ability to affect the mean value of a thing can feed into the notion of salience. Many facts that make the connection have to do with the nearness of a person and a thing, or the presence of a person on land. It often will be difficult to determine how much this is psychological and how much the control that nearness affords makes the person especially suited to draw value from it. Even Hegel's and other "will" theories of possession and Locke's famous labor theory are not incompatible with salience and practicality. Thus, for Hegel one acquires objects through possession by imposing one's will on them, but this will must be expressed physically, either by grasping, imposing form, or marking (Hegel 1820: §§ 51–58; Knowles 1983: 49–51). Each of these methods makes the possessor special with respect to the resource in terms of both notice and usefulness.

Perhaps the most difficult question is whether possession can rest on nearness alone. Some would say that control and an intent to control are necessary for possession (Savigny 1848). However, some forms of

---

also Cheung (1970: 67) ("An exclusive property right grants its owner a *limited* authority to make [decisions] on resource use so as to derive income therefrom."); Demsetz (1967: 347) ("An owner expects the community to prevent others from interfering with his actions, provided that these actions are not prohibited in the specifications of his rights."); Eggertsson (1990: 33) (stating that "[w]e refer to the rights of individuals to use resources as *property rights*" and quoting Alchian's definition).

marking may happen without a high degree of control. Customs of first possession lie along a sliding scale of required control. For resources that might be dissipated by continued competition and where one person early on in the process can be designated the winner, we might expect a tendency to award possession without much control (Lueck 1995). Here the designation of the early winner is again a matter of comparative likelihood to win, as well as psychological salience. If a group's ongoing norms of mutual respect are more robust, then requirements of control and continuing control in defining possession can be relaxed. Consider Holmes's (1888: 235) example of the child on the sidewalk who picks up a pocketbook while a "powerful ruffian" is within equal reach and sight. Does the child possess the pocketbook? Surely, the ruffian is stronger and would win a struggle. Sugden (2004 [1986]: 91–92, 101–03) gives a similar example of North Sea oil, most of which Norway owns, despite being much less powerful than the Soviet Union, which got none. But in a society in which there is much mutual forbearance, we can say that the child's relation to the pocketbook is salient and easily generalizable – at least until the man takes it from the child. Salience is a relative matter, and it fits in a pattern of generalization: people are looking for patterns. In a Hobbesian state of nature, perhaps the ruffian would be deemed the possessor, while in our society the child would. It is natural to take the existence of society as the starting point for normative questions of possession, and in modern society, the generalization that might makes right is less prominent than who is closest or holding an object.

This consideration of the salience of relations between persons and things raises the question of what a thing is. For our legal ontology, we need a theory of what counts as a person and what as a thing, along with whatever connections there might be between the former and the latter. Sometimes, in the simplest cases, the notion of a legal thing will track a thing from everyday ontology: chairs, foxes, and the like. More difficult will be situations in which the extent of a collection of attributes could come out one way or another. Is an attached bookshelf part of a house or not? A pencil includes its attached eraser, but unattached erasers are separate things, unless they share some design features with pencils (as in a desk set). The salience theory also addressed this question in terms of notions of the lesser going with the greater, known sometimes as accession. Here we have a similar process of salience and practicality in determining what goes with what, and which the possessor in turn possesses. Hume devotes considerable attention to accession, as does

Sugden. Again, the rules for the lesser going with the greater are interpreted psychologically as an association of ideas in Hume and as a selection of equilibria based on salience in Sugden. Thus, the Orkneys go with Britain and the calf with the mother cow, and not the other way around. In the doctrine of accession, labor must have a certain prominence in terms of transformation or relative value in order to entitle the good faith improver to keep the thing and pay damages.[4] Now consider Locke again. To get from even productive labor to property rights, we need a notion of accession, as Locke seems to have realized, when he claimed that "labour makes the far greatest part of the value of things" (Locke 1689: 297; see also Claeys 2013; Smith 2007: 1767–68). Why does productive labor lead to exclusion rights, rather than merely to use rights, rights to the current flow of the resource (a *profit-à-prendre*), or a right to trace the contribution of labor with some sort of lien (Epstein 1979)? Here, too, some combination of psychological salience and practical usefulness does the work. In the Humean process of mutual forbearance, the emergence of the possession convention goes in tandem with the emergence of accession conventions. In general, first possession involves accession. (Or, one might say vice versa. This is perhaps what Blackstone [1766: 258] means when he says that one always takes ownership by occupancy – because he regards accession as part and parcel of the notion of occupancy.)[5]

In a hypothetical state of nature, we would have persons with varying strengths and talents and a multitude of attributes that might be grouped together in various ways. In Barzel's theory, we might expect that people would be assigned a collection of attributes whose mean return they had

---

[4] *Wetherbee v. Green*, 22 Mich. 311 (1871); see also Chang (2015 forthcoming); Merrill (2009); Newman (2009: 86–93).

[5] Even Merrill (2009: 474–75), who treats accession as an acquisition principle that stands as an alternative to first possession, acknowledges that accession and first possession are closely related. Merrill asserts that accession only works when property rights exist, but this assumes that accession is limited to being an acquisition principle. Something like accession is what determines what a thing is, a possible object for possession (and ownership) in the first place (Newman 2009: 86–93; Smith 2007). Interestingly, in his insightful theory of which chattels can be taken as up for grabs, Corriel (2013) lumps aspects of possession and accession together, using notions reminiscent of salience. For Corriel, whether an object can be acquired depends on how unique and identifying it is, whether it "nests" with other objects to send a strong signal together, and whether notice overrides what otherwise would be the signal. Thus, a five-dollar bill is fungible, non-identifying, and so up for grabs, but in a private place or next to a driver's license in a public place, it is not. Defaults that can be overridden by further nesting or notice are consistent with the theory of possession offered here.

a special ability to affect. We cannot say that this starting point is ideal: some people will be stronger than others. Some families or clans will be more powerful than others. And some will be lucky enough to be located near better resources. It would also be a mistake to think this is a world without property rights of any kind. People's natural talents and opportunities mean that they will have the ability to consume some resources without interference. In Umbeck's (1981: 39) famous example for the capacious New Institutional Economics definition of property rights, if someone is the only one who knows how to climb a tree, he has property rights (*de facto*, not *de jure*) in the coconuts. Umbeck based his theory of property rights on the ability to commit violence. This may be too narrow, and theorists of the formation of society disagree as to whether we should think of early arrangements, either the hypothetical ones of philosophers or the actual ones we can reconstruct, as coercive or more balanced. (Compare Moselle and Polak 2001 with Olson 1993.) Moreover, we will be most interested in those "property rights" that have gained legitimacy in the eyes of third parties. (See Chapter 2.)

For our purposes, it makes sense to stick with description and explanation, with side glances in a normative direction. It is no accident that Hume's theoretical justificatory account and Barzel's economic explanation converge, and that both accord with current basic customary norms and morality.[6] To capture this connection, Friedman (1994) offers an account of property rights in terms of Schelling points – equilibria that are chosen because of their uniqueness. (The uniqueness can be seen as resulting from salience, and Friedman (1994: 2) notes the similarity to Sugden's account.) Friedman argues that people will use Schelling points to contract out of the Hobbesian state of nature step by step, where previous contracting changes the Schelling points (Schelling 1960). Friedman argues that there is a convergence among a libertarian form of morality, efficiency, and (roughly) the social orders that have evolved, because the contracting process that generates rights leads to all three – morality, efficiency, and social order. But, as Friedman notes, these norms are only "locally efficient." This is true of the whaling

---

[6] Hume insists that his theory of justice and property is based on psychology and not a sense of the public interest (Hume 1739–40: 496, 502, 504 n. 1). But when it comes to the rules of possession he does admit that "[w]e are said to be in possession of any thing, not only when we immediately touch it, but also when we are so situated with respect to it, as to have it in our power to use it; and may move, alter, or destroy it, according to our present pleasure or advantage" (Hume 1739–40: 506).

norms discussed by Ellickson (1991): they were adopted to deal with conflict between two whaling crews meeting on the ocean, not in the interest of conserving whales. As we will see, some of Ellickson's most arresting examples are possessory, and the Hume/Sugden theory elaborates on Schelling in showing how a convention could have emerged based on salience. In the process of contracting based on Schelling points, conventions will not be adopted because they are moral or efficient overall but because they serve the interests of the contracting parties, as Friedman argues. To this, we might add that the morality is also a local one, corresponding to corrective justice and local distributive justice, rather than societal distributive justice. Private law is easier to explain in corrective justice terms because it is local, in part for information-cost reasons (Gold and Smith ms.). This is reflected in its hypothetical and perhaps actual history. Norms that have a local moral and practical appeal are scaled up. This scaling up involves a persistent focus on individual interaction horizontally. As in modular systems, one can build up a system of great complexity while still allowing the local simplicity of interaction of earlier stages of the system: we need only build on it. Perhaps the main difference between libertarians and statists is the degree to which they differ as to whether morality persists as we scale up. We need not resolve this debate here in order to pursue the information-cost theory, which is mainly explanatory. That its more general module of possession accords with local morality and its more designed and refined modules reflect more global considerations is suggestive, but I am not making any foundational normative claims here.

In the next sections, I will show how numerous features of possession can be explained by the modular information-cost account. Possession as a basic module makes sense of several of its striking features. Possession is the aspect of property that most resembles animal territoriality (see, e.g., Peterson 2011: 156–72). It is also the one that children learn first (Friedman and Neary 2009). The modular structure of customary and legal concepts allows possessory concepts to play a simple and widespread role in the system. Possession remains close to its roots in biology, morality, and custom while interacting with more complex aspects of a modern legal system. The close association of possession with custom is both historically and functionally a result of the ability of close-knit groups to get on the same page as far as the nature of things and the connection of persons to things. Like all custom, the customs of possession tend to become formalized as they apply to larger and more impersonal groups.

A famous example of this process of formalizing custom as it becomes more general is the doctrine of the *pedis possessio*. Originally, the *pedis possessio* was a custom among miners that allowed one who was working a "spot" to work it exclusively without interference from forcible, fraudulent, and clandestine intrusions, as long as he kept working the spot. What constituted a spot – a kind of "thing" – and what counted as continuous work were a matter of custom, and, in the context of a close-knit miners' camp, a general understanding could easily arise (and change as needed with circumstances). As case law and then federal statutes grew up in mining, they borrowed heavily from mining customs. As I have argued elsewhere, the process of custom becoming applicable to wider and more impersonal audiences leads those designing the law to strip the custom down, and make it more formal, in the sense of being less responsive to context (Smith 2009). The *pedis possessio* is a prime example. The General Mining Law of 1872 provides that mining claimants must satisfy requirements of both location and discovery, in order to have a valid unpatented mining claim (a property right less than a fee simple). These requirements are essential for rights against the United States.[7] As for rights against other miners who might interfere with a claim, the legal doctrine of the *pedis possessio* allows such rights even if a claim has not yet been validly located. When courts adapted the custom, the boundary of the spot was identified with the boundary of the claim.[8] By contrast, under the older custom, the boundary of a "spot" was not the entire claim but a fuzzy area that one was considered to be working.[9] The more formal boundary of the claim would be easier for outsiders to understand, commensurate with its more in rem aspect and its use in courts.

Nor is this a matter of mere expansion: more recently, courts have refused to expand the *pedis possessio* beyond the boundaries of a claim, despite the need in industries like uranium for much larger "spots" in the exploratory phase. There may be a custom in the uranium industry to extend the *pedis possessio* beyond the boundary of a single claim. The Supreme Court, however, has held that the *pedis possessio* does not extend to claims adjacent to the one being worked, and courts that have tried to extend the *pedis possessio* in this fashion have been severely

---

[7] 30 U.S.C. § 23 (2000).
[8] *Field* v. *Grey*, 25 P. 793, 794 (Ariz. 1881); *Miller* v. *Chrisman*, 73 P. 1083, 1086 (Cal. 1903), aff'd, 197 U.S. 313 (1905); see also Finberg (1982: 1036).
[9] *Union Oil* v. *Smith*, 249 U.S. 337 (1919). See, e.g., Forman, Dwyer, and Fox (1970).

criticized.[10] The "test" adopted by a minority of courts for the expanded *pedis possessio* winds up being vague and unworkable, requiring the evaluation of claims for similar geology and reasonable size, discovery work under state law, an overall work program, diligent pursuit of the work program, and economic impracticability on the narrow version of *pedis possessio*.[11] The mainstream approach is to reject the wider *pedis possessio*, as in the well-known case of *Geomet Exploration, Limited* v. *Lucky Mc Uranium Corp.*,[12] and to limit the doctrine to the bounds of a claim. The "thing" – here the claim – does a lot of work.

Possession forms the link between *de facto* (pre- or extra-legal) and *de jure* property rights. As I will argue, part of the problem besetting accounts of possession has been the attempt to derive all the legal manifestations of possession from first principles. This has been especially so in civil law countries, where Roman law was a starting point and concessions to practicality have been made with ostensible reluctance. Even in common law, forcing possession into rigid templates like the relativity of title and the older forms of the theft offenses have tied commentators in knots. It would be simpler to start with pre-legal possession and then ask how it is modified and stretched to form part of the law of property.[13] As we will see, keeping possession pre-legal and based on salience, psychological and practical, allows us to explain many features of both possession and the social and legal architecture into

---

[10] *MacGuire* v. *Sturgis*, 347 F. Supp. 580 (D.C. Wyo. 1971); see also *Continental Oil Co.* v. *Natrona Service, Inc.*, 588 F.2d 792, 798 (10th Cir. 1978).
[11] *MacGuire* v. *Sturgis*, 347 F. Supp. at 584.   [12] 601 P.2d 1339 (Ariz. 1979).
[13] The germ of the theory sketched here can be found in Dernburg's treatise on the Roman law Pandects (Justinian's *Digest*, which in Germany was – and to some extent still is – treated as a way into the current law). As Dernburg argues, "Possession – *possessio* – is the actual control over valued things. Possession is not, as many suppose, law. It is rather a phenomenon that stands outside the law, even if laws are linked to it." (All translations the author's.) See also Pollock (1896: 168). Dernburg makes the point that even if law were removed, possession would remain, because it is a "condition of securing human existence" (Dernburg 1900: 1–2). In arch-Prussian fashion, Dernburg (1900: 7) goes on to say that our actual distribution of goods must be "sacrosanct" as a condition of ordered coexistence. One need not go this far to recognize the importance of stability of possession. It features in Hume's hypothetical history and justificatory theory. Moreover, widespread lack of respect for possession is a step toward social chaos. As in Hume's account, for Dernburg (1900: 6–7), "possession is the actual social order, the given allocation of valued objects. It directly affords the individual the tools for his activities, the means to satisfy his needs." The salience theory coupled with the New Institutional Economics can do even better than Dernburg's account at showing how possession is linked with the law.

which it fits. By breaking things down into their constituent valued attributes, a Humean version of New Institutional Economics can explain how property gets started. It also accounts for why things are important in the law of property and why property law draws on possession to a great extent.

3. The generalization of possession

De facto possession as accounted for in the modular theory forms a platform for successive layers of legal superstructure. In this section, I show how the law regulates possession as a legal concept, starting with how the law secures possessory rights. The law affords greater durability to possession than it can achieve in pre-legal convention. I show how possession and ownership are related, through layering of the latter on the former. For extending possession beyond its roots, the notion of a thing is crucial, because it allows for the formalization needed in more in rem contexts, for greater durability, and for enhanced alienability.

In the modular architecture of property, possession is the basic module, in the sense of a regime connecting persons to objects for purposes of rights availing against others. As a module, it needs to plug into the rest of property law in a defined way, such that much of the internal working of possession need not be relevant to duty bearers and enforcers, as long as it provides answers to a useful set of questions. The set of concepts in property is nearly decomposable in the sense of Simon (1981: 210), because they group situations into clumps whose constituents intensively interact (internally), but which interact only weakly with other situation-clumps (externally). Formalizing them further takes this compartmentalization further. As we will see, the interaction of possession with other regimes is one of a general module (basic possession) being partially trumped by more specific ones (refined possession, title, ownership).

3.1. Extended possession

As touched on earlier in the discussion of custom and the *pedis possessio*, the law adapts conventions of possession by making them more formal. What is salient to a close-knit group may or may not be salient to the larger society. Thus, when the law affords a legally enforceable possessory right, it does not merely adopt possessory customs wholesale and unaltered. The more the possessory notion has to govern a wide and impersonal set of duty bearers – the more it is classically in rem – the more possession has to be divorced from parts of its context (Merrill and Smith 2000, 2001a; Smith 2003). It is too much to expect nonlocal miners to know what a "spot" is for the *pedis possessio*, but the boundaries of a claim are relatively easy to process. Possession law, like all law, is a form of communication and as such faces a trade-off: one can communicate in an intensive way with a more intimate audience or in a less information-dense way with a more extensive audience (Smith 2003, 2013; Heylighen 1999: 27, 49–53). In closer social contexts, much information can be implicit, thereby making the amount of information per unit of communicative effort very high. This is true of what linguists call pragmatics: there are principles of conversation that allow one to infer (in a loose, defeasible way) from "It's cold in here" to a request to close the window (Grice 1989; Levinson 2000). In other words, for audiences that are more in rem – large and indefinite, and so unlikely to share as much background knowledge – the communication has to be more formal, that is, relatively invariant to content (Smith 2003). Formalism is a matter of degree, and we expect more formal communication to in rem audiences. When we move from *de facto* and customary possession to the law of possession, this formalization is part of the process.

Not all extra-legal possessory norms are particular. On the contrary, much of what goes under the heading of possession is very basic and not particular even to one society. Ellickson notes how striking it is that the most basic possessory norms are common across cultures, or rely on salience that often makes it possible for an outsider to interpret property signals (Ellickson 2011). Fences and the like are easy to process, and the use of broken furniture and other objects to mark shoveled snow spots after major snowstorms is but one (very prominent) example: even those from warm climates can guess what the claim is (Epstein 2002: 528–33; Rose 1985: 81). Again, it is a version of the possessory module here that is the most general, which allows it to reach the widest and most impersonal audiences. Law pushes this process further when necessary.

One key to formalizing possessory customs is the notion of a thing. As we saw earlier, possession and accession both involve – even give rise to – the notion of a thing: which attributes go with which, and are in turn associated with which person or persons. As possession binds more socially distant parties, it becomes more important for them to process the information about this duty *through the thing itself*. Thus, "in rem" is not just etymologically "relating to a thing": it is the thing that promotes the de-contextualization needed to extend norms of possession into legal norms (Smith 2012b).

Custom or law can extend *de facto* possession into more durable rights to possess. This is cost-effective as long as the marginal benefits of better tailoring of the possessory rights exceed the marginal costs of communication and foregone multiple use. One very cost-effective dimension is duration. With more durable rights, one can leave a thing with no immediate control over it without losing the right to possess it. This legal durability is an extension of the process of making customary possession more durable: the miners customs allowed miners to leave to get supplies without losing rights under the *pedis possessio*. Thinghood makes the persistence of possession easier, so that possession can be maintained with less effort, also allowing more specialization. The thing makes processing by duty bearers less costly: it is easier for others to know what is off limits even when the possessor is absent if they can rely on the boundaries of the thing to tell them the content of their duty.

More durable rights to possess also can be transferred, with the addition of the formalities of transmission. Even *de facto* possession can be transferred by a sort of directional abandonment. But as possession becomes more formal, the delivery of some surrogate thing like a twig or even a document can effect the transfer (see Chapter 8). (As discussed later, moving beyond possession, the formalities associated with ownership, and title records in particular, further facilitate transfers of rights.)

First possession is an area of the law where custom plays an unusually large role. First possession as an acquisition principle latches onto a pre- or extra-legal social fact. Further, the custom as enforced by courts is a somewhat more formal version of the one that subgroups of society might employ among themselves. In the (somewhat artificial) classic of possession law, *Pierson* v. *Post*,[14] this issue of communication is not far from the surface (Rose 1985; Smith 2003). It may well be that hunters among themselves might recognize rights of one in hot pursuit of a fox. The question is whether nonhunters should be held to know this.

---

[14] 3 Cai. R. 175 (N.Y. Sup. Ct. 1805). A recent outpouring of scholarship suggests that *Pierson* was artificial and unusual in many ways. (See Berger 2006; Ernst 2009; Fernandez 2009a, b; McDowell 2007).

Whaling customs relied on background knowledge of whalers, but they also show a pattern of nested default rules, with more general ones being more formal and easier for nonexperts to deal with. Two whaling crews meeting on the high seas can be presumed to know the customs of possession of whales. As Ellickson (1989, 1991) argues, these rules were good for managing the interaction of members of the community (whalers), but they might cause out-group externalities (and whales indeed were overhunted). Likewise, as Friedman (1994) notes, norms of possession are adopted for reasons that do not include their being good or efficient overall (see also Cosmides and Tooby 2006: 187). Even here, we arguably see nested default rules: under the "fast fish loose fish" rule, the whale belonged to the first one to harpoon it as long as the harpoon was attached to the whaler's boat. By contrast the "first iron" rule gave the first harpooner exclusive rights as long as fresh pursuit continued. The "first iron" rule is further from the kind of salience that would appeal to nonwhalers and it was adopted in high-stakes contexts, for sperm whales, which were both valuable and especially dangerous. Indeed the "fast fish loose fish" rule appears to have been the general custom and "first iron" (and other rules like those for finback whales) a departure from it.

Adverse possession is another extension of possession, and it shows this process of formalization based on a thing. Because it competes with an existing claim of ownership, the salience required for ouster is greater than in other contexts (like liability for rent in co-ownership). Not just any possession will count; it must be open and notorious, actual, continuous and under a claim of right. The standard here is higher than the possession a rightful possessor needs to maintain, or a wrongful possessor against a subsequent wrongful possessor.

Adverse possession also is formalized in ways similar to the *pedis possessio*, but adverse possession is more complicated because of the owner's pre-existing claim. The boundaries of a parcel do have a gravitational pull, but the adverse possessor's claim and its relation to the boundaries are only part of the picture: the larger is the adverse possessor's claim, the smaller is the original owner's. In the case of a building encroachment, the salient rule is occupation of the footprint of the encroaching structure. When it comes to cultivation or other kinds of use, salience probably does refer to the boundaries of a parcel, but also with regard to the owner's activities and interests. Thus, if an adverse possessor possesses a plot that the owner is partially occupying, the adverse possessor gets a minimal claim. An adverse possessor who is using a parcel of an absentee owner will probably not have a hard time establishing a claim over the whole parcel unless the use is quite confined to a part. If the adverse possessor is acting as a gatekeeper, the likely presumption is that possession is over the entire parcel. Use is highly salient in the activities of both the adverse possessor and the owner, which gives rise to criticisms that adverse possession has an anti-conservation bias built into it (Sprankling 1996: 538–40). Finally, adverse possession is formalized beyond the physically salient facts on the ground. Having a defective deed to the whole parcel makes it easier to adversely possess an entire parcel by using a part of it. A parcel requires demarcation and so is more artificial than a chair or a pencil. In the case of land, the legal thing is further from the thing furnished by pre-legal ontology. Again, the parcel as a legal thing, boosted here by some documentary evidence, does some important work.

The case of the wrongful possessor brings us to the topic of the relativity of title. This theory, which has enjoyed a vogue in the common law since the nineteenth century, is sometimes thought to be characteristic of common law (Holmes 1881; Pollock and Wright 1888). Civil law, by contrast, emphasizes ownership and is more grudging about recognizing lesser rights (Chang and Smith 2012). In the next section, I will use the modular theory to explain some of the differences between common and civil law in their approach to possession and ownership. For now, we can analyze relativity of title as one, but only one, solution to layering ownership on top of possession.

The essence of relativity of title is that a possessor's rights against those with later (or lesser) possessory rights mimic the owner's even better rights. To be sure, in a possessory action, the owner beats all others, and a possessor beats subsequent possessors (although there is some doubt as to whether a wrongful possessor beats a subsequent rightful possessor). Relativity of title goes a step further and identifies the content of the owner's right with the content of the lesser rights of the other possessors (if any). Most often this content is identified with the right to exclude, with "natural" extensions to rights to use and transfer (e.g., Chapter 6; McFarlane 2008: 146; Chapter 1). The owner is simply the one with the best right to exclude. As Gordley and Mattei (1996) point out, one can recognize a possessory right without identifying the content of the right with ownership in this fashion. They further argue that relativity of title was invented in the nineteenth century, and is not a fully accurate picture of common law. One main difference between possessory rights and ownership is durability. It is easier for possessors who have left actual physical control to lose their rights than it is for owners. Recall that ownership is a legal extension of possessory rights, here along the dimension of durability. Nothing in the theory rules out other extensions. Ownership rights are more likely to be subject to registries, which allow further distance between the state of title and visible facts on the ground. Title, too, is formal, in the sense of decontextualization.

3.2. Possession and ownership

Why protect both possession and ownership, or even have two concepts at all? This has been a puzzle in both common and civil law, although the reaction tends to be very different in the two systems. The modular theory of possession allows us to see where possession does and does not fit in the overall architecture of property. First, the customs of possession still operate most of the time (Chapter 1). It would be too expensive and not worthwhile to have registries for objects like paper cups, shoes, and watches. Ordinary potential violators most often need not know anything about possible divergences between ownership and title in order to respect the modular package of rights. Keeping off – a message sent largely, but not entirely, by the thing itself – is usually enough. Because this regime is already there, the law can piggyback on it, with some formalization around the edges as needed.

Even in the case of land, possession works most of the time. Getting permission (in order to avoid being a trespasser) usually involves asking the one in possession. This even extends to gaining access to land with permission of security guards, who have no property interest at all. Most of the time the stakes are low enough in seeking access so that we stick with the cheap solution of allowing the one in possession to give permission. One can accept a dinner invitation without consulting land records. For high-stakes problems like building encroachments, more onerous requirements come into play: one must commission a survey, which is keyed to ownership rights and not possession.

Because it is more formalized, ownership can do better much of what possession does, albeit at greater cost. Ownership is keyed to an even more formalized version of the thing than is possession, and so ownership rights are more easily alienable than are possessory rights. Yes, one person can hand over possession to another. But it is very difficult to know from a third-party perspective whether all the rights are being handed over, whether possession is given temporarily, or whether the possessor is giving mere permission to enter (a license). The problems here are so great that possession cannot serve to identify multiple unqualified in rem rights in the same thing (see Chapter 8; see also Chapter 7). With ownership, the thing is depersonalized to a degree that one person can step in the shoes of another without much trouble for third parties (Smith 2012b: 1710–11, 1724). Indeed, this process has inspired some to identify ownership as an office (Essert 2013; Katz 2010). No one argues that possession is an office. I have argued that the depersonalization of the relationship between owners and others made possible by thing-definition is what allows for alienability and the other features that make the notion of an office of "owner" attractive (Smith 2013: 337–38). Ownership is different from and more formal than possession in this respect.

Being more formal than possession, ownership makes certain bailments feasible, again at greater cost. The greater durability and formalization of ownership make it easier to give lesser possessory rights without the ambiguity of a possessor-to-possessor transfer. This feature of ownership comes at a cost: the ownership records that make transfers less ambiguous are costly. Think of the difference between an informal bailment of a coat at a coat check and the bailment of a fine painting. Ownership records are relevant to the latter but not the former. In between is a car at an auto repair shop: possession is usually enough, but in cases of doubt registration will need to be produced.[15] Again, there is a sliding scale of formality (and its attendant cost) from possession to ownership.

3.3. Solving the mystery of possession

Possession's role in property theory stems in part from the general lack of attention in the common law world, especially in the United States, to the thing over which property is defined. Rights to things are considered naïve and inaccurate (see, e.g., Cohen 1935: 815; Grey 1980: 69–70, 80). Because things are (on this view) out of the picture, and the notion of the relation between a person and a thing is downplayed (especially in American law), people invoke possession as the next-best thing. Because possession thus implicitly assumes a notion of the thing, the thing is being smuggled in when what we really need is the thing itself.

---

[15] The trouble that can be caused by non-owners contracting for repairs is well illustrated in *Tappenden v. Artus*, (1964) 2 Q.B. 185, (1963) 3 All E.R. 213 (Ct. App.).

Common law has long emphasized possession. The system of estates was built around present and future possession, and at its heart was the concept of seisin, which was close to the notion of possession. On the modular account, this approach may hang together because the possessory notions are doing the work of defining a thing for purposes of property.

Commentary in common law has veered all over the lot on whether things are important to property, and possession has played a complementary role. The most influential commentator of modern times, William Blackstone (1766), employed a civilian inspired organization, with Volume 2 of his *Commentaries* devoted to "Of the Rights of Things." Adam Smith in his *Lectures on Jurisprudence* (1762–63: 11) adopted a civilian-style distinction between real (or in rem) and personal (or in personam) rights, noting, "[w]e may observe that not only property but all other exclusive rights are real rights." More recently, the bundle of rights theory has downplayed things. The bundle picture of property comes in different versions, some of which emphasize a thin notion of the right to exclude (Cohen 1954; see also Mossoff 2011). Even more recently, many theorists, seeking to get beyond the vacuity of the bundle theory and seeking a theme in property, have emphasized the right to exclude, or close variants (Merrill 1998).[16] I agree that exclusion strategies are important as a unifying thread, and a characteristic one, for property (Smith 2002; Smith 2005). Part of the reason for this is the importance of the thing to property, which has not been widely appreciated. One might say that the attention lavished on the right to exclude and on possession is a symptom of the lack of attention to the thing. Possession and the right to exclude are related to trespass, which closely tracks the thing. Talking about trespass is a way of invoking things without having to do so explicitly.

Civil law, by contrast, defines ownership more directly, and spends a great deal of explicit effort defining things (Chang and Smith 2012). In a fashion reminiscent of the ontology of norms we sketched earlier, Roman law divided the world into persons, things, and actions (remedies). Property is the prototypical law of things, and this notion has persisted into the modern civil codes (Foster and Sule 2010: 493; Yiannopoulos 2001: §§ 12, 15). Chapter 4 shows how reducing possession to a minimum (the author argues for physical control) allows possession to plug into the

---

[16] Penner (1997) usually is classified as an exclusion theorist, but, unlike most commentators, he equally emphasizes his separation thesis (and thing definition).

set of other concepts in civil law. The modular theory also provides the solution to older debates over why possession is protected in civil law, even though ownership is so elaborately defined (and defended as a concept). In both common and civil law, basic *de facto* possession is a modest but potentially far-reaching starting point. Common law extends it under the heading of possession, building up incrementally from basic possession through related possessory notions, to a version of ownership. In civil law, ownership appears quite distinct and distant from possession, which would seem to suggest that a module based on basic *de facto* possession does not play much role. Nevertheless, Chapter 4 shows how defining a minimal module of possession based on control of a person over a thing would plug into the rest of the civil law of possession. The contrast in the style of delineation of ownership and possession is an important difference between civil and common law, even if it is functionally important only around the edges (Chang and Smith 2012, 2015). Ultimately, it is the architecture and its function that count, not the labels – "possession" or something else – that we attach to the modules.

4. The persistence of possession

Possession persists in importance because it is the basic module in a system of property. How it is expressed is not a matter simply of finding first principles – whether grounded in morals or efficiency – for defining "possession" as a legal matter. Rather, possession is a formalized version of possessory custom, which is the ultimate default regime for assigning things to persons. Built on top of possession are various other rules of property, which modify and override basic possession in situations in which actors, private and public, have found it worthwhile to go beyond possession. These more refined regimes tend to reflect more conscious design than basic possession. Moreover, they are layered on the basic module and trump it in specific environments. They tend to make disconnected refinements to basic things and so give many the impression that things as defined by basic possession and accession are no longer important – and that property itself is a disjointed grab bag (a bundle of rights, one might even say). Nevertheless, possession and things retain their importance in less "refined" contexts, where the basic default layer shows through. Because of this layering architecture of modular property, possession winds up being a heterogeneous category, one that governs in an "elsewhere" pattern – when nothing more specific applies.

4.1. Layering and the modularity of possession

Many of the most striking and difficult features of possession are easily captured on the modular theory of possession. Because possession is the most basic layer and the law employs it unless another part of the system overrides it, possession is close to its roots in custom. It is also a cheap and rough way to treat property questions on an ongoing basis. Possession also has a gravitational pull corresponding to its status as the ultimate default regime within property.

Possession is the general default regime, with other rules layered on it.[17] Much of what is layered on top of basic possession is a matter of law, but not everything. In the so-called "small property" market in Shenzen, China, some real property changes hands despite its technically illegal status. Qiao (2014) analyzes this regime as resting on focal points, including an expectation of reform, which would represent an extension of the mechanism behind possession into the realm of alienability. Most of the familiar transition from possessory customs to the rest of property law is a matter of layering formal rules relating to title, which allows more complex forms of ownership to displace the basic possessory regime. Other displacing rules relate to use. Possession, because it is based closely on thing definition, is tightly bound up with exclusionary strategies. When these prove inadequate, possession and possessory remedies – instantiations of the exclusion strategy – will give way to more refined rules and standards focusing in on particular uses, in a governance strategy (Smith 2002). These more refined devices in a governance strategy can take the forms of contracts, off-the-rack nuisance law, and zoning and other regulation. In the case of personal property, governance usually takes the form of contracts or beneficial interests layered on top of basic legal title.

Layering is the result of the specific-over-general principle. A rule whose description properly contains that of another rule will displace it. This is a widespread device in human language (Hayes 2009; Sag, Wasow, and Bender 2003; Smith 1996). For example, the *-ed* rule is the general way to form past tense in English, but more specific rules exist, such as the *-ing, -ang, -ung* rule (*sing, sang, sung; ring, rang, rung*), and even more specific rules like *bring, brought* (Pinker 1999: 13–19).[18] The *-ed*

---

[17] In a vaguely similar fashion, Heck (1930: §§ 1, 3) posits possession as a "provisional order" that is confirmed or overridden by a system of definite rights to things.
[18] The simplifying type of analogy works in the direction of the more general rules: verbs that used a subrule or were irregular adopted *-ed*, but generally not vice versa (*dive, dove,* came to alternate with *dive, dived*, in a process many verbs have completed, such as the

rule applies "elsewhere" in the highly diverse set of circumstances not falling under any other more specific rule. Human language grammar employs this device of specific-over-general pervasively, and the notion of nested defaults, or "default hierarchies," was borrowed by linguistics from computer science (see, e.g., Holland et al. 1986: 18–19; Dorigo 1991: 221–22). Human knowledge, especially that built up inductively (like possession), can be organized into default hierarchies, in which "the rules that constitute a category do not provide a *definition* of the category. Instead, they provide a set of expectations that are taken to be true only as long as they are not contradicted by information that is more specific. In the absence of additional information these 'default' expectations provide the best available sketch of the current situation" (Holland et al. 1986: 18; citing Minsky 1975).[19] For example, knowing that an animal is a bird produces a default expectation that it can fly, which can be overridden by more specific – for example, penguin-specific – information. A similar, well-known principle in contract law includes the system of default rules explored in the law and economics literature (Ayres and Gertner 1989).[20] A version of the specific-over-general principle also applies in statutory interpretation: if two provisions might apply, the more specific one trumps (Manning 2011: 2012). The modular theory allows us to see that nested default rules are pervasive in many areas of law.

Like other basic general rules, possession exhibits an "elsewhere" pattern: possession is defined by not being anything else (Smith 2012a). That is, this most basic rule or regime applies in a disparate collection of scenarios, when nothing else does, like the *-ed* rule for past tense in English. Consider fencing in versus fencing out. Under the former, a farmer has possessory rights against trespasses by wandering cattle, and under the latter, ranchers have no duty to keep wandering cattle from

---

verb *help*). Other linguistic processes create new specific rules (Smith 1996: 221–58; Hopper and Traugott 2003). The costs and benefits of creating, maintaining, and discarding rules differ between language and law, but the specific-over-general architecture captures some similarities.

[19] A set of categories is more modular if a subcategory inherits its features from only one path of supercategories ("single inheritance"). I leave open exactly how far modularity can be pushed in analyzing property concepts.

[20] *Smoot v. United States*, 237 U.S. 38, 42 (1915) (Holmes, J.) ("In general, specific or individual marks prevail over generic ones."); *DCV Holdings, Inc. v. Conagra, Inc.*, 889 A.2d 954, 961 (Del. 2005) ("Specific language in a contract controls over general language, and where specific and general provisions conflict, the specific provision ordinarily qualifies the meaning of the general one").

entering others' land. Ellickson (1991) found that regardless of whether the formal law was fencing in or fencing out, the informal norm in Shasta County was for animal owners to take responsibility. The norm conformed to the most general possessory default (also reflected in the general law of trespass). We can further hypothesize that fencing in would be more widespread than a narrow area-by-area comparison of the value of farming versus ranching would lead one to expect (Merrill and Smith 2001b).

Another example from property of nested defaults is the relationship of the principle of *nemo dat quod non habet* ("one cannot give that which one does not have") to rules favoring good faith purchasers. In the case of property rights in transfer, the system is more simply described as *nemo dat* subject to exceptions like those for certain good faith purchasers, rather than taking some other rule as basic and capturing most of we think of as *nemo dat* more directly. Levmore (1987) hypothesized that the different rules for good faith purchaser were close to each other in their efficiency and that this was the reason for the variety of rules among systems in some situations involving good faith purchasers. (Other, clearer situations showed uniformity.) Here, too, we can analyze this pattern as layering, just as with possession. As I have argued elsewhere, *nemo dat* is the basic rule – and incidentally the one most easily integrated with the possessory regime (Smith 2013). Rules favoring good faith purchasers are layered on top of this. The displacement can numerically be very pervasive, but the more basic rule persists in an elsewhere pattern. The system is much easier to describe using *nemo dat* (like possession) as the basic rule and good faith purchaser as the more specific, and therefore trumping, rule (along with other more specific rules). In addition, we would predict that as a legal system breaks down, *nemo dat* (like possession) would remain longest. We should expect that children would learn *nemo dat* before rules such as good faith purchaser. Also, like possession, *nemo dat* has a gravitational pull for situations not covered by the system. Finally, it is to be expected that at the edges of the more refined module, whether *nemo dat* versus good faith purchaser or possession versus title, we would find close cases, in the pattern that Levmore noticed.

The relationship between possession and more refined rules of title works similarly. Thus, we can protect actual possessors, but someone with title will beat a possessor. Explicit arrangements like landlord-tenant and estates and future interests can be built on the principle that present possession is not the last word. But absent any such overlay, possession still shines through. Thus, the search for a comprehensive principle for possession is a wild goose chase. Unlike ownership and other overlays, possession is described most economically as the ultimate default, leading to the "elsewhere" or "otherwise" pattern and the gravitational pull possession still exerts in close contexts. Moreover, because possession is the ultimate default, different systems will add more or fewer overriding modules on top of possession. The addition of the last such overriding module should be a close case: modules should be added up to the point where marginal benefit no longer exceeds marginal cost. Therefore, at the margin, one would expect there to be close cases whether it is worthwhile to employ another module based on a more refined notion, like title, or to stick with basic possession.

As with *nemo dat*, whether to employ possession or some more refined rule relating to title is bound to be close, precisely because the more refined rule is layered on top of possession. Title rules have wider or narrower scope and can be added or subtracted from the system, with possession picking up the slack. Thus, if the system is close to efficient, whether through evolutionary pressures or by design, in those situations it will be close to the margin in terms of costs and benefits.

Before turning to other examples of layering, it is worth emphasizing what the specific-over-general principle and consequent layering do and do not mean. Being more basic does not mean superior, more important, and the like. (This point seems to escape the notice of many commentators. See, e.g., Alexander 2009; Dagan 2011: 37–55.) If anything, within their domain, strategies of governance and rules relating to title reflect the importance of a problem, such that it calls for particular treatment. This particular treatment comes at a cost, so that the basic regime – possession, exclusion, and the things of property – does have some presumptive force. The more general default exerts a greater gravitational pull than do other rules. When it comes to property, possession promotes a general stability and mutual respect in Humean fashion, and correspondingly possession is associated with a local but widespread form of morality (Merrill and Smith 2007). Again, this does not mean that possession and exclusion are morally superior to other forms of legal intervention. It does mean that they are more spontaneous and widespread, and they will predominate where numbers are high and the stakes of any given interaction are low.

It also bears emphasizing that possession operates in much of everyday life. This is not to say that possession is simple on some absolute metric, whatever that would mean. It may or may not be identifiable with the

System 1 (S1) propounded by a variety of psychologists, in which people use simple and often virtually automatic heuristics, as opposed to System 2 (S2), which involves more reflection and sustained attention (Chapter 6; see also Kahneman 2011). Whether there is one kind of S1 style process in cognition is controversial to begin with (Evans 2008), and the cognition involved in possession may partake of multiple processes. Even basic notions about possession may partake of both S1 and S2 (to the extent those labels are valid), but the more basic *de facto* parts of possession nonetheless draw on knowledge that is widely shared among members of society. This is particularly true of thing definition in many cases, as well as many relations of persons to those things. Possession is keyed to signals that are easily observed and processed (Corriel 2013), allowing for quick judgments. (It is also a default that can be overridden by more refined rules, in a fashion analogous to the way S2 sometimes overrides S1 in some models, at some cost in effort. See Evans 2008: 261–63, 271). As we saw earlier, considerations of value and efficiency do enter into what counts as salient. I know not to take a newspaper from the newsstand but am free to take one from a train seat. Abandonment is the reverse of possession, in terms of control and intent; as in possession, control and intent in abandonment draw on conventions fed by salience and practicality. Sometimes coordination can happen without a firm convention here, too.

4.2. *Elsewhere and the layering principle*

From the specific-over-general principle and possession's status as the most general default regime, we can explain the characteristic patterns of possession. General defaults apply when nothing else does. Thus, unlike the subrules that displace them, general defaults hang together mainly in what they are not. Within their large domain, they apply when nothing else does. It is simpler and more explanatory to capture the system by giving a succinct account of the subrules and letting the general one apply otherwise or "elsewhere" (see, e.g., Hayes 2009; Smith 1996; Smith 2012a). The set of situations covered by the general rule may be small, if the rule is displaced a lot, but with a large number of unrelated subrules (more specific defaults), the general rule will not be easily captured by formulating these situations of application more directly. The general regime, in this case basic possession, applies "otherwise" or "elsewhere" and tends to be the simpler and cheaper approach, albeit less effective where effectiveness depends on tailoring.

Possession closely relates to exclusion, especially when it is protected by trespass. Both possession and exclusion are general defaults that are cheap, rough, and displaceable in important contexts, by rules of title and governance, respectively. Governance regimes give rise to multiple rights in the same asset, which are difficult to keep track of through possession alone (Chapter 8; Baird and Jackson 1984: 303). Possession as a fact and then as a custom likely antedates the law, and the law of possession may well have developed before that of ownership (Pollock 1896: 176). Like possession, in many cases exclusion is the historically prior method of delineating property rights, and is supplemented and partially supplanted when it proves inadequate (Smith 2002; see also Rose 1991). If a governance rule – like a stint on the number of sheep or liability in nuisance for a particular activity – is dropped, say, because it is no longer worthwhile, we fall back on possession and trespass in an exclusion strategy.

Further examples of specific-over-general abound in property law, and they are not unrelated to possession. One possible example would be open access and various kinds of property. Open access might be earlier and more general, although displaced very extensively by property (private, common, and public). As noted in Demsetz (1967) and the literature it inspired, property rights can be seen as the result of extra effort when extra effort is worthwhile; otherwise open access prevails. When horses became less valuable after the advent of cars, many horses were allowed to run wild (Anderson and Hill 1975: 170–76; see also Haddock and Kiesling 2002). Or as Barzel (1997: 16–32) would say, when attributes are not worth the effort to delineate property rights in them, they are left in what he calls the "public domain," free to be captured by anyone. Again, nondelineation of property rights is the ultimate default.

Another example of nested regimes is law versus equity. It might be surprising to invoke law versus equity, because civil law never had separate equity jurisdiction. By "equity," I mean a defined, equitable decision-making mode that reserves ex post discretion (possibly supplemented by prophylactic rules) to deal with opportunism, and, in more expansive versions, to fix problems of law owing to the law's generality (Smith ms.). This decision-making mode in its narrower and broader forms traces back to Aristotle, who defined equity (*epieikeia*) as an invocation of justice where law fails because of its generality (Aristotle 1980 ed.: 133). As such, it is present in civil law, in the form of interpretive approaches and the doctrine of abuse of right (Yiannopoulos 1994: 1192–93). Aristotle's formulation suggests that equity is more specific and trumps law only when there is a compelling need for it.

The architectural theory of property with possession as a basic module suggests a different way to explain possession. As I mentioned earlier, the conventional approach to possession is either to look for coherent first principles or to evaluate rules of possession one by one in a functional light. Alternatively, from the earliest days of Legal Realism, commentators have voiced doubts that there is any unifying thread to possession (Bingham 1915: 638; Shartel 1932: 615). Law and economics carries on this skeptical tradition, with much of the current commentary on possession seeking to explain possession "rules" individually and separately, and asking if they are efficient or fair. For example, Posner (2000) evaluates different approaches to possession and first acquisition from the point of view of economic efficiency, especially using considerations of rent seeking. His aim is a functional explanation of the "contours" of possession. He criticizes earlier commentators like Savigny for grudgingly considering function. He also argues that Holmes simply lacked the economic tools to get very far with a more functional approach. Posner contrasts his approach based on "social need" with earlier thinkers (and civilians) looking for an "inner logic" to possession (Posner 2000: 551, 564, 566–67). The modular architecture of possession suggests that possession rules apply when something more specific does not, but the possession rules are not free standing. They comprise a very general system that benefits from its scope, rather than being a collection of disparate rules. As in modular systems generally, the system of concepts including possession may have an "inner logic" in part for functional, even economic, reasons (Goldberg 2012: 1652–58; Smith 2012a). These reasons have a lot to do with managing complexity through modularity.

Indeed, the "social need" is one that is widespread and basic. Posner (1976: 601) once noted that the difference between Blackstone and his fierce critic Bentham was in part one of focus. Blackstone appeared complacent to Bentham because Blackstone was emphasizing the problem of basic social order, whereas Bentham was concerned with welfare. Bentham's focus on welfare called for attention to more refined issues that need to be solved once basic order is achieved and then more complex forms of social organization demand solutions that are more complex. It is easy to overlook that the refined parts of property are the apex of a pyramid of social order (Merrill and Smith 2001b), and that possession forms a large part of the base. That possessory base is keyed to the things of property that we encounter and make use of conceptually all the time, but which legal theory tends to downplay and obscure. Possession is extended and partially displaced by the complex rules of property, tort, and contract, which tend to receive attention from commentators. As Hume recognized, possession is a solution to one of the most basic problems of social order, and it is correspondingly easy to miss.

Conclusion

The key to understanding possession is that there is less and more than meets the eye. Possession is extremely basic and simple, and is part of the first cut at a legal ontology. It involves the elements of private law – persons, things, and the relations between them. It uses the thing to mediate relations between persons. Possession can be extended, especially through the further depersonalization made possible by thing definition, to notions like rights of possession and durable possession culminating in ownership. Possession still is used when it is all we need – a rough and ready system to handle numerous, low-stakes interactions. Its connection to custom continues its pervasive role. Possession is one of the most basic modules of property law.

References

Alberti, Federica, Sugden, Robert, and Tsutsui, Kei 2012. "Salience as an Emergent Property," *Journal of Economic Behavior & Organization* 82:379–94.
Alchian, Armen A. 1965. "Some Economics of Property Rights," *Il Politico* 30:816–29, reprinted in Alchian, Armen A. 1977. *Economic Forces at Work* 127–49. Indianapolis: Liberty Press.
Alexander, Gregory S. 2009. "The Social-Obligation Norm in American Property Law," *Cornell Law Review* 94:745–820.
Anderson, Terry L. and Hill, P.J. 1975. "The Evolution of Property Rights: A Study of the American West," *Journal of Law & Economics* 18:163–80.
Aristotle, *The Nicomachean Ethics*, translated by David Ross trans., revised by J.L. Ackrill and J.O. Urmson. Oxford University Press, 1980.
Arruñada, Benito. Chapter 8, this volume. "The Titling Role of Possession."
Austin, Lisa M. 2013. "Possession and the Distractions of Philosophy," in *The Philosophical Foundations of Property Law*, J. E. Penner and Henry E. Smith, (eds.), Oxford University Press, pp. 182–201.
Ayres, Ian and Gertner, Robert 1989. "Filling in Gaps in Incomplete Contracts: An Economic Theory of Default Rules," *Yale Law Journal* 99:87–130.
Baird, Douglas and Jackson, Thomas 1984. "Information, Uncertainty, and the Transfer of Property," *Journal of Legal Studies* 13:299–320.

Baldwin, Carliss Y. and Clark, Kim B. 2000. *Design Rules: The Power of Modularity*. Cambridge, MA: MIT Press.

Barzel, Yoram 1997. *Economic Analysis of Property Rights*. 2nd edn. Cambridge University Press.

Berger, Bethany R. 2006. "It's Not About the Fox: The Untold History of *Pierson v. Post*," *Duke Law Journal* 55:1089–43.

Bingham, Joseph W. 1915. "The Nature and Importance of Legal Possession," *Michigan Law Review* 13:535–65.

Blackstone, William 1766. *Commentaries on the Laws of England*, vol. 2. Oxford: Clarendon.

Chang, Yun-chien 2015 forthcoming. "An Economic and Comparative Analysis of *Specificatio* (the Accession Doctrine)", European Journal of Law and Economics 39.

   Chapter 4, this volume. "The Economy of Concept and Possession."

Chang, Yun-chien and Smith, Henry E. 2012. "An Economic Analysis of Common versus Civil Law Property," *Notre Dame Law Review* 88:1–55

   2015 forthcoming. "Structure and Style in Comparative Property Law," in *Research Handbook on Comparative Law and Economics*, Giovanni B. Ramello and Theodore Eisenberg (eds.), Northampton: Edward Elgar.

Cheung, Steven N.S. 1970. "The Structure of a Contract and the Theory of a Non-Exclusive Resource," *Journal of Law & Economics* 13:49–70.

Claeys, Eric R. 2013. "Productive Use in Acquisition, Accession, and Labour Theory," in *Philosophical Foundations of Property Law*, James Penner and Henry E. Smith (eds.), Oxford University Press, pp. 13–46.

Cohen, Felix S. 1935. "Transcendental Nonsense and the Functional Approach," *Columbia Law Review* 35:809–49.

   1954. "Dialogue on Private Property," *Rutgers Law Journal* 9:357–87.

Corriel, Matt 2013. "Up for Grabs: A Workable System for the Unilateral Acquisition of Chattels," *University of Pennsylvania Law Review* 161:807–60.

Cosmides, Leda and Tooby, John 2006. "Evolutionary Psychology, Moral Heuristics, and the Law," in *Heuristics and the Law*, G. Gigerenzer and C. Engel (eds.), Cambridge, MA: MIT Press.

Dagan, Hanoch 2011. *Property: Values and Institutions*. Oxford University Press.

Demsetz, Harold 1967. "Toward a Theory of Property Rights," *American Economic Review* 57(2):347–59

Dernburg, Heinrich 1900. *Pandekten*, vol. 1, part 2. 6th edn., with the assistance of Johannes Bierman. Berlin: H.W. Müller.

Dorigo, Marco 1991. "New Perspectives About Default Hierarchies Formation in Learning Classifier Systems," in *Trends in Artificial Intelligence: 2nd Congress of the Italian Association for Artificial Intelligence*, Edoardo Ardizzone et al. (eds.) 218–27.

Eggertsson, Thráinn 1990. *Economic Behavior and Institutions.* Cambridge University Press.

Ellickson, Robert C. 1989. "A Hypothesis of Wealth-Maximizing Norms: Evidence from the Whaling Industry," *Journal of Law & Economics* 5:83–97.

    1991. *Order without Law: How Neighbors Settle Disputes.* Cambridge, MA: Harvard University Press.

    2011. "The Inevitable Trend Toward Universally Recognizable Signals of Property Claims: An Essay for Carol Rose," *William & Mary Bill of Rights Journal* 19:1015–32.

Epstein, Richard A. 1979. "Possession as the Root of Title," *Georgia Law Review* 13:1221–44.

    2002. "The Allocation of the Commons: Parking on Public Roads," *Journal of Legal Studies* 31:S515–44.

Ernst, Daniel R. 2009. "*Pierson* v. *Post*: The New Learning," *Green Bag (2nd ser.)* 13:31–42.

Essert, Christopher 2013. "The Office of Ownership," *University of Toronto Law Journal* 64:418–61.

Evans, Jonathan St. B. T. 2008 "Dual-Processing Accounts of Reasoning, Judgment, and Social Cognition," *Annual Review of Psychology* 59:255–78.

Fernandez, Angela 2009a. "The Lost Record of *Pierson* v. *Post*, The Famous Fox Case," *Law and History Review* 27:149–78.

    2009b. "*Pierson* v. *Post*: A Great Debate, James Kent, and the Project of Building a Learned Law for New York State," *Law & Social Inquiry* 34:301–36.

Finberg, James M. 1982. "The General Mining Law and the Doctrine of *Pedis Possessio*: The Case For Congressional Action," *University of Chicago Law Review* 49:1026–49.

Forman, William J., Dwyer, Robert G., and Fox, C. Robert 1970. "Judicial Uncertainties in Applying the Mining Doctrine of 'Pedis Possessio'," *Natural Resources Lawyer* 3:467–74.

Foster, Nigel G. and Sule, Satish 2010. *German Legal System and Laws.* 4th edn. Oxford University Press.

Friedman, David. 1994. "A Positive Account of Property Rights," *Social Philosophy and Policy* 11(2):1–16.

Friedman, Ori and Neary, Karen R. 2009. "First Possession Beyond the Law: Adults' and Young Children's Intuitions About Ownership," *Tulane Law Review* 83:679–90.

Gold, Andrew S. and Smith, Henry E. ms. "How Private Law is Simply Moral."

Goldberg, John C.P. 2012. "Introduction: Pragmatism and Private Law," *Harvard Law Review* 125:1640–63.

Gordley, James and Mattei, Ugo 1996. "Protecting Possession," *American Journal of Comparative Law* 44:293–334.

Grey, Thomas C. 1980. "The Disintegration of Property," in *NOMOS XXII: Property*, J. Roland Pennock and John W. Chapman (eds.), New York University Press, pp. 69–85.
Grice, Paul H. 1975. "Logic and Conversation," in *Speech Acts (Syntax and Semantics 3)*, Peter Cole and Jerry L. Morgan (eds.), New York: Academic Press, pp. 41–59. Reprinted in Grice, Paul 1989. *Studies in the Ways of Words*. Cambridge, MA: Harvard University Press, 22–40.
Haddock, David D. and Kiesling, Lynne 2002. "The Black Death and Property Rights," *Journal of Legal Studies* 31:S545–87.
Hayes, Bruce 2009. *Introductory Phonology*. Malden, MA and Oxford: Wiley-Blackwell.
Heck, Philipp 1930. *Grundriß des Sachenrechts*. Tübingen: Mohr.
Hegel, Georg Wilhelm Friedrich 1820. *Hegel's Philosophy of Right*, translated by T.M. Knox. Oxford University Press, 1952.
Heylighen, Francis 1999. "Advantages and Limitations of Formal Expression," *Foundations of Science* 4:25–56.
Holland, John H., Holyoak, Keith J., Nisbett, Richard E., and Thagard, Paul R. 1986. *Induction: Processes of Inference, Learning, and Discovery*. Cambridge, MA: MIT Press.
Holmes, Oliver Wendell 1881. *The Common Law*. Boston: Little, Brown.
Hopper, Paul J. and Traugott, Elizabeth Closs 2003. *Grammaticalization*. 2nd edn. Cambridge University Press.
Hume, David 1739–40. *A Treatise of Human Nature* L.A. Selby-Bigge (ed.), Oxford: Clarendon Press, 1896.
Katz, Larissa 2010. "The Moral Paradox of Adverse Possession," *McGill Law Journal* 55:47–80.
Kelly, Daniel B. 2015. "Dividing Possessory Rights," in Law and Economics of Possession, Yun-chien Chang (ed.) Cambridge: Cambridge University Press.
Knowles, Dudley 1983. "Hegel on Property and Personality," *Philosophical Quarterly* 33:45–62.
Krier, James E. 2009. "Evolutionary Theory and the Origin of Property Rights," *Cornell Law Review* 95:139–59.
Krier, James E., Christopher Serkin, 2015. "Possession and Ownership," in Law and Economics of Possession, Yun-chien Chang, (ed.) Cambridge: Cambridge University Press.
Langlois, Richard N. 2002. "Modularity in Technology and Organization," *Journal of Economic Behavior & Organization* 49.19–37.
Levinson, Stephen C. 2000. *Presumptive Meanings: The Theory of Generalized Conversational Implicature*. Cambridge, MA: MIT Press.
Levmore, Saul 1987. "Variety and Uniformity in the Treatment of the Good-Faith Purchaser," *Journal of Legal Studies* 16:43–65.
Lewis, David 1969. *Convention: A Philosophical Study*. Cambridge, MA: Harvard University Press.

Locke, John 1689. *Two Treatises of Government*, Peter Laslett (ed.), New York: Cambridge University Press, 1988.

Lueck, Dean 1995. "The Rule of First Possession and the Design of the Law," *Journal of Law & Economics* 38:393–436.

Manning, John F. 2011. "Separation of Powers as Ordinary Interpretation," *Harvard Law Review* 124:1939–2040.

Maynard Smith, John 1982. *Evolution and the Theory of Games*. Cambridge University Press.

McDowell, Andrea 2007. "Legal Fictions in *Pierson v. Post*," *Michigan Law Review* 105:735–78.

McFarlane, Ben 2008. *The Structure of Property Law*. Oxford: Hart Publishing.

Merrill, Thomas W. 1998. "Property and the Right to Exclude," *Nebraska Law Review* 77:730–55.

   2001a. "The Property/Contract Interface," *Columbia Law Review* 101:773–852.

   2001b. "What Happened to Property in Law and Economics?" *Yale Law Journal* 111:357–98.

   2007. "The Morality of Property," *William & Mary Law Review* 48:1849–95.

   2009. "Accession and Original Ownership," *Journal of Legal Analysis* 1:459–510.

   2015. "Possession and Ownership," in Law and Economics of Possession, Yun-chien Chang, (ed.) Cambridge: Cambridge University Press.

Merrill, Thomas W. and Smith, Henry E. 2000. "Optimal Standardization in the Law of Property: The *Numerus Clausus* Principle," *Yale Law Journal* 110:1–70.

Minsky, Marvin 1975. "A Framework for Representing Knowledge," in *The Psychology of Computer Vision*, Patrick Henry Winston (ed.), New York: McGraw-Hill.

Moselle, Boaz and Polak, Benjamin 2001. "A Model of a Predatory State," *Journal of Law, Economics, & Organization* 17:1–33.

Mossoff, Adam 2002. "Locke's Labor Lost," *University of Chicago Law School Roundtable* 9:155–64.

   2011. "The False Promise of the Right to Exclude," *Econ Journal Watch* 8 (3):255–64.

Newman, Christopher M. 2009. "Patent Infringement as Nuisance," *Catholic University Law Review* 59:61–123.

Olson, Mancur. 1993. "Dictatorship, Democracy, and Development," *American Political Science Review* 87:567–76.

Qiao, Shitong. 2014. "Small Property, Big Market: A Focal Point Explanation" (February 21, 2014). *American Journal of Comparative Law* 63, No. 1 (2015) Available at SSRN: http://ssrn.com/abstract=2399675.

Penner, J.E. 1997. *The Idea of Property in Law*. Oxford: Clarendon Press.

Peterson, Dale 2011. *The Moral Lives of Animals*. New York: Bloomsbury Press.

Pinker, Steven 1999. *Words and Rules: The Ingredients of Language*. New York: Basic Books.

Pollock, Frederick 1896. *A First Book of Jurisprudence*. New York: Macmillan.
Pollock, Frederick and Wright, Robert Samuel 1888. *An Essay on Possession in the Common Law*. Oxford: Clarendon Press.
Posner, Richard A. 1976. "Blackstone and Bentham," *Journal of Law & Economics* 19:569–606.
  2000. "Holmes, Savigny, and the Law and Economics of Possession," *Virginia Law Review* 86: 535–67.
Rixecker, Roland and Säcker, Franz Jürgen. 2012. *Münchener Kommentar zum Bürgerlichen Gesetzbuch*. Munich: C.H. Beck.
Rose, Carol M. 1985. "Possession as the Origin of Property," *University of Chicago Law Review* 52:73–88.
  1991. "Rethinking Environmental Controls: Management Strategies for Common Resources." *Duke Law Journal*:1–38.
  2015. "The Law is Nine-tenths of Possession: An Adage Turned on its Head," in Law and Economics of Possession, Yun-chien Chang, (ed.) Cambridge: Cambridge University Press.
Sag, Ivan A., Wasow, Thomas, and Bender, Emily M. 2003. *Syntactic Theory: A Formal Introduction*. 2nd edn. Stanford: CSLI.
Savigny, Friedrich Carl von 1848. *Von Savigny's Treatise on Possession; or the Jus Possessionis of the Civil Law*. Translated by Sir Erskine Perry. 6th edn. London: S. Sweet.
Schelling, Thomas C. 1960. *The Strategy of Conflict*. Oxford University Press.
Shartel, Burke 1932. "Meanings of Possession," *Minnesota Law Review* 16:611–37.
Simon, Herbert A. 1981. *The Sciences of the Artificial*. 2nd edn. Cambridge, MA: MIT Press.
Smith, Adam 1762–63. *Lectures on Jurisprudence*, R.L. Meek et al. (eds.), Oxford: Clarendon Press, 1978, pp. 9–86.
Smith, Henry 1996. *Restrictiveness in Case Theory*. Cambridge University Press.
Smith, Henry E. 2002. "Exclusion Versus Governance: Two Strategies for Delineating Property Rights," *Journal of Legal Studies* 31:S453–87.
  2003. "The Language of Property: Form, Context, and Audience," *Stanford Law Review* 55:1105–91.
  2005. "Self-Help and the Nature of Property," *Journal of Law, Economics & Policy* 1:69–146.
  2007 "Intellectual Property as Property: Delineating Entitlements in Information." *Yale Law Journal* 116:1742–1822.
  2009. "Community and Custom in Property," *Theoretical Inquiries in Law* 10:5–41.
  2012a. "On the Economy of Concepts in Property," *University of Pennsylvania Law Review* 160:2097–128.
  2012b. "Property as the Law of Things," *Harvard Law Review* 125:1691–1726.

2013. "Emergent Property," in *Philosophical Foundations of Property Law*, James Penner and Henry E. Smith (eds.), Oxford University Press, pp. 320-38.

ms. "An Economic Analysis of Law versus Equity."

Sprankling, John G. 1996. "The Antiwilderness Bias in American Property Law," *University of Chicago Law Review* 63:519-90.

Sugden, Robert 2004 [1986]. *The Economics of Rights, Co-operation and Welfare.* Houndmills, Basingstoke, Hampshire; New York: Palgrave Macmillan.

2011. "Mutual Advantage, Conventions and Team Reasoning," *International Review of Economics* 58:9-20.

Swinnen, Koen 2012. "Property Law Accessories under the DCFR," in *The Draft Common Frame of Reference: national and comparative perspectives*, Vincent Sagaert, Matthias Storme, and Evelyne Terryn (eds.), Cambridge: Intersentia, pp. 289-302.

Umbeck, John 1981. "Might Makes Rights: A Theory of the Formation and Initial Distribution of Property Rights," *Economic Inquiry* 19:38-59.

Waldron, Jeremy 1983. "Two Worries About Mixing One's Labour," *Philosophical Quarterly* 33:37-44.

Yiannopoulos, A.N. 1994. "Civil Liability for Abuse of Right: Something Old, Something New...," *Louisiana Law Review* 54:1173-97.

2001. *Louisiana Civil Law Treatise: Property*, vol. 2, 4th edn. St. Paul: West.

4

The economy of concept and possession

YUN-CHIEN CHANG

1. Introduction

The "styles" of possession in civil and common property law are very different.[1] In American property law, possession is not a self-contained topic. Possession is discussed and defined in the context of specific legal issues, such as the rule of first possession and the rule of adverse possession. One cannot find a chapter in a casebook or hornbook on US property law titled "possession." In contrast, possession is often one independent chapter in the civil code (mostly in the book on the "law of things"[2]) in civil-law countries. Interestingly, sometimes the possession chapter is the first (for example, civil codes in Germany and Japan) and sometimes the last or penultimate chapter (for instance, civil codes in Italy, Switzerland, and Taiwan) in the book on property.[3] Moreover, in civil law countries, the

---

Associate research professor and Co-Director of the Center for Empirical Legal Studies, Institutum Iurisprudentiae, Academia Sinica, Taiwan. J.S.D., New York University School of Law. I thank John Goldberg, Daphna Lewinsohn-Zamir, Thomas Merrill, Shitong Qiao, Henry Smith, Yongqin Su, and participants at the Private Law Speaker Series at Harvard Law School and the 5th Law and Economic Analysis Conference for helpful comments on previous drafts. Charline Jao and Christine Yuan provided valuable research assistance. Ministry of Science and Technology (grant number 101-2410-H-001-020-MY3) provides financial support. Any errors are mine.

[1] A "style is a manner of doing things that is characteristic of a particular culture. Often artifacts exhibiting different styles (think of the design of pots or the shape of automobiles) can serve the same function. Common and civil law can be thought of as families of legal cultures, in which a function, here delineating property rights and setting up interlocking property doctrines, can be served in multiple ways" (Chang and Smith 2012: 12).

[2] In civil law countries, especially those influenced by the German Civil Code, the book on property is called "the law of things" (in German, *Sachenrecht*). See Smith (2012b) for arguments that property law should be viewed as a law of things.

[3] Similarly, Barry (2004: 180, 184) observes, "In civil law, there is an attempt to distinguish *ownership* from *possession*, which is not a crucial feature of common law" (emphasis original) and that "common law does not make a great deal of difference between possession and ownership; they are treated as much the same. But in civil law, ownership is very important, and a code's emphasis on it has prevented efficient property rights from developing."

difference between ownership and possession is highlighted – ever since Roman law – while in the common law, this distinction is not a crucial feature (Barry 2004: 180, 184; Hinteregger 2012: 98). Adverse possession is generally recognized as a possession issue, though it is often stipulated not in the possession chapter, but in the chapter on ownership or general principle.[4] On the other hand, good-faith purchase is often stipulated in the possession chapter in civil codes (for example, civil codes in Japan, Taiwan, Italy, Spain, and Switzerland), whereas good-faith purchase is dealt with in contract law, sales law, or commercial law in the United States, probably due to the influence of the Uniform Commercial Code.[5] Furthermore, the two legal traditions emphasize different issues under the broadly defined possession problem. First possession is deemed an important issue in American property law (Austin 2013) and receives important analysis by first-rate scholars (e.g., Epstein 1979; Rose 1985). As the legal and philosophical foundation of property rights, first possession is often the first thing 1L students learn about property law.[6] In civil law systems, in contrast, first possession is almost an afterthought. Possession theorists in civil law countries seem to prefer devoting time to the conceptual perspective of possession (e.g., Steiner 2010: 393–94), in which modern American jurists have almost no interest. Simply put, while property scholars in civil law countries are zealous in searching for the general principle and debating the conceptual framework of possession, property scholars in the United States are far more interested in dealing with specific possession doctrines.

The styles of delineating possession within the civil law tradition are far from unified and perhaps more divided than the styles of delineating ownership.[7] To name a few differences in styles here, civil codes in Japan (art. 180) and Korea (art. 192) regard possession as a right, while civil

---

[4] The French Civil Code and civil codes influenced by it (such as the Portuguese Civil Code), as well as the Italian Civil Code, stipulate doctrines on prescriptive acquisition (the closest civil-law term for adverse possession) in the chapter on possession. The French Civil Code even puts possession and prescriptive acquisition as the joint title of the chapter. See, e.g., Bell, Bell, and Boyron (2008: 277–78). The German Civil Code and its progeny, such as the Taiwan Civil Code, tend to put the relevant doctrines outside the possession chapter. China's Property Law of 2007, though, is a notable exception, as it does not allow adverse possession at all (Chang 2012: 360–62).

[5] For example, Schwartz and Scott (2011), two contract scholars, recently made an important contribution to understanding the good-faith purchase problem.

[6] The title of the first chapter in Dukeminier et al. (2010) is first possession. Merrill and Smith (2012) start the second chapter with first possession.

[7] See Chang and Smith (2012, 2015a) for the different styles of delineating ownership in civil law and common law.

codes in Germany (art. 854) and Taiwan (art. 940) view possession as a fact. Do possessors have to hold a specific "intent to possess"? Theorists since Savigny (1848), a German scholar, and Holmes (1881), an American jurist, cannot agree.[8] Civil codes in Germany (art. 854) and Taiwan (art. 940) define possession as actual control, period. Nonetheless, many property scholars in these jurisdictions prefer a narrower definition with subjective elements. In contrast, under civil code in Japan (art. 180), possession comprises actual control and intent to control for oneself. Civil codes in France, Austria (art. 309), and the Netherlands (art. 3:107) distinguish possession from "detention,"[9] based on whether actual control is retained with *animus domini* (intent to be owners). Civil codes in Germany (art. 855), Korea (art. 195), and Taiwan (art. 942) call a person who has detention "an agent in possession" who is not considered a possessor. This is not the end of the complications. As it turns out, actual control is not even a necessary condition for possession, because in Germany (art. 868), France (art. 2255), Taiwan (art. 941), and the Netherlands (art. 3: 107), to name a few, indirect possession is recognized as possession. For instance, a landlord who does not have the key to her rented house also qualifies as an indirect possessor.

Drawing on Smith's (2012a) economy of concept theory, this chapter argues that possession in civil property jurisprudence should be re-conceptualized. Smith (2012a) points out that concepts help economize information by suppressing some context, but not all concepts serve the function of economizing information equally well. "Even with extensional equivalence, one set of concepts can lower information costs more than another" (Smith 2012a: 2106). In addition, "reductions in the information costs of using the system are reflected in the economy of description of that system ... A better theory ... will capture known facts in a shorter description that simultaneously exposes the theory to counterevidence; the shortness of the description will correspond to a generality that makes claims about new cases" (Smith 2012a: 2107). Smith's theory suggests that the variations of possession concepts in civil-law

---

[8] See a review and critique of Savigny's and Holmes's possession theory in Posner (2000).
[9] Detention is the literal counterpart of the French term, but in the context of Anglo-American property law, the term detention could be misleading – though Epstein (1999: 29) and Chapter 8 use the term detention as it is understood in civil law. Custody should be a more apt term for British and American lawyers (Gambaro and Mattei 2002: 286). In this chapter, I use the term "detention" when referring to the European and Asian civil codes that entertain this concept, mostly in order to be in line with the prior comparative law literature.

jurisdictions discussed in this chapter[10] are sub-optimal, as they are unnecessarily complex. As the following analysis will show, the new concept of possession proposed here is of almost the same "extensional equivalence" as the possession concept in any civil code. My new concept, however, is much more concise, thus reducing the information costs of those using the system of property.

The concept of possession under my framework is very straightforward – possession is actual control.[11] No exceptions. To the best of my knowledge, this simplified concept has not been advanced before, because three closely related yet different concepts have been conflated: possession as a fact, (subsidiary) possessory right,[12] and possession as a basis for acquiring or relinquishing property rights. Once these three concepts are disentangled, the conceptual framework of possession will be crystal clear rather than muddy – to paraphrase Rose (1988).

Possession as a fact is the fundamental concept for civil lawmakers and civil scholars. The universal consensus is that actual control is the *corpus* (the physical element) of possession. Since actual control is an objective fact, many scholars claim that possession is not a *right*. Scholars in the other camp, as well as lawmakers in Japan and South Korea, perceive possession as more than a fact, claiming that possession instead be conceptualized as a right to justify the protection the law awards to the possessor. These two views, however, confuse possession as a fact with the "subsidiary possessory right."[13]

---

[10] The jurisdictions include, but are not limited to, Germany, France, the Netherlands, Switzerland, Spain, Portugal, Italy, Austria, Japan, Korea, and Taiwan. China's Property Law of 2007 is located at the other end of the concept spectrum. With just five brief articles, it focuses only on unauthorized possession without ever defining possession.

[11] That is, I contend that the mental element should be removed from the definition of possession; even awareness of the fact of physical possession is not necessary. In most cases, possessors are aware of the fact, so my objective standard would not create any problems. In exceptional scenarios, because possessors are not necessarily owners, and actual control is rarely, if ever, a sufficient condition for any liability, my possession concept will not lead to perverse results. For example, if John inadvertently controls Mary's mobile phone, John will not and should not be considered Mary's bailee before he is aware of the fact. How much control constitutes actual control here, to a certain extent, can vary by contexts and be determined by customs and social norms. Nevertheless, the variance has to be limited; otherwise possession cannot be decontextualized enough to be easily understood by most people, as it is the general applicability that makes possession a basic modular concept. See Chapter 3.

[12] For more discussion on possessory rights, see Chapter 7.

[13] I call it a subsidiary right because the possessory right is not a self-contained, independent right. More on this to come.

To understand the distinction and the nature of the latter, we have to start with the nature of ownership. In short, ownership (rather than property) is a bundle of subsidiary rights. A full owner of land or chattel keeps various subsidiary rights, depending on the division of ownership. These rights include the subsidiary possessory right, subsidiary right to use, subsidiary right to profit, subsidiary right to transfer, and so forth. (cf., e.g., Honoré 1961). Subject to the constraint of the *numerus clausus* principle (Merrill and Smith 2000; Hansmann and Kraakman 2002; Smith 2011b; Chang and Smith 2015b), the owner can only chop these various subsidiary rights and package them into standardized forms (lesser property interests) and transfer them to others. The subsidiary possessory right is contained in some of the property forms (such as life estate, possessory lien, or *superficies*) but not others (such as mortgage). Hence, in this sense, possession is a right for its holder to have actual control over a specific thing. Possession as a fact and possession as a subsidiary right are closely related, but different, concepts. The latter concept is implied in the structure of (civil) property law, whereas the former concept is explicitly dealt with in the possession chapter in civil codes.

The variations in the "intent to possess" requirements in the civil law system came into being because civil lawmakers confused possession as a fact and possession as a basis for title transfers. Again, possession as actual control is fundamental. One can gain or lose actual control without legal implication. John may spot something on the ground and pick it up just to find out what it is but lose interest and throw it away. John gains and then loses actual control, but he does not acquire or relinquish titles to it, as John never intends to be a keeper of that thing. For cases like this, whether John is qualified as a possessor can, and should, solely depend on whether John has actual control. Not all cases are this simple. In adverse possession, first possession, good-faith purchase, and abandonment issues, the intent of the possessor is critical. *The key point is that intent only matters when possession is part of the conditions for acquiring or relinquishing property rights.* The legal system should not concern itself with the exact intent of a possessor until a transfer of property rights (through adverse possession for instance) is involved.

Moreover, possession is a critical doctrinal component in many property issues and quite a few torts, contract, and unjust enrichment issues. The doctrines often require different possession intents and other possession conditions, such as conspicuous and continuous possession.

Using the least common denominator (actual control) to define possession, and then tailoring requirements on top of the common possession definition, is much less information-intensive than adding to or subtracting from a baseline definition of possession.[14] Put differently, the least common denominator approach better enables the concept of possession to interact with other doctrines. The add-or-subtract approach will instead spawn a parade of complicated possession-related (sub)concepts, to fit the needs of other legal contexts.[15]

Finally, theoretically, there might be several different ways to define possession in an equally low information-intensive fashion. Nevertheless, possession as actual control still has an advantage over other definitions, because there is substantive economic reason to put the legal burden or give the legal benefit to a party who has actual control. Defining possession as actual control thus maximizes the use of the bare-bones possession concept.

In the following, I elaborate on these points. Section 2 delineates the contour of the possessory right. Section 3 distinguishes possession as a fact and possession as a basis for title transfers. Section 4 argues for discarding the cerebral concept of possession, and that possession as actual control makes economic sense beyond the economy of concept.

2. The nature of possessory rights

Most civil codes, such as those in Germany (Kohler 2005: 233), France, Taiwan, and China, consider possession a fact. Japan and South Korea, however, specifically regard possession as a right. Nonetheless, other than characterizing possession as a right, the stipulations in the possession chapter in the civil codes of Japan and South Korea resemble those in Germany and Taiwan, where possession is a fact. From the scholarly literature and the civil codes in Japan and South Korea themselves, it is unclear what type of right possession is, and in what way possession as a right provides possessors with more protection.[16]

This section demonstrates that lawmakers in Japan and South Korea unfortunately have conflated possession as a fact and the possessory

---

[14] In a similar vein, Chapter 3 argues that possession is the general default regime, with other rules layered on it.
[15] The animal keeper tort liability in German law is a case in point. See Section 4.2.2.
[16] For a brief economic analysis of possession in Japanese law, see Ramseyer and Nakazato (1999: 23–25). They do not touch on the issues in question here.

right. Scholars in other civil law countries sometimes over-emphasize the factual aspect of possession, ignoring the possessory right implied in their civil codes. Perhaps the unpopularity of the bundle of rights metaphor in civil law countries contributes to their ignorance. Since the nature of possession as a fact is straightforward, this section will focus on analyzing the nature of the subsidiary possessory right. Sub-section 2.1 explains that the possessory right is one stick in the ownership bundle of subsidiary rights. Sub-section 2.2 advances a dichotomy of in rem and in personam possessory rights. Sub-section 2.3 argues that unlawful possessors should not be entitled to sue in court to recover possession.

2.1. One stick in the ownership bundle

The bundle of rights concept is not useless, but it better describes ownership.[17] In Chang and Smith (2012, 2015a) and Smith (2011a, 2012b), Smith and I argue that property is not a bundle of rights (but compare Ellickson 2011; Epstein 2011); rather, property is a structured bundle of relations. Chang and Smith (2012) distinguish the concepts of property and ownership. Simply put, ownership is just one type of property right. Lesser property interests such as mortgage, pledge, servitude, superficies, and so forth are also property rights. More importantly, lesser property interests are all subdivisions of ownership (in French, *démembrement*). Both ownership and lesser property interests can be divided into more basic components, such as the right to transfer, the right to use, and the possessory right. To avoid confusion with property rights, this chapter calls these component rights "subsidiary rights."

But for the *numerus clausus* principle, owners can freely chop and divide the subsidiary rights and transfer them to other willing parties (see Chapter 7). With the constraints on property forms, the subsidiary rights can be packaged only into certain prescribed lesser property interests (cf. Fennell 2012). The subsidiary possessory right is an essential component in some, but not all, lesser property interests. For instance, in leasehold and usufruct, the subsidiary possessory right (or the right to actually control a specific thing) is part of what the owner gives up in exchange for the price the other party pays. By contrast, in mortgage, the owner/mortgagee keeps the subsidiary possessory right.

---

[17] This idea is not entirely new. Ellickson (1993: 1371), for example, points out that "The fee simple, by contrast, is a default bundle of rights. " But it seems that this point has not been emphasized.

Therefore, in one specific sense, possession is a (subsidiary) right, not just a fact. Because the subsidiary possessory right is an implicit feature in civil property law and civil codes, prior theorists on possession tend to over-emphasize possession as a fact to the extent of total denial of possession as a right. Scholars in Japan and South Korea do not appear to recognize the sophisticated difference between possession as a fact and the possessory right. My contribution to the fact-right debate is the elaboration that possession is both a fact and a right because actual control and the subsidiary possessory right are distinct concepts.

2.2. In rem and in personam possessory right

The shadow example of the subsidiary possessory right above is an in rem possessory right. In the civil law system particularly, it is important to emphasize that possessory right can be in personam. A subsidiary possessory right is in rem if it is contained in a property form such as ownership and *superficies*. The in rem possessory right, as part of the property right, is protected against any unlawful interfering party. By contrast, a subsidiary possessory right is in personam if the possessor acquires such a right through contracts such as lease, which is a type of contract in most, if not all, civil-law jurisdictions. During the term of the lease contract, the owner/lessor has a contractual obligation not to interfere with the possession of the possessor/lessee. The lessee has an in personam possessory right against the lessor. The lessee, however, does not necessarily have a possessory right against a third party. The lessee's claim is shaped by the stipulations in the civil code regarding protection of possession (not protection of property rights). Put differently, law selectively protects possession, and when the actual controller has only an in personam possessory right, the law does not always protect him or her. Taking German Civil Code art. 868, Taiwan Civil Code art. 962, and Swiss Civil Code art. 927 as examples, the in personam possessory right is only protected when the possession is "violently deprived."[18] If Jane unintentionally leaves an umbrella she borrowed from a friend at a restaurant, and the restaurant refuses to return it, Jane cannot sue the restaurant to restore possession, because the restaurant has not forcefully deprived her of possession. Therefore,

---

[18] In France, a party who has enjoyed possession or detention for *over a year* can be protected from nonviolent dispossession (Hinteregger 2012: 109) (emphasis added). Italian Civil Code (art. 1170) contains a similar stipulation.

conceptually and practically, it is important to distinguish the in rem possessory right from the in personam possessory right, as the court would favor holders of the latter in a possession recovery lawsuit only if they have been violently deprived of their possession.

It is worth noting that the *modern*[19] function of the right of action for recovering possession[20] – called *interdict unde vi* in Roman law (Bouckaert and Geest 1998: 153; Gordley and Von Mehren 2006: 154) – is to protect possessors who only have in personam possessory rights,[21] rather than those with in rem possessory rights.[22] Other scholars justify actions for recovering possession with other rationales.[23] One popular theory is that possessors are often owners, but ownership is hard to prove – the so-called *probatio diabolica* (devil's proof) (Terre and Philippe 2006: §67). That is, we protect ownership through protecting possession, and doing so saves information costs. This theory is not convincing, because registration or recording systems have made proof of ownership manageable. Moreover, civil codes generally presume possessors to be owners[24] or parties with legitimate interests.[25] This presumption is sufficient to make the devil's proof moot.[26] Another theory is that possession is protected to respect possessors' wills. As Gordley (2006: 56) argues, this theory does not explain why the earlier possessor (rather than the later possessor) should win, or why physical possession matters.

The third theory, from Savigny, is that protecting possession maintains public order, particularly when possessors are not owners (Gordley 2006: 53). As I elaborate in sub-section 2.3, self-help also maintains public order. More importantly, the concern of public order is insufficient to justify protection of unlawful possessors. Finally, *interdict unde vi* is a property-rule protection, but public order can also be preserved

---

[19] I am not trying to explain the function in *interdict unde vi* in Roman times.
[20] See the Taiwan Civil Code art. 962, China's Property Law of 2007 art. 245, the German Civil Code arts. 861–862, the French Civil Code art. 2282, the Dutch Civil Code art. 3: 125, and Japan Civil Code arts. 197–199. For more discussion on recovery of possession under Roman law, see Chapter 8.
[21] See Chapter 1 for a slightly different view.
[22] Holders of usufruct, who have in rem possessory right, can use *vindicatio* (more on this later) to retrieve their possession. See German Civil Code art. 1065 and Taiwan Civil Code art. 767.
[23] Chapter 1 discusses the same issue. Our arguments are different but not contradictory.
[24] See, e.g., the German Civil Code art. 1006 and the French Civil Code art. 2276.
[25] See, e.g., the Austrian Civil Code art. 323.
[26] Note, however, that *probatio diabolica* appears to be a real problem in Italy, see Gambaro and Mattei (2002: 308–10).

through a liability-rule system or administrative measures. As Gordley (2006: 55) points out, original possessors' incentive to defend public order by bringing legal actions "depend[s] on the value of what he has lost, a consideration which, by hypothesis, has nothing to do with the extent to which public order has been disrupted." Therefore, maintaining public order should not be the main reason for protecting possession.

2.3. Unlawful possession

A person, like a thief, can be an unlawful possessor[27] who has neither in rem nor in personam possessory right. Yet both the relativity title theory in common law and the possession protection stipulations in civil law protect the actual control of an unentitled party against those who do not have (superior) titles. Because possession appears to be protected for its own sake, Gordley (2006: 60) argues that possession should be a right, not just a fact. I have distinguished possession as a fact from possession as a right. Here I focus on whether unlawful possession should be protected.

I argue that the domain of self-help (Epstein 2005; Smith 2005) should be broad and include protection for unlawful possessors, while only a party with a possessory right has a legal claim against other parties for restoring possession. The net of self-help should be widely cast because forceful transfer of possession by private parties should be discouraged, and a stronger right to self-help gives nonpossessors weaker incentive to use force. *Ex ante*, sometimes even the possessor and the potential taker cannot be sure whether the former has a possessory right. Judges are unlikely to be present at the self-help scene to proclaim whether the current possessors are entitled. Hence, if the legal rule of self-help does not afford protection for unlawful possessor, incidents of forceful takeover of possession will increase, harming the entitled possessors.

The case for giving an unlawful possessor a cause of action is different. The theory of relativity of title and the civil-law stipulations are in place to deal with the problem of proving titles in chattels. That is, even after a lengthy litigation, a judge may still be unable to tell whether one party has a legitimate property right. It is a common complaint that title survey in real estate is difficult. What if title survey is also required for personal properties? Hence, these aforementioned theories and other supporting

---

[27] For more discussion on unlawful possession, see Chapter 5.

doctrines enable courts to presume that the prior possessor has a relative title against the subsequent possessor.

That said, it is not necessary for possession law to go all the way to give a known unlawful possessor (for example, a conceded thief or an apparent converter) a right to restore possession from another unlawful possessor, for the following reasons. Unlike self-help, the dispute of restoring possession takes place when a new social order (the defendant controlling the thing) is being established. Courts have ample time to investigate evidence and find out whether any of the litigating parties has a legitimate property interest. If it turns out that neither has good title, there is no reason in returning possession to the plaintiff/prior possessor. Dismissing the case reduces frivolous lawsuits brought by people without legitimate interests and further discourages unlawful possession in the first place.[28] On the other hand, the rule of self-help still applies and largely could prevent reciprocal taking between unentitled parties. In Hohfeldian terms, an unlawful possessor may have the *privilege* to possess, but not the *possessory right*.

3. Possession as a basis for acquiring or relinquishing titles

My argument in this section is simple: *animus* (the mental element) is required only when titles change. It is surprising to me that no scholar since Savigny has viewed the conceptual framework of possession this way. Instead, many argue that the mental element is a built-in component of the concept of possession, although there is no consensus as to what type of intent is required. Sub-section 3.1 outlines the scholarly debate and the choices made by civil lawmakers. Sub-section 3.2 argues that possession as purely about actual control is more economizing on information. Mental elements come to the forefront when changes in actual control affect titles to the things in question. Ultimately, the possession law built on my concept of possession does not deal with possession issues differently from the possession stipulations found in contemporary civil codes. Nonetheless, as Smith (2012a) points out, concepts with the same

---

[28] In the United States, there are few reported decisions involving lawsuits between two converters. See Merrill and Smith (2012: 220–26) for discussing the leading case and a few other reported cases. In one case, *Russell v. Hill*, 34 S. E. 640 (N.C. 1899), the court dismisses the case brought by a converter against another converter – consistent with my thesis. I have surveyed six years (2006–2011) of court cases in Taiwan and I have not found any cases of converter versus converter.

extensions may imply different information costs. This part demonstrates that my simplified concept of possession is more economizing.

3.1. The debate on intent to possess

Actual control is the necessary physical element of possession. But civil codes differ over whether a specific mental element should be required. Civil codes in Germany (art. 854) and Taiwan (art. 940) appear content with an objective standard, while civil codes in France (arts. 2256–2257) and the Netherlands (art. 3: 107) require *animus domini* (intent to possess as an owner).[29] Japan's Civil Code (art. 180) stipulates that possessor must have "intent to possess on one's own behalf" (*Eigenbesitzer* in German).

Scholars have debated the intent issue for more than a century. The German legal historian Friedrich Carl von Savigny (1848) insists that *animus domini* is necessary. His contemporary Rudolf von Jhering requires only the "intent to exercise some right over the thing." The great American jurist Oliver Wendell Holmes, Jr., in his influential book, *The Common Law,* criticizes Savigny's approach and argues that the "intent to exclude others from interfering with one's uses" should be enough (Holmes 1881: 186–222; Posner 2000: 547). Fast forward. Two of the most influential legal thinkers of our time have jumped on the bandwagon. Posner (2000: 559) argues that Savigny is wrong "to suppose that [intent to possess as an owner] should be required *always* to be present a possessory right to be recognized" (emphasis original). Epstein (1998: 63), in the context of first possession, argues that "the mental element and the overt acts have to combine in order to establish the initial possession that lies at the root of legal ownership" and that possession "requires that the putative possessor desire to keep exclusive possession of the thing in question, with the idea of acquiring ownership." Posner and Epstein are on the right track. Their arguments suggest that the mental element can vary across contexts, and that establishing

---

[29] In France and the Netherlands, one with actual control but not *animus domini* is a *detenteur* who has only detention (Kleijn et al. 2006: 106; Steiner 2010: 393). The distinction between possession and detention has practical import because only possessors can bring actions to recover possession. Italian scholars have tried to introduce *animus* into the definition of possession in the Italian Civil Code (Gambaro and Mattei 2002: 286).

legal titles requires specific mental elements. Their analyses, however, are not comprehensive. This is not surprising, as American jurists traditionally do not analyze possession as a general principle. The following sub-section fills this gap.

3.2. Actual control as the least common denominator

Mental elements are universally required when possession is a basis for acquiring titles and when giving up possession is the basis for abandoning titles (see Strahilevitz 2010, 2011). The specific elements, however, differ. While first possession and adverse possession of ownership prescribe *animus domini*, prescriptive acquisition of lesser property interests (such as a passage easement) requires the intent to become a holder of a lesser property interest, rather than *animus domini*. Moreover, when a bailee or a lease tenant gains actual control of a thing, their possession generally does not depend on their intent to be a bailee or a tenant. Therefore, if the definition of possession includes any mental element, that definition will be inapplicable in certain contexts. That is, if *animus domini* is a prerequisite for possession, a lease tenant is not a possessor. One can coin other terms to refer to parties who have actual control but not *animus domini*, which would unnecessarily increase the complexity of the conceptual system of possession.

I propose simply to define possession by elements that are the least common denominator of all possession-related issues. Actual control is such an element. If actual control is removed from the definition, possession as a concept could become an empty set for lack of a physical element. If any other element is added to the definition, additional terms (such as agents in possession and detention/custody) will be needed to refer to "incomplete" or "atypical" possession. Possession as actual control should thus be what Smith (2012a) would describe as having an "optimal level of generality."

Another reason for simply defining possession as actual control, regardless of intent, is information cost. Courts would have a hard time verifying the intent of possessors. A third party cannot tell from the fact that Paul unlawfully possesses Mary's land whether Paul intends to acquire prescriptively Mary's ownership, to acquire only a usufruct, or to use it temporarily. When the stakes are high, such as when titles to resources change hands, it is justifiable to look into the actual intents of possessors. In other contexts, as I will demonstrate, possessors' intents often do not matter, or are not worth the verification effort.

This simplified concept of possession does not in any way alter the doctrines of first possession and adverse possession. My theory just streamlines the conceptual framework of possession. This is particularly meaningful for civil-law property theory, as civil codes are constructed from abstraction to concreteness. Take prescriptive acquisition as an example. To adversely acquire ownership or a lesser property interest, the possessor has to maintain the specific type of actual control as prescribed by the doctrine (open, notorious, conspicuous, and so forth); in addition, throughout the period of statutory limitation, the possessor has to have *animus domini* or the intent to become a holder of lesser property interests. My conceptual framework does not affect whether any given adverse possessor can gain title. Nevertheless, my theory lightens the mental burden on the practitioners of possession law.

In light of this new concept of possession, the conceptual mishaps in many civil codes become apparent. For instance, a number of civil codes stipulate that possession can be inherited and tacked (e.g., German Civil Code art. 857; Portuguese Civil Code arts. 1255 and 1256; Korean Civil Code art. 199; and Taiwan Civil Code art. 947). Nevertheless, inheritance of possession is hard to reconcile with the baseline definition of possession as a fact.[30] Tacking and inheritance of possession are, in fact, issues only in adverse possession, and they should not be generalized to other possession issues. In other words, tacking and inheritance of possession should not be stipulated in the possession chapter in the book of the law of things, lest practitioners be misled to believe that possession in every context can be inherited.

To give another example, some civil codes, such as Japan Civil Code art. 186 and Taiwan Civil Code art. 944, presume that possessors have *animus domini* and the possession is good faith, peaceful, and conspicuous. Peaceful and conspicuous possession is relevant only in adverse possession issues. The presumption of good-faith (unentitled) possession of registered real estate does not make sense, as it nullifies the notice function of real estate registries, and overshoots by presuming entitled possessors to be unentitled. The presumption, though, saves courts a lot of work in judging the mental state of possessors in matters such as adverse possession of chattels. In addition, presuming all possessors to have *animus domini* is overly broad as it applies to possessors, such as lease tenants, and to adverse possessors who aim

---

[30] Portuguese Civil Code art. 1255 even explicitly prescribes that a descendent becomes a possessor regardless of actual control.

to prescriptively acquire an easement. In short, civil lawmakers tend to over-generalize in possession stipulations. Presumptions about possessions in different contexts should vary. Civil lawmakers, however, often impose a one-size-fits-all possession concept. A superior alternative is to define possession as simply actual control[31] and add presumptions regarding possession in specific doctrines.

4. Possession as a fact

Now we return to possession as a fact. Even without the confusion with the subsidiary possessory right, or the concerns with acquiring and relinquishing titles, civil codes still manipulate the concept of possession. The diseconomy of concept of possession does not appear to bother civil lawmakers and civil property scholars, as they seem to embrace a more "cerebral" concept as more sophisticated. Sub-section 4.1 discusses issues regarding acquiring and maintaining actual control. Sub-section 4.2 delineates the contour of the cerebral concept and critiques the justification for deviation from the simple possession concept of actual control. Sub-section 4.3 argues that the actual controller of things becomes the focus of various private law doctrines for substantive economic reasons.

4.1. Actual control and continuous possession

Once a party gets possession of a thing through actual control, the next question is how to maintain possession. The standard for continuous possession is critical, especially for adverse possessors. They, unlike first possessors, do not acquire title immediately. Moreover, the statute of limitation starts over when possession is deemed discontinued. My solution: adverse possessors do not lose possession until another party (be it the owner or a third party) takes actual control (cf. Epstein 1998: 63). Most adverse possessors are not always present in the properties they control. Whether they should be considered to be terminating adverse possession may be context – or social-norm-dependent. But the bottom line is that once another party gains stronger control over the property in question, the adverse possessor's possession ends.

For property interest holders, whether they are regarded as possessors generally does not matter (unless it is difficult to prove titles other

---

[31] See Chapter 5 for the possibility that actual control might be context-dependent to a certain extent.

than being a possessor), since losing possession is not coterminous with losing title. If the law adopts a stringent standard for (continuous) possession, so that homeowners lose possession when going out to work during the day, property owners still would work away from home, as long as they keep their titles and are able to exclude infringers based on their in rem rights.[32]

Nonetheless, there is no obvious benefit in adopting a stringent standard of continuous possession, particularly when we take into account parties with only in personam possessory rights. Lease tenants in most civil law countries only have in personam possessory rights, protected by law under certain conditions (such as violent deprivation). A stringent standard for (continuous) possession (say, again, treating tenants who go out to work as terminating possession) would create legal hurdles for possessors without any conceivable benefit.[33] Hence, to sum up, a party who acquires actual control would not lose possession until another party gains actual control. The abstract standards for defining continuous possession in adverse possession law and other property contexts converge. This simple standard is also consistent with the baseline definition of possession as actual control.

4.2. (Noneconomizing) cerebral concept

Civil laws complicate the concept of possession by manipulating it in two directions. On the one hand, actual control is swept aside, and an indirect possessor is dubbed a possessor. On the other hand, actual control is not enough, as an agent in possession is not regarded as a possessor. I critique the two concepts in turn.

4.2.1. Indirect possession

"A person who possesses property which is held for him by another has indirect possession," as stipulated in the Dutch Civil Code (art. 3: 107). The Netherlands is not alone, as civil codes in Germany (art. 868), Taiwan (art. 941), and France (art. 2255) contain similar provisions.

---

[32] This is not the case in jurisdictions where clear and formal titling regimes are absent. Empirical studies in Peru demonstrate that increases in possession protection lead to increases in employment outside the home (Field 2003: 858; Fennell 2010: 10–4).

[33] A gangster who enters into a lease tenant's house by force during working hours would not be violently depriving the latter of possession, since under the stringent standard, the latter has given up actual control.

Thus, an indirect possessor (such as a landlord) and a direct possessor (such as a tenant) are both possessors, but they are not co-possessors. This definition clearly defies the aforementioned civil codes' definition of possession as actual control. The indirect possessor does not have actual control in the way this term can be understood (if he or she does, the concept of indirect possession would be redundant). German scholars thus admit that the concept of possession is "cerebral" (*vergeistigt*). Three theories have been offered to justify this concept. First, indirect possessors have better incentive to bring the actions of recovering possession (Epstein 1998: 67). Second, *constitutum possessorium*[34] can be used in chattel transactions (Wang 2010: 551). Finally, indirect possession also serves the notice function (Wolf 2001: Rn. 185).[35] Each rationale has its own problems.

The problem with the incentive rationale is as follows: indirect possessors are usually owners. Owners can bring actions for recovery (called *vindicatio* in Roman law) and do not have to rely on their status as indirect possessors. Even in cases of movables, ownership of the indirect possessors can be presumed based on their past direct possession.[36] If indirect possessors are not owners or holders of lesser property interests, giving them a cause of action is inconsistent with other possession rules. As discussed previously, (direct) possessors have a cause of action only when their possession is violently deprived. Indirect possession cannot be violently deprived – perhaps only in a cerebral fashion. Moreover, even when direct possession is violently deprived, indirect possessors can hardly do anything, because doctrinally speaking, indirect possession disappears when a direct possessor loses possession (Hinteregger 2012: 105). That is, an indirect possessor loses "possession" just when he needs it the most.

Granted, when the indirect possessors have in personam (rather than in rem) possessory rights, their legal interests warrant legal protection in some way. In my view, since there must be a contractual relation between the direct possessor and indirect possessor, the better institutional design is to enable the indirect possessor to be subrogated to the

---

[34] According to Black's Law Dictionary, *constitutum possessorium* is a "type of constructive delivery in which mediate possession is transferred while the immediate control or custody remains in the transferor."
[35] For other ways to frame the function of possession, see Bouckaert and Geest (1998: 152).
[36] Swiss Civil Code art. 930 clearly specifies this presumption. It is implied in other civil codes.

direct possessor's claim against the third party, should the direct possessor elect to do nothing. A number of civil law countries (e.g., Japan Civil Code art. 423; Taiwan Civil Code art. 242) have recognized this design, which has at least two advantages. First, there will not be inconsistency between the claims brought by direct possessors and those by indirect possessors. Second, subrogation is a general design applicable in many contexts; thus, unlike indirect possession, it is not an ad hoc design that would complicate the private law system.

The other two rationales are easier to refute. The second rationale concerns whether constructive delivery, including attornment, *constitutum possessorium*, and *traditio brevi manu*, is efficient. Nevertheless, in any case, *constitutum possessorium* is a type of *constructive* delivery; thus, recognizing indirect possession as possession is *not* a necessary condition for allowing *constitutum possessorium*. Again, constructive delivery is just one specific possession issue. Recognizing indirect possession as a general concept (applicable to all possession contexts) is overshooting in terms of justifying constructive delivery. The final rationale is as cerebral as can be. How could Peter know from Paul's direct possession of a boat that Mary is the indirect possessor? Notice serves to reduce information costs, and recognizing indirect possession as possession does just the opposite.

In short, even if indirect possession is not considered real possession, other existing doctrines such as subrogation and in rem possessory rights should be able to provide the "indirect" possessor with ample protection. If civil codes have not yet stipulated such supporting doctrines, perhaps it is better to enact them than to stretch the limits of the concept of possession.

4.2.2. Agent in possession

An agent in possession is a person who exercises actual control over a thing for another person in the latter's household, trade or business or in a similar relationship, and must follow the instructions from the latter. Civil codes in Germany (art. 855) and Taiwan (art. 942) specifically exclude agents in possession as possessors. In France and the Netherlands, agents in possession are by definition *detenteur*, thus not possessors to begin with.[37] In jurisdictions like Germany and Taiwan, however,

---

[37] There is, however, a further complication. In French law, for example, a usufructuary "has a double position. In respect of ownership he is a detentor, but with respect to his limited property right he holds the object as a possessor" (Hinteregger 2012: 100).

excluding agents in possession (who have actual control) as possessors makes the possession concept even more cerebral (Baur and Stürner 2009: Ch. 7 Rn. 4).

German scholars worry that if agents in possession are considered possessors, they will enjoy the protection of possession and shoulder the responsibility of possessor (Baur and Stürner 2009: Ch. 7 Rn. 62). My response is, why not? The relation between an agent in possession and a principal is regulated by their contract. As long as contractual terms prevail between agents in possession and possessors/principals, and the former cannot employ their possession protection against the latter, I see no reason for excluding an actual controller from the protection of possession, which is used against third parties. In addition, the liabilities of the agents in possession in torts and unjust enrichment law should not be influenced by whether they are conceptualized as possessors – at least from a law-and-economic perspective.

In Taiwan, however, within a family, only the family head is considered a possessor, while other members are agents in possession. If the whole family lives in another person's house without prior permission, only the head of the household would be responsible for paying back the unjust enrichment. Although treating minors as agents in possession can, in some cases, protect them from this kind of liability, this does not always work, as a minor can be the sole controller of a neighbor's land against his or her parent's will (and thus inevitably be considered the possessor). A better institutional design in civil law is to stipulate a general vicarious liability doctrine that puts the burden and duty mostly on the parents, rather than prescribing a narrow vicarious rule in tort law and then inventing the concept of agency in possession to deal with vicarious issues in property law and unjust enrichment law. The basic point is that possession law and the concept of possession are only part of the many concepts, doctrines, and rules in any civil code. A complicated concept of possession at the most abstract level is not the only way to deal with the questions at hand, as other doctrines can often take care of them.

The necessity of carving out agents in possession can be further called into question when one considers places where a civil code refers to possessors or the like. Here are two examples: self-help and tort liability for animal keepers. Civil codes in Germany and Taiwan start with the baseline approach: only real possessors can exert the right of self-help (German Civil Code §859 and Taiwan Civil Code §960). But in the next article (German Civil Code §860 and Taiwan Civil Code §961), the lawmakers give the right of self-help to agents in possession. Under my framework, this is unduly complicated. An actual controller of things should be equipped with the right of self-help (for reasons elaborated earlier), and possessor should be coterminous with actual controller.

As for animal keepers' tort liability, the civil codes in Germany and Taiwan converge, but from different paths. Taiwan Civil Code §190 stipulates that possessors of animals are responsible for the damage caused by the animals. Scholars, however, interpret the possessor in this context to include agents in possession. An agent in possession is generally the least-cost avoider, so it makes economic sense to put the burden on the party who has actual control. On the other hand, German lawmakers, probably sensing the absurdity of explicitly designating agents in possession as possessors, first hold the "animal keeper" responsible (German Civil Code §833), and then put the prevention task to the party "who by contract assumes the supervision of an animal for the animal keeper" (German Civil Code §834) – read: agents in possession. Hence, civil lawmakers first oust agents in possession and eventually welcome them back – so frequently that one wonders whether the banishment or the greeting is the exception.[38]

A crystal clear conceptual system is important in any jurisdiction, but perhaps more so in civil law. In American common law, there may be no urgent need to distinguish possession and first possession, or to define possession precisely, as the common-law approach would allow the same term to be defined and used in slightly different ways. This is not the case in civil law. A civil code is an internally connected system. The intension and extension of a legal concept are shaped by other related legal concepts in the civil code. Thus, in this sense, the economy of concept is an even more important virtue in civil law. An overly complicated concept affects both the issue it prescribes and other private-law issues. As shown before, once the concept of agents in

---

[38] In this context, it is perhaps clearer why the animus of possessors should not matter. For information-cost reasons, the court has a hard time verifying the real animus of anyone, and animus could be a product of the legal rules. Moreover, given that actual controllers are least-cost avoiders and should thus shoulder the responsibility of curbing the animals, it should not matter what types of intents the possessors have. If a certain animus is built into the definition of possession, either tort law has to carve out another exception for the concept of possession, or tort law has to discard the term possession and use other essentially equivalent terms to replace it.

possession is recognized, not only does property law have to make additional efforts to clean up the mess (such as recognizing the self-help rights of agents in possession), but tort law and unjust enrichment are also made more complicated than is necessary.

4.3. Simple concept: economizing in information and efficient in substance

The preceding analysis has shown that there appears to be no need to complicate the concept of possession.[39] This sub-section further argues that defining possession as actual control makes economic sense beyond conceptual clarity and simplicity. Indeed, private laws, including contract, torts, property, and unjust enrichment, need to refer to a legal party who has actual control in many contexts. For example, in the law of sale contract, the default rule for the risk of destruction or deterioration to pass from the seller to the buyer is usually that the risk passes when actual control of the goods changes hand. In addition, in unjust enrichment law, a party who controls and uses others' real property without prior consent is liable for restitution of the benefits (saved rent) to the latter (Chang, Chen, and Lin 2014). Of course, the tort liability for animal keepers, discussed previously, is another case in point.

The legal conditions converge on actual control for a very good reason: a party who has actual control (not cerebral or constructive control) over the thing in question can best curb the animal, use the land, and protect the goods. In other words, a party with actual control is generally the "least cost avoider" in terms of preventing contractual breach, damage, and tortious actions from happening. Civil lawmakers often sense the need to induce the actual controllers of things to internalize the damage

---

[39] In German Civil Code and civil codes influenced by it, there are other possession-related concepts – such as *Eigenbesitzer* (a person who holds a thing for herself), *Fremdbesitzer* (a person who holds a thing for another), and quasi-possession (for instance, possession of a right) – and discussions on whether a natural will is required to transfer or acquire possession (Hinteregger 2012: 104–07). For similar reasons elaborated in this book chapter, I think these distinctions are overly complex. In addition, many civil codes stipulate how possession can be gained, transferred, and lost (e.g., Portuguese Civil Code arts. 1263 and 1267; Spanish Civil Code arts. 460–462). In my theory, these stipulations are redundant. One gains and loses possession by getting and relinquishing actual control. Any other definition is inconsistent with the baseline definition of possession as actual control.

they cause and to provide them with sufficient protection. For example, pursuant to the French Civil Code (art. 2278), a "detentor" who has actual control but not the intent to be owner also enjoys possessory protection against third parties (Hinteregger 2012: 108). Again, animal keepers in Germany and Taiwan include possessors and agents in possession. In these civil codes, agents in possession and detentors are the exceptions to the baseline definition of possessors, and the doctrines that embrace them as possessors are exceptions to the exception. These exceptions and exceptions to the exception do not exist under my simple conceptual framework of possession. In sum, to increase social welfare, actual controllers often become the center of legal responsibility. A clear conceptual framework would label actual controllers as possessors without exception and leave adjustments of possessors' responsibility (if ever needed) to specific contexts.

Conclusion

This chapter has demonstrated that a concise definition of possession – as actual control with no exception – has an optimal level of generality and economizes on information costs for users of the legal system.[40] As Kahneman (2011) has shown, our System 2 is lazy. Lawmakers and scholars should avoid using unnecessarily complex concepts, which take a heavy toll on our brainpower. Civil property scholars might feel uncomfortable in a world without a parade of possession terms. As this chapter has shown, a change in concepts does not lead to a substantive change in the various possession doctrines. The prescribed conditions for, say, adverse possession and first possession are still the same.

My analysis may also explain why there is hardly any discussion of possession as a general concept in common law – because it is unnecessary. Possession as actual control is intuitive and does not need a statute and a series of cases to elaborate it. What the American jurisprudence of possession informs civil lawyers about is that the contents of the specific possession doctrines, such as adverse possession, first possession, and good-faith purchase, are more important. Now that the conceptual bushes are trimmed, civil lawyers should turn their focus to these challenging issues.

---

[40] See Chapter 5 on opposite contention to broaden the concept of possession.

References

Austin, Lisa M. 2013. "Possession and the Distractions of Philosophy," in *The Philosophical Foundations of Property Law*, James E. Penner and Henry E. Smith, (eds.) Oxford University Press, pp. 182–201.
Barry, Norman 2004. "Property Rights in Common and Civil Law," in *The Elgar Companion to the Economics of Property Rights*, Enrico Colombatto, (ed.) Northampton, MA.: Edward Elgar, pp. 177–96.
Baur, Jürgen and Stürner, Rolf 2009. *Sachenrecht*. 18th edn. München: Beck.
Bell, John, Bell, Andrew and Boyron, Sophie 2008. "Property Law," in *Principles of French Law* John Bell, Sophie Boyron and Simon Whittaker, (eds.) Oxford University Press, pp. 269–93.
Bouckaert, Boudewijn and De Geest, Gerrit 1998. "The Economic Functions of Possession and Limitation Statutes," in *Essays in Law & Economics IV*, Claus Ott and Georg von Wangenheim, (eds.) Antwerpen: Maklu, pp. 151–68.
Chang, Yun-chien 2012. "Property Law with Chinese Characteristics: An Economic and Comparative Analysis," *Brigham-Kanner Property Rights Conference Journal* 1:345–72.
Chang, Yun-chien, Chen, Kong-pin, Lin and Lin, Chang-ching 2014. "Anchoring Effect in Real Litigation," *working paper*.
Chang, Yun-chien and Smith, Henry E. 2012. "An Economic Analysis of Common versus Civil Law Property," *Notre Dame Law Review* 88 (1):1–55.
  2015a "Structure and Style in Comparative Property Law," in *Research Handbook on Comparative Law and Economics*, edited by Giovanni B. Ramello and Theodore Eisenberg, (eds.) Northampton: Edward Elgar.
  2015b "The *Numerus Clausus* Principle, Property Customs, and the Emergence of New Property Forms," *Iowa Law Review* 100, forthcoming.
Dukeminier, Jesse, Krier, James E. Alexander, Gregory S. and Schill, Michael H. 2010. *Property*. 7th edn. New York, NY: Aspen Publishers.
Ellickson, Robert C. 1993. "Property in Land," *Yale Law Journal* 102:1315–1400.
  2011. "Two Cheers for the Bundle-of-Sticks Metaphor, Three Cheers for Merrill and Smith," *Econ Journal Watch* 8 (3):215–22.
Epstein, Richard A. 1979. "Possession as the Root of Title," *Georgia Law Review* 13:1221–44.
  1998. "Possession," in *The New Palgrave Dictionary of Economics and the Law*, Peter Newman, (ed.) New York, NY: Stockton, pp. 62–68.
  1999. *Torts*. New York, NY: Aspen.
  2005. "The Theory and Practice of Self-Help," *Journal of Law, Economics & Policy* 1:1–31.
  2011. "Bundle-of-Rights Theory as a Bulwark Against Statist Conceptions of Private Property," *Econ Journal Watch* 8 (3):223–35.
Fennell, Lee Anne 2010. "Possession Puzzle," in *Powell on Real Property*, Michael Allan Wolf, (ed.) New York, NY: Lexis-Nexus, pp. WFL10–1–WFL10–20.
  2012. "Lumpy Property," *University of Pennsylvania Law Review* 160:1955–93.

Field, Erica 2003. "Property Rights, Community Public Goods, and Household Time Allocation in Urban Squatter Communities: Evidence from Peru," *William & Mary Law Review* 45:837–87.
Gambaro, Antonio and Mattei, Ugo 2002. "Property Law," in *Introduction to Italian Law*, Jeffrey S. Lena and Ugo Mattei, (eds.) The Hague: Kluwer Law International, pp. 283–316.
Gordley, James 2006. *Foundations of Private Law: Property, Tort, Contract, Unjust Enrichment*. Oxford University Press.
Gordley, James and Von Mehren, Arthur Taylor 2006. *An Introduction to the Comparative Study of Private Law: Readings, Cases, Materials*. Cambridge University Press.
Hansmann, Henry and Kraakman, Reinier 2002. "Property, Contract, and Verification: The Numerus Clausus Problem and the Divisibility of Rights," *Journal of Legal Studies* 31:S373–S420.
Hinteregger, Monika 2012. "The Protection of Property Rights," in *Cases, Materials and Text on Property Law*, Sjef Van Erp and Bram Akkermans, (eds.) Oxford: Hart, pp. 97–210.
Holmes, Oliver Wendell 1881. *The Common Law*. Cambridge, MA: Harvard University Press.
Honoré, A.M. 1961. "Ownership," in *Oxford Essays in Jurisprudence: A Collaborative Work*, A.G. Guest, (ed.) Oxford University Press, pp. 107–47.
Kahneman, Daniel 2011. *Thinking, Fast and Slow*. New York, NY: Farrar, Straus and Giroux.
Kleijn, W.M. Jordaans, J.P. Krans, H.B. Ploeger, H.D. and Steketee, F.A. (revised by J.M.J. Choros) 2006. "Property Law," in *Introduction to Dutch Law*, J.M.J. Chorus, Piet-Hein Gerver and Ewoud Hondius, (eds.) The Hague: Kluwer Law International, pp. 103–34.
Kohler, Jürgen 2005. "Property Law (Sachenrecht)," in *Introduction to German Law*, Joachim Zekoll and Mathias Reimann, (eds.) The Hague, The Netherlands: Kluwer Law International, pp. 227–49.
Merrill, Thomas W. and Smith, Henry E. 2000. "Optimal Standardization in the Law of Property: The Numerus Clausus Principle," *Yale Law Journal* 110:1–70.
  2012. *Property: Principles and Policies*. 2nd edn. New York, NY: Foundation Press.
Posner, Richard A. 2000. "Savigny, Holmes, and the Law and Economics of Possession," *Virginia Law Review* 86:535–67.
Ramseyer, J. Mark and Nakazato, Minoru 1999. *Japanese Law: An Economic Approach*. University of Chicago Press.
Rose, Carol M. 1985. "Possession as the Origin of Property," *University of Chicago Law Review* 52:73–88.
  1988. "Crystals and Mud in Property Law," *Stanford Law Review* 40: 577–610.

Savigny, Friedrich Carl von 1848. *Von Savigny's Treatise on Possession; or the Jus Possessionis of the Civil Law*. Translated by Sir Erskine Perry. 6th edn. London: S. Sweet.

Schwartz, Allan and Scott, Robert E. 2011. "Rethinking the Laws of Good Faith Purchase," *Columbia Law Review* 111:1332–84.

Smith, Henry E. 2005. "Self-Help and the Nature of Property," *The Journal of Law, Economics & Policy* 1:69–146.

    2011a. "Property Is Not Just a Bundle of Rights," *Econ Journal Watch* 8(3):279–91.

    2011b. "Standardization in Property Law," in *Research Handbook on the Economics of Property Law*, Kenneth Ayotte and Henry E. Smith, (eds.) Cheltenham, UK; Northampton, MA: Edward Elgar, pp. 148–73.

    2012a. "On the Economy of Concepts in Property," *University of Pennsylvania Law Review* 160:2097–128.

    2012b. "Property as the Law of Things," *Harvard Law Review* 125:1691–726.

Steiner, Eva 2010. *French Law: A Comparative Approach*. Oxford University Press.

Strahilevitz, Lior 2010. "The Right to Abandon," *University of Pennsylvania Law Review* 158:355–420.

    2011. "Unilateral Relinquishment of Property," in *Research Handbook on the Economics of Property Law*, Kenneth Ayotte and Henry E. Smith, (eds.) Cheltenham: Edward Elgar, pp. 125–47.

Terre, Francois and Philippe, Simler 2006. *Droit Civil: Les Biens*. 7th edn. Paris: Dalloz-Sirey.

Wang, Tze-chien 2010. *Taiwan's Property Law*. Taipei: San Min Press.

Wolf, Manfred 2001. *Sachenrecht*. 18th edn. Muenchen: Beck.

5

What behavioral studies can teach jurists about possession and vice versa

DAPHNA LEWINSOHN-ZAMIR

1. Introduction

For nearly five decades, the economic analysis of property law has occupied a central place in the property literature. After laying down the main economic justifications for private property (for summaries see Posner 2011: 40–42; Shavell 2004: 11–23), and deriving basic rules – such as those relating to takings compensation – from these ideas (e.g., Michelman 1967), scholars have turned to ever more sophisticated and complex analyses that are sometimes less applicable to actual property conflicts (Lewinsohn-Zamir 2001: 98–101). In contrast, the behavioral analysis of property law is still relatively novel. Research in this field is in the early stage of testing or applying basic insights and theories, and it currently covers rather limited or sporadic issues.

The behavioral property literature can be divided into two categories, which partially correspond with two different periods. One category consists of (mostly earlier) studies that did not conduct independent, law-related experimental research, but rather relied on general results from the vast corpus of psychological literature. These applications were based on common-sense reasoning and analogies, rather than on direct testing of property law topics. Thus, Fennell (2003) used phenomena like the omission and regret-avoidance biases (Baron and Ritov 1994; Ritov and Baron 1990, 1992), to explain why, despite the popular opposition to estate taxes, people do not dispose of their property during their lifetime. The second category of behavioral studies is characterized by endeavors to carry out experimental research explicitly tailored to legal issues. Scholars

Louis Marshall Professor of Environmental Law, Faculty of Law, Hebrew University of Jerusalem. For their helpful comments and suggestions, I am grateful to Dan Kelly, Eyal Zamir, and the participants in the 5th Law and Economic Analysis Conference at Academia Sinica, Taiwan.

have either designed their own experiments or relied on studies that directly examined law-related topics. Thus, for example, Nadler and Diamond (2008) investigated the adequacy of market-value compensation for the expropriation of residences, by expressly asking subjects about the sum of money above market value that would be required for them to sell their home (with the understanding that if negotiations fail, the government would exercise its eminent domain powers to compel the transfer). The authors found that respondents indeed required compensation surpassing market value and that the length of time the residence had been in the family significantly affected the difference between market value and the hypothetical sale price (Nadler and Diamond 2008: 729–30, 743–44).

Both types of behavioral studies suffer from limitations that are due to the nascent stage of this theoretical and methodological perspective. One major limitation is the excessive focus on certain types of assets and property rights. For instance, a substantial part of the literature is occupied with the home, and whether it indeed merits special legal protection (Barros 2006; Blumenthal 2009: 617–21, 640–41; Godsil 2004; Kelly 2006; Nadler and Diamond 2008; Stern 2009, 2010). Put differently, contemporary research concentrates on owners who physically possess their place of residence, but largely overlooks other important issues, such as the cases of nonowners and vacant lands. Consequently, it has not examined the extent to which certain psychological findings are relevant to fungible or nontangible property, and to possessors who do not own the property.

This chapter uses the concept of "possession" to discuss the gaps in the literature and the ways they may be filled. In doing so, it demonstrates the potential for the mutual enrichment of behavioral studies and legal analysis.

Within the legal arena, "possession" typically is perceived as tangible, and property owners often receive greater protection against interference with their physical possession than against interference lacking any physical attribute. A good example is eminent domain compensation. Some American states require compensation surpassing market value for expropriation of occupied residences. In a similar vein, scholars have recommended that such compensation be tied to the length of the owner's possession.[1] However,

---

[1] Thus, condemnors in Indiana are required to pay 150 percent of fair market value for occupied residences, and Michigan's constitution states that compensation for takings of a principal residence must not be less than 125 percent of market value. See IND. CODE § 32–24–4.5–8(2)(A); MICH. CONST. art. X, § 2. Merrill (2005) has suggested that owners of homes, businesses, and farms would receive a one-percentage bonus above fair market value for each year they have continuously occupied the property.

psychological studies indicate that people's notion of "possession" is not always physical, but may extend to intangible entitlements and expectations. If, indeed, the impact of nonphysical injuries is not necessarily qualitatively different from that of physical ones, the law should consider updating and broadening its understanding of possession.

Psychological studies usually do not differentiate between ownership and possession, often conflating the two (e.g., van Dijk and van Knippenberg 1998). Consequently, it is unclear whether their findings are attributable to the existence of ownership, possession, or both. Only few psychological studies have begun to examine the distinction between ownership and possession, with thus far partial results. Legal scholars, of course, have long been aware of the distinction, as well as that between lawful and unlawful possession. Yet some jurists have applied findings that did not test those nuances in situations where ownership and possession were not vested in the same person. Implementing the distinction between ownership and different types of possession in future behavioral studies would enhance their accuracy and relevancy for both legal and nonlegal debates.

The chapter opens with a discussion of experimental findings that support a less physical conception of possession (Section 2.1). Section 2.2 applies this broader notion of possession to the issues of takings and first possession. Section 3.1 demonstrates the inadequacy of existing data on the relative impact of possession and ownership in cases of adverse possession. After surveying preliminary evidence of a "possession effect," Section 3.2 offers tentative observations regarding self-help measures to recover property and rights of long-term tenants. The chapter concludes with remarks on the prospects for debiasing, and recommendations for future research.

2. Nonphysical possession

An example for the centrality of tangibility in legal possession goes back to the famous case of *Pierson* v. *Post*, which involved a dispute between two hunters over a fox.[2] Post was pursuing the unowned wild animal across a deserted beach, when Pierson rode up and physically caught it. Post demanded that Pierson hand over the fox, based on the doctrine of first possession. That is to say, Post claimed that his hot pursuit of the animal counts as "possession," and hence that he was already the fox's owner at the time that Pierson seized it. The majority ruled in favor of

---

[2] 3 Caines 175 (N.Y. 1805).

Pierson, holding that possession requires strong tangible manifestations: if not actual bodily capture, then at least mortal wounding or securing in a trap. Until today, the definition of possession includes a significant physical element: taking in hand, occupying, or some other sort of physical control (Epstein 1998: 63). A modern-day illustration of this conception is the claim that the "possessiveness instinct" and the notion of "trespass" are irrelevant to intellectual property disputes (e.g., Lemley 2005: 1036–37). Psychological findings question this perception of possession.

2.1. Psychological evidence of nontangible possession

One of the most robust phenomena explored by behavioral studies is the endowment effect (EE). Numerous experiments have shown that people value an entitlement they already have much more than an identical entitlement they have an opportunity to acquire (Camerer 1995: 665–70; Hoffman and Spitzer 1993; Kahneman, Knetsch and Thaler 1990, 2008; Knetsch and Sinden 1984). A major explanation for the EE is loss aversion. Parting with an entitlement is perceived as a loss, whereas acquiring the same entitlement is viewed as a gain. Since losses loom larger than gains, people's selling price is significantly higher than their purchase price (Camerer 1995: 668; Kahneman 1992; Korobkin 2003: 1250–55; Zamir 2012: 835–40).[3]

Many of the EE experiments involved physical possession of tangible goods, such as mugs, pens, and chocolate bars. Some scholars, however, have explored the possibility that an EE can also exist in relation to intangible goods, or without physical possession of the relevant good. Thus, for example, an EE was found with respect to intangible entitlements like hunting rights (Hammack and Brown 1974), working hours (Ortona and Scacciati 1992), promotional coupons for restaurants (Sen and Johnson 1997), academic chores (Galin, Gross, Sapir, and Kela-Egozi 2006), and default rules (Korobkin 1998; Sunstein 2002). Furthermore, experimental studies have shown that the mere expectation of receiving a tangible or intangible resource can create an EE. Feldman, Schurr, and Teichman (2013) have demonstrated that the gains a party expects to realize from a contract produce an EE, and hence the disutility associated

---

[3] But see Plott and Zeiler (2005, 2007), who argue that the EE is due to subject misconceptions caused by the specific procedures used to elicit valuations. For criticism of these studies, see Isoni, Loomes, and Sugden (2011).

with not realizing those gains is similar to that of losing goods already in possession. For example, promisors who viewed unrealized expectations as a loss were more likely to interpret their contractual obligation in a self-serving manner. In a similar fashion, Marzilli-Ericson and Fuster (2011) found that expectations determined by the probability of receiving a mug created an EE: subjects who had a high (80 percent) chance of obtaining a mug, valued it 20–30 percent higher than subjects who had only a low (10 percent) chance of obtaining the asset.[4]

Experiments with online auctions are also informative for our purposes. Various studies (e.g., Ariely and Simonson 2003; Heyman, Orhun, and Ariely 2004) have shown that participants who were the highest bidders for a certain period of time developed an EE with respect to the auctioned item, even before they became its actual owners or physical possessors. The possibility of being outbid by others was perceived as a loss, which in turn increased their valuation of the item.[5] Another relevant line of research concerns consumers' behavior in online and offline purchases. Byun and Sternquist (2008, 2012) examined the effect of product-marketing techniques that induce perceptions of limited availability (by using such phrases as "limited time only," "while stock lasts," and so forth). They found that consumers perceive not buying as the loss of an opportunity that they currently have. Consumers react to this feeling of loss by hoarding numerous items in their shopping cart, which eventually leads to excessive purchases. In other words, aversion to losing an intangible opportunity increases instances of physical possession and ultimately ownership. In a similar vein, Tom, Lopez, and Demir (2006) observed an EE in both retail purchases (where the product is usually delivered on the spot) and direct marketing purchase (where the product is bought online or through a catalog). In the latter case, an EE was found even though the product was purchased remotely and physical possession obtained only after a period.

Finally, Peck and Shu (2009) and Peck, Barger, and Webb (2013) discovered that asking nonowners to *imagine* touching an object could produce an EE. It appears that even imagination can sometimes substitute for actual ownership or physical possession.

---

[4] For additional studies of expectations as reference points for evaluating gains and losses see Camerer, Babcock, Loewenstein, and Thaler (1997); Abeler, Falk, Goette, and Huffman (2011).

[5] In addition, it was proven that this higher valuation could not be explained by an "opponent effect," that is, a competitive impulse to win the auction.

These diverse experimental data support the claim that people's notion of "possession" is not confined to physical occupation, holding, or control of tangible assets. Rather, feelings of possession may relate to intangible assets, entitlements and expectations, and may exist in the absence of any physical proximity to a tangible asset.[6] The next section discusses possible implications of these findings.

2.2. "The new possession" in law?

In his seminal article "The New Property," Charles Reich (1964) argued that government largess in the form of welfare benefits, licenses, franchises, subsidies and the like, should be regarded as "property." The main motivation for including intangible, government-created entitlements in the institution of property was to improve their protection against injurious state interference. Reich claimed that increased protection is necessary in light of the fact that an ever-increasing portion of individuals' wealth comprises of government largesse rather than traditional types of property. In a somewhat analogous fashion, we may want to consider "The New Possession." If perceptions, preferences, and reactions conventionally associated with physical possession are also manifested without physical control and with respect to intangible entitlements and expectations, then we may need to broaden our definition of legal possession.

Recognizing a wider, more flexible notion of possession may have implications for legal debates. A good example is the takings issue. In the United States (and elsewhere), there is a sharp distinction between physical and nonphysical injuries to land. Landowners are afforded much wider protection against physical injuries (such as the taking of possession or the elimination of existing uses on the land) than against nonphysical injuries (such as the restriction of unrealized development rights or the prohibition of future uses). Whereas in the former case even a small injury requires compensation, in the latter enormous reductions in value are legitimized without compensation (Lewinsohn-Zamir 1996: 114–19).[7]

---

[6] *Cf.* Brenner, Rottenstreich, Sood, and Bilgin (2007: 375–76), who state that "the notion of possession is somewhat fuzzy" and that "it is no accident that statements like 'I *have* a headache' or '*My* commute is very long' use possessive verbs and pronouns."

[7] The physical/nonphysical distinction is not universal. Countries such as Germany and Israel recognize a broad right to compensation for both types of injury. For a comparative study of land use regulation and compensation in several countries see Alterman (2010).

Some scholars have justified these rules by relying on the EE phenomenon. Ellickson, for example, rationalized that a physical injury to land would ordinarily be viewed as a loss. In contrast, a nonphysical injury is likely to be perceived as an unattained gain. Therefore, the former type of injury is worthier of protection than the latter (Ellickson 1989: 35–38). In a similar vein, Serkin claimed that elimination of an existing use is experienced differently from the prohibition of a future use – the former as an out-of-pocket cost, and the latter as a foregone gain. Consequently, existing uses deserve more protection than prospective uses, like development rights (Serkin 2009: 1267–69). Both explanations justify the physical/nonphysical distinction by tying restriction of development rights to people's psychological reaction to unattained profits. These arguments are based on the crucial assumption that nonphysical injuries are usually perceived as foregone gains. However, the above experimental evidence of intangible possession indicates that this may not necessarily be the case. Why wouldn't landowners experience downzoning as a loss of formerly "held" development rights? This presumption seems especially plausible if the land's purchase price reflected the value of the development rights. Absent direct testing of the matter, one cannot presume one way or the other.[8]

Another possible implication of acknowledging intangible possession is that the majority view in *Pierson* v. *Post*, which conditioned the doctrine of first possession on there being almost a certainty of attaining physical possession, is too stringent.[9] The minority view, which sufficed with a reasonable likelihood of physical capture, may better accord with people's perception of possession.[10] The latter test also supports the claim that the similar dispute involving a million-dollar home-run-record-breaking baseball should have been resolved in favor of the first person

---

[8] Note that even if restriction of development rights is viewed as an unattained gain – and thus the injury to the landowner is smaller than if such restriction were regarded as a loss – the injury may still be substantial enough to warrant compensation.

[9] See Chapter 2 for a more demanding understanding of "first possession." Accordingly, possession must be such as to provide a clear and acceptable signal to others that the possessor intends to control the asset and claim it as her property.

[10] Interestingly, the minority judge explicitly uses the language of expectations when he conditions the first hunter's ownership on his having "a reasonable prospect" of capturing the fox. Epstein (1979: 1231) notes that the custom of hunters in the region to regard "hot pursuit as giving rights to take an unimpeded first possession," may justify the reversal of the court's decision. Furthermore, Epstein (1979: 1230–31) describes a universal maritime custom that assigned an escaped whale to the fishing crew that first stuck a harpoon into it, rather than to the crew that first physically captured it.

who stopped the flight of the ball with his glove, but was thrown to the ground by other spectators in the game before he could physically secure it in his hand. However, the court held that the ball should be sold and its proceeds divided equally between the above individual and the person who eventually picked it up (who did not take part in the scuffle over the ball).[11]

In sum, behavioral studies cast doubt on the assumption that "possession" necessarily requires a significant physical component. Such understanding of possession may sometimes be overly rigid, since people may perceive themselves as possessors of intangible entitlements and expectations, and as nonphysical possessors of tangible assets.

Two important caveats are in order. First, it is not claimed that notions of intangible possession always exist or that they invariably equal in strength to those of physical possession. Further – and law-related – experimentation is necessary in order to map out the circumstances giving rise to nonphysical perceptions of possession and to assess their relative intensity. For example, it may transpire that nonphysical notions of possession occur when a person has high expectations of receiving (but has not yet received) physical possession, or when the object of possession is itself intangible. In contrast, we may discover that such notions do not arise when the owner of a tangible asset voluntarily decides to part with its physical possession, as is the case when a landlord leases her property to a tenant.

Second, even when perceptions of intangible possession exist, it does not automatically follow that they should have normative implications. The legal system may have good reason not to acknowledge these perceptions, and countervailing considerations – varying according to the specific issue at stake – may eventually prevail. For instance, the unwillingness to encourage fetishism or the high administrative costs of identifying and catering to nonphysical possession may limit the law's consideration of this phenomenon. However, if one holds that enhancing human welfare is a central goal of legal policymaking, and if one espouses a theory of welfare that is concerned with preference fulfillment, then it is important to be aware of the potential flaws of an overly physical definition of possession.[12] Furthermore, to the extent that the magnitude

---

[11] See *Popov v. Hayashi*, No. 400545, 2002 WL 31833731 (Cal. Super. Ct. Dec. 18, 2002).

[12] This is particularly true for efficiency analysis, which aims to maximize people's welfare as measured by the extent to which their preferences are satisfied (Shapiro and McClennen 1998). It also holds for objective theories of well-being (since they accept that fulfilling people's wishes is one element of human welfare) and deontological theories

of an individual's losses is relevant to the pertinent legal rule, and to the extent that the law's protection of possession assumes that possessors feel more strongly about assets than non-possessors,[13] then we should take into account that such reactions may be present even without tangible possession.

3. Possession versus ownership

Ownership and possession are basic building blocks of property law, and every so often, they vest in the same person. Legal scholars, however, are well aware of the importance of the distinction between ownership and possession, and of the fact that the two may diverge. In addition, jurists acknowledge the significance of distinguishing between lawful and unlawful possession, as well as between actual and prospective possession. Thus, a case of adverse possession may involve an owner and an unlawful possessor; and a trespass scenario may pit a person with a right to receive possession against a person who possesses in fact. Indeed, conflicts between owners and possessors – both lawful and unlawful – are not uncommon.

The legal treatment of such situations could benefit from behavioral research. Moreover, the relevance of psychological data goes beyond disputes between owners and possessors. In creating legal rules, it would be helpful to know, for instance, whether the attitudes and reactions of tenants (both short- and long-term) to property resemble or markedly differ from those of owners. Regrettably, however, psychological studies usually do not differentiate between ownership and possession. Notwithstanding, jurists rely on such non-nuanced experiments in their analysis of conflicts between owners and possessors, as will be demonstrated.

3.1. Legal use of incomplete data

Behavioral studies often conflate ownership and possession. Consequently, we do not know whether their findings are attributable to

---

(since they do not deny the importance of consequences, including human welfare). For discussion of objective theories of well-being and their application to property law, see Lewinsohn-Zamir (2003).

[13] Some reasons for respecting possession may be relevant only for physical possession. For example, Rose (1985: 81–82) argued that possession is socially useful because it gives clear notice of who the owner of the asset is, which in turn facilitates trade and minimizes resource-wasting conflicts.

ownership, possession, or both. A major manifestation of this difficulty is found in experimental studies of the EE. Typically, subjects are informed that they are owners of some object (such as a mug, a pen, or a chocolate bar), which they also physically possess. The value of the endowed object is elicited and often compared to the value of some alternative object, which subjects neither own nor possess (Kahneman, Knetsch, and Thaler 1990, 1991; Kahneman 1992; Knetsch and Sinden 1984; Morewedge, Shu, Gilbert, and Wilson 2009; van Dijk and van Knippenberg 1996, 1998). Terms pertaining to both ownership and possession are often used interchangeably throughout the studies. The potential differences between lawful and unlawful possession were not investigated at all. Hence, to date, we do not really know to what extent the EE is an "ownership effect" or a "possession effect," and what happens when ownership and possession diverge.

These shortcomings of current behavioral research should have limited their applicability to law-related issues, yet legal studies do apply such general data to owner-possessor disputes. A prominent example is the discussion of adverse possession. According to this doctrine, a trespasser may gain title to the land or immunity from an ejection suit, if his or her possession is adverse to the owner's interest (that is, does not stem from the owner's right and is without the owner's permission), and is actual, open and notorious, exclusive, and continuous for the statutory period of limitation. Cohen and Knetsch (1992: 751–52), Ellickson (1989: 38–39) and Stake (2001: 2423–32), rely on the EE and loss aversion to justify adverse possession. The long-time possessor, so the argument goes, would perceive giving up the land as a loss, whereas the owner would view not receiving it back as a foregone gain. Since losses loom larger than gains, incurring the second cost – rather than the first – maximizes the parties' joint welfare. Stake (2001: 2459–64) also addresses the possibility that the non-possessing owner may perceive the rejection of his or her suit as a loss (rather than an unattained gain), but believes that this loss would be smaller than the corresponding loss to the possessor. This is because the latter's loss of a tangible object would be greater than the former's loss of what he or she probably sees as only an intangible financial asset.

These claims may be plausible, yet without direct behavioral research it is difficult to know whether owners would view themselves as being in the domain of gains or in the domain of losses (Korobkin 2003: 1259–62; Rose 2000: 489), or if they would perceive their land as merely a financial resource. Arguably, a registered landowner who loses title or the ability ever to use the land may perceive this outcome as the loss of a non-fungible asset. Moreover, regardless of whether the situation is framed as an unattained gain or as a loss, a crucial factor is the magnitude of these gains and losses.[14] In real life, the owner may have purchased the land in the past for its market price and therefore will be deprived of this value, whereas the possessor may have knowingly trespassed on unpaid-for land. The value of the foregone gains or losses to the owner may surpass the value of the losses to the possessor. In sum, one should be cautious in applying behavioral findings to legal issues, absent a good "fit" between the two.

Note that even after these issues are resolved, the case for adverse possession would not be automatically settled one way or the other. The possible asymmetry in the subjective costs to each party – highlighted by behavioral studies – is but one relevant consideration among many. Thus, for example, the high costs of adjudicating old cases to all parties involved – plaintiffs, defendants, and courts – support the statute of limitation.[15] However, in countries where adverse possession does not extinguish the owner's title, acknowledgement of the possessor's right to remain on the land would obstruct the accuracy of the information in the land registry, and the possibility of future purchasers to rely on it. For this reason, Israeli law, for example, does not recognize adverse possession claims in lands that have undergone a settlement of title procedure.[16]

3.2. *Preliminary evidence of a "possession effect" and potential implications*

Behavioral research has not tested the relative strength of possession vis-à-vis ownership directly – by pitting owners against possessors. However, a small number of experiments support the possibility that possession may sometimes be the more crucial factor psychologically.

A few studies have demonstrated the effect of mere possession. Knetsch and Wong (2009) found an EE when subjects were offered a

---

[14] To the extent that the possessor has improved the land, he or she may be reimbursed for these costs, at least in cases where the encroachment was in good faith. See Sterk (1987: 80–81); *Somerville v. Jacobs*, 170 S.E.2d 805, 807, 813 (1969).
[15] For discussion of the traditional justifications for adverse possession, see Merrill (1985: 1128–33).
[16] See section 159(b) of the Land Law, 5729-1969, 23 LSI 283, 311.

choice between an object (a mug or a pen) that they possessed but were expressly told that they did not own, and an alternative object (a pen or a mug, respectively) that they neither possessed nor owned yet. Subjects strongly preferred to become owners of the object that they possessed: only 14 percent of the initial penholders traded it for a mug, and only 33 percent of the initial mug possessors traded it for a pen (Knetsch and Wong 2009: 411–12). In a similar vein, experiments have shown that touch alone increases the valuation of objects for both owners and non-owners. Peck and Shu (2009) examined, inter alia, the effect of touching a mug on its valuation by potential buyers. Subjects who had a mug placed in front of them but did not touch it, offered lower prices for the mug than subjects who had an opportunity to touch it before indicating their willingness to pay. Likewise, opportunity to touch increased owners' valuation of the pen they owned, making them more reluctant to trade it, in comparison to owners who did not touch the owned object.[17]

Another behavioral study demonstrated the effect of length of physical contact with an unowned object. Wolf, Arkes, and Muhanna (2008) varied the amount of time during which participants could examine an item before bidding for it in an online auction. Half of the subjects inspected the coffee mug for ten seconds and the other half for thirty seconds. It was found that this small difference in duration of touching the object significantly increased non-owners' valuation of the mug and the amount of their bids.[18]

The study coming closest to testing the relative significance of possession and ownership is that of Reb and Connolly (2007). The authors elicited the monetary valuations of chocolate bars in four groups of subjects: the first group had both ownership and possession of the object; the second group owned the object but did not possess it; the third group possessed the object but did not own it; and the fourth group neither possessed nor owned the object. The results revealed a significant main

---

[17] Interestingly, studies on the behavior of territorial animals found that defenders of a territory invariably overcome intruders of the same species who try to take over their territory (Alcock 2009: 278–84; Bradbury and Vehrencamp 1998: 711–30). Obviously, animals have no notions of legal ownership and thus these studies attest to the strong, instinctive protection of possession.

[18] Experimental studies have also shown that length of ownership increases the valuation of objects. However, the owners in these studies were also possessors of the valued asset, and thus ownership and possession were not contrasted. (See Shu and Peck 2011: 443–44; Strahilevitz and Loewenstein 1998).

effect for possession. That is to say, participants gave the chocolate bar a higher monetary value when they possessed it than when they did not possess it. Ownership, in itself, did not produce a similar significant effect. These results were replicated with coffee mugs (Reb and Connolly 2007: 109, 111). Although Reb and Connolly's study is unique in its attempt to disentangle the effects of ownership and possession, it did not directly contrast the two. Owners and possessors did not interact with each other, for example to negotiate a sale or exchange. Thus, we still lack data regarding direct competitions between owners and possessors.

In sum, the available findings indicate that mere possession may suffice for creating an EE, even when people are aware that they are not the owners of the asset they possess. Furthermore, it appears that the duration of possession increases this effect, even after a very short period. Current literature has not yet tested scenarios in which ownership and possession are pitted against each other, although one study lends initial support to the possibility that the possession effect may sometimes be stronger than the ownership effect. Pierce, Kostova, and Dirks (2003: 88–93) theorized that feelings of ownership (without formal ownership) are induced by controlling an asset, becoming familiar with it (through actual or imagined use), and/or investing one's self into it (for example, through labor). To the extent that this theory is true, it can explain why non-owning possessors (including consciously unlawful possessors) develop strong attachments to the property, whereas non-possessing legal owners may not always experience similar feelings of psychological ownership.[19] The state of the available data on this issue requires much caution when moving from laboratory results to legal applications. Nevertheless, let me offer some tentative observations.

The apparent strength of possession per se, justifies most of the prevailing rules regarding self-help measures to recover possession. Ordinarily, a person whose proprietary rights have been violated must turn to the judicial and enforcement systems of the state. Nevertheless, the law sometimes allows individuals to forcefully reclaim their property. This privilege of self-help often operates as a defense against what would otherwise be a tort of assault or battery (Keeton, Dobbs, Keeton, and

---

[19] For general studies of the connection between possessions and people's identity, self-development and extended self, see Beggan (1992); Belk (1988); and Csikszentmihalyi and Rochberg-Halton (1981).

Owen 1984: 131).[20] Self-help is limited to reasonable force and can be exercised only as an immediate response to an attempted – or very recent – invasion of property rights. The main prerequisite is that the force-user be the lawful and actual possessor of the property.[21] Mere ownership or right to receive possession does not suffice (Dobbs 2000: 182). Thus, an owner of a vacant parcel cannot forcibly expel a wrongful possessor, and a landlord usually cannot evict defaulting tenants by herself (Friedman 1997: 1246–47).

To the extent that possession – rather than ownership – is the main driving force of the EE and of people's powerful inclination to gain possession by force, we may want to consider expanding self-help to unlawful possessors as well, at least vis-à-vis subsequent trespassers (if not also against the true owner of the property). This recommendation is in harmony with the common law rule that does not allow defendants-wrongdoers to raise an ius tertii claim against plaintiffs-possessors (Epstein 1998: 65). Like the latter rule, awarding self-help to unlawful possessors would reduce the incidence of public disorder from successive attempts to dispossess current possessors.[22] In a similar vein, assuming that the welfare loss of nonpossessing owners due to the absence of a self-help remedy is relatively small in comparison to that of possessing owners, it may be justifiable to hold that defaulting tenants' right to a judicial eviction proceeding cannot be contractually waived. Currently, some American states permit such waivers, which allow the landlord to use self-help to regain possession of the tenement (Friedman 1997: 1248–49; Schoshinski 1980: 403).

Another possible implication of the preliminary data on possession is that the law should examine whether certain rights and protections afforded to owners also should be given to tenants, and particularly to long-term tenants (see Barros 2006: 300–05).[23] This is largely the practice in Israel, where most lands are held in public ownership and individuals usually

---

[20] In other countries, such as Israel, a direct right to self-help is acknowledged in the property legislation itself. See Land Law § 18, 5729–1969, 23 LSI 283, 285 (1968/69).

[21] See Restatement (second) of Torts §§ 77, 81, 91, 94, 103, 106; Keeton, Dobbs, Keeton and Owen (1984: 131, 137–40).

[22] For a somewhat different justification for extending self-help to unlawful possessors, see Chapter 4.

[23] In a different context, Stern (2011) relied on empirical data to argue that owners and tenants of comparable residential duration perform quite similarly on certain citizenship measures such as community organizational participation and certain forms of collective action.

receive only long-term leases. Israeli law often extends the rules applying to ownership – for example, with respect to statutory rights of first refusal and rights of redemption – to leases for a term that exceeds twenty-five years. Moreover, recognizing that these tenants most probably regard themselves as owners and that it would be politically unfeasible to require them to vacate the land at the end of the lease, or else pay the full market value of a new lease, has led the state to gradually transfer ownership in developed urban lands to the long-term tenants (rather than perpetually renewing the lease without requiring payment from the tenants).

Conclusion

This chapter has discussed behavioral literature that is relevant to the legal concept of "possession." The discussion revealed two phenomena that seem to be partially in tension: people's notion of possession may extend to intangible entitlements and expectations, and to assets that they do not physically hold. Concomitantly, preliminary evidence suggests that mere physical possession can have a psychological effect similar to that of ownership, and that the effect of possession may sometimes be stronger than the effect of ownership.

A question that commonly arises with respect to experimental findings is whether the law should attempt to "debias" people and steer them in a more rational direction (for general discussions of debiasing through law, see Blumenthal 2007; Jolls and Sunstein 2006).

The answer to this question is necessarily context dependent. Sometimes, there is no justification for legal intervention. For instance, if people experience feelings of loss not only with respect to tangible goods, but also with regard to intangible ones, there is no compelling reason to try to eliminate the latter type of perceptions, as there is nothing, in principle, objectionable or irrational about them. In other cases, an attempt to debias may not succeed, due to the relative rareness of the type of loss involved in people's lives. Take, for example, ownership of land. If most owners develop their parcels according to plan and do not experience significant downzoning, it would be hard for the law to educate them that restriction of their development rights constitutes merely unattained gains rather than losses. Similarly, as Justice Holmes famously stated,[24] we cannot reasonably expect individuals to curb their

---

[24] See Holmes (1881: 213): "Law, being a practical thing, must found itself on actual forces. It is quite enough, therefore, for the law, that man, by an instinct which he shares with the

powerful instinct to respond to dispossession with force. Therefore, the law cannot avoid acknowledging some forms of self-help behavior.

In closing, a comment on future behavioral studies of possession is in order. The existing body of research has undoubtedly contributed to our understanding of possession. At the same time, further work must be done to improve the relevance and fruitfulness of these studies for the law. There is a need for experimental and empirical studies that directly examine legal situations involving possession. Our ability to draw useful insights and conclusions from studies unrelated to the law is necessarily limited. For instance, it would be worthwhile to discover the legal contexts giving rise to intangible perceptions of possession and to design scenarios that test the relative strength of physical and nonphysical possession. Such studies would help us understand – and, one hopes, resolve – the partial tension between the two phenomena discussed in this chapter. In a similar vein, legal scholars should design experiments that expressly employ distinctions between ownership and possession, between lawful and unlawful possession, and between short-term and long-term possession. Of course, laboratory experiments' ability to test the latter distinction is very limited. Empirical studies are likely to give us far better knowledge about the effects of long-term possession by non-owners of property.

References

Abeler, Johannes, Falk, Armin, Goette, Lorenz and Huffman, David 2011. "Reference Points and Effort Provision," *American Economic Review* 101:470–92.

Alcock, John 2009. *Animal Behavior: An Evolutionary Approach*. 9th edn. Sunderland: Sinauer Associates.

Alterman, Rachelle 2010. *Takings International: A Comparative Perspective on Land Use Regulations and Compensation Rights*. Chicago: American Bar Association Publishing.

Arieli, Dan and Simonson, Itamar 2003. "Buying, Bidding, Playing, or Competing? Value Assessment and Decision Dynamics in Online Auctions," *Journal of Consumer Psychology* 13:113–23.

---

domestic dog ... will not allow himself to be dispossessed ... of what he holds, without trying to get it back again. Philosophy may find a hundred reasons to justify the instinct, but it would be totally immaterial if it should condemn it and bid us surrender without a murmur. As long as the instinct remains, it will be more comfortable for the law to satisfy it in an orderly manner, than to leave people to themselves. If it should do otherwise, it would become a matter for pedagogues, wholly devoid of reality."

Baron, Jonathan and Ritov, Ilana 1994. "Reference Points and Omission Bias," *Organizational Behavior and Human Decision Processes* 59:475–98.
Barros, D. Benjamin 2006. "Home as a Legal Concept," *Santa Clara Law Review* 46:255–306.
Beggan, James K. 1992. "On the Social Nature of Nonsocial Perception: The Mere Ownership Effect," *Journal of Personality and Social Psychology* 62:229–37.
Belk, Russell W. 1988. "Possessions and the Extended Self," *Journal of Consumer Research* 15:139–68.
Blumenthal, Jeremy A. 2007. "Emotional Paternalism," *Florida State University Law Review* 35:1–72.
  2009. "'To Be Human:' A Psychological Perspective on Property Law," *Tulane Law Review* 83:609–44.
Bradbury, Jack W. and Vehrencamp, Sandra L. 1998. *Principles of Animal Communication.* Sunderland: Sinauer Associates.
Brenner, Lyle, Rottenstreich, Yuval, Sood, Sanjay and Bilgin, Baler 2007. "On the Psychology of Loss Aversion: Possession, Valence, and Reversals of the Endowment Effect," *Journal of Consumer Research* 34:369–76.
Byun, Sang-Eun and Sternquist, Brenda 2008. "The Antecedents of In-Store Hoarding: Measurement and Application in the Fast Fashion Retail Environment," *The International Review of Retail, Distribution and Consumer Research* 18:133–47.
  2012. "Here Today, Gone Tomorrow: Consumer Reactions to Perceived Limited Availability," *Journal of Marketing Theory and Practice* 20:223–34.
Camerer, Colin 1995. "Individual Decision Making," in John H. Kagel and Alvin E. Roth (eds.), *The Handbook of Experimental Economics.* Princeton University Press, pp. 587–703.
Camerer Colin, Babcock, Linda, Loewenstein, George and Thaler, Richard 1997. "Labor Supply of New York City Cabdrivers: One Day at a Time," *Quarterly Journal of Economics* 112:407–41.
Cohen, David and Knetsch, Jack L. 1992. "Judicial Choice and Disparities between Measures of Economic Values," *Osgoode Hall Law Journal* 30:737–70.
Csikszentmihalyi, Mihaly and Rochberg-Halton, Eugene 1981. *The Meaning of Things: Domestic Symbols and the Self.* Cambridge University Press.
Dobbs, Dan B. 2000. *The Law of Torts.* St. Paul: West Publishing Company.
Ellickson, Robert C. 1989. "Bringing Culture and Human Frailty to Rational Actors: A Critique of Classical Law and Economics," *Chicago-Kent Law Review* 65:23–56.
Epstein, Richard A. 1979. "Possession as the Root of Title," *Georgia Law Review* 13:1221–43.
  1998. "Possession," in Peter Newman (ed.), *The New Palgrave Dictionary of Economics and The Law,* vol. 3. New York: Stockton Press. pp. 62–68.

Feldman, Yuval, Schurr, Amos and Teichman, Doron 2013. "Reference Points and Contractual Choices: An Experimental Examination," *Journal of Empirical Legal Studies* 10:512–41.

Fennell, Lee Anne 2003. "Death, Taxes, and Cognition," *North Carolina Law Review* 81:567–652.

Friedman, Milton R. 1997. *Friedman on Leases*. 4th edn. New York: Practicing Law Institute.

Galin, Amira, Gross, Miron, Kela-Egozi, Irit and Sapir, Sigal 2006. "The Endowment Effect on Academic Chores Trade-Off (ACTO)," *Theory and Decision* 60:335–57.

Godsil, Rachel D. 2004. "Viewing the Cathedral from Behind the Color Line: Property Rules, Liability Rules, and Environmental Racism," *Emory Law Journal* 53:1807–85.

Hammack, Judd and Brown, Gardner M. Jr. 1974. *Waterfowl and Wetlands: Toward Bioeconomic Analysis*. Washington DC: RFF Press.

Heyman, James E., Orhun, Yesim and Ariely, Dan 2004. "Auction Fever: The Effect of Opponents and Quasi-Endowment on Product Valuations," *Journal of Interactive Marketing* 18:7–21.

Hoffman, Elizabeth and Spitzer, Matthew 1993. "Willingness to Pay vs. Willingness to Accept: Legal and Economic Implications," *Washington University Law Review* 71:59–114.

Holmes, Oliver Wendell 1881. *The Common Law*. Cambridge MA: Harvard University Press.

Isoni, Andrea, Loomes, Graham and Sugden, Robert 2011. "The Willingness to Pay—Willingness to Accept Gap, the 'Endowment Effect', Subject misconceptions, and Experimental Procedures for Eliciting Valuations: Comment," *American Economic Review* 101:991–1011.

Jolls, Christine and Sunstein, Cass R. 2006. "Debiasing Through Law," *Journal of Legal Studies* 35:199–241.

Kahneman, Daniel 1992. "Reference Points, Anchors, Norms, and Mixed Feelings," *Organizational Behavior and Human Decision Processes* 51:296–312.

Kahneman, Daniel, Knetsch, Jack L. and Thaler, Richard H. 1986. "Fairness and the Assumptions of Economics," in Robin M. Reder and Melvin R. Hogarth (eds.), *Rational Choice: The Contrast between Economics and Psychology*. University of Chicago Press, pp. 101–16.

1990. "Experimental Tests of the Endowment Effect and the Coase Theorem," *Journal of Political Economy* 98:1325–48.

1991. "The Endowment Effect, Loss Aversion, and Status Quo Bias," *Journal of Economic Perspectives* 5:193–206.

2008. "The Endowment Effect: Evidence of Losses Valued More than Gains," in Charles R. Plott and Vernon L. Smith (eds.), *Handbook of Experimental Economics Results*, vol. 1, Amsterdam: North-Holland publishing, pp. 939–55.

Keeton, W. Page, Dobbs, Dan B., Keeton, Robert E. and Owen, David G. 1984. *Prosser and Keeton on the Law of Torts.* 5th edn. St. Paul: West Publishing Company.

Kelly, James J. Jr. 2006. "'We Shall Not Be Moved': Urban Communities, Eminent Domain and the Socioeconomics of Just Compensation," *St. John's L. Rev.* 80:923–90.

Knetsch, Jack L. and Sinden, J. A. 1984. "Willingness to Pay and Compensation Demanded: Experimental Evidence of an Unexpected Disparity in Measures of Value," *Quarterly Journal of Economics* 99:507–21.

Knetsch, Jack L. and Wong, Wei-Kang 2009. "The Endowment Effect and the Reference State: Evidence and Manipulations," *Journal of Economic Behavior and Organization* 71:407–13.

Korobkin, Russell B. 1998. "The Status Quo Bias and Contract Default Rules," *Cornell Law Review* 83:608–87.

2003. "The Endowment Effect and Legal Analysis," *Northwestern University Law Review* 97:1227–93.

Lemley, Mark A. 2005. "Property, Intellectual Property, and Free Riding," *Texas Law Review* 83:1031–76.

Lewinsohn-Zamir, Daphna 1996. "Compensation for Injuries to Land Caused by Planning Authorities: Towards a Comprehensive Theory," *University of Toronto Law Journal* 46:47–127.

2001. "Contemporary Property Law Scholarship: A Comment," *Theoretical Inquiries in Law* 2:97–105.

2003. "The Objectivity of Well-Being and the Objectives of Property Law," *New York University Law Review* 78:1669–1754.

Marzilli Ericson, Keith M. and Fuster, Andreas 2011. "Expectations as Endowments: Evidence on Reference-Dependent Preferences from Exchange and Valuation Experiments," *Quarterly Journal of Economics* 126:1879–1907.

Merrill, Thomas W. 1985. "Property Rules, Liability Rules, and Adverse Possession," *Northwestern University Law Review* 79:1122–54.

2005. The Kelo Decision: Investigating Takings of Homes and Other Private Property: Hearing Before the Senate Committee on the Judiciary. 109th Congress 122 (testimony of Thomas W. Merrill, Professor, Columbia University Law School).

Michelman, Frank I. 1967. "Property, Utility and Fairness: Comments on the Ethical Foundations of 'Just Compensation' Law," *Harvard Law Review* 80:1165–1258.

Morewedge, Carey K., Shu, Linda L, Gilbert, Daniel T. and Wilson, Timothy D. 2009. "Bad Riddance or Good Rubbish? Ownership and not Loss Aversion Causes the Endowment Effect," *Journal of Experimental Social Psychology* 45:947–51.

Nadler, Janice, and Seidman Diamond, Shari 2008. "Eminent Domain and the Psychology of Property Rights: Proposed Use, Subjective Attachment, and Taker Identity," *Journal of Empirical Legal Studies* 5:713-49.
Ortona, Guido and Scacciati, Francesco 1992. "New Experiments on the Endowment Effect," *Journal of Economic Psychology* 13:277-96.
Peck, Joann and Shu, Suzanne B. 2009. "The Effect of Mere Touch on Perceived Ownership," *Journal of Consumer Research* 36:434-47.
Peck, Joann, Barger, Victor A. and Webb, Andrea 2013. "In Search of a Surrogate for Touch: The Effect of Haptic Imagery on Perceived Ownership," *Journal of Consumer Psychology* 23:189-96.
Pierce, Jon L., Kostova, Tatiana and Dirks, Kurt T. 2003. "The State of Psychological Ownership: Integrating and Extending a Century of Research," *Review of General Psychology* 7:84-107.
Plott, Charles R. and Zeiler, Kathryn 2005. "The Willingness to Pay—Willingness to Accept Gap, the 'Endowment Effect', Subject Misconceptions, and Experimental Procedures for Eliciting Valuations," *American Economic Review* 95:530-45.
   2007. "Exchange Asymmetries Incorrectly Interpreted as Evidence of Endowment Effect Theory and Prospect Theory?," *American Economic Review* 97:1449-66.
Posner, Richard A. 2011. *Economic Analysis of Law*. 8th edn. New York: Aspen Publishers.
Reb, Jochen and Connolly, Terry 2007. "Possession, Feelings of Ownership and the Endowment Effect," *Judgment and Decision Making* 2:107-14.
Reich, Charles 1964. "The New Property," *Yale Law Journal* 73:733-87.
Ritov, Ilana and Baron, Jonathan 1990. "Reluctance to Vaccinate: Omission Bias and Ambiguity," *Journal of Behavioral Decision Making* 3:263-77.
   1992. "Status-Quo and Omission Biases," *Journal of Risk and Uncertainty* 5:49-61.
Rose, Carol M. 1985. "Possession as the Origin of Property," *University of Chicago Law Review* 52:73-88.
   2000. "Left Brain, Right Brain and History in the New Law and Economics of Property," *Oregon Law Review* 79:417-92.
Schoshinski, Robert S. 1980. *American Law of Landlord and Tenant*. Rochester: The Lawyers Cooperative Publishing Co.
Sen, Sankar and Johnson, Eric J. 1997. "Mere-Possession Effects without Possession in Consumer Choice," *Journal of Consumer Research* 24:105-17.
Serkin, Christopher 2009. "Existing Uses and the Limits of Land Use Regulations," *New York University Law Review* 84:1222-91.
Shapiro, Scott and McClennen, Edward F. 1998. "Law-and-Economics from a Philosophical Perspective," in Peter Newman (ed.) *The New Palgrave Dictionary of Economics and the Law*, vol. 2, New York: Macmillan Reference Limited, pp. 460-65.

Shavell, Steven 2004. *Foundations of Economic Analysis of Law*. Cambridge MA: Harvard University Press.

Shu, Suzzane B. and Peck, Joann 2011. "Psychological Ownership and Affective Reaction: Emotional Attachment Process Variables and the Endowment Effect," *Journal of Consumer Psychology* 21:439-52.

Stake, Jeffrey E. 2001. "The Uneasy Case for Adverse Possession," *Georgetown Law Journal* 89:2419-74.

Sterk, Stewart E. 1987. "Neighbors in American Land Law," *Columbia Law Review* 87:55-104.

Stern, Stephanie M. 2009. "Residential Protectionism and the Legal Mythology of Home," *Michigan Law Review* 107:1093-1144.

2010. "The Inviolate Home: Housing Exceptionalism in the Fourth Amendment," *Cornell Law Review* 95:905-56.

2011. "Reassessing the Citizen Virtues of Homeownership," *Columbia Law Review* 111:890-938.

Strahilevitz, Michal A. and Loewenstein, George 1998. "The Effect of Ownership History on the Valuation of Objects," *Journal of Consumer Research* 25:276-89.

Sunstein, Cass R. 2002. "Switching the Default Rule," *New York University Law Review* 77:106-34.

Tom, Gail, Lopez, Stephanie and Demir, Kivilcim 2006. "A Comparison of the Effect of Retail Purchase and Direct Marketing on the Endowment Effect," *Psychology and Marketing* 23:1-10.

Van Dijk, Eric and van Knippenberg, Daan 1996. "Buying and Selling Exchange Goods: Loss Aversion and the Endowment Effect," *Journal of Economic Psychology* 17:517-24.

1998. "Trading Wine: On the Endowment Effect, Loss Aversion, and the Comparability of Consumer Goods," *Journal of Economic Psychology* 19:485-95.

Wolf, James R., Arkes, Hal R. and Muhanna, Waleed A. 2008. "The Power of Touch: An Examination of the Effect of Duration of Physical Contact on the Valuation of Objects," *Judgment and Decision Making* 3:476-82.

Zamir, Eyal 2012. "Loss Aversion and the Law," *Vanderbilt Law Review* 65:829-94.

6

The possession heuristic

JAMES E. KRIER AND CHRISTOPHER SERKIN

1. Introduction

A heuristic, as Daniel Kahneman (2011: 98) observes, "is a simple procedure that helps find adequate, though often imperfect, answers to difficult questions." Kahneman is a psychologist, one of a handful of scholars who have brought heuristics to the attention of a general audience, thanks in large part to several books (Kahneman, Slovic, and Tversky 1982; Gilovich, Driffin, and Kahneman 2002). Just as Thomas Kuhn's 1962 ideas about paradigms in the history of science are fodder for academics in all sorts of fields (this for better or worse), so too for Kahneman and company's ideas about heuristics, and legal academics are among the wide audience of consumers. Witness a host of articles and several books, including the recently published *Heuristics and the Law* (Gigerenzer and Engel 2006; see also, e.g., Chapter 5; Sunstein 2000; Kelman 2011).

We join the crowd here, examining the role of possession as a heuristic in the law of property. While heuristics-and-the-law is the subject of considerable scholarship, much of the work is mainly about heuristics, drawing in occasional examples from the law. Examples from property law in general, let alone possession in particular, usually figure very little. Thus, we have found no mention of a possession heuristic in the legal literature, although there are scattered references in work by psychologists.[1] But we are talking about property law, particularly the role it assigns to possession. Our discussion of possession as a heuristic is informed more by theories of possession than by theories of heuristics, and our aim is a contribution to the former, not the latter. We take heuristics in the sense Kahneman suggests. They are simple decision-making strategies devised to solve complex problems. Since the law of

---

Krier is Earl Warren DeLano Professor, University of Michigan Law School. Serkin is Professor of Law, Vanderbilt Law School.

[1] See, e.g., Friedman and Neary (2008: 829), discussing a "first possession" heuristic whereby people treat things as belonging to the person who first possessed them.

property is essentially the law of belongings, its first task is to determine to whom things belong. There are all sorts of complicated inquiries that could be undertaken to figure out and justify an incredible range of answers to this question. Alternatively, there is a simple inquiry that provides a simple answer: a thing belongs to its possessor.

This is the possession heuristic.

2. Evolution and the possession heuristic

2.1. Regarding animals (other than humans)

Evolutionary game theory suggests why there might be a possession heuristic. Consider an account by John Maynard Smith (1982). His model supposes two animals of the same species, each of which aims to occupy a particular breeding site. The value of that site to its occupant is the gain it promises in reproductive fitness as compared to the next best alternative site. The probability that either of the two animals will be the first to occupy the site is given as equal, and either animal might be either an aggressive Hawk or a passive Dove. Hawks fight over territory until one is injured and retreats, and in a Hawk/Hawk contest, each competitor has an equal chance of winning or losing. Losing carries the cost of reduced reproductive fitness. Doves do not fight; they avoid injury by giving in to Hawks or by sharing with other Doves. On these assumptions, Maynard Smith argues, natural selection will lead the species to evolve in the direction of a Hawk-Dove hybrid, a "Bourgeois" type that acts as a Hawk when in possession but as a Dove when not – this because the Bourgeois strategy (whereby animals protect what they possess but defer to what others possess) is better than any alternative. Bourgeois types "avoid more damaging encounters than the pure Hawks and win more encounters than pure doves" (Krier 2009: 153). Bourgeois strategy is said to be evolutionarily stable, meaning that once it is established, natural selection forecloses invasion by any mutant strategy.[2]

Two points must be noted: first, the outcome described above depends on a stock of breeding sites of sufficient number that the value of sites is less than the cost of fighting over them.[3] Second, and more pertinent for

---

[2] The discussion of evolution and the possession heuristic is drawn from Krier (2009), which itself relies heavily on the literature cited in this section.
[3] Notice the contrast with Demsetz's (1967) argument that property rights develop in response to resource scarcity. See also Ellickson (2013: 9 n.41) for the suggestion that increasing scarcity might be accompanied by heightened defense of resources, increasing the costs of fighting to the point that they remain larger than the value of the resources in question.

our purposes, the outcome depends on the asymmetry of occupant and latecomer, which signals to a contestant the role (Hawk or Dove) an opponent is likely to play. Where this asymmetry holds, a behavioral pattern (a "norm") of deference to possessors can develop spontaneously and persist simply as the consequence of self-interested individual action.[4]

2.2. Regarding human animals

The late Jack Hirshleifer, though skeptical to some degree of the Hawk-Dove-Bourgeois account, conceded, "[o]n the human level, a corresponding environmental situation might be expected to lead to a 'social ethic' supporting a system of property rights" (Hirschleifer 1982: 23). Robert Sugden (2004 [1986]) pursues that line of thought in a book published a few years after Hirshleifer's remark. Sugden alters Maynard Smith's (1980) model to fit the human context by substituting utility for reproductive fitness, and by assuming that effective strategies develop through imitation and learning as opposed to biological natural selection. Having done so, he reaches conclusions much like those of Maynard Smith: repeated play would likely lead to a convention – a *de facto* rule – of deference to possessors. David Hume, he notes, had long ago anticipated his argument.[5]

Of particular interest to us is Sugden's discussion of possession as the crucial asymmetry. Given any number of asymmetries (the difference between a strong contestant and a weak one, an attractive contestant and an ugly one, a loud contestant and a quiet one, a greedy contestant and a generous one, a rich contestant and a needy one, and so on), why settle on possession as the decisive factor? Sugden's answer begins with the observation that the purpose of a convention is to guide behavior. To perform that function, the asymmetry underlying the convention must be prominently apparent. Hume thought possession worked well in this

---

[4] That the behavioral pattern can develop does not mean that it will, and it is a fact that there seem to be few examples of species known to defer to possession. This could mean that the underlying model is not developed in a sufficiently discriminating fashion, or it could mean that appearances are not what they might at first seem.

[5] Unlike Thomas Hobbes and John Locke, who imagined modes of governance reached by group agreement or imposed by central authorities, Hume argued that decisions made by self-interested individuals each choosing on his own could lead to successful strategies for cooperation and coordination; Hume called these strategies "conventions" (Hume 1978 [1740]: bk. 3, pt. 2, §2).

respect (its salience led people to converge on it), and Sugden agrees. The idea is to find a simple strategy for assigning objects to people, and there is "a natural prominence to solutions that base the assignment on some pre-existing relation between persons and objects," namely possession, which, because it is usually unambiguous, provides a clear indication of the status of any claimant (Sugden 2004 [1986]: 95–107).

The norm of deference to possession, in its simplest form, did not amount to much in terms of what it provided; it would have been "problematic in the case of land ... and also when attention switches from the acquisition to the maintenance of possession" (Posner 2000: 545–46). As to land, the norm would seem to protect only what the possessor physically occupies, and even then only so long as the possessor is actually there. As to chattels, one can actually possess only a few. In both cases, then, ongoing vigilance and control could be relaxed only at the peril of losing what one had managed to obtain. This fault was fixed by extending the essence of possession to include *constructive* possession evidenced by prominent signals that identified things as subject to a standing claim – branding and such in the case of chattels; building, fencing, and tilling in the case of land. Actual physical occupation was no longer necessary to trigger the possession heuristic, meaning the security it provided was "permanent" rather than "transient" (Blackstone 1765–69: *3–7).

3. Possession, priority, and ownership

The foregoing suggests how early humans arrived at a *de facto* norm of deference to possession (eventually including constructive possession) well before the appearance of formal legal systems.[6] We can be confident that adherence to the norm was hardly perfect. Probably deference was most regular among small, close-knit groups (Ellickson 1991: 177–78), whose members we might liken to conspecifics in the case of nonhuman animals. And group members probably differentiated between insiders and outsiders, deferring to possessors in their clan, but not to those in other clans.[7] Hence, conflict could co-exist with cooperation, thanks in

---

[6] See also Epstein (1979, 2006: 147–49) and Rose (1985).
[7] A striking example is the taking of North America by European settlers. Deference to possession was standard practice on the continent (put aside the occasional war), but not when it came to dealings with such primitives as the Native Americans. The settlers rested their claim to America on discovery (a conventional means by which to acquire property),

particular to the invention of constructive possession. Simply picture the situation where a possessor is temporarily absent, and another person comes along and takes possession, whether because of misunderstanding or bad intentions. In either event, the result is a new possessor who might claim the right to what in fact another already (constructively) possesses. The resolution is plain: if constructive possession is to mean anything, it must mean that as between the two contestants, the first possessor should prevail.

We do not know how this principle was put into operation in *de facto* regimes that had developed a norm of deference but had not yet arrived at something like a "government" to resolve disputes of the sort described. What is clear, however, is that *de facto* became *de jure* with the gradual emergence of governing authorities (in other words, of states), and formal property regimes have regularly adopted as legal rules what primitives had adopted as customs. Those legal rules protect possession, including constructive possession, and formalize a principle of priority to resolve contests arising from sequential possession. Exactly as we should expect, the principle considers the claim of the prior possessor to be superior to the claim of the subsequent possessor. The superior claimant is said to have "title" to the thing in question – relative, at least, to the second possessor, and absent a voluntary transfer by the former to the latter.[8]

This doctrine of relative title is sometimes said to give a possessor "title good as against all but the true owner," but that is misleading: the "true owner" is no one but the prior possessor relative to the subsequent possessor. If we put context aside, "true owner" simply designates the person whose possession is subsequent to no one's. As Holmes put the point, rights acquired by possession "continue to prevail against all the world but one, until something has happened sufficient to divest ownership" (Holmes 1831/1938: 238). Holmes saw where his observation led. "The consequences attached to possession are substantially those attached to ownership," at least according to the common law (Holmes

---

notwithstanding that natives already inhabited the discovered land. This was unproblematic for the settlers, who reasoned that the natives were mere occupants, not possessors, and that move spelled end game. The settlers were entitled, if necessary, to enforce their rights of possession by conquest. It was left to Chief Justice Marshall to explain (and apologize) in *Johnson v. M'Intosh*, 21 U.S. (8 Wheat.) 543 (1823).

[8] This conclusion holds even where the prior possessor had acquired the item in question by earlier stealing it from a third party, a point discussed more fully in Section 4.2.

1831/1938: 241).[9] We venture to say, however, that the proposition holds more or less in the case of virtually any property regime, formal or informal; it is a cultural universal. Possession kick starts property.

So what is "property"? To put the question in terms like Holmes', what are "the rights acquired by possession," the "consequences ... attached to ownership"? Conventionally, they are three: the right to exclude, the right to use, and the right to transfer (the last two rights would seem to follow necessarily from the first) (Merrill 1998). None of these rights is without limitation,[10] but each is extensive, and the force of the state backs all.[11] The package of rights can be justified, or on the other hand criticized, on various grounds, but we leave those matters to our concluding section.

4. Applications, problems, and fixes

Here we consider some examples of the possession heuristic at work in the common law of property, look at some problems to which the heuristic gives rise, and consider some fixes. By and large, our examples are drawn from relatively simple situations, because they are the most illustrative. They come from four doctrinal categories, and each category tends to put its own particular light on the possession heuristic. With respect to all of the categories, however, we see the courts more or less taking the possession heuristic as it developed *de facto* and applying it *de jure*.[12] The courts, in short, made the heuristic their own to a considerable degree. Perhaps they thought it wise to inform the law by looking to

---

[9] Throughout this chapter, we focus our discussion on the common law, as opposed to the civil law of many countries. For comparative discussions of possession in the common and civil law, see, e.g., Holmes (1938: 206–46); Posner (2000: 535–67); Gordley and Mattei (1996: 293–334); Chapter 4 and Smith (2012).

[10] For example, the right to exclude is limited by rules privileging trespass in the event of necessity, and by prohibitions against racial discrimination in certain circumstances; the right to use is limited by the law of waste and the law of nuisance; the right to transfer is limited by (again) prohibitions against racial discrimination, and by rules against restrictions on alienability.

[11] The rights could exist, of course, yet not be backed by the state, but instead by self-help that the state explicitly or implicitly allows.

[12] *De jure* adoption by courts of a *de facto* heuristic used by ordinary people in everyday affairs has figured at least a little in the heuristics literature. A "group report" on the subject (Haidt 2006) supposes, as have we, that common law courts might have relied considerably on informal lay heuristics in carrying out their formal legal work, because the lay heuristics are simple and often work in practice to achieve what the courts saw as desirable ends, although normative constraints limit to some degree what courts may and should do.

lay intuitions and norms; perhaps they considered the heuristic to be, in any event, an apt means to resolve the conflicts that came before them; or perhaps for both of these reasons, or for others not apparent to us.

4.1. Capture

Under the common law, and consistent with the possession heuristic, landowners have possession (or constructive possession) of any resources on, over, and under their parcels. Notice the incentives that result. Since any landowner reaps all the gains from using his parcel wisely, and bears all the losses from neglect, we expect he will manage his belongings wisely, if for no reason other than a self-interested aim to maximize their value to him. This is a neat picture from the standpoint of efficiency, but it frays at the edges. Even the most diligent landowners will find it difficult or impossible to manage all that they possess, because land parcels often have on them some resources, which, unlike the land itself, are not fixed in place; hence, they can escape an owner's possession. Who owns them, once they are removed from the land?[13]

The answer is provided by the rule of capture, the domain of which is so-called fugitive resources like wild animals, water, oil, and gas. Provided such resources are captured off a landowner's parcel, they belong to the capturer as first possessor. We will modify this statement shortly, but first observe its consequences. Once resources move off an owner's land, they change status from the owner's private property to everybody's common property (the default rule of common property is that anyone may take and use the resources free of interference by anyone else). This changes incentives for the worse, because anyone who exploits a common resource gets all the gains therefrom, yet (unlike the situation of an individual owner) bears only a fraction of the losses, since they are spread over all the commoners. The predictable consequence is socially wasteful overconsumption.

Whether or not the common law courts fully appreciated this disturbing feature of the possession heuristic, they acted as if they did,

---

[13] The discussion in this and later sections takes a lesson from the arguments in Section 3, and thus uses the term "owner" to designate the person with the relatively best title in the circumstances under examination. Moreover, we regard the owner as having *individual* (not shared) ownership of a particular parcel of land or other resource. At the other extreme is the open-access or universal commons, open to all; this is not really a property regime since no one has the right to exclude. In between the extremes is the limited-access commons. (See Section 4.3.)

developing rules that helped counter the problems presented by fugitive resources. As one might expect, these adaptive new rules usually operated by extending the idea of constructive possession. The rules were nice but also limited fixes and they were sometimes applied in clumsy and unsatisfactory ways. We can illustrate both observations by looking first at some examples regarding wild animals, and then considering oil and gas (with a glance at water, another fugitive resource).

Suppose an owner of a large parcel of land frequented by deer. The deer, while on that parcel, are in the constructive possession of the landowner, as we have seen. But suppose further that the landowner has granted permission to various hunters to hunt for the deer on this land, and that one of those hunters has snared a deer and taken it home alive, hoping eventually to build a small herd of deer to be corralled on his, the hunter's, own land. That hunter who first captured the deer becomes its owner by virtue of the possession heuristic. It matters not that some other hunters had also tried to capture the deer in question – indeed had begun their efforts before the successful hunter began his. The common law rule, illustrated by the famous case of *Pierson* v. *Post*,[14] is that the animal goes to the first hunter to capture it, whether by kill, mortal wound, or trap. The dissenting judge in the case was of a different mind, arguing that the first hunter to chase with a reasonable prospect of capture should be entitled to the animal if his efforts ultimately succeed. He reasoned (incorrectly) that otherwise no one would hunt.[15] The majority (correctly) thought otherwise, and in any event believed that the dissenting judge's rule would be too difficult to apply. It chose the first-to-capture rule "for the sake of certainty," noting that the alternative rule of first-to-pursue "would prove a fertile source of quarrels and litigation." (This statement illustrates an important feature of the possession heuristic already noted: a claim based on possession is relatively cheat-proof, difficult to feign, as compared to claims based on who was first to pursue, who was most likely to capture, and so on.)[16]

---

[14] 3 Cai. R. 175, 2 Am. Dec. 264 (1805).
[15] The idea that no one would hunt calls to mind Yogi Berra's idea that nobody eats at a certain restaurant because it is too busy. In fact, the rule of capture generally has led not to inactivity but rather to over-exploitation and over-investment in capture technology in any number of documented instances.
[16] Consider also the rule of increase, according to which the owner of a female animal also owns her offspring, no matter who owned the male animal. The rule so holds, in part, because it is easier to determine the female source of the offspring than it is the male source.

Back to our hunter who snared a deer. He eventually realizes his hopes of building a herd. His deer reproduce, and they develop a comfortable attachment to the corral that is their home. Matters reach the point where the hunter can let his deer out during the day to graze wherever they like, because they return habitually in the evening. They have acquired, as the law speaks of it, the *animus revertendi*. They have been domesticated.

But a domestic species of animal (such as a cow) is one thing, and a domestic individual of a wild species another.[17] Suppose a person hunting for deer under just the circumstances of our original situation comes upon one of the domestic deer and captures it, only to have his possession challenged by the hunter who built the herd and kept it corralled each night. Now the rule is that, because the deer in question had the *animus revertendi*, it belongs still to the owner of the herd. This is a considerable extension of constructive possession; it lets an owner of domesticated animals secure his possession of them with a very long but entirely invisible leash. The doctrine of *animus revertendi* is untroubling in the case of domestic species (cows again), because it is reasonable to attribute to hunters knowledge that certain animals are not wild and up for grabs. The doctrine is also untroubling in instances where the domesticated individual of a wild species is clearly marked in a way that suggests its status – a bell on a collar around its neck, a prominent brand on its side. In both of these instances, the existence of a prior possessor is apparent – an important feature in the development and application of the possession heuristic. Yet the courts seem not always to insist on such measures, nor commentators to criticize their failure to do so. Probably they accept *animus revertendi* as a suitable means to reach a productive end, namely domestication of animals. Yet when so clumsily applied, the rule results in uncertainty, the costs of which the owners of the animals in question can most cheaply avoid.

A related example of the possession heuristic in the case of animals has to do with a wild animal that has no habit of return and is taken by a hunter out of the animal's native territory. The animal has escaped the clutches of an owner keeping it and its kind for commercial purposes. The owner shows up to claim the animal from the hunter, and the question boils down to whether the animal's status as a foreigner put the hunter on notice that it belongs to someone, and forecloses the hunter's objection

---

[17] For an evolutionary account of the domestication of animals, see, e.g., Ellickson (2013: 1–25).

that the animal has returned to its natural state. The answer is easy and obvious in the case of a hunter who shoots a giraffe grazing in an Iowa cornfield. It is more difficult in the case of a silver fox native to Canada, owned by a fur rancher in Colorado, and captured by a trapper in the latter state. Our sense of the cases is that courts have some interest in protecting important local industries, so the Colorado trapper might well lose to the Colorado rancher. And perhaps it is right to suppose that trappers should know whereof they seek, just as we expect fishermen to be aware of the difference between a largemouth bass regulated by one set of fishing rules and a smallmouth bass regulated by another.

Legislative and administrative regulation is the chief means by which the legal system aims to alleviate an undesirable consequence of the rule of capture in the case of wild animals – overhunting. If anything, the common law rules have worked as much to provoke undue consumption as to limit it, as is evident in judge-made rules regarding interference with capture. Allegations of interference with capture are bound to arise from the very nature of the rule of capture itself. A hunter is after wild game, and just as he readies for the kill an interloper appears and kills first. Or, a hunter is after wild game, and just as he readies for the kill an interloper scares the animal off. The difference between the two cases has been important to the courts, which tend to rule that in the first case the interloper wins, whereas in the second the hunter has a remedy, say in damages equal to the value of the lost opportunity. The point of the set of rulings is clear: in the first case, there is a successful capture, whereas in the second there is not, and since capture seems to be the purpose in mind (after all, hunting laws license the activity), the courts are happy to judge in light of the consequences. If the outcome of a contest is that, despite the interference, one person or another has managed to make the kill, all to the good; but if, thanks to the interference, neither has, all to the bad.[18] Unless, of course, the resource in question is scarce, in which case conservation, as opposed to capture, might be the better social end. Yet common law courts have been reluctant to consider scarcity in applying their rules about interference with capture. In short, judges were content to invent the rule of capture in regimes of abundance that made it sensible, yet unwilling to change their minds when the foundations of the rule of capture began to crumble, and thanks in part to the judges' invention!

---

[18] See *Keeble v. Hickeringill*, 103 Eng. Rep. 1127 (1707); Krier (1997).

A response, of course, is that legislatures *have* intervened in various respects (hunting regulations, conservation laws to protect endangered species, and so forth), but the effective reach of these measures is limited in that legislative jurisdiction has an insufficient reach in some important instances. The best example, perhaps, is ocean fisheries, productive management of which calls for international cooperation of a sort difficult to realize. And so we witness overfishing, and overinvestment in fishing capital, each a predictable consequence of the rule of capture.

Now consider the rule of capture as applied to oil and gas resources. The story here is much the same as that for wild game, so our account can be brief. Oil and gas resources were discovered to be useful long after the basic rules of capture of wild animals were laid down, but their fugitive nature led the courts to treat them in the same fashion. So, in an early case the court reasoned that oil and gas were, after all, just like foxes and deer – resources *ferae naturae* – in that "they have the power and the tendency to escape without the volition of the owners." What followed from the analogy (which the court hoped was "not too fanciful") was plain:

> [Oil and gas] belong to the owner of the land, and are part of it, so long as they are on and in it, and are subject to his control; but when they escape, and go into other land, or come under another's control, the title of the former owner is gone. Possession of the land, therefore, is not necessarily possession of the gas [and oil]. If an adjoining, or even a distant, owner drills his own land, and taps your gas [or oil], so that it comes into his well and under his control, it is no longer yours, but his.[19]

From the standpoint of efficient use, this extension of the rule of capture was not always problematic. If the pool of oil or gas happened to be located entirely within the boundaries of an owner's land (which boundaries are said, with some hyperbole, to stretch up to the heavens and down to the center of the earth), then, as noted in Section 3, we could expect productive management. But usually oil and gas are found in vast common pools that lie under many parcels of land belonging to many individual owners. The rule of capture as applied by the court in *Westmoreland* turned these common pools into common property, thus inviting the sorts of ills we considered earlier in connection with wild animals. Drillers could be expected to capture as much as they could before others did so, and, as part of that aim, to overinvest in capture

---

[19] *Westmoreland & Cambria Natural Gas Company v. DeWitt*, 18 A. 724, 725 (Pa. 1889).

technology, drilling multiple wells where a single owner would use fewer; they could store what they captured in tanks to save the resources for another day. However, an owner of a private pool could store more economically by leaving the resources in the ground until demand justified extraction.

The ills of common ownership were in principle avoidable, though perhaps at the cost of undue concentrations of wealth in lucky drillers. The courts could have said that the first to tap into a pool owns all of its contents, whatever their reach – in short, that the first to drill successfully had captured not just the flow from the pool, but the stock of the pool itself (Lueck 1995: 396–97, 422).[20] But given the state of the relevant sciences in the nineteenth century, this approach would have been difficult if not impossible in practice. There was no reliable means to identify the boundaries of any given pool, and thus to differentiate one stock from another.

Courts did do what little they could to privatize common pools, primarily by way of the so-called bottoming rule. A landowner (or his licensee) could drill down only through his own parcel, never crossing over into the subterranean territory of neighbors (who had the right to exclude). Assuming one could accurately monitor the angle of a well (and it seems the courts thought this possible), the bottoming rule helped avoid common-pool problems. The rule protected pools that were in fact private (located entirely under a single parcel of land) from lateral drilling, and the rule turned *de jure* common pools into *de facto* private ones in instances where drilling was not practical on neighboring land perched over a common pool, say because of natural barriers such as impenetrable rock. So the bottoming rule helped alleviate common-pool problems, but did not overcome them entirely. Observing this, at least a few courts aimed at a fuller remedy, limiting excessive drilling into and extraction from what could be identified as common pools. Eventually, however, and as with wild animals, legislative bodies stepped in to regulate extraction, primarily by unitization of oil and gas fields. Unitization aims to achieve efficient management of common pools by forcing multiple owners to act, in essence, as a single owner would.[21]

---

[20] Compare underground caves that extend beneath many parcels of land. On one view, the cave belongs in common to all owners of the overlying land. On another view, the entire cave belongs as a stock to the owner of the land on which sits the entrance to the cave, or to the first landowner to discover the cave and open it to access. See *Edwards* v. *Sims*, 24 S.W.2d 619 (Ky. 1929); *Edwards* v. *Lee's Admr.*, 96 S.W.2d 1028 (Ky. 1936).

[21] For a discussion of similar problems and responses in the case of ground and surface waters, see Dukeminier, Krier, Alexander, and Schill (2010: 37–38).

4.2. Finders

The folk saying is "finders keepers, losers weepers," and no doubt this is often the reality. The law, however, runs to the contrary. Early in the eighteenth century, an English court announced the rule that has prevailed ever since: a finder does not have "absolute property or ownership, yet he has such a property as will enable him to keep it against all but the rightful owner."[22] We noted in Section 3 that this statement is misleading, if not flat-out wrong, as the law of finders illustrates. Suppose that A is "the rightful owner" of an item and loses it, that B finds the lost item and takes possession but then loses it, and that C then finds it. B learns of C's find and sues to recover the item. The statement from the *Armory* case clearly holds that B wins against C, but it also clearly holds that C wins against B. Each of them, after all, is a finder, and neither of them is "the rightful owner"! The absurd result is avoided by stating the rule correctly: a finder wins as against all but prior possessors. Therefore, B prevails over C, and A over B, according to the doctrine of relative title discussed in Section 3.

It is interesting to note that the doctrine of relative title holds even if a person in the chain of title is a thief, provided the theft was not committed against the person making a claim.[23] If, in our example above, C in the suit by B wishes to show that B had stolen the item in question from A, the evidence will not be heard, and for good reason. If C were allowed to show that B had stolen the item, it would follow that B should be allowed to show that A had stolen it as well, from X, and A to show that X also had stolen it, from Y, and so on. Efforts to disallow protection of a thief's prior possession could result in an endless enterprise.

This is why courts hold, in a suit by a prior possessor against a subsequent possessor, that the latter may not use a *jus tertii* defense in support of his own possessory title by showing that his adversary's title is in fact in some third party (*jus tertii* means "a right of a third party"). Yet even astute observers seem to overlook the point of this sensible rule. So Judge Richard Posner asks whether a "wrongful possessor" should prevail over a subsequent lawful finder, and answers, "Presumably not; depriving him of possession is the only feasible sanction for his initial wrongful act, and the prospect of such deprivation may be the only feasible deterrent

---

[22] *Armory* v. *Delamirie*, 1 Strange 505 (1722).
[23] Yun-chien Chang, in Chapter 4, offers a different view of wrongful possession, and sees no reason to protect prior wrongful possessors.

against wrongful takings"(Posner 2000: 557). But how does Posner know that the "wrongful possessor" was indeed wrongful? He knows only because he asks in his example for us to "suppose" this! Hypothetical problems make life so much simpler than reality, as judges should well understand. In any event, how does Posner know that the wrongful possessor did not get possession by finding what had been lost by another wrongful possessor? He doesn't.

A particularly interesting feature of finders cases is that "the rightful owner" (the most prior of all possessors) is seldom on the scene. There are few reported finders cases arising from suits by "rightful owners," no doubt in part because their claims are indisputable and thus not litigated. Most commonly, the cases involve a series of possessors each claiming not to own but only to have rights of possession relatively better than their adversaries have, by virtue of being prior in time. And usually, but not always, this means lawsuits between a finder and the owner of the locus where an item was found. The English common-law judges made a proper spectacle of themselves as they struggled to determine who, as between locus owner and finder, was the prior possessor of the item in question, for it always came down to that – prior possession. (Unhappily, their reasoning spread like a virus to the New World.) Was it the locus owner by virtue of constructive possession, or the finder by virtue of actual possession? Might it matter (it might) whether the found item was attached to or under the ground or lying on the surface? Was the locus a private place, a public one, or something in between? (The intentions of the locus owner, judges thought, might vary as a function of this, although sometimes they said it was irrelevant.) Was the find by a servant of the locus owner, and, if so, was the servant in the course of service, or outside it? Did the locus owner know of the thing found? (Sometimes this mattered and sometimes not, judging from various opinions.) Did it appear that the found item had been abandoned, meaning there was no "true owner"?

These questions, and the various and often contradictory answers courts developed in response, are bewildering. Consider the plight of the judge in *Hannah* v. *Peel*, an English case.[24] His job was to determine whether it was the finder, or rather the locus owner, who was the prior possessor of a brooch found by the former in the home of the latter. After working dutifully through the precedents, he concluded with a startling

---

[24] [1945] K.B. 509.

but perfectly understandable observation: "A discussion of the merits," he said, "does not seem to help"!

What, exactly, are the merits? One answer, incontestable as far as we can see, is that the great first principle of the law of finders is to protect the rights of "true owners," which is to say, in this instance, the person who lost possession of the item in question. We presume that the common law rules of finders developed with this end in mind, yet no one (we include ourselves) has been able to see or to show how the design of the rules reflects or advances that ambition. The conventional law – at least, the common law rules, as opposed to various legislative measures – displays a formalistic architecture, as opposed to an instrumental or functional one. At least a few courts have noted this and have chosen to design alternative rules by self-consciously and transparently reasoning from desired ends to suitable means.

An example of the instrumental approach is *McAvoy* v. *Medina*,[25] which involved a wallet found on a table by a customer in a barbershop. The judge noted the usual rule "that the finder of lost property has a valid claim to the same against all the world but the true owner." But here, the judge observed, the wallet was not lost but *mislaid*; its owner voluntarily placed it on the table. Accordingly, the finder was not entitled to take the wallet from the shop; rather, the barber had a duty to hold it safely until its owner returned. "We accept this," the judge concluded, "as the better rule, and especially as one better adapted to secure the rights of the true owner." The reasoning is clear: the real owner, realizing the absence of his wallet, will retrace his steps and find it where he left it.

That does seem plain on first glance, but it doesn't stand up to closer observation. Instrumental reasoning is fine if it is informed by careful attention to how people actually think and behave under the constraints of legal rules. The judges who created the *mislaid* rule, however, were careless in these respects.

First, the *mislaid* rule requires a judge to determine whether a found item was lost, or rather was mislaid, a task easy enough on the facts of *McAvoy* but not in a host of other cases that might arise (a woman's purse under the chair where she sat in a restaurant; a small package found under the seat in a theater, and so on).

Second, there is no reason to engage in costly musing over ambiguous facts when the purpose behind the mislaid rule shows it to be

---

[25] 93 Mass. (11 Allen) 548 (1866).

unnecessary. Consider: whether found items were mislaid or lost, surely their owners would try to retrace their steps. Owners who have mislaid might be more likely to succeed than owners who have lost, but owners who have lost are *much* more likely to find their items if they remain where they were lost than if they do not! Hence, the *McAvoy* rule should be applied regardless.

Third, perhaps it should not be applied at all. Courts commonly read the rule to hold that "a finder of property acquires no rights in mislaid property."[26] If the owner retraces, the property is his; if he does not, it remains where it was mislaid. The owner of the locus gets to keep it forever. Hence, finders announce their find at their peril, which hardly gives them incentives to disclose, and disclosure is the crucial first step in protecting the rights of owners who have lost or mislaid their goods.

We would say that the *McAvoy* case is that rare thing, a perfectly incorrect decision. This hasn't stopped learned authorities from agreeing with it. The late Walter Wheeler Cook (1935: 524) considered it "obvious [note the confidence!] that from the point of view of social policy the shopkeeper ought to be preferred to the customer, as in that event the article would be more likely to get back into the possession of the real owners."[27] Judge Posner (2000: 556) also seems to endorse the lost-mislaid distinction to some degree, although he wonders why the finder of a mislaid item could not just leave his name and address so that the owner of the item can track him down. But that could be done as well in cases of lost goods, a point Posner leaves unmentioned, perhaps because he takes "lost" to mean, "that the owner doesn't realize the property is missing," and so "is unlikely to search for it." Posner has a strange definition of lost, and an odd sense of how losers act.

Since protection of the possessory interests of those who lose or mislay belongings depends on disclosure by finders, we have to consider their incentives to disclose. They might be inclined to disclose on pain of being charged with theft, but the probability of such charges in most cases will be almost zero; or they might be inclined to disclose on pain of feeling guilty, which depends on how well they have been socialized. In any event, the law puts finders in a double bind: they are cheaters if they don't disclose and fools if they do. Finders would have heightened incentives to

---

[26] See, e.g., *Michael v. First Chicago Corp.*, 487 N.E.2d 403, 409 (Ill. App. 1985).
[27] Cook should have known better. After all, he had both legal and scientific training (mathematics and physics) and was a specialist in the application of scientific methods to the study of law. He taught at such august law schools as Chicago, Columbia, and Yale.

disclose if owners were required to pay a reward in order to reclaim possession. Some civil law countries do this, but the common law requires no reward unless one had been promised. One could argue also that finders are encouraged to disclose by the fact that they will win in the end, guilt free, if no true owner shows up (which is probably often the case). The problem is that even in those circumstances there is no guarantee, since found items might be awarded to locus owners instead, either because the items are judged mislaid, or because the owner of the locus is judged to be the prior possessor. One could escape the latter difficulty by barring claims by locus owners, but doing so would dash the justified expectations of people who figure, usually with good reason, that what is on their land belongs to them, at least as against mere finders.

The possession heuristic as conventionally applied by the courts leaves them incapable of resolving the dilemmas of finders law, and for a very simple reason. The courts see possession as all or nothing: either the finder is the prior possessor and thus prevails, or the locus owner is the prior possessor and thus prevails, period. The consequence of this formalistic viewpoint is that it forecloses what would almost always be the best outcome – that each party has a claim to half as between themselves, and ultimately as to the so-called true owner of the item if he does not appear to make a claim within a reasonable time. If the true owner does show up within that time, we would require that he pay a reasonable reward, itself to be divided between the finder and the owner of the locus. In the meantime, found items, whether deemed lost or mislaid, should be held either in a public repository, or in the place where they were found. This is plain common sense, on any number of grounds. It is the way we would expect well-socialized individuals to resolve the matter on their own. It would increase the incentives of finders to disclose. It would acknowledge the expectations of locus owners. It would provide closure.[28]

4.3. Shared possession

The case we just made for sharing between finders and locus owners rests on purely instrumental reasoning. Some commentators, looking for a doctrinal hook on which to hang the approach, find it in "the concept of joint finding" (Helmholtz 1983: 324). However expressed,

---

[28] For a similar proposal, see Helmholtz (1983).

the result is (at least for a time) a regime of shared possessory rights, a kind of concurrent ownership.

Concurrent ownership is a regular feature of property law as to both land and personal property (bank accounts, for example). It appears in several forms in the common law system – the most ordinary being tenancy in common and joint tenancy – but the distinctions between the two are not important to our discussion. The important feature is that both forms involve shared possession, and it should be apparent from our discussion in Section 4.1 that concurrent ownership (as with so-called common property generally) can be problematic from the standpoint of efficient resource management. Good management requires concurrent owners to cooperate – to act, in essence, as would a single owner – but this can be difficult to achieve, especially when there are many individuals sharing possession, but also when there are few.[29] The common law contains some default rules presumably designed to cope with this problem. The underlying principle is that the possessory rights of co-owners are undivided, meaning each is entitled to use all of the property subject only to the exact same entitlement in the others. Regularly, though, one co-owner's use necessarily conflicts with another co-owner's use, yet the principle provides no guidance whatsoever on the question of who should prevail.[30] This is probably why the default rules developed to animate the principle are confusing, inconsistent, and unpredictable in their application, meaning co-owners would be well advised to sidestep the rules by making agreements among themselves. If they cannot agree, then – happily – the law leaves a way out. Every joint tenant or tenant in common has a unilateral right to exit by partition, which results in divided ownership in severalty.[31] This is one of the great default rules of the common law.

---

[29] This is not to say that co-owners of a limited-access commons (open to members only) never manage to coordinate, even when there is a considerable number of them. See, e.g., Ostrom (1990). Nor should it be taken to suggest that such commons do not have considerable virtues, such as economies of scale, risk spreading, and the pleasures of working in consort.

[30] The same difficulty arises from the central (and useless) principle of nuisance law, that one should use one's own property in such a way as not to injure the property of another.

[31] Some states recognize tenancy by the entireties, a form of co-ownership available only to husband and wife. In a tenancy by the entireties, neither husband nor wife may act unilaterally with respect to the property. Perhaps this encourages cooperation, but if it fails in this respect, partition is not an option unless both spouses agree. During their joint lives, the only unilateral move available to either is divorce.

Concurrent ownership is a productive regime provided the owners are people who tend to get along well together. If the messy default rules of the common law have a virtue, it is that they nudge uncooperative types to get out of the co-owner game altogether.

4.4. Adverse possession

Adverse possession doctrine holds that an owner can lose his land to a subsequent possessor who enters without the owner's permission, provided the entry is actual, apparent, hostile, and continuous for a period set by a statute of limitations.[32] The result is, effectively, a forced transfer, seemingly inconsistent with the possession heuristic and its set of rights. Actually, the contrary is the case. It is true that adverse possession doctrine compromises security of possession, but it is equally true that it also enhances security of possession – namely in all cases where the claim to some belonging happens to trace back to the actions of a distant dispossessor. The aim of the doctrine – and of statutes of limitations generally – is closure, and for good reasons. With the passage of time and the accompanying deterioration of relevant evidence, the facts of the *status quo ante* become increasingly difficult to determine. Moreover, during that same time various transactions in the property usually will have been made in reliance on appearances. Reversing these, especially given uncertainty about what really occurred back at the outset, would usually be unsettling, and in the case of land, particularly so. Hence, adverse possession helps more than it hurts, once the social benefits of quieting title are taken into account. Adverse possession is not an indispensable means to achieving closure (see, e.g., Stake 2001), but it is a useful one.

Still, the doctrine does effectuate forced transfers, and this has moved its defenders to develop several other justifications for adverse possession over the years, each of them aiming to show that the transfers are a good thing in themselves, without regard to the aim of quieting title.[33] One such argument is that an erstwhile owner has no grounds to complain,

---

[32] We should mention that constructive possession also comes into play in adverse possession law. Under the "color of title" doctrine, one who actually enters just a portion of land, under a deed or other instrument that purports to convey all the land but happens to be ineffective, nevertheless is said to possess all the land that is described in the instrument, subject to various limitations.

[33] The forced transfers lead critics, especially lay critics, to complain that adverse possession amounts to "legalized theft." The complaint overlooks the fact that theft itself is legalized theft once a statute of limitations forecloses criminal prosecution for theft and civil

having left his land idle while he slept on his rights. A second argument looks at the other side of the matter, holding that the adverse possessor has earned his reward by putting the land to productive use.[34] These views – sometimes called the "sleeping" and "earning" theories, respectively – have introduced undesirable distractions into the American law of adverse possession. For example, and probably thanks to both theories, judicial decisions and legislative requirements commonly reflect the view (at times only implicit) that active use of land is especially meritorious, when in fact leaving land undeveloped is often the more efficient course. Beyond that, the earning theory in particular has led some jurisdictions to require good faith as an element of adverse possession,[35] and to require privity among a series of adverse possessors in order for them to tack together their periods of "earning" ultimate title. The English law does neither, because it wisely views adverse possession as a means to quiet title, and nothing more.

5. Possession and property

As we noted in the Introduction, the law of property is the law of belongings, and its first task is to determine to whom things belong. The possession heuristic provides the answer: a thing belongs to its possessor.[36] That person, being an owner in the sense described in our discussion, has rights that necessarily accompany the status of owner – to exclude, to use, and to transfer. A virtue of the possession heuristic (of any heuristic) is its simplicity. It calls for no attention whatsoever to any number of considerations that could be relevant to determining who in

---

actions for conversion of the item in question. Yet it seems that only when the item in question is land do people get their backs up.

[34] A third (and more recent) argument (in two variations, both offering interpretations of Holmes [1897: 476–77]) asserts that, given the passage of time, the adverse possessor likely gains more utility in keeping the land than the former owner loses in having to give it up (Posner 2011: 98; Ellickson 1989: 39; see also Stake 2001: 2455–71).

[35] In odd contrast, some jurisdictions insist on bad faith on the part of adverse possessors, requiring them to prove that they knew the land in question did not belong to them when they entered it. In our view (and that of many courts), any inquiry into the subjective mental state of adverse possessors is undesirable, since it is usually impossible to assess what was the actual state of mind of the adverse possessor at the time of entry. In any event, there was a cause of action against the entrant no matter his mental state, so the statute of limitations should begin to run.

[36] For discussions in the same vein, though not cast in terms of heuristics, see Epstein (1979) and Rose (1985).

society is entitled to what – who in any particular instance might justly deserve the entitlement, have the greatest need for it, attach the highest value to it, or make the most efficient use of it. That the possession heuristic ignores these factors does not mean that it serves nothing but convenience. Quite to the contrary, the rules on possession and the rights that accompany it (to exclude, use, and transfer) are commonly justified in terms of desert (e.g., Sugden 2004: 99–101); efficiency (e.g., Posner 2011: 41), individual autonomy (e.g., Friedman 1962: ch. 1) and human flourishing generally (e.g., Alexander 2009a). In particular instances where applying the possession heuristic seems unjustified from the viewpoint of any of those terms, modifications can be (and regularly are) made, whether by courts or legislatures.

In the language of the heuristics literature, the modifications are usually products of a switch from one system of problem solving to another, the two being referred to as System 1 and System 2 (see, e.g., Kahneman 2011: 20–21). S1 refers to problem solving by means of heuristics, whereas S2 is characterized by self-conscious attention to a variety of considerations. S1, then, is simple, and S2 is complex. The law of property, writ large, employs both systems, meaning property amounts to more than just possession and its default incidents.

Discussions of S1 and S2 run throughout the heuristics literature, but it is best for our purposes to focus instead on an ongoing debate among property theorists about the comparative advantages and disadvantages of the two systems. The debate is not framed in terms of S1 and S2, but it could as well be. The debate, as we see it, is about simplicity versus complexity, and how to realize the virtues of each. Here we present the contending views in a brief and somewhat stylized account, drawing on some of the work of Tom Merrill and Henry Smith, who favor S1, and Gregory Alexander and Hanoch Dagan, who favor S2.[37] For convenience, we refer to the two camps as M&S and A&D, respectively.

M&S begin with the in rem nature of property rights. The rights are good against the world, and this requires that their substantive content be readily accessible and intelligible to third parties to guide them in their behavior and expectations – in particular, to inform them what belongs to them and what does not, and with what consequences. M&S construct an entire theory of property based on this observation, a theory with both descriptive and normative elements. For example, they have argued, on

---

[37] Alexander (2009a); Dagan (2007); Merrill and Smith (2003, 2000); Smith (2012, 2009).

the basis of many examples, that the law of estates is designed to limit the forms of ownership to a short and conventional list, this in order to minimize the information costs that would arise if owners and others had to deal with a large collection of novelties (Merrill and Smith 2000: 8). They claim elsewhere that this constraint is rooted in morality. "Property can function as property only if the vast preponderance of persons recognize that property is a moral right ... [and] the morality upon which it rests must be simple and accessible to all members of the community" (Merrill and Smith 2007: 1850). While few would characterize the law of estates as "simple" or "accessible to the community," their central insight is persuasive: property's moral and practical force depends on its overall intelligibility.

A&D, on the other hand, consider property to be a complex, context-dependent set of rights and obligations intended to promote "human flourishing" (Alexander 2009a: 760). They build on the legal realists, who characterized property as a "bundle of sticks," a set of relational interests that might be personal and not solely in rem. For example, property usually includes the right to exclude, but need not always do so if exclusion is inconsistent with larger social concerns. So the court in *State v. Shack*[38] was justified in thwarting the wishes of a landowner who wanted to exclude social workers seeking to speak with migrants laboring on his land. And property can (and, they argue, does) entail, as a "social obligation," an affirmative duty to preserve open space or to share resources that are sufficiently important to the community (Dagan 1999: 768–78; Alexander and Peñalver 2009: 148). The content and normative underpinnings of these claims are well developed in the literature, so we need not rehearse them here (Serkin 2013). It is plain that their method of resolving conflicting property claims can sometimes involve far more complex analysis than does the M&S method, which usually relies on a simple right of exclusion.[39]

Notice that each point of view has some key elements. M&S object to the relational approach (in personam as opposed to in rem) at least in part because it is neither easy to apply nor easy to discern. The approach uses uncertain standards that make property rights contingent and relatively uninformative for everyday purposes. Usually it is better to

---

[38] 277 A.2d 369 (N.J. 1971).
[39] Merrill and Smith both separately acknowledge the important role of complexity in legal systems, but reject it for the possession and the creation of bare property rights (Chapter 1; Smith 2012: 1694).

use simple rules to govern behavior and avoid disputes. A&D object to the narrow-mindedness of the foregoing; they are willing to tolerate more complexity in the content and specification of property rights, in order to take account of social welfare considerations too often ignored by simple rules.

Actually, the differences between the debaters are not as stark as our outline suggests, nor as the protagonists claim to believe. Their arguments (and it is worth noting that each side tends to caricature the views of the other side) are cast in the form of deep ontological disagreement about the very nature of property, about its "core" versus its "periphery." Framing the debate in such high-stakes terms is a distraction. The reality is that property, in form and practice, is a mixed system, as both sides acknowledge.[40] Merrill expands this very point in his contribution to this book, offering an information-cost account of the relationship between property and possession (Chapter 1). Property reflects no singular ideological commitment. Methodologically, it reflects a division of labor between S1 and S2 problem solving. It is, to be sure, more rule-bound than most of the common law, and no doubt for the reasons M&S suggest. Yet it repeatedly resorts to standards, as any property scholar knows. Sometimes the switch from bright-line rules to more vague standards occurs precisely where S1 thinking breaks down.[41] We speculate that careful investigation would show that S1 dominates some substantive areas of property law (such as the law of capture and finders), and S2 others (the law of servitudes comes to mind). We also speculate that observed patterns of dominance could usefully be explained by reference to the very ideas brought out in the work of M&S and A&D alike (see, e.g., Sterk 2013).

To us, the interesting question is the degree to which the two different approaches to resolving property disputes can be accommodated in a manner that compromises the central concerns of neither. The sort of property system envisioned by M&S – a system that relies considerably

---

[40] For example, M&S concede there are occasional limitations on the right to exclude (e.g., Smith 2009: 971), and A&D acknowledge the ongoing relevance of a general right to exclude in most cases (e.g., Alexander 2009b: 1063–69). Moreover, A&D's examples of "affirmative obligations" usually are not affirmative at all; rather they take the form of additional limitations on the right to exclude, regarding which recall the discussion in footnote 10.

[41] It is possible – as one of us has argued – that bright-line protection for existing uses, as opposed to the ad hoc protection of prospective uses, is best justified by similar behavioral intuitions (Serkin 2009: 1267–70).

on the S1 methodology – is robust. It works well most of the time, meaning that a switch to the S2 methodology called for by A&D seldom would be necessary. Adding occasional complexity to the core understanding of property hardly undermines its utility as a simple and instructive system. Even decisions based on S2 methodology can fit themselves into the basic S1 system. In particular categories of cases, standards can be applied in a manner so regular and consistent as to become in essence rules, such that the ex post approach evolves into ex ante rules, while still leaving some flex in the system.

An interesting feature of the property debate sketched in this section is that the contending parties both present a view based not just on normative but also on positive theory. Each side, that is, claims to be describing how our present property system actually works. And each side is correct. If property law required people in all their interactions to depend on S2 reasoning instead of S1 intuitions, the friction in the system would soon become unbearable; but so too, if the situation were turned the other way around. However, the study of heuristics demonstrates that there is a role for both methods, simultaneously, and our property system works all the better for it.

References

Alexander, Gregory S. 2009a. "The Social-Obligation Norm in American Property Law," *Cornell Law Review* 94: 745–819.
  2009b. "The Complex Core of Property," *Cornell Law Review* 94: 1063–71.
Alexander, Gregory S. and Peñalver, Eduardo M. 2009. "Properties of Community," *Theoretical Inquiries in Law* 10: 127–60.
Blackstone, William 1765–1769. *Commentaries on the Laws of England*. Various Publishers.
Bowles, Samuel 2004. *Microeconomics: Behavior, Institutions, and Evolution*. Princeton University Press.
Chang, Yun-chien and Smith, Henry E. 2012. "An Economic Analysis of Civil Versus Common Law Property," *Notre Dame Law Review* 88: 1–55.
Cook, Walter Wheeler 1935. "Ownership and Possession." in *Encyclopedia of the Social Sciences* 11: 521.
Dagan, Hanoch 1999. "Takings and Distributive Justice," *Virginia Law Review* 85: 741–804.
  2007. "The Social Responsibility of Ownership," *Cornell Law Review* 92: 1255–73.
Demsetz, Harold 1967. "Toward a Theory of Property Rights," *American Economic Review (Papers and Proceedings)* 57: 347–57.

Dukeminier, Jesse, Krier, James E., Alexander, Gregory S., and Schill, Michael H. 2010. *Property*. 7th edn. New York, NY: Aspen Publishers.

Ellickson, Robert C. 1989. "Bringing Culture and Human Frailty to Rational Actors: A Critique of Classical Law and Economics," *Chicago-Kent Law Review* 65: 23–55.

  1991. *Order without Law*. Cambridge, MA: Harvard University.

  2013. "Stone-Age Property in Domestic Animals," *Brigham-Kanner Property Rights Journal* 2: 1–25.

Epstein, Richard A. 1979. "Possession as the Root of Title," *Georgia Law Review* 13: 1221–43.

  2006. "The Optimal Complexity of Legal Rules" in Gigerenzer and Engel (eds.) (2006) 141–58.

Friedman, Milton 1982. *Capitalism and Freedom*. University of Chicago Press.

Friedman, Ori and Neary, Karen R. 2008. "Determining Who Owns What: Do Children Infer Ownership from First Possession?," *Cognition* 107: 829–49.

Gigerenzer, Gerd and Engel, Christoph (eds.) 2006. *Heuristics and the Law*. Cambridge, MA: MIT Press.

Gilovich, Thomas, Griffin, Dale, and Kahneman, Daniel (eds.) 2002. *The Psychology of Intuitive Judgment*. Cambridge University Press.

Gordley, James and Matte, Ugo 1996. "Protecting Possession," *American Journal of Comparative Law* 44: 293–334.

Haidt, Jonathan (Rapporteur) 2006. "Group Report: What Is the Role of Heuristics in Making Law?" in Gigerenzer and Engel (eds.) (2006) 239–57.

Hirschleifer, Jack 1982 "Evolutionary Models in Economics and Law: Cooperation Versus Conflict Strategies," *Research in Law and Economics* 4: 1–60.

Holmes, Oliver Wendell, Jr. 1881/1938. *The Common Law*. Boston: Little, Brown and Company.

  1897. "The Path of the Law," *Harvard Law Review* 10: 457–78.

Hume, David 1740/2005. *A Treatise of Human Nature*. New York, NY: Barnes & Noble.

Huskinson, Lucy and Schmidt, Bettina E. 2010. "Introduction" in *Spirit Possession and Trance*, Lucy Huskinson and Bettina E. Schmidt) (eds.) New York, NY: Continuum International Publishing Group, pp. 1–15.

Kahneman, Daniel, Slovic, Paul, and Tversky, Amos (eds.) 1982. *Judgment under Uncertainty: Heuristics and Biases*. Cambridge University Press.

Kahneman, Daniel 2011. *Thinking Fast and Slow*. New York, NY: Farrar, Straus and Giroux.

Kelman, Mark 2011. *The Heuristics Debate*. New York, NY: Oxford University Press.

Krier, James E. 1997. "Capture and Counteraction: Self-Help by Environmental Zealots," *University of Richmond Law Review* 30: 1039–54.

  2009. "Evolutionary Theory and the Origin of Property Rights," *Cornell Law Review*, 95: 139–59.

Kuhn, Thomas S. 1962. *The Structure of Scientific Revolutions*. University of Chicago Press.

Lueck, Dean 1995. "The Rule of First Possession and the Design of the Law," *Journal of Law and Economics* 38: 393–436.

1998. "Property and the Right to Exclude," *Nebraska Law Review* 88: 730–55.

Merrill, Thomas W. and Smith, Henry E. 2003. "The Morality of Property," *William and Mary Law Review* 48: 1849–95.

2000. "Optimal Standardization in the Law of Property: The Numerus Clausus Principle," *Yale Law Journal* 110: 1–70.

Ostrom, Elinor 1990. *Governing the Commons: The Evolution of Institutions for Collective Action*. Cambridge University Press.

Posner, Richard A. 2011. *Economic Analysis of Law*. 7th edn. New York, NY: Aspen Publishers.

2000. "Savigny, Holmes, and the Law and Economics of Possession," *Virginia Law Review* 86: 535–67.

Rose, Carol M. 1985. "Possession as the Origin of Property," *University of Chicago Law Review* 52: 73–88.

1986. "The Comedy of the Commons: Custom, Commerce, and Inherently Public Property," *University of Chicago Law Review* 53: 711–81.

Serkin, Christopher 2013. "Affirmative Constitutional Commitments: The State's Obligations to Property Owners," *Brigham-Kanner Property Rights Conference Journal* 2: 109–33.

2009. "Existing Uses and the Limits of Land Use Regulations," *New York University Law Review* 84: 1222–91.

Smith, Henry E. 2012. "Property as the Law of Things," *Harvard Law Review* 125: 1691–1726.

2009. "Mind the Gap: The Indirect Relationship Between Ends and Means in Property Law," *Cornell Law Review* 94: 959–89.

Smith, John Maynard 1982. *Evolution and the Theory of Games*. Cambridge University Press.

Stake, Jeffrey E. 2001. "The Uneasy Case for Adverse Possession," *Georgetown Law Journal* 89: 2419–74.

Sterk, Stewart E. 2013. "Moral Obligations of Landowners: An Examination of Doctrine," *Brigham-Kanner Property Rights Journal* 2: 135–57.

Sugden, Robert 2004. *The Economics of Rights, Cooperation and Welfare*. 2nd edn. New York, NY: Palgrave Macmillan.

Sunstein, Cass (ed.) 2000. *Behavioral Law and Economics*. Cambridge University Press.

7

Dividing possessory rights

DANIEL B. KELLY

1. Introduction

Property owners have a right to *exclude* others from their property, to *use* their property for various purposes, and to *transfer* their property by sale or gift. In addition, owners may *divide* their property in various ways, including by space, time, or function (Ellickson 1993: 1371–75). However, with a few notable exceptions (see, for example, Shavell 2004: 27–32; Stake 2010), there is little economic analysis of how owners divide their possessory rights.[1]

The issue of dividing possessory rights has emerged in several recent controversies and debates. For example, one factor in the mortgage crisis was the use of complex financial instruments such as mortgage-backed securities and collateralized-debt obligations. These financial instruments not only permit the separation of a possessory right from a security interest but also enable parties to carve up a security interest numerous times among multiple owners. The complexity of such instruments, and the difficulty of modifying or combining them, may have contributed to the financial crisis (Dana 2010; Judge 2012; Note 2012; Schwarcz 2012).

Professor of law and co-director, Law and Economics Program, Notre Dame Law School. J.D., Harvard Law School; B.A., University of Notre Dame. For helpful comments, I am grateful to Abraham Bell, Joseph Bauer, Margaret Brinig, Yun-chien Chang, Robert Ellickson, Nicole Garnett, Richard Garnett, Daniel Klerman, Daphna Lewinsohn-Zamir, Dean Lueck, Thomas Merrill, John Nagle, Shitong Qiao, Claire Priest, Steven Shavell, Henry Smith, Katrina Wyman, Stephen Yelderman, and participants at the American Law and Economics Association, Harvard/Stanford/Yale Junior Faculty Forum, New York University School of Law Workshop on Property Law and Theory, North American Workshop on Private Law Theory, Notre Dame Law School Faculty Workshop, and the Taiwan Law and Economic Analysis Conference. This chapter draws on several themes developed in Kelly (2014), which analyzes how property may serve not only to exclude but also to include.

[1] Shavell (2004: 9) defines a "possessory right" as a right to commit, or prevent others from committing, some act regarding the use, or nonuse, of things. For a comparison of possessory rights and possession as a fact, see Chapter 4.

Likewise, scholars have focused on the costs of dividing possessory rights in several recent debates in property law. In analyzing the *numerus clausus* principle, Merrill and Smith (2000) and Hansmann and Kraakman (2002) discuss why property law, unlike contract, restricts customizability and authorizes only a limited number of forms. In investigating the tragedy of the anticommons, Heller (1998) emphasizes that, if property becomes excessively fragmented, transaction costs may prevent an efficient assembly of rights. Other scholars are skeptical of arguments for restricting division based on simplifying transactions or preventing fragmentation. They argue that restrictions on dividing may prohibit valuable divisions of property, without a clear economic justification.

This chapter analyzes the socially optimal division of property rights, investigates why owners may choose to divide or not to divide their property, and examines the extent to which the private incentive to divide property converges with the optimal level of division. I also evaluate the primary justifications for the various legal restrictions on dividing property.

I contend that law in general and property law in particular should focus largely on ensuring that owners have an adequate incentive to divide their property rights and thereby include others in the use of their property. Economic logic suggests that, under most circumstances, private owners will not have an incentive to divide their property excessively. The reason is straightforward: owners typically internalize the costs, as well as the benefits, of a division. Thus, owners usually will not divide their property too much. To the extent that information costs increase complexity or bargaining costs may impede private consolidation, the law should compare the institutional arrangements for minimizing such costs, rather than necessarily restricting the division of property.

A division of possessory rights can be socially beneficial because it allows multiple parties to obtain benefits from a single property. A property owner may divide property by *space*. For example, a private developer may divide her property into ten parcels and sell the parcels to ten homeowners. The value of the parcels to the homeowners may exceed the value of the land to the developer. An owner also may divide property by *time*. For example, a settlor may create a trust and give an equitable life estate in a home to her spouse followed by a future interest, a remainder, in their child. The value of the spouse's life estate plus the value of the child's future interest may exceed the value of the home in fee simple to either the spouse or child. In addition to dividing property by space and time, owners also may divide their property by *function* or *use*. For example, a homeowner may grant a neighbor an easement over the homeowner's land to provide the neighbor with access to a beach for swimming and boating. Moreover, divisions can involve tangible property, like leases and easements, or intangible property, like intellectual property licenses and mortgage-backed securities.

To facilitate the division of possessory rights, owners can utilize various legal mechanisms, including contracts, property, and organizational forms. Of course, if contracts were complete or property rights could be perfectly specified and enforced, the owner's private incentive to divide would correspond with the socially desirable result. An owner might divide property if and only if the social benefits exceeded the social costs. But, given that contracts are incomplete and property rights are imperfect, there is a danger of either too little division or too much division.

Too little division occurs if the owner's incentive to divide property rights is suboptimal. An owner may have an insufficient incentive to divide for several reasons. First, because division creates multiple interests in the property, there is a greater likelihood that disputes may arise over how to use the resource. Second, parties who benefit from a division, as well as the owner who does the dividing, may attempt to expand the scope of their rights strategically. Third, if division entails a principal-agent relationship (such as a landlord and tenant, shareholder and director, or settlor and trustee), division includes costs associated with shirking (by an agent) and monitoring (by a principal). Fourth, any division entails certain delineation and enforcement costs.

As noted above, property owners normally internalize the costs of a division. This cost internalization reduces the risk of excessive fragmentation by ensuring the private incentive to divide does not exceed the socially optimal level of division. Moreover, to the extent that owners may not fully internalize the costs of division, the law employs a range of anti-fragmentation rules (Dana 2010: 109–14; Ellickson 1993: 1374). Some rules limit the division of property ex ante; other rules facilitate private consolidation ex post. Moreover, if property that is divided optimally becomes suboptimally divided, owners often have an incentive to assemble fragmented rights if the benefits of assembling such rights exceed the costs.

However, excessive fragmentation, i.e., too much division, is possible for several reasons. First, a property owner may be myopic and divide her property even though doing so is contrary to her self-interest. The problem is imperfect information: if the owner was not subject to bounded rationality, the owner would not make this type of mistake. Second, circumstances may change in a way the owner did not anticipate, meaning a division that was optimal has become suboptimal. The problem is again imperfect information: if the owner had known what the optimal division would be in all future periods, the owner would incorporate those future values of the asset and divide the property accordingly. Third, even if an owner has perfect information, division may be excessive if dividing property entails external costs on third parties. For example, an excessively complex division might impose administrative costs on courts or information costs on other market participants.

Finally, it is worth noting that there may be significant differences between the division of property interests by private owners and the division of property interests by public officials (whether in administrative agencies, legislatures, or courts). If public officials, not private owners, are responsible for dividing property interests, there is a risk that officials may not internalize the economic costs and benefits of division. Consequently, the government may divide property either too little or too much.

In addition to their financial incentives not to divide property excessively, many private owners may have a psychological disposition not to divide property too much. Specifically, there is some evidence suggesting that owners may prefer full rights in a resource rather than rights that are partial, contingent, or divided. This proclivity not to divide may apply especially to tangible property that owners can physically possess, like homes and chattels, as opposed to intangibles, like mortgages and intellectual property rights. Thus, the extent to which legal intervention is necessary to prevent excessive division may depend not only on financial incentives but also on the owners' psychological inclinations, which may vary based on context and the type of property at issue.

Section 2 summarizes the ways that owners divide possessory rights, by space, time, and function. Sections 3, 4, and 5 seek to explore three questions about divisibility. Section 3 asks under what circumstances the private incentive to divide possessory rights may be insufficient (why might we see too little division). I examine situations in which the incentive to divide is suboptimal due to coordination difficulties, strategic behavior, and agency costs. Section 4 asks under what circumstances the incentive to divide possessory rights may be excessive (why might we see too much division). I analyze situations in which excessive division may occur but contend that owners usually will not have an incentive to divide too much. Section 5 asks why the law may restrict division, even if a division is mutually beneficial (what are the justifications for legal restrictions on division). I briefly explore two justifications: preventing excessive fragmentation (due to bargaining costs) and simplifying sales transactions (due to information or verification costs). I also explore the effect of possession on dividing property rights and suggest that owners may be less likely to divide property they can physically possess. Section 6 examines several applications.

Overall, I contend the private incentive to divide property usually converges with the optimal level of division. The primary reason is that, in deciding whether to divide, owners bear the costs of a division as well the benefits. Consequently, owners usually have an economic incentive not to divide their property rights too much. Moreover, excessive fragmentation may be especially unlikely in the context of certain types of tangible property because, all else being equal, owners may prefer undivided possession of tangible property. Finally, if bargaining costs impede the private assembly of divided rights or information costs increase the complexity of property, the legal system should compare the institutional arrangements for minimizing these costs rather than necessarily restricting division.

2. Types of division

In the economic analysis of property, one of the first examinations of dividing property rights is by Ellickson (1993: 1371–75). Ellickson notes that a fee simple in property is a "*default* bundle of rights, which its owner by and large is free to modify by contract, gift, will, or otherwise." He describes how landowners can tailor this default bundle by dividing land along several dimensions, including territory (for example, parking spaces), time (for example, leases), and use-privileges (for example, easements). More recently, Ellickson (2011) states: "Property rights in a particular resource commonly are splintered among different owners."[2] While acknowledging the potential drawbacks of such fragmentation, Ellickson explains that "the carving out of partial interests in a resource can be value-enhancing."[3]

Shavell (2004: 27–32) briefly discusses the "Division of Property Rights" as well. Like Ellickson, Shavell describes several types of division,

---

[2] Ellickson (2011) suggests owners may fragment property rights along five dimensions: subdivision into parcels of lesser acreage; decomposition of particular privileges of use (mineral rights, grazing leases, easements); temporal limitations on entitlements (leases and future interests); concurrent ownership; and security interests.

[3] See also Heller (1999: 1165) noting, "People often create wealth when they break up and recombine property in novel ways."

including divisions of possession and use (for example, easements), divisions based on contingencies (for example, conditional gifts), rental arrangements that divide property over time (for example, leases), and the division of possessory and transfer rights (for example, trusts). In considering the advantages and the disadvantages of dividing property, Shavell notes that division often can be socially valuable because different parties may derive different benefits from the same property.

In analyzing the "Decomposition of Property Rights," Stake (2010) surveys the economically oriented literature on dividing property rights into packages of less than full ownership. Stake argues that, given the importance of property and the attention to transaction costs, it is odd that "particular rules of English property law, which impose costs on land transactions, have received relatively little attention from economists." He notes, "The rules governing subdivision or decomposition of property rights have received some attention from law and economics scholars" but cites only the prior analysis by Shavell (2004: 27–32).

Stake also maintains that owners may divide land in several ways. First, owners may divide land spatially. Spatial division may be horizontal (dividing one parcel into ten parcels) or vertical (separating surface rights from mineral rights or air rights). Stake points out that "the law and economics literature on spatial division of rights in land is not extensive." Second, owners may divide land temporally. The classic example is the distinction between present interests (such as a life estate) and future interests (for example, a reversion or remainder). Stake notes that there is also a "substantial literature" in landlord-tenant law on the division of property by time. Third, owners may divide property rights according to use, including private division through covenants, equitable servitudes, easements, and profits and government division via zoning.[4] I discuss spatial, temporal, and functional division in turn.

2.1. Spatial division

Spatial division usually applies to real property, rather than personal property or intellectual property. For example, the world is divided into many countries; each country has land that is divided into territorial units such as states or provinces; and each state or province is divided

---

[4] On divisions by use, see Ellickson (1973); Epstein (1982); Stake (1988); Sterk (1988). Stake (2010) also points out that an owner may divide property via a trust. On the agency costs of dividing property in trust, see Sitkoff (2004); see also Hansmann and Mattei (1998).

further into cities, townships, and unincorporated areas. Similarly, a city may divide its land into various areas for residential, commercial, and industrial use; a developer in a residential area may further divide a particular subdivision into individual lots for single-family homes; and a homeowner may then divide a home into several rooms.

Spatial division can be vertical as well as horizontal. For example, a landowner may sell subsurface rights, including mineral rights, to an energy company. Conversely, the owner of a building may seek to transfer development rights in the air above its building to a real estate developer.

The government also may own divided property rights or regulate the division of property along a horizontal as well as a vertical dimension. In its capacity as landowner, a state government may own submerged lands beneath tidal waters. In its capacity as regulator, the federal government may allow airlines to fly at 30,000 feet above millions of parcels without obtaining permission from the landowners below.

2.2. Temporal division

Divisions by time may apply to real property or personal property including intellectual property. For example, in a residential lease, a tenant has a right to possess the apartment for a limited period, while the landlord enjoys a reversionary interest after the tenant's interest expires. In a trust containing real estate, an owner may separate a present possessory interest in the land (for example, a life estate) from a future interest (such as a remainder).

With personal property, an owner may lease property to lessees for a specified period. For instance, an automobile dealer may lease a car to a driver for thirty-six months. Or an office supply company may lease copiers and other office equipment to small businesses on an annual basis. Likewise, in a bailment, the owner of personal property may transfer temporary possession of her car to a parking garage valet or her watch to a jeweler. An owner also may divide intangible personal property like patents and copyrights by time. A software license may expire after several months or several years.

2.3. Functional division

In addition to dividing property by space and time, owners often divide their property by function or use. For example, by granting a revocable license or an easement, a landowner may allow a neighbor to use her driveway. In entering a commercial lease, a landlord may allow a tenant to use a factory or an office building for one purpose but not another. In licensing intellectual property rights, the owner of a patent may license the patent but limit the scope of the license so the licensee may use the patent only for certain specified purposes.

Consider as well the various types of entity property, such as leases, trusts, and corporations. Each type of entity property entails a division of property that facilitates specialization. A lease entails the separation of ownership and possession: the landlord may own a suburban mall in which each of the mall's tenants operates an individual store or outlet.[5] A trust entails a separation of the burdens and benefits of ownership: a settlor transfers ownership of property to a trustee who manages and invests the property for the benefit of beneficiaries.[6] Finally, a corporation entails the separation of ownership and control: shareholders elect a board of directors, and the board hires managers (the CEO and CFO) who operate the firm on a day-to-day basis.[7]

Owners also may have an incentive to separate possessory rights from transfer rights. Shavell (2004: 30) points out that it may be beneficial to separate possessory and transfer rights "when the holder of possessory rights does not have a proper incentive to transfer them," such as a tenant who may rent an apartment from a landlord but is prohibited from assigning possession rights to another party. Similarly, owners often separate possessory rights from security interests. For example, because of the social value of mortgages and other types of security interests, owners may have an incentive to divide their possession of their property (e.g., in a home or car) from a security interest in the property.[8]

3. Private incentive to divide may be suboptimal

In considering the optimal division of property, a division is socially desirable if the overall benefits of division exceed the costs of division.[9]

---

[5] On the separation of ownership and possession in leases, see Lueck and Miceli (2007).

[6] On the issue of divided interests in trusts, see Sitkoff (2004); see also Scott et al. (2006) (noting how trusts "separate the benefits of ownership from the burdens of ownership").

[7] On the separation of ownership and control in corporations, see Berle and Means (1991); see also Manne (1967) (discussing efficiency of specialization in the corporate form).

[8] On mortgages, security interests, and other property interests in financial contracts, see Ayotte and Bolton (2011); Bowers (2010).

[9] If the aggregate value of property interests, as divided, exceeds the value of the undivided whole, then a division is socially desirable. As Stake (2010: 41) puts it: "The basic economic

An owner's private incentive to divide may converge with what is socially desirable. In deciding whether to divide, an owner will weigh the private benefits and costs. Typically, if a division is desirable, an owner will agree to divide property with another party in a mutually beneficial exchange.

However, in certain circumstances, the private incentive to divide may diverge from what is socially optimal. An owner may have an insufficient incentive to divide her property if the owner anticipates coordination problems, fears strategic behavior, or worries about agency costs. If the law is incapable of providing effective mechanisms to reduce such costs, there may be too little division.

An owner's ability to specify the terms of a division is not adequate to deter conflicts or opportunism. As I discuss elsewhere (see Kelly 2014), if contracts were complete or property rights were perfectly specified and enforced, the division of property rights might be straightforward. But, ex ante specification is difficult because of the inability to foresee all contingencies that may arise. Moreover, even if foreseeable, it is costly for parties to specify additional terms in an agreement. In addition, in defining access or use, parties may be unable to observe if they have a common understanding of the terms or conditions. Finally, even if parties have a common understanding, either party may act strategically, and it is costly for parties to rely on courts or other mechanisms to verify each party's compliance with this understanding. Because contracts and property rights are incomplete and imperfect, I have argued that dividing possessory rights creates several interrelated problems, including coordination difficulties, strategic behavior, and agency costs.[10]

If a single party, *A*, owns property in fee simple, there is little or no difficulty in coordinating how to use the property. *A* can use her property in whatever way, and to whatever extent, she believes to be best (assuming the use is lawful). However, suppose that *A* decides to divide her property by including *B*. Now *A* and *B* must coordinate how to use the property. *B* may have a limited right to use the property for a certain

---

rationale for allowing the set of all rights to use a piece of land to be carved up into small packages of rights [is that] the sum of the parts can be worth more than the whole." By contrast, if the value of the undivided whole exceeds the aggregate value of property interests, as divided, then a division is socially undesirable.

[10] For a more comprehensive discussion of these problems, including additional examples involving the inclusion of others in one's property, see Kelly (2014: 879–82). The analysis that follows regarding the problems with division is an abbreviated version of this more extensive discussion concerning the problems with inclusion.

purpose (as in a license), with A retaining the right to use it for all other purposes. Or B may have the right to possess the property for a limited time (as in a lease), with A reserving the right to retake possession when B's interest ends. In each situation involving more than one party (whether a license, lease, or other arrangement), there is a higher likelihood that disputes will arise because of the difficulties of coordination.

The possibility of strategic behavior or "opportunism" (see Williamson 1985) exacerbates the coordination problems associated with dividing property rights. For example, an owner may want to divide property for one purpose, but it may be difficult for the owner to limit access for that purpose. As a result, nonowners may seek to expand the scope of their rights. Moreover, unauthorized parties may attempt to expand the scope of a division by using property for an authorized purpose. In short, dividing property exacerbates two problems with exchange: observability and verifiability.[11] If the expected costs of dividing rights are too high, then owners may decide not to divide their property at the outset.[12]

A particular type of opportunism that often arises in dividing possessory rights is the problem of agency costs (Jensen and Meckling 1976). Agency costs are the costs that arise because agents (such as managers, trustees, or tenants) may shirk their duties or mismanage and misappropriate property interests that rightfully belong to the principal (shareholders, settlors, or landlords). Agency costs also include the costs that a principal may incur in attempting to mitigate the problems of shirking, mismanaging, and misappropriating. Thus, in many situations, the division of property entails agency costs that can reduce the likelihood of value-maximizing transactions.

Of course, notwithstanding the possibility of coordination difficulties, strategic behavior, and agency costs, division does occur in many situations. Leases, including residential, commercial, and agricultural leases, are a common economic arrangement (Lueck and Miceli 2007). Licenses in real and personal property, as well as intellectual property, are ubiquitous. Moreover, dividing property through business entities, including trusts, corporations, and partnerships, involves literally trillions of

---

[11] For a summary of the issues of observability and verifiability in the context of dividing property rights, see Hansmann and Kraakman (2002). Even if dividing property rights is feasible, parties often will have to incur additional costs in specifying the terms of division in order to reduce the possibility of misunderstandings or opportunism. See also Chapter 8.

[12] In addition, once a division occurs, either party may exit, or threaten to exit, strategically, which may deter parties from dividing interests ex ante. See Dagan and Heller (2001).

dollars. In each of these situations, a property owner has determined that the benefits of dividing their property rights exceed the costs. However, in the absence of effective legal and non legal mechanisms for assuring owners and nonowners that a division of possessory rights will not result in disputes, opportunism, and malfeasance, the overall level of division is likely to be suboptimal.

Therefore, as I discuss elsewhere (see Kelly 2014: 882–95), it is important for the law to help facilitate the division of possessory rights through several mechanisms, including informal arrangements, contractual agreements, and property forms. Relying on informal arrangements to divide property – a gratuitous license to attend a dinner party or rights to use a library carrel – is common. Yet, these informal arrangements are sometimes inadequate for dividing property in other transactions. Thus, formal mechanisms, including contracts and property forms, are necessary to bolster the private incentive to divide possessory rights. Indeed, Shavell (2004: 31) notes that people can "divide property rights as they please by means of contracts [or] through recognized devices of property law."

The ability to divide property rights through *either* contract *or* property law devices raises an interesting question. As Stake (2010) asks, why is it necessary for the law to provide "multiple doctrines with differing rules by which rights are subdivided"?

Division by contract relies on contractual rights and remedies. These contractual rights and remedies provide parties with more certainty than informal division alone. As a result, parties often divide possessory rights by contract if transaction costs are not prohibitive, if there is a risk of high-value opportunism, and if social norms or reputational concerns are unlikely to deter such opportunism. However, despite their ability to divide property by means of contract, owners may have an insufficient incentive to divide because contracts deter opportunism only imperfectly.[13]

To reduce the costs of opportunism even further, the law recognizes a number of property forms by which owners may divide their possessory rights. These forms include leases, easements, bailments, and trusts. I argue elsewhere (Kelly 2014) that these proprietary forms, while similar to contracts in several respects, may bolster an owner's private incentive to divide property rights. For example, because property rights are in rem

---

[13] See Kelly (2014: 885–89); see also Posner (2006: 762) (noting that the "traditional model of contract law is inadequate" because rational individuals would act differently "if they could rely on the courts to deter opportunism in contractual relationships").

and typically run with the land, property forms provide greater certainty and information for third parties, including successive owners and users. Moreover, while contracts deter certain types of opportunism, the property forms often provide additional protection through mandatory rules (consider the implied warranty of habitability in lease law) or fiduciary duties (consider the duty of loyalty and duty of care in trust law). Finally, unlike contracts, which rely primarily on compensatory damages, property forms often entail supracompensatory remedies (including injunctions, punitive damages, and restitution), which may help to deter strategic behavior as well.

Thus, allowing owners to divide possessory rights informally and formally through both contractual arrangements and property forms facilitates cooperation by ensuring that the private incentive to divide does not diverge too far below the socially optimal level of division.[14]

4. Private incentive to divide may be excessive

4.1. Why incentive to divide is generally not excessive

In general, owners should not have a private incentive to divide their possessory rights too much. The reason why the owner's incentive to divide usually is not excessive is that owners typically internalize the costs as well as the benefits of a division. Thus, in deciding whether to divide their possessory rights, owners will weigh the expected costs and benefits of division.

Other scholars have recognized this point, especially in analyzing the *numerus clausus* principle. Merrill and Smith (2000: 28) point out that explanations for the *numerus clausus* that are "based on classes of

---

[14] The division of property, like a transfer of property, may be involuntary or voluntary. Two examples of involuntary transfer are adverse possession (by a private party) and eminent domain (by the government). Similarly, two examples of involuntary division are prescriptive easements and compulsory licenses. Consider as well the doctrines governing necessity, airplane overflights, and fair use in copyright law. In each case, the law effectively imposes a division of property rights, even though the owner has not agreed to the division. This type of involuntary division is common if transaction costs are high. More broadly, it is possible to conceptualize almost any regulation of property that rearranges existing entitlements as an involuntary division. Hence, if the state prevents an owner from using coal beneath the surface or from building an office tower above the surface, the owner may argue that these types of division constitute a taking. See Stake (2010: 34). Indeed, whether an owner's takings claim is likely to succeed may depend on how the court calculates the denominator of what is being divided.

individuals within the zone of privity have difficulty identifying costs that are not impounded into the price facing those who make the decision whether to create the fancy in the first place." In discussing the "anti-fragmentation objection" to their theory, Merrill and Smith (2002: 52) note that owners are allowed to fragment their property interests: "the law does not prevent an anticommons but rather leaves it up to parties to choose the degree of fragmentation they wish, and to bear the costs of any mistakes they might make." Similarly, Hansmann and Kraakman (2002: 418) conclude: "It is generally not in the interest of property owners to fragment their rights inefficiently since they will bear the costs of that fragmentation."[15] Thus, in many circumstances, because owners internalize the costs of division, the private incentive to divide possessory rights is not excessive.[16]

4.2. Reasons excessive fragmentation may occur

Although the incentive to divide property is generally not excessive, a property owner's incentive to divide possessory rights may exceed what is socially optimal in certain situations. Specifically, an owner may divide property too much due to a mistake, a change in circumstances, or an externality. In addition, government ownership or control of property may result in excessive fragmentation if public officials do not bear the economic costs of division.

4.2.1. Private owners

One reason why private owners may divide their possessory rights too much is simply that they make a mistake (Hansmann and Kraakman 2002: 418). Whether or not to divide real, personal, or intellectual property may entail a complex calculation about what is optimal at any given time. Given bounded rationality and other human limitations,

---

[15] One exception is retransfer externalities: "After an initial division of property rights in an asset, the holder of one of the partial rights does not bear the full anticommons-type costs of further subdivision of that right, since those costs will in part fall on other holders of the previously divided partial rights in the asset." (Hansmann and Kraakman 2002: 418).

[16] Future work might compare the mechanisms of capitalization. Although owners may internalize the benefits and costs of division, what are the key mechanisms, including property rights, by which the benefits and costs are capitalized? These mechanisms of capitalization entail certain costs, including establishment and enforcement costs. While the future costs and benefits of an owner's actions are often impounded in the price of the land or other asset, the costs of the capitalization mechanisms may not be.

owners may not have the necessary information or may not be capable of processing this information in a cost-effective manner. As a result, an owner may decide to divide possessory rights even though a division is suboptimal. Conversely, an owner may decide not to divide possessory rights even though a division would be optimal.

Owners also may divide property rights too much because of changed circumstances. A division of property rights that was optimal in period 1 may be suboptimal in period 2 if the property's highest use has changed. For example, in many cities, the optimal size of commercial parcels may have been relatively small when family-operated stories dominated the urban landscape. Decades later, to compete with suburban malls and big-box retailers, many developers argue that increasing the lot size of city parcels is necessary for effective urban planning. Of course, with perfect foresight, owners would not divide their property too much. Instead, owners would incorporate the value of all future uses, discounted by the probability of each contingency, in deciding whether or how to divide. But owners, like most human beings, rarely have this level of foresight.[17]

Owners also may divide possessory rights too much because some types of division may entail negative effects or "externalities" on third parties.[18] For example, an owner's dividing possessory rights may impose costs on others by creating excessively complex interests. Posner (2011: 95) maintains, "People who create excessively complex interests burden the courts as well as themselves and their grantees, so there is some externality that might warrant public intervention." To a certain degree, in deciding whether divide, owners will consider the costs of complexity on the value of their property. An owner will divide property if and only

---

[17] See Fennell (2006: 1092) ("because human foresight is imperfect, decisions about land use cannot be made once and for all, never to be revisited"); cf. Dooley (1992: 465); Sterk (1988: 957). It is worth noting that bounded rationality may result in either too much or too little division, and I thank Shitong Qiao for pointing out that there is no reason to believe a priori that bounded rationality is more likely to result in too much rather than too little division. I briefly discuss why owners may psychologically prefer full rights in resources, especially in tangible property, in section 5.4.

[18] There are competing definitions of the term "externality" in the literature. Compare Coase (1988: 24) (defining externality as "effect of one person's decision on someone who is not a party to that decision"), with Demsetz (1967) (defining externality as an effect that a party does not have an incentive to internalize). For an overview of the debate, see McChesney (2006). For present purposes, I follow Coase (and most commentators) in adopting the traditional definition of externality as an external effect on another person. See Shavell (2004: 77). For an interesting perspective on this debate, see Fennell (2013).

the expected benefits of dividing the property exceed the expected costs of doing so, including the costs of fragmentation.

In analyzing the *numerus clausus* principle, the idea that property, unlike contract, entails a limited number of forms, Merrill and Smith (2000) and Hansmann and Kraakman (2002) examine a related question: what is the functional justification for restricting or regulating the ability of owners to customize their property rights? Merrill and Smith argue that some degree of standardization via a menu of forms reduces information costs. Hansmann and Kraakman contend that the law regulates the types and degree of notice for establishing different kinds of property to minimize verification costs. However, as I will discuss in section 5, the focus of both theories is whether allowing owners to divide their property without any limitations entails external harm on others.[19]

4.2.2. State actors

Finally, it is worth noting that, unlike private owners, public officials do not necessarily internalize the economic costs and benefits of dividing possessory rights (cf. Levinson 2000; Chang 2009). Rather, public officials tend to focus on the political costs and benefits of their decisions. As a result, state actors may divide too little or too much.

To illustrate the idea of an anticommons, Heller (1998) uses the example of a Moscow storefront. In doing so, Heller highlights the role of state actors and agencies in dividing property rights: "Within the legal and institutional context of the Moscow storefront, the main actors are a wide variety of state and quasi-state organizations." Heller notes how "local and regional government agencies emerged as the key players, with nearly monopolistic control over property such as commercial real estate." Consequently, there were "numerous competing claims among local, regional, and federal authorities."[20] Heller contends that this division of ownership and authority among governmental actors was a significant factor in the underutilization of the Moscow storefront.

As Heller's example suggests, an anticommons or excessive fragmentation of property rights may arise more easily if a party dividing the property rights does not fully internalize the costs of the division. In deciding how to divide property rights along a number of dimensions,

---

[19] For additional analysis of the debate regarding the *numerus clausus* principle, see also Davidson (2008); Dorfman (2011); Lewinsohn-Zamir (2003: 1730–39); Merryman (1963); Mulligan (2013); Rudden (1987); and Smith (2011).

[20] For an alternative perspective on the existence of Moscow kiosks, see Lametti (2013).

public officials may not internalize the costs of division, to the extent officials are motived by political rather than economic considerations. Thus, government decisions about whether to assemble or divide property may result in not only too little division if the government has an incentive to assemble property through eminent domain (Kelly 2006) but also too much division if the government has an incentive to divide but does not bear the full costs of the division (Heller 1998).

4.3. Legal rules that prevent or mitigate excessive division

Insofar as the incentive to divide possessory rights may exceed what is socially optimal, the law employs a number of rules that prevent the excessive division of property (Ellickson 1993: 1374–75; see also Dana 2010: 110–14; Heller 1999: 1169–87). Ellickson observes that owners may divide land too much: they may "splinter rights in a fee simple bundle into bits that are far less valuable than the pre-splintered whole." To deter such "destructive decompositions of property," the legal system maintains a "complex set of paternalistic rules," including anti-fragmentation rules and assembly mechanisms.

Anti-fragmentation rules prevent or inhibit parties from dividing their property ex ante, that is, before fragmentation occurs. Examples of anti-fragmentation rules include the rule against perpetuities,[21] the presumption that conveyances to railroads are easements,[22] and the principle that trustees retain legal title to trust property.[23] Assembly rules assist owners in assembling property ex post, that is, after fragmentation has occurred. Examples of assembly rules include the government's power of eminent domain,[24] the laws governing oil and gas unitization,[25] and a court's ability to order a partition by sale.[26]

---

[21] On the rule against perpetuities, see Stake (1990).
[22] For a recent U.S. Supreme Court case discussing related issues, see *Marvin M. Brandt Revocable Trust v. United States*, 134 S. Ct. 1257 (2014).
[23] The trust form allows settlors to divide their property in almost limitless ways but largely contains any adverse effects on third parties. See Heller (1999: 1178); Merrill and Smith (2000: 57); see also Sitkoff (2004: 629 n.31) ("A further useful feature of trust law is its amenability to the creation of exotic beneficial interests without dividing legal title").
[24] On the use of eminent domain in assembling land, see Merrill (1986); Kelly (2006); Kelly (2011); see also Chang (2013).
[25] On unitization of oil fields in Oklahoma, Texas, and Wyoming, see Libecap (1989).
[26] On partition, see Chang and Fennell (2014).

As Heller (1999) suggests, these types of "boundary doctrines" help to prevent excessive division.

In most circumstances, legal rules do not prevent division entirely, but instead mitigate the costs of property that, for one reason or another, has become excessively fragmented. Posner (2011: 95) notes that, at times, "undivided ownership is ... facilitated by automatic reuniting of divided land once the reason for the division has ceased." Likewise, Hansmann and Kraakman (2002: 418–19) point out that the "law's approach is generally not to prevent ... fragmentation, but rather to facilitate its elimination when it gets out of hand ... through a broad range of familiar doctrines." Hansmann and Kraakman argue that "[t]o prevent these problems by prohibiting division of rights ex ante is to throw out the baby with the bath water."

Thus, there is a legitimate concern that owners may not consider the full costs of dividing possessory rights, but this concern should not be overstated. Owners often have an incentive to incorporate the costs of division in deciding whether to divide their property. When they do not, the law employs a range of devices and doctrines that either impede division or facilitate consolidation.

5. Theories justifying restrictions on division

5.1. A puzzle for economic thinking

As discussed previously, the private incentive to divide possessory rights usually converges with the socially optimal level of division. If anything, owners may have an incentive to divide their property rights too little. But, because owners internalize the costs as well as the benefits of dividing their property, they normally do not have an economic incentive to divide their possessory rights too much. However, as mentioned, the law imposes restrictions on the ability of owners to divide their property, even in situations in which doing so might be mutually beneficial. This presents a puzzle for economic thinking: if owners usually do not have an incentive to divide their property excessively, what is the economic justification for such legal restrictions?

In analyzing the division of property, Shavell (2004) compares the socially optimal division of property with its actual division. He concludes: "One would expect the actual division of property rights by private parties generally to reflect the socially optimal division. The fundamental reason is that when the transfer of certain rights would be socially desirable, there will typically exist a mutually beneficial private exchange involving the rights." However, as Shavell points out, the law serves a dual function. The law not only "tends to aid the division of property rights that parties wish," but also "places various limitations on division of property rights." Why does the law place such limitations on an owner's ability to divide?

5.2. Preventing excessive fragmentation

One justification for restricting the divisibility of possessory rights is to prevent excessive fragmentation. In recent years, property scholars have focused on excessive fragmentation in the context of the "tragedy of the anticommons." In analyzing the anticommons, Heller (1998, 2008) and Heller and Eisenberg (1998) highlight how fragmented property may result in gridlock and the underutilization of resources. For example, if a developer wants to assemble multiple parcels of land for a shopping center, each landowner can thwart the project by refusing to sell. If a firm needs to acquire several patents to develop a new drug, any patent holder can refuse to license a patent, resulting in the drug not being developed. Heller (2008: 27) states that he "coined the term *tragedy of the anticommons* to help make visible the dilemma of overly fragmented ownership."[27] Likewise, Parisi (2002, 2003), Depoorter and Parisi (2003), and Schulz, Parisi, and Depoorter (2003) have emphasized the "unidirectional" nature of fragmentation in property.[28]

To illustrate his theory, Heller relies on several anecdotes, for example, street kiosks in Moscow (see section 4.2.2) and patents for an Alzheimer's drug. Yet, as Heller (2011) acknowledges, empirical analysis of the anticommons is thin: "Anticommons theory is now well established, but empirical studies have yet to catch up. How hard is it to negotiate around ownership fragmentation? How much does ownership fragmentation slow down technological innovation? ... We are just starting to examine these conundrums."[29] To the extent scholars have examined the difficulty

---

[27] Recognition of the economic idea underlying the anticommons goes back at least as far as the analysis of the "complimentary oligopoly" problem in Cournot (1838).
[28] For additional work on the tragedy of the anticommons, see Buchanan and Yoon (2000); Fennell (2011); Heller (2011); and Kieff and Paredes (2007). For a skeptical analysis of the anticommons concept, see Epstein (2011) and Lametti (2013).
[29] To my knowledge, there is only one article exploring the scope of the anticommons in real property, an article on the tenancy in common in Taiwan (Chang 2012).

of negotiating around fragmented ownership, it is primarily in the context of intellectual property.[30]

Shavell (2004) briefly considers the excessive fragmentation of property as a justification for legal restrictions on division. But he is skeptical. Specifically, Shavell "wonders why consolidation by private parties would not usually occur (why, for example, a person would not ordinarily succeed in purchasing different individuals' time shares if an apartment is more valuable when lived in year round by a single person)." He concludes: "A satisfactory answer to this basic question has not been provided, even though it is possible that in some situations problems in bargaining might retard or prevent beneficial private consolidation." Shavell is thus relatively optimistic about the ability of parties to consolidate divided rights, even if the property rights are fragmented. Yet because bargaining costs could impede assembly in some situations, there is an underlying empirical question about the ability of private parties to consolidate fragmented property interests.

Perhaps a more fundamental objection to the argument for limiting division based on the parties' inability to consolidate fragmented rights is that this justification does not explain why owners initially would have an incentive to divide their property excessively. The anticommons literature emphasizes bargaining costs. Bargaining costs may impede the consolidation of property that already is divided. But bargaining costs do not cause excessive fragmentation. Thus, one empirical question is determining the magnitude of bargaining costs, in a range of circumstances, including assembling land and intellectual property rights, and how often these costs prevent desirable consolidation (Chang 2012). However, an antecedent question is determining how often, and under what circumstances, owners actually decide to divide their property rights too much at the outset.

5.3. Simplifying sales transactions

Another set of justifications for restrictions on division is based on simplifying sales transactions. As noted earlier (see section 4.2.1), Merrill and Smith (2000) suggest that third-party *information costs* are a reason why property law, unlike contract, does not allow owners to customize

---

[30] See, for example, Barnett (2009: 428–29 & n.103), collecting and discussing empirical literature on the anticommons in patent law. For experimental investigations of the anticommons, see Depoorter and Vanneste (2006) and Murray and Stern (2007).

property rights. Alternatively, Hansmann and Kraakman (2002) suggest that *verification costs* explain the need to regulate the divisibility of property rights.

5.3.1. Information costs

One theory for the *numerus clausus* or the closed number of forms in property law is that some degree of standardization via a menu of forms reduces information costs. Merrill and Smith (2000: 28–33) argue that, if two parties were able to create idiosyncratic property rights, these rights would impose information or measurement costs on third parties, including potential trespassers, other buyers and sellers, and creditors. On a broad scale, these other market participants must "ascertain the legal dimensions of property rights in order to avoid violating the rights of others and to assess whether to acquire the rights of others" (id. at 69). They contend that "compulsory standardization of property rights" controls the "external costs of measurement to third parties." Thus, allowing owners to divide property without limitation could entail an externality. In deciding whether, and to what extent, to divide their property rights, owners would not have an incentive to incorporate these third-party information costs.

In arguing that third-party information costs explain standardization, Merrill and Smith (2000) frame the issue not in terms of why the law provides default rules but why property, unlike contract, does not allow parties to opt out of the default rules and freely customize their property rights.[31] Having framed the issue, Merrill and Smith contend that most explanations of the *numerus clausus* "focus on the effect of novel property rights on the originating parties and the potential successors in interests." For Merrill and Smith, these explanations are inadequate because the costs of creating a complex interest, including the costs of any future transactions (discounted by their probability), will be "impounded into the price facing those who make the decision whether to create the [interest] in the first place." Thus, Merrill and Smith conclude that any explanation for the *numerus clausus* must involve costs *external* to the original parties and their successors. Specifically, they contend that the "much more straightforward problem of externalities associated with the creation of idiosyncratic property rights" is the effect on "other market participants." In the absence of standardization,

---

[31] On the boundary between property and contract rights, see Merrill and Smith (2001).

these parties would incur greater information costs in the course of purchasing property or ensuring that they are not violating others' rights.

Shavell (2004) is skeptical of this argument given the possibility of notice. Regarding third-party information costs, he states, "This problem, if significant, seemingly could be met by either of two types of legal rules that do not bar individuals from dividing property rights if that is what they wish." First, Shavell suggests the legal system could impose "a rule under which a division of property rights is not enforced unless the division is made explicit in the sales documents." Under this rule, he argues, "there could be no concern about hidden interests." Second, and alternatively, Shavell suggests the legal system could impose "a rule under which a division of property rights is not enforced unless the division has been entered into a registry, and possibly a fee has been paid for so doing." The purpose of the fee would be "to induce those who obtain the rights to take into account the cost that others will bear in checking the registry."

In defending their claim, Merrill and Smith (2000: 44) anticipate this objection. They argue that "[m]aking the running of a fancy depend solely on the original parties' intent and on notice – even recorded notice – to subsequent parties acquiring property assumes that notice is the most cost-effective method to minimize third-party information costs." However, in their view, "notice of idiosyncratic property rights is costly to process, and, although land registers furnish notice at far lower cost than would a doctrine of constructive notice, even they can require lengthy and error-prone searches." Thus, the disagreement between Shavell and Merrill and Smith seems to be a disagreement about whether, empirically, it is more cost-effective to control information costs through explicit disclosure or a registry of divided interests, on the one hand, or by limiting the number of forms, on the other.

5.3.2. Verification costs

Another theory for the *numerus clausus* principle is that the law regulates the types and degree of notice for establishing different kinds of property to minimize verification costs. Hansmann and Kraakman (2002) argue that verification costs, not information costs, explain the *numerus clausus*. They acknowledge, "third-party information costs are central to the law's regulation of property rights." However, they contend that restrictions on creating property "serve not to facilitate communication among persons who transact in rights, but rather to facilitate verification of ownership of the rights offered for conveyance."

Hansmann and Kraakman (2002: 382–83) argue that, in transferring property from one owner to another, parties confront a verification problem. To solve this problem, each party "needs assurance that the other will not opportunistically assert rights that properly belong to the other." As they point out, the problem of verification in property differs from the problem of verification in contract. For contractual rights, the principal means of verification is the contract itself. By contrast, for property rights, because "two or more holders of property rights in a given asset may not be in privity of contract," the law "addresses the verification problem by presuming that all property rights in a given asset are held by a single owner." The law then allows "a partitioning of property rights across more than one owner" but only "if there has been adequate notice of that partitioning to persons whom it might affect."

Shavell's argument that the law should permit the division of possessory rights if notice is adequate seems largely consistent with Hansmann and Kraakman's focus on verification costs. However, in subsequent work, Smith argues that information costs "include but are not limited to verification costs" (Smith 2004: 1768 n.174) and criticizes Hansmann and Kraakman's "narrow focus" on verification costs (Smith 2011: 170 n.4). That is, other types of information costs – in addition to verification costs – may be significant and, if so, the law must take into account these costs in the institutional design of property. For example, Merrill and Smith (2000) discuss potential trespassers as well as other market participants as parties who may incur information costs in the absence of a *numerus clausus*. If verification costs are a subset of information costs, then, as Smith (2011) argues, Hansmann and Kraakman's account may be inadequate to explain mandatory standardization in property law. Thus, it appears that once again a comparative institutional analysis is necessary to determine the optimal arrangement for governing the division of possessory rights.

5.4. *The effect of possession on division*

The foregoing analysis suggests that, in theory, the private incentive to divide possessory rights usually converges with what is socially optimal. An owner's incentive to divide may be insufficient but is usually not excessive. However, in some circumstances, legal restrictions on division may be justifiable because of bargaining costs or information costs. In these situations, there is a need for more analysis of the institutional mechanisms for minimizing such costs.

In addition to the financial incentives to divide or not to divide, there is some evidence that property owners are psychologically disposed to prefer full rights in a resource. Nash and Stern (2010: 470) provide experimental evidence suggesting that individuals prefer property that is packaged as discrete assets. Ellickson (2011: 218) points out that Nash and Stern "devised a survey instrument to test the effects of what they call 'property frames.'" The respondents in Nash and Stern's survey "expressed a relative dissatisfaction with policies that confer less than full ownership."

Fennell (2012) also examines the "lumpiness" of property rights. She notes, "[a] good may exhibit lumpiness either because it is considerably less valuable when divided or because it is very expensive to divide (or to produce in smaller units in the first instance)." Fennell provides a number of examples in which property is lumpy, even when we might expect owners to slice up their property in various ways: "In the housing realm, for example, marked gaps exist on the tenure spectrum, leaving out a range of innovative hybrid arrangements that would blend elements of renting and owning." Fennell observes that the law itself often plays a role in maintaining property's lumpy nature. For instance, in housing, she points out that "hybrids do exist, but they are limited in scope and are not well supported by current tax and regulatory regimes."

Given these findings about people's preferences for full ownership and the lumpiness of property, as well as earlier work on how certain types of property such as homes and wedding rings are more closely related to personhood (Radin 1982), it is possible that excessive fragmentation may be less problematic with regard to certain kinds of property. Consider the distinction between tangible and intangible property. It may be that, all other things being equal, fragmentation is less likely for tangible property – property that owners can physically possess – than intangible property. To be sure, even with intangible property, such as mortgage-backed securities or intellectual property rights, owners might have a financial incentive not to divide their property too much.[32] But, with tangible property, such as homes or rings, in addition to having a private financial

---

[32] Of course, these financial incentives may be perverse or skewed if the actors deciding whether to divide do not bear the full costs of their decisions, as may have been the case with the securitization of mortgages during the financial crisis. See infra Section 6.2. The prior literature on mortgages has focused primarily on the pitfalls of excessive division. A notable exception is Fennell (2009), who explores the potential benefits of reconfiguring rights in homeownership.

incentive not to divide excessively, owners may have a psychological proclivity to maintain full ownership. Thus, owners may be especially unlikely to divide excessively property that they can possess physically.

6. Applications

In this section, I offer a few preliminary observations about how owners tend to divide (or not to divide) several types of property, including homes, mortgages, tangible personal property like cars and watches, and intellectual property rights like patents. Of course, additional empirical and experimental research is needed to understand the economic as well as the psychological factors that may motivate owners to divide each of these assets in a variety of settings.

6.1. Homes

Although homeowners may divide their property in certain respects, they rarely do so in other ways. For example, physical division of a house, that is, actually cutting a house in two, is exceedingly unusual, although it has occurred.[33] Moreover, at least in the United States, co-ownership of a home gives each co-owner a right to occupy the whole, regardless of the owner's fractional share of the underlying property interest. Of course, multi-member households engage in many types of informal division, for example, allocating bedrooms to family members. Yet, even in situations involving such divisions, the law does not intervene directly; rather, it gives homeowners broad discretion in how best to divide, for example, in deciding if two children should share a room.[34]

Several types of division discussed earlier entail dividing possessory rights in the home. Renting one's house entails a division of possession over time. Hosting a dinner party entails informal division. Many homes are subject to easements, for example, easements on driveways that neighbors may utilize. Perhaps most notable is the existence of time-share arrangements in which multiple owners each have an ownership interest in a dwelling for a specified period (for example, one week per

---

[33] See, for example, Cambodia #49 – News: Split House in Divorce (Oct. 13, 2008), at www.youtube.com/watch?v=n4ErrsOeZCY (couple together for forty years separates and decides to divide their house, concluding, "It is the best solution they can think of for now").

[34] On property rights and informal ordering around the home, see Ellickson (2010).

year). As Dubord (1980) explains, "What is novel about time-sharing is the division of joint ownership rights into binding periods of exclusive use and possession."[35] Historically, the market for time-shares in the United States has focused primarily on shares in vacation homes and condominiums.[36] With leases, licenses, easements, and times shares, economic incentives seem to play a key role in determining whether homeowners decide to divide their property rights.

However, in other situations in which one might expect new forms of divided ownership to emerge, it seems that homeowners continue to exhibit a strong preference for undivided homeownership. Indeed, the preference among owners for not dividing property they can possess may help to explain the relative lack of interest in land trusts and other novel ways of dividing homeownership. Fennell (2008, 2009) also has proposed shared equity arrangements and various other forms of divided ownership, part of what she calls "Homeownership 2.0." Yet, it remains to be seen whether homeowners will find these innovative arrangements to be psychologically attractive, irrespective of their potential economic benefits.

6.2. Mortgages

Another type of division is the separation of possessory rights in a home from a security interest in the underlying asset. Security interests in homes, that is, mortgages, are a longstanding financing device for homeowners. However, in recent decades, including the years prior to the financial crisis, a new type of division emerged: slicing and dicing security interests into financial products like mortgage-backed securities and collateralized-debt obligations. As Dana (2010: 103) points out: "By virtue of the financial alchemy of Wall Street, a single mortgage could be – and often has been – transformed into tens or hundreds or even thousands of distinct investment interests." Given their complexity, these fragmented mortgages, in addition to increasing information costs, have made it difficult to modify many underwater mortgages.

It is interesting to consider why, unlike the resistance to new forms of homeownership, there was so little hesitation in dividing intangible assets in home mortgages. One explanation is based on financial incentives. The investment bankers and other proponents of securitized mortgages may

---

[35] On time shares, see also Peirce and Mann (1983).
[36] For a comparative perspective on time-shares and other forms of fragmented property holding in South Africa, see Pienaar (2010).

have had perverse incentives to divide too much. Under this theory, the parties that divided these assets did not bear the full costs of the division.[37] Yet another part of the explanation may involve the lack of any inhibition about dividing intangible assets, as opposed to tangible ones.

6.3. Cars, watches, and other personal property

Unlike excessive fragmentation in the mortgage industry, excessive division does not seem to be a problem for automobiles, jewelry, or other types of personal property. Most people do not divide possessory rights in cars. There are some exceptions involving leases and co-ownership. Car dealerships may lease a new automobile to a customer for three years or 36,000 miles. Rental car companies also enable business travelers and tourists to rent a car for a shorter period of several days or weeks. Barzel (1997: 57–58) also discusses the shared ownership of taxicabs, in which two cab drivers share ownership of one cab. Barzel notes that these co-owners may divide certain attributes of the cab, such as fuel payments or driving shifts, relatively easily. But there are other aspects of ownership, for example, the wear and tear on the engine or the interior, that are likely to remain common property because of the difficulty of dividing property.

Another example of divided rights in personal property is Merrill and Smith's hypothetical of a watch that different individuals may own on different days of the week. Merrill and Smith (2000: 27) posit: "[S]uppose *A* wants to create a 'time-share' in the watch, which would allow *B* to use the watch on Mondays but only on Mondays (with *A* retaining for now the rights to the watch on all other days)." They continue, "As a matter of contract law, *A* and *B* are perfectly free to enter into such an idiosyncratic agreement. But *A* and *B* are not permitted by the law of personal property to create a property right in the use of the watch on Mondays only and to transfer this property right from *A* to *B*." Merrill and Smith note that the *numerus clausus* principle prevents time-shares in personal property, thereby reducing information costs for third parties. However, even if legally permitted to do so, it is doubtful whether many owners would have an economic incentive to divide the property rights in their watches in this way. Moreover, owners of watches, wedding rings, jewelry,

---

[37] On incentives in the market for mortgage-backed securities, see Black and Gervais (2010).

and other types of personal property may have a psychological inclination not to divide their personal property by time, space, or function.

6.4. Patents and other intellectual property

Intellectual property (IP) rights are intangible rights in information. The government often authorizes IP rights. For example, in the United States, Congress authorizes patents, copyrights, and trademarks under federal law. These two attributes of intellectual property – that the government often authorizes them and that they entail intangible (as opposed to tangible) rights – have implications for analyzing whether the division of intellectual property will converge with what is socially optimal.

First, because the government creates IP rights, the initial division of rights might be inefficient. As noted earlier, state actors do not necessarily have the same incentives in weighing the costs and benefits of division as private parties. As a result, the government's allocation of IP rights, and its delineation of the scope of such rights, might be inefficient.

Second, once an intellectual property right exists, a private owner of the intellectual property may decide to divide the property. For example, a biotechnology firm that owns a drug patent or a movie studio that owns the copyright to a film may decide to license its IP rights to others. On one hand, the firm may divide its property too little; as a monopolist, the company may charge the monopoly price in negotiating a license. On the other hand, the firm may divide too much, creating an anticommons, especially if owners are relatively uninhibited in dividing intangible property. Thus, dividing intellectual property is especially interesting, and worthy of further investigation, because it involves dividing intangible property and entails division by public as well as private actors.

Conclusion

In analyzing the socially optimal division of possessory rights, I have examined the benefits and costs of division. I also investigated the circumstances in which the private incentive to divide may converge with, or diverge from, what is socially optimal. The social desirability of dividing possessory rights depends on whether the sum of the parts is greater than the whole. Yet, in certain circumstances, an owner's private incentive to divide possessory rights may diverge from what is socially desirable.

By authorizing division via contracts and certain recognized forms of property, the law attempts to minimize disputes, prevent strategic behavior, and reduce agency costs, and thus ensure that owners have a sufficient incentive to divide. Moreover, because owners internalize the costs as well as the benefits of division, the private incentive to divide usually does not exceed the optimal level of division. To the extent owners do not fully internalize the costs of division, the law employs anti-fragmentation and assembly rules that either limit division or facilitate consolidation. Therefore, the law both facilitates division (via contracts and forms of property) and restricts division (through anti-fragmentation and assembly rules) to approximate more closely the conditions necessary for achieving the socially optimal division of property.

However, if owners generally do not have an incentive to divide their property too much, legal restrictions on the divisibility of property rights present a puzzle for economic thinking. Two of the primary justifications for restricting division are preventing excessive fragmentation (if parties are unable to consolidate fragmented rights due to bargaining costs) or simplifying sales transactions (due to information or verification costs). To understand the circumstances in which these costs may justify limitations on division, legal scholars and economists must engage in further empirical analysis and comparative analysis to determine which legal and institutional mechanisms are superior for minimizing such costs. For tangible property that owners can physically possess, dividing property too much may be especially unlikely. With tangible property, owners may not only have an economic incentive to avoid excessive fragmentation but also a psychological inclination for undivided ownership.

References

Ayotte, Kenneth and Bolton, Patrick 2011. "Optimal Property Rights in Financial Contracting," *Review of Financial Studies* 24(10): 3401–33.

Ayotte, Kenneth and Smith, Henry E. (eds.) 2011. *Research Handbook on the Economics of Property Law*. Cheltenham: Edward Elgar.

Barnett, Jonathan M. 2009. "Property as Process: How Innovation Markets Select Innovation Regimes," *Yale Law Journal* 119: 384–456.

Barzel, Yoram 1997. *Economic Analysis of Property Rights*. Cambridge University Press.

Berle, Adolf A. and Means, Gardiner C. 1991. *The Modern Corporation & Private Property*. Rev. edn. New Brunswick, NJ: Transaction.

Black, Bernard and Gervais, Simon 2010. "Incentives in the Market for Mortgage-Backed Securities," *working paper*.

Bouckaert, Boudewijn (ed.) 2010. *Property Law and Economics*. Cheltenham: Edward Elgar.

Bowers, James W. 2010. "Security Interests, Creditors' Priorities, and Bankruptcy," in Bouckaert (ed.), pp. 270–317.

Buchanan, James M. and Yoon, Yong J. 2000. "Symmetric Tragedies: Commons and Anticommons," *Journal of Law and Economics* 43: 1–13.

Chang, Yun-chien 2009. "Empire Building and Fiscal Illusion? An Empirical Study of Government Official Behaviors in Takings," *Journal of Empirical Legal Studies* 6(3): 541–84.

    2012. "Tenancy in 'Anticommons'? A Theoretical and Empirical Analysis of Co-Ownership," *Journal of Legal Analysis* 4: 515–53.

    2013. *Private Property and Takings Compensation: Theoretical Framework and Empirical Analysis*. Cheltenham, UK: Edward Elgar.

Chang, Yun-chien and Fennell, Lee Anne 2014. "Partition and Revelation," *University of Chicago Law Review* 81: 27–51.

Coase, R.H. 1988. *The Firm, The Market, and The Law*. University of Chicago Press.

Cournot, Augustin 1838. *Researches into the Mathematical Principles of the Theory of Wealth*. New York: MacMillan (reprinted in 1897).

Dagan, Hanoch and Heller, Michael A. 2001. "The Liberal Commons," *Yale Law Journal* 110: 549–623.

Dana, David A. 2010. "The Foreclosure Crisis and the Antifragmentation Principle in State Property Law," *University of Chicago Law Review* 77: 97–120.

Davidson, Nestor M. 2008. "Standardization and Pluralism in Property Law," *Vanderbilt Law Review* 61: 1597–1664.

Davidson, Nestor M. and Dyal-Chand, Rashmi 2010. "Property in Crisis," *Fordham Law Review* 78: 1607–60.

Demsetz, Harold 1967. "Toward a Theory of Property Rights," *American Economic Review*, Papers and Proceedings 57: 347–59.

Depoorter, Ben and Parisi, Francesco 2003. "Fragmentation of Property Rights: A Functional Interpretation of the Law of Servitudes," *Global Jurist Frontiers* 3(1): 1–41.

Depoorter, Ben and Vanneste, Sven 2006. "Putting Humpty Dumpty Back Together: Experimental Evidence of Anticommons Tragedies," *Journal of Law, Economics and Policy* 3: 1–23.

Dooley, Michael P. 1992. "Two Models of Corporate Governance," *Business Lawyer* 47: 461–527.

Dorfman, Avihay 2011. "Property and Collective Undertaking: The Principle of Numerus Clausus," *University of Toronto Law Journal* 61: 467–520.

Dubord, David R. 1980. "Time-Share Condominiums: Property's Fourth Dimension," *Maine Law Review* 32: 181–236.

Ellickson, Robert C. 1973. "Alternatives to Zoning: Covenants, Nuisance Rules, and Fines as Land Use Controls," *University of Chicago Law Review* 40: 681–781.

1993. "Property in Land," *Yale Law Journal* 102: 1315–1400.
2010. *The Household: Informal Order Around the Hearth*. Princeton University Press.
2011. "Two Cheers for the Bundle of Sticks Metaphor, Three Cheers for Merrill and Smith," *Econ Journal Watch* 8: 215–22.

Epstein, Richard A. 1982. "Notice and Freedom of Contract in the Law of Servitudes," *Southern California Law Review* 66: 1353–68.
2011. "Heller's Gridlock Economy in Perspective: Why There is Too Little, Not Too Much Private Property," *Arizona Law Review* 53: 51–82.

Fennell, Lee Anne 2006. "Efficient Trespass: The Case for 'Bad Faith' Adverse Possession," *Northwestern University Law Review* 100: 1037–96.
2008. "Homeownership 2.0," *Northwestern University Law Review* 102: 1047–1118.
2009. *The Unbounded Home: Property Values Beyond Property Lines*. New Haven, CT: Yale University Press.
2011. "Commons, Anticommons, Semicommons," in Ayotte and Smith (eds.), pp. 35–56.
2012. "Lumpy Property," *University of Pennsylvania Law Review* 160: 1955–1993.
2013. "The Problem of Resource Access," *Harvard Law Review* 126: 1471–1531.

Garnett, Nicole Stelle 2001. "On Castles and Commerce: Zoning Law and the Home-Business Dilemma," *William & Mary Law Review* 42: 1191–1244.

Hansmann, Henry and Kraakman, Reinier 2000. "The Essential Role of Organizational Law," *Yale Law Journal* 110: 387–440.
2002. "Property, Contract, and Verification: The *Numerus Clausus* Problem and the Divisibility of Rights," *Journal of Legal Studies* 31: S373–S420.

Hansmann, Henry and Mattei, Ugo 1998. "The Functions of Trust Law: A Comparative Legal and Economic Analysis," *New York University Law Review* 73: 434–79.

Heller, Michael A. 1998. "The Tragedy of the Anticommons: Property in Transition from Marx to Markets," *Harvard Law Review* 111: 621–88.
1999. "The Boundaries of Private Property," *Yale Law Journal* 108: 1163–1223.
2008. *The Gridlock Economy: How Too Much Ownership Wrecks Markets, Stops Innovation and Costs Lives*. New York: Basic Books.
2011. "The Anticommons Lexicon," in Ayotte and Smith (eds.), pp. 57–74.

Heller, Michael A. and Eisenberg, Rebecca S. 1998. "Can Patents Deter Innovation? The Anticommons in Biomedical Research," *Science* 280: 698–701.

Jensen, Michael C. and Meckling, William H. 1976. "Theory of the Firm: Managerial Behavior, Agency Costs and Ownership Structure," *Journal of Financial Economics* 3: 305–60.

Judge, Kathryn 2012. "Fragmentation Nodes: A Study in Financial Innovation, Complexity, and Systemic Risk," *Stanford Law Review* 64: 657–725.

Kelly, Daniel B. 2006. "The 'Public Use' Requirement in Eminent Domain Law: A Rationale Based on Secret Purchases and Private Influence," *Cornell Law Review* 92: 1–65.

2011. "Acquiring Land Through Eminent Domain: Justifications, Limitations, and Alternatives," in Ayotte and Smith (eds.), pp. 344–71.
2014. "The Right to Include," *Emory Law Journal* 63: 857–924.
Kieff, F. Scott and Paredes, Troy A. 2007. "Engineering a Deal: Toward a Private Ordering Solution to the Anticommons Problem," *Boston College Law Review* 48: 111–48.
Lametti, David 2013. "The Concept of the Anticommons: Useful, or Ubiquitous and Unnecessary?" in Howe, Helena R. and Griffiths, Jonathan (eds.), *Concepts of Property in Intellectual Property Law*. Cambridge University Press, pp. 232–57.
Levinson, Daryl 2000. "Making Government Pay: Markets, Politics, and the Allocation of Constitutional Costs," *University of Chicago Law Review* 67: 345–420.
Lewinsohn-Zamir, Daphna 2003. "The Objectivity of Well-Being and the Objectives of Property Law," *New York University Law Review* 78: 1669–1754.
Libecap, Gary D. 1989. *Contracting for Property Rights*. Cambridge University Press.
Lueck, Dean and Miceli, Thomas J. 2007. "Property: Leases," in Polinsky, A. Mitchell and Shavell, Steven (eds.), *Handbook of Law and Economics*, vol. 1. Amsterdam: Elsevier, pp. 217–23.
Manne, Henry G. 1967. "Our Two Corporation Systems: Law and Economics," *Virginia Law Review* 53: 259–84.
McChesney, Fred S. 2006. "Coase, Demsetz, and the Unending Externality Debate," *Cato Journal* 26: 179–200.
Merrill, Thomas W. 1986. "The Economics of Public Use," *Cornell Law Review* 72: 61–116.
Merrill, Thomas W. and Smith, Henry E. 2000. "Optimal Standardization in the Law of Property: The *Numerus Clausus* Principle," *Yale Law Journal* 110: 1–70.
2001. "The Property/Contract Interface," *Columbia Law Review* 101: 773–852.
2012. *Property: Principles and Policies*. 2nd edn. New York: Foundation Press.
Merryman, John Henry 1963. "Policy, Autonomy, and the *Numerus Clausus* in Italian and American Property Law," *American Journal of Comparative Law* 12: 224–30.
Mulligan, Christina 2013. "A Numerus Clausus Principle for Intellectual Property," *Tennessee Law Review* 80: 235–90.
Murray Fiona and Stern, Scott 2007. "Do Formal Intellectual Property Rights Hinder the Free Flow of Scientific Knowledge? An Empirical Test of the Anti-commons Hypothesis," *Journal of Economic Behavior & Organization* 63: 648–687.
Nash, Jonathan Remy and Stern, Stephanie M. 2010. "Property Frames," *Washington University Law Review* 87: 449–503.
Note 2012. "The Perils of Fragmentation and Reckless Innovation," *Harvard Law Review* 125: 1799–1821.

Parisi, Francesco 2002. "Entropy in Property," *American Journal of Comparative Law* 50: 595–632.
  2003. "Freedom of Contract and the Laws of Entropy," *Supreme Court Economic Review* 10: 65–90.
Pienaar, G.J. 2010. *Sectional Titles and Other Fragmented Property Schemes*. Cape Town: Juta.
Peirce, Ellen R. and Mann, Richard A. 1983. "Time-Share Interests in Real Estate: A Critical Evaluation of the Regulatory Environment," *Notre Dame Law Review* 59: 9–60.
Posner, Richard A. 2006. "Common-Law Economic Torts: An Economic and Legal Analysis," *Arizona Law Review* 48: 735–47.
  2011. *Economic Analysis of Law*. 8th edn. New York: Aspen.
Radin, Margaret Jane 1982. "Property and Personhood," *Stanford Law Review* 34: 957–1015.
Rudden, Bernard 1987. "Economic Theory v. Property Law: The *Numerus Clausus* Problem," in Eekelaar, John and Bell, John (eds.), *Oxford Essays in Jurisprudence*. Oxford: Clarendon Press, pp. 239–363.
Schulz, Norbert, Parisi, Francesco, and Depoorter, Ben 2003. "Fragmentation in Property: Towards a General Model," *Journal of Institutional and Theoretical Economics* 158: 594–613.
Schwarcz, Steven L. 2012. "Structuring Responsibility in Securitization Transactions," *Capital University Law Review* 40: 803–19.
Scott, Austin Wakeman, Fratcher, William Franklin, and Ascher, Mark L. 2006. *Scott and Ascher on Trusts*. 5th edn. New York: Aspen.
Shavell, Steven 2004. *Foundations of Economic Analysis of Law*. Cambridge, Mass.: Belknap Press of Harvard University Press.
Sitkoff, Robert H. 2004. "An Agency Costs Theory of Trust Law," *Cornell Law Review* 89: 621–84.
Smith, Henry E. 2004. "Property and Property Rules," *New York University Law Review* 79: 1719–98.
  2011. "Standardization in Property Law," in Ayotte and Smith (eds.), pp. 148–73.
Stake, Jeffrey E. 1988. "Toward an Economic Understanding of Touch and Concern," *Duke Law Journal* 1988: 925–74.
  1990. "Darwin, Donations, and the Illusion of Dead Hand Control," *Tulane Law Review* 64: 705–81.
  2010. "Decomposition of Property Rights," in Bouckaert (ed.), pp. 126–60.
Sterk, Stewart E. 1988. "Foresight and the Law of Servitudes," *Cornell Law Review* 73: 956–70.
Williamson, Oliver E. 1985. *The Economic Institutions of Capitalism*. New York: Free Press.

8

The titling role of possession

BENITO ARRUÑADA

1. A general theory of impersonal exchange

1.1. Possession and property in economics and law

Distinguishing ownership from possession, or control, is essential to understand the institutions supporting property, and to be effective when creating and reforming them. In property law, "ownership is pre-eminently a right. Possession, on the other hand, expresses the physical relation of control exercised by a person over a thing" (Holdsworth 1927: 123). Separation of ownership and possession has also been the subject of economic analysis since at least Adam Smith, who studied separation of ownership and control not only in corporations but also in land (Smith 1776: 391–92). However, until recently, not much attention has been paid to possession in the economic analysis of institutions. In fact, even prominent authors in the economics of so-called property rights identify possession with ownership (for example, North 1990: 33; Demsetz 1998: 144).[1]

Pompeu Fabra University and Barcelona GSE. This work has benefitted from exchanges with Avi Bell, Daniel Klerman, Yun-chien Chang, Thomas Merrill, Pedro Pernas, Henry E. Smith, Georg von Wangenheim and other participants at the 5th Law and Economic Analysis Conference, Academia Sinica (Taipei), the 2013 annual meeting of the German Law & Economic Association (Bozen), and the 18th annual conference of the International Society for New Institutional Economics (Duke University). Usual disclaimers apply. It presents an original application to possession of the framework developed in Arruñada (2012), from which it borrows some examples and applications. It received support from the Spanish Ministry of the Economy and Competitiveness, through grant ECO2011-29445.

[1] With respect to economics, Steiger even claims that "the fundamental flaw in New Institutional Economics [is] missing the distinction between possession and property" (2006: 194). It has also been claimed that possession has lost the prominence it had in legal scholarship during the last part of the nineteenth century (Epstein 1988). This may well be so in developed economies; however, squatting is still a major issue in developing economies.

This lack of attention is unsurprising. Economic analysis has mainly focused on the political aspects of property. As emphasized by North and his co-authors, a well-organized polity will preclude violence and confiscation, and subject owners' expropriation to strict conditions, including proper compensation.[2] Moreover, as analyzed by many works influenced by Coase (1960), the law and, largely, government and politics set the initial allocation of rights, which enables parties to easily transact in the market and thus achieve better allocation of resources. Many of these economic analyses focus on how political failures lead to bad institutions.[3] Their central concern is that property may be endangered by political failure because most governments not only prove unable to allocate "property rights" clearly, and to preclude violence and defend private rights against private encroachment: they are also prone to confiscating their citizens' property.

Property law, instead, focuses on private aspects. In particular, it is mainly concerned with the fact that property can also be endangered by market failure, when individuals misuse market transactions to grab the property of others. This may happen because most owners acquire their property from someone else and will, at some point and especially in a modern economy, transfer it to others. But transfers pose risks to both owners and acquirers, so that owners will fear being dispossessed of their rights and acquirers will fear being cheated on their acquisition. To prevent their mutual fears and encourage them to invest, specialize and trade, a market economy requires institutions providing more than initial allocation of rights and a non-confiscatory State. Institutions must also achieve an efficient mix of property enforcement and transaction costs, as I will explain.

1.2. The conflict between property enforcement and transaction costs

Many economic analyses simplify property enforcement as making sure that rights to property are not taken by force, either unimpeded or exerted by a failed polity. Consequently, they neglect the basic conflict arising between property enforcement and transaction costs when one considers that rights can also be taken because of market actions.

---

[2] See mainly North and Thomas (1973), North (1981, 1990), and North, Wallis, and Weingast (2009).

[3] These economic analyses have helped illuminate a wide variety of important issues (see some examples in Arruñada 2012: 236 n. 13).

They fail to provide a productive foundation for analyzing the institutions of property law that make it possible to solve such conflict. In particular, they fail to consider the central feature of property enforcement: the distinction between remedies in rem and in personam, between the two basic types of rights: contract rights and property rights. (Their use of the term "property rights" only adds to the confusion.)

A fruitful economic analysis of the institutions of property must therefore start by considering these concepts, by understanding how property is actually enforced. In principle, given that property rights are the foundation of economic incentives and prosperity, one may think that they should be enforced strictly, so that, in case of conflict with acquirers, goods are always returned to their owners unless they had granted their consent – treating them as rights in rem. However, such strict enforcement would increase transaction costs by worsening the information asymmetry suffered by acquirers of all sorts of rights, who would always have to gather the consent of the previous owners without even knowing who they are. Strictly enforcing property rights would therefore endanger trade. Moreover, it would also endanger specialization, because specialization is often based on having agents acting as owners' representatives, and, with universal strict enforcement, acquirers would have reasons to doubt the legal authority of sellers.

Economic growth therefore requires this conflict between property enforcement and transaction costs to be optimized, so that both current owners and acquirers are efficiently protected. Protecting owners' property rights encourages investment, and reducing the transaction costs faced by acquirers encourages them to trade impersonally and thus improves the allocation and specialization of resources. Owners' consent must be preserved but enforced in a way that makes trade possible. And current owners have an interest in tackling the conflict, not only because they are potential sellers but also because, being acquirers with respect to the previous owners, they could eventually lose their title.

The nature of the problem can be clarified by considering that most economic transactions are interrelated sequentially, as most transactions legally interact with previous transactions. In the simplest sequence, with only two transactions, one or several "economic principals" – such as owners, employers, shareholders, creditors, and the like – voluntarily contract first with one or several economic "agents"– possessors, employees, company directors, and managers – in an "originative" transaction. Second, the agent then contracts "subsequent" transactions with third parties.[4] Understandably, it is necessary to optimize the total costs of transacting, considering both originative and subsequent transactions.

Sequential exchange is necessary to specialize the tasks of principals and agents – between landowners and farmers, employers and employees, shareholders and managers, and so on in the originative contract. But it also gives rise to substantial transaction costs, because, when third parties contract with the agent in the subsequent contract, they suffer information asymmetry regarding not only the material quality of the goods or services being transacted but also the legal effects of the previous originative contract. In particular, third parties are often unaware if they are dealing with a principal or an agent, or if the agent has sufficient title or legal power to commit the principal.

Moreover, principals face a commitment problem when trying to avoid this asymmetry because their incentives change after the third party has entered the subsequent contract. In an agency setup, before contracting, principals have an interest in third parties being convinced that agents have proper authority. However, if the business turns out badly and there are no further incentives in place, principals will be inclined to deny such authority.[5] The typical dispute triggered by the sequential nature of transactions is one in which the principal tries to

---

[4] This use of "agency" language for describing property cases may puzzle readers familiar with the legal concept of agency. However, it is convenient to generalize the argument, encompassing all types of transactions. The agency structure is clearer for those business transactions for which there is an explicit agency or employment relationship. In contrast, for property transactions, which party plays the role of agent or of principal even depends on the type of potential deception considered. But the agency structure is also present in all property transactions. Observe, for instance, that in a second sale the seller is acting as an economic agent for the first buyer, even if this use of the agency concept is unconventional in legal terms, since the first buyer does not intend the seller to act in this capacity and the seller does not portray herself as an agent of the buyer. In addition to making a more general argument, talking of principals and agents avoids the confusing labeling of some claimants (usually the first in some contractual event) as "legal" or "true" rightholders, without them necessarily being the ones held as such by the law.

[5] This is easy to grasp in a legal agency setup as, e.g., when contemplating the relationship between a shareholder (principal), a corporate representative (agent) and a corporate lender (third party). A typical property conflict is that between a first buyer (principal), a seller (agent) and a second buyer (third party). In such a case, the commitment refers to the seller's promise not to sell twice. Ex ante, she is interested in committing herself, in order to encourage the buyer to buy; but her incentives change after the sale. The text could therefore read: Before the originative sale contract, sellers (i.e., agents) have an interest in buyers (i.e., principals) being convinced that they will not cheat through a subsequent transaction (e.g., a second sale), but their incentives change after the first sale.

elude obligations assumed by the agent in the principal's name, whether the agent had legal authority or not.

In principle, judges may adjudicate in such disputes in favor of the principal or the third party. I will refer to favoring the third party as enforcing "contract rules," as opposed to the seemingly more natural "property rules" that favor the principal.[6] The effects of these rules are clear. Take the simple case in which an agent exceeds his legal powers when selling a good to an innocent third party (i.e., a good-faith party who is uninformed about the matter in question). When applying the "property rule" that no one can transfer what he does not have, judges have the sold good returned to the previous owner, who is therefore granted a right *in rem*, and give the innocent third party a mere claim in personam against the agent. Conversely, judges may apply an indemnity or "contract rule" so that the sold good stays with the acquiring third party and the owner-principal only wins a personal claim against the agent.

The difference in the value of these legal remedies– real or personal– is substantial because the enforceability of these two types of right is often markedly different. While rights in personam are only valid against specific persons, *inter partes*, rights *in rem* are valid against all individuals, *erga omnes*. The latter, therefore, provide the strongest possible enforcement: without the consent of the rightholder, rights *in rem* remain unaffected. When the thing is a parcel of land, the difference in value often ranges from full value for the party being adjudicated the land, to zero value for the party being given a claim to be indemnified by an insolvent person. (Similar differences arise in business and corporate

---

[6] These labels parallel the legal origin of the dichotomy and should avoid confusion with related but drastically different concepts. In particular, the rules are similar but distinct from the "property" and "liability" rules defined in the influential work by Calabresi and Melamed (1972) because, instead of a taking that affects only two parties, here the rules are defined in the context of a three-party sequence of two transactions. Moreover, my analysis focuses on the role played by the parties in each transaction, disregarding that current third parties will often act as principals in a future sequence of transactions. Consequently, when good-faith third parties win a dispute over their acquisitive transaction (i.e., when they are given a property right), they do not win as a consequence of applying a property rule, which—by definition—would have given the good to the original owner. In such a case, the third party does not pay any monetary damages to the original owner, as in Calabresi and Melamed's liability rule. A final difference is that Calabresi and Melamed's property rule is weaker, referring only to the ability to force a would-be taker to bargain for a consensual transfer similar to specific performance, which thus arguably has little to do with a right *in rem* (Merrill and Smith 2001a).

contexts, where a parallel distinction is often made, but framed in more general terms: not in terms of rights but in terms of legal priority.)

If judges apply a property rule, maximizing property enforcement, owners will feel secure with respect to future acquisitions but all potential acquirers will suffer greater information asymmetry with respect to legal title, endangering trade. Conversely, if judges apply a contract rule, minimizing information asymmetry for potential acquirers, they weaken property enforcement, making owners feel insecure, endangering investment and specialization. The choice of rule therefore involves a conflict between property enforcement and transaction costs– more generally, a conflict between the transaction costs of originative and subsequent contracts.

This chapter examines how legal systems rely on possession for solving this conflict. I first outline a theory on the efficacy and limitations of possession as evidence for property titling and propose a taxonomy of the roles played by possession and two hypotheses about how it works (Section 2). I then analyze in Sections 3 to 5 three partly overlapping areas in which possession plays relevant but diverse roles: those of (1) movable and (2) immovable property, as well as (3) documentary possession. The purpose of this analysis, if not to test the hypotheses, is to explore at least their consistency in the main types of institutional solutions. What emerges is a nuanced view of the titling function of possession, which depends on the availability of institutions (mainly, registries), the type of asset (movable versus immovable), the type of transaction (commercial versus noncommercial) and the multiplicity of rights.[7]

2. Hypotheses on reliance on possession as evidence for titling

To overcome the conflict between in rem property enforcement and transaction costs, expanding the set of viable contractual opportunities with minimal damage to property rights, different solutions will be appropriate, depending on the circumstances of each type of right and

---

[7] This titling function of possession does not tie in with stark separations of possession and ownership, such as the view expressed in the first five sections of Merrill (Chapter 1). To the extent that the exercise or delivery of possession plays a titling function – either directly, with respect to third-party good-faith acquirers; as a consequence of *usucapio* and other forms of acquisitive prescription; or through the publicizing element of delivery – possession becomes highly relevant even for the "audience" interested in exchanging property rights.

transaction. The legal system may directly choose to enforce some rights in a certain way or, more generally, give freedom to rightholders about which rule to apply. However, when rightholders are free to choose, the legal system must guarantee their commitment, which in some cases is automatic as a byproduct of market interactions but in others requires costly formal institutions such as public registers.

In general, for judges to apply property rules, which favor owners, owners must have publicized their claims or their rights, which should protect acquirers. That is, owners can opt for a property rule to make their rights stronger, but, thanks to publicity, acquirers suffer little information asymmetry. Conversely, for judges to apply contract rules, which favor acquirers, owners must have granted their consent, which should protect them. That is, when it is in the owners' interest to reduce transaction costs, they choose a contract rule, so that acquirers' rights are stronger, whereas owners' rights are weaker. This weakening of property is safeguarded by the fact that it is owners – in general terms, principals – who choose the agent to whom they entrust possession or appoint as their representative, this being the same moment when they implicitly opt for a contract rule. However, commitment to their choice is also necessary.

Smooth operation of this conditional application of rules poses varying degrees of difficulty for different transactions. The difficulty is relatively minor when the originative transaction produces verifiable facts, such as the physical possession of movable goods by a merchant or a house by a lessee. For these cases, judges can base their decisions on this public information, which is produced without any explicit formal intervention. What judges or legislatures have to do is only to clearly define the rules to be applied.

The difficulty is greater when the originative transaction produces less verifiable facts, making private (contractual, as opposed to institutional) solutions harder to apply. Such private solutions may even be impossible if all the information on the transaction remains hidden and its consequences are not verifiable. Consider, for example, the difficulties for using land as collateral when hidden mortgages are enforced on the basis of contractual documents. Given the possibility of antedating mortgage deeds, judges would be basing their decisions on unreliable information, and lenders would be reluctant to contract for fear of previous mortgages emerging. In such a context, rules alone are not enough because applying them requires verifiable information on the titling-relevant elements of originative contracts. To produce such information, it is necessary to

Table 1. *Main types and examples of reliance on possession*

Action	Possession of goods	Possession of documents
Exercise of possession	Commercial trade, overriding lease, Roman *usucapio* (acquisitive prescription)	Money, negotiable instruments, powers of attorney, property deeds
Delivery of possession	Livery of seisin, demonstration of boundaries in Roman conveyance by *mancipatio*	Granting of powers of attorney, property deeds, etc.

enforce only those mortgages that have been made public, usually by entering them into a public register.

As illustrated in Table 1, possession produces varying levels of publicity and verifiability in different circumstances, as it is present in four different strategies, based on public knowledge that possession is being exercised or has been transferred, or on delivery and possession of documentary representations of property rights.[8]

The actual exercise of physical possession (that is, the mere control or holding of the good, sometimes referred to as "detention") can act as a titling mechanism when some key circumstances of their possession or use are publicly observed in a verifiable manner. This is, for example, the case of movables being sold by merchants, as well as some rights on immovables, such as all rights connected to use or occupation (such as real property leases and rights of way). In these cases, the exercise of possession by the agent of the originative contract informs observers about the titling-relevant elements of such an originative contract. It becomes one of those "publicly observable states of fact" (Merrill and Smith 2001b: 803) effective in communicating information about potentially affected parties. If needed, judges verify possession (and, crucially for movables, that the seller is a merchant) and use it as evidence on titling-relevant consequences of the originative transaction when adjudicating property rights in a conflict triggered by a subsequent transaction. Consequently, if rules about the titling consequences of originative contracts are clear, as possession is also observable by potential parties, they can use it as a basis for their contractual decisions. Therefore,

---

[8] I will mostly deal with possession as a fact. For possession as a right, see, e.g., Chang (Chapter 4) and Kelly (Chapter 7), and, more generally, Smith (Chapter 3).

Publicity hypothesis: *Exercise of possession is effective as a titling mechanism when independent parties observe it, thus providing publicity and verifiability of the titling-relevant elements contained in originative contracts.*

The exercise of physical possession can only inform about who holds the particular right being exercised: "It can support only a single form of ownership that encompasses all useful rights in the object – a simple unitary property right" (Hansmann and Kraakman 2002: 385). Such information may affect acquiring third parties positively or negatively. For example, possession of movable goods by a merchant usually informs that the merchant has legal authority to transfer ownership to an innocent third party acquirer (positive information). On the contrary, in many jurisdictions, buyers of residential real estate are burdened with the possessory rights of tenants even if unregistered. In both cases, possession informs about a single right: multiple rights may exist but either they are in personam rights (the right held by the merchandise owner) or they are in rem rights burdened by the possessory right (the right of the real property subject to the lease). In the first case, previous in rem rights were made in personam to facilitate trade. The price of using possession positively (ensuring the full and in rem nature of the rights that innocent third parties acquire) is to dilute property rights in contractual rights. In the second case, the opposite happens: the in personam tenant's right is made in rem to ensure enforcement. The price of using possession negatively is to increase the transaction costs of acquirers, who are obliged to search for such potentially contradictory possessory rights.[9] Therefore,

Dilution hypothesis: *Given that possession is only effective to inform about a single in rem right, direct and automatic reliance on the exercise of possession for titling requires that all other rights be diluted to in personam status or be burdened by the possessory in rem right.*

Given its informational limitations, when the exercise of possession is used as a basis for titling, all other in rem rights are either transformed into in personam rights or burdened with the possessory right. Consequently, when it is optimal to enforce multiple rights in rem, legal systems rely on more elaborate titling solutions, in many of which either

---

[9] I am omitting from the discussion the fact that legal systems often rely on possession as a source of information and legal evidence regarding the physical extent of property rights. This tends to be the case, even in systems with registration of rights, with respect to the demarcation of land parcel boundaries.

the public transfer and/or the public exercise of possession is a key element. For instance, in order to guarantee publicity and verifiability, it has been common in many legal cultures to rely on formal ceremonies for land transactions, such as, for example, those of the *mancipatio* in classic Roman law and the livery of seisin of medieval England. In essence, these ceremonies produce a public conveyance that is separate from the private contract, the two-step contracting process characteristic of property, as emphasized by Arruñada (2003a). The public step plays at least two major roles. First, it triggers the start of a prescription period that can also be understood as a purging procedure. Contradictory in rem rights are downgraded to in personam status unless rightholders oppose the intended transaction either during the ceremony or within the prescription period. Second, it provides the basis for future legal procedures, as the law usually grants substantial procedural advantages to possessors against other claimants. Therefore, in a context of multiple rights,

Corollary I: *Public knowledge of the delivery of possession is required for possession to play a public titling function.*

When property rights are embodied in contractual documents such as property deeds or negotiable instruments, possession of these documents can have similar legal effects to those of possession of goods. It offers the advantage that delivering possession is easier for documents than for goods. For instance, documents can be delivered far from the goods, which should facilitate trade. However, given that, in principle, one of the parties keeps contractual documents, they are subject to possible manipulation and contradictory documents may therefore easily emerge. Consequently, they are more reliable when held by the party in need of protection. This limits its usefulness to documents reflecting only a single in rem right, such as negotiable instruments and powers of attorney; and leads to serious difficulties in the presence of multiple and hidden rights, as illustrated by the chain of title deeds in real property. Therefore,

Corollary II: *Documentary possession is only effective as a public titling mechanism in the absence of multiple rights in rem.*

3. The informational value of physical possession in commercial exchange

Contract rules protecting innocent third parties are applied in the main type of business exchange, when transferring the ownership of movable property. When you buy a new computer in a store, you do not check whether the salesperson has the legal power to sell it; and, when you pay for it, you do not worry that the salesperson might keep the money instead of giving it to the store or that the store might not pay the manufacturer. Even if the employees or the store fails to comply with their duties, you know that you will keep the computer. The store would have to recover the money from the salesperson and the manufacturer from the store. But you would keep the computer; thus for you the relationships among the salesperson, the store, and the manufacturer are almost irrelevant. In fact, many other possible relationships are also irrelevant. For instance, most stores are now part of corporations, legal entities that simplify a complex web of legal relationships. When you contract with their representatives, such as managers and salespersons, all these relationships are also irrelevant. These simplifications greatly facilitate exchange and, in particular, impersonal exchange: as a customer, you can focus on the physical quality of the computer, because proper legal institutions make sure that you are able to buy a property right on it, a right in rem.

You are protected because in most business contexts, the law enforces contract rules, granting in rem rights to innocent third parties and greatly facilitating impersonal exchange. This protection of acquiring third parties dilutes current or previous owners' property rights, but this dilution is controlled by owners' decisions: it is owners who select and monitor the agents whose conduct might trigger the economic consequences of dilution. In the example, it is the computer manufacturer that selects its distributors, and it is the store owner that selects its agents and salespersons.

This is so in most commercial contexts, in which the judge will confirm ownership for an innocent third party who bought the good from a "merchant" (in practice, now a business firm) who had been entrusted with possession. For example, the Uniform Commercial Code (UCC) in the United States, adopted by almost all states, establishes that "any entrusting of possession of goods to a merchant who deals in goods of that kind gives him power to transfer all rights of the entruster to a buyer in ordinary course of business" (UCC §2–403[2]). Something similar happens in civil law jurisdictions.[10] This means that the former legal owner will only hold a personal indemnity claim on the selling merchant and will not recover the good bought for value and in good faith by the third party.

---

[10] Compare, e.g., for Germany, the German Civil Code or *Bürgerliches Gesetzbuch* (BGB), §§932 and 935, with the German Commercial Code or *Handelsgesetzbuch* (HGB), §366.

In this context, contract rules are generally efficient because the enforcement advantage that alternative property rules would provide is less valuable than the cost of the information asymmetry they cause. Therefore, owners are willing to dilute their claims in order to reduce the acquirers' information asymmetry and obtain higher prices. This is highlighted by the specific nuances and exceptions used when enforcing the rule. In particular, legal systems tend to attribute the property right to the good-faith purchaser only *when the owner is a merchant*. This makes sense because application of one rule or the other alters purchasers' incentives to determine the true legal ownership, as well as owners' incentives to protect their property. And both the cost and the effectiveness of these activities of information and ownership protection change depending on whether the owner is a merchant.[11] Thus, when the owner is a merchant, not only the cost of searching title is high; the merchant-owner also faces a comparatively low cost of protecting property. First, if the owner is a merchant, it is usually more difficult for the purchaser to search the ownership of the good, because in most cases there will have been a whole chain of transactions, such as those between manufacturers and wholesale and retail distributors.[12] Second, merchants are better able to protect their ownership because owners who are merchants are in a good position to choose reliable sellers.[13] Therefore, retaining a property right over the goods would be less valuable to them than to owners who are not merchants. The key element is not only possession of goods is public as that the merchant nature of the seller is also public.[14]

---

[11] Therefore, the argument considers the effects of allocation rules on both property enforcement and transaction costs. These two effects have been extensively analyzed in the literature on good-faith purchasers (see, e.g., Medina 2003: 344 for an introduction), often under extreme and opposite assumptions minimizing one of the two effects. For instance, many works assume that third parties' willingness to pay remains unaffected by the choice of legal rule since they will also become principals and thus will be affected by both rules. This assumption seems particularly inadequate for situations of voluntary agency (instead of a fraud or theft), as it is principals' decisions that trigger rule switching and it is therefore principals' performance in, for instance, selecting agents that defines the costs they will bear.

[12] As Sauveplanne (1965: 652) asserts, "the rapid circulation of movables makes it difficult, if not impossible, to trace their legal origin. If every purchaser were compelled to investigate his predecessor's title, the circulation of movable property would be seriously hampered".

[13] As argued, e.g., by Weinberg (1980: 588–91), for cases in which there is fraud and the owner's agent behaves incorrectly.

[14] The rationale for applying a contract rule in commercial transactions on movable property depends on the commercial nature of the owner of the good, although the legal

Exceptions to application of the contract rule in commercial contexts confirm the argument. In many countries, a property rule is applied to some transactions with merchants, including sometimes the obligation for the owner to compensate the purchaser for the price paid by the latter to the seller. Such exceptions are commonly applied to transactions in which the selling merchant's supplier – usually the owner of the good – is an individual and not another merchant, as in used goods stores, art galleries, and auction or pawnshops. As a result, even innocent purchasers lose ownership of the goods they have acquired in such establishments when a prior owner appears whose right had been violated. For example, when defining whether a purchaser acts "in ordinary course of business," UCC §1–201(9) requires the seller, in addition to good faith and lack of knowledge, to be "in the business of selling goods of that kind." And its mention of pawnbrokers was interpreted as creating an exception (Baird and Jackson 1984: 307 n. 22), an interpretation that was later confirmed by the revision of the UCC. Moreover, purchases in art galleries are generally treated in the United States as those in auction houses and pawnbrokers, so that a good-faith purchaser of a stolen work of art will probably have to relinquish it if the prior owner appears.[15] Certainly, in many countries, the prior owner is entitled to restitution but only after refunding the price paid for the good by the good-faith purchaser.[16]

Other typical exceptions violate basic assumptions of the general problem under analysis. This happens in particular for the good faith and knowledge exceptions, which relate to the breakdown of the information asymmetry assumption; and the theft case, which violates the assumption of voluntary agency. Understandably, many jurisdictions,

---

formulation for its application is often approximated in terms of the commercial or noncommercial nature of the seller or of the transaction, thus using subjective or objective criteria (Tallon 1983). Considering that delivering possession switches the applicable legal rule, clearly defining who is a merchant is essential. Fortunately, this is now easy even without registration (Arruñada 2012: 86). See also Klerman (Chapter 10) for a discussion of the property disputes over stolen arts.

[15] See, e.g., Caruso (2000), as well as Landes and Posner (1996), for a defense of application of the property rule, and Merryman (2008), who argues in favor of granting legal entity status to the register of lost works of art.

[16] This applies for lost or stolen movables that have been purchased in a public sale, as well as those bought from authorized pawnbrokers. For example, Article 464 of the Spanish Civil Code, partially amended by Article 61.1 of Law 7/1996 on the organization of retail trade.

including most of the United States, apply the property rule to commercial purchases of stolen goods, but the contract rule to goods that have been separated through fraud, deceit, or coercion, where a voluntary, though imperfect, element is present. Similarly, some business transactions rely on registers but are not commercial or not about movables. Corporate and secured transactions affect the relative position of the merchant's creditors but are less relevant for the rights of third parties acquiring merchandise from the merchant. Finally, registries for high-value identifiable assets such as cars, ships, and airplanes are sometimes used during their distribution to reduce transaction costs and lower the cost of financing inventories (Fernández del Pozo 2004: 105–78).[17] They provide an interesting borderline case with immovable property both with respect to the nature of the assets and the costs and benefits of preserving in rem rights in them.

Overall, the standard practice for commercial transactions in movable goods is consistent with both the publicity and dilution hypotheses: public knowledge of who is a merchant makes it possible for possession to play a titling function, protecting innocent acquirers, even if at the price that all conflicting rights are implicitly diluted to in personam status. In a sense, the key element is not possession itself but the merchant nature of the possessor.

4. The informational value of possession in real property exchange

In the standard commercial transaction on movable goods, the *exercise* of physical possession by a merchant suffices to trigger the application of a contract rule that benefits the innocent third party acquirer. However, all conflicting rights are diluted to in personam rights. For real property, such general dilution would usually be inefficient; therefore, possession plays more nuanced roles: (1) Delivery of legal possession is usually part of public conveyancing processes, with or without judicial intervention, which publicize the intended transaction and provide an opportunity to defend and purge conflicting rights. (2) Possession serves to define the type of legal actions available to the different types of claimants and to

---

[17] Not by chance, these assets, together with land, come close to including what classical Roman law considered *res mancipi* and therefore required a formal conveyancer by *mancipatio* or *in iure cessio*. The Roman solutions are further analyzed in Arruñada (forthcoming).

grant ownership after a certain period (the Roman *usucapio*, a form of acquisitive prescription or adverse possession). And (3) the exercise of physical possession provides sufficient notice to acquirers on negative in rem interests, as happens with some overriding interests for registered land.

4.1. Publicity in the delivery of possession

Delivery of possession has been a key element in traditional conveyancing and titling procedures. Since 1066, English conveyances followed the continental practice of delivering possession through a ritual known as "livery of seisin." In essence, the seller gave the buyer a clod of earth from the land, a twig, or a key, and loudly said that he was conveying the estate. In the Roman *mancipatio*, the seller and the acquirer appeared upon the property before a person holding a scale and five witnesses. The acquirer then boasted that he declared the property to be his, stroke a token coin against the scales and handed it to the seller, who said nothing. It seems that "in England an actual livery of vacant seisin was required ... partly [because] it helped to promote publicity of conveyance and thus to prevent the frauds which secrecy of conveyance renders possible" (Holdsworth 1927: 112–13). In contrast, *mancipatio* did not in principle require delivery of possession (Buckland 1912: 95–96; Gaius 170: IV.131). However, rights on provincial land were conveyed by delivering possession and, even for Italic land, the transferor had a duty to deliver possession (Honoré 1989: 139). Moreover, if the transferee did not obtain possession publicly, it was not protected against dispossessors by possessory interdicts, a speedy procedure by which the judge would adjudicate on possession without looking at title, forcing possible owners to rely on a more cumbersome action, *vindicatio* (Nicholas 1962: 108–09). Similarly, in English law, since the twelfth century the action for *novel disseisin* (recent dispossession) opted for possession: even though owners could rely on another action, called *writ of right*, this was more costly and allowed parties to present all sorts of evidence to support their claims (Simpson 1986: 39). Both Roman and medieval law also provided safer access to ownership through judicial procedures such as the *in iure cessio* and *fine*, in which delivery of possession was an essential step. For instance, conveyance by *fine* "was the most secure of all medieval conveyances ... [because] so long as one of the parties was seised of the lands no one could dispute the fine after a period of a year and a day from the execution of it, except those under some disability," as well as, if accompanied by proclamations, strangers after five years (Simpson 1986: 124).

These ceremonies had a titling function as they publicized conveyances,[18] but also served to gather the consents of affected rightholders and therefore purge conflicting claims either at once or after a certain period. Numerous witnesses were required, and this "was probably needed not so much to prove that the act had taken place as to give it publicity so that any defect of title (which in a small society would be likely to be known to the witness) could be investigated immediately" (Nicholas 1962: 256).[19] In contrast, creating rights in personam by formal *stipulatio* did not require any witnesses (Nicholas 1962: 104). A key element for purging were boundary disputes. For this, in Rome, "though not a legal requirement, it was standard practice to call the neighbours to witness a conveyance by delivery. This allowed the transferee to verify that the transferor and his neighbours agreed on the boundaries, or, if they did not, to pinpoint the area/s of dispute. If the dispute was not settled at the time, the conveyance could be confined to the agreed area, or if necessary postponed" (Honoré 1989: 139). This customary practice of boundary demonstration in the presence of neighbors may have become formally required after the reforms enacted by Constantine in 313–23 (Honoré 1989: 142–49). The purging potential is also clearer in the livery of seisin, as witnesses originally had to be neighboring, and therefore potentially affected, rightholders (Blackstone 1765–1769: 315–16). Their presence was likely playing a similar function to the "secondary sellers" found in old land transactions in Babylonia (Silver 1995: 122–27) and was reminiscent of the custom of paying so-called witnesses, found in other transactions in some primitive tribes (Diamond 1951: 259). Lastly, the requirements of repeated proclamations and waiting periods for the conveyance to reach in rem effects cannot be explained as mere providers of contractual proof to transactors. This was clear in the practices followed in other European regions, where laws mandated sophisticated procedures of publicity "before the church" and "at the gate of town walls" for rural and urban land, respectively, as well as some judicial registration (Patault 1989: 205–08, Oliver y Esteller 1892). Historical evidence on similar forms of publicity dates back to

---

[18] "The delivery of seisin must be an actual delivery of vacant possession and not a mere symbolic delivery alone ... It is obvious that this mode of conveyance gave to dealings in land a notoriety which no symbolic delivery or delivery of a deed could ever give" (Simpson 1986: 118).

[19] "These *testes* or *superstites*, as they were called, were not witnesses in our sense, expected later to testify to what they had seen or read, but judges, expected to stop an act at the time of its making if the performance were flawed" (Meyer 2004: 118).

the ancient societies of the Middle East, around 2500 BC (Ellickson and Thorland 1995: 383–84).

Public ceremonial conveyances therefore served for providing publicity, gathering consents and purging property rights. However, they probably became less efficient with economic development, as I will analyze in Section 6.[20] First, their cost becomes higher as parties move more and may need to purchase from a distance. Second, they are more effective in local markets, where transactions take place between neighbors, as was common in rural societies, than in wider markets. For example, "the six participants in the *mancipatio* though adequate enough for a small community, could constitute no hindrance to secrecy in so a vast a society as the imperial Rome" (Nicholas 1962: 104). Indeed, for neighbors, it is easy to notice announcements and public deals, especially for the kinds of rights common in rural societies, many of which are linked to family matters. Probably less so for non-neighbors. This conjecture is consistent with the existence of rules that granted lesser effects to these and similar procedures for strangers and disabled parties (e.g., in the English *fine*, according to Simpson 1986: 124). Similarly the effect of publicity "before the church" and "at the gate of town walls," was immediate for the rightholders who were present but was delayed for one year and one day for those absent (Patault 1989: 205–8, Oliver y Esteller 1892). Costlier knowledge was apparently balanced with longer time, suggesting that these systems could hardly support more distant and impersonal trade.

4.2. *Exercise of possession as access to ownership: the Roman* usucapio

To the extent that the exercise of possession has observable consequences, it provides the basis for titling by having it upgraded to ownership with the lapse of time – by acquisitive prescription or *usucapio*.[21]

---

[20] Moreover, two other factors may be present, at least in the short term. On the one hand, there is a permanent demand for privacy by economic agents, because of reputational concerns and tax avoidance, a demand that could be uncorrelated to economic growth. As argued by Nicholas, "there was a similar struggle to achieve secret conveyancing in English law, culminating early in the seventeenth century in the recognition of the device of a bargain and sale for a term followed by a release" (1962: 104 n. 3). On the other hand, conveyancers – mainly lawyers – may have an interest in privacy solutions to the extent that they increase the demand for their professional services.

[21] This provides a solution in very different contexts. A modern application of this solution is the registration of possessory rights, a standard procedure commonly used when

For Romans, undisturbed possession of land and other capital goods for only two years (one year for other movables) led to ownership if acquired in good faith and based on proper cause, even if conveyed by simple *traditio* (delivery of possession) without *mancipatio*.[22] Furthermore, during the late Republic, the Praetor enhanced the protection enjoyed by the good faith possessor on the way to *usucapio* by granting him an action that ensured he succeeded even against the formal owner (if the possessor's title was formally defective: a recipient of land by informal delivery or *traditio* instead of formal *mancipatio*) or against everyone but the owner (if the title was substantively defective because, for example, he had bought from a non-owner). As a consequence, "the recipient of a *res mancipi* by *traditio* was for nearly all practical purposes in the position of an owner" (Nicholas 1962: 127). It is believed that, thereafter, informal delivery by *traditio* replaced formal *mancipatio*.[23]

A key element for *usucapio* to work is that the exercise of possession provides claimants with the information they need to litigate and protect any property rights infringed by the intended transaction (e.g., Rose 1985: 78–81). It therefore implicitly provides the basis to start a selective purge and acquirers need to check only if the seller has effectively been in possession for the prescription period. In this context, doubts about the information provided by possession may easily emerge, especially if the delivery of possession is unobservable. For instance, in Roman law, *traditio* was increasingly made without any visible transfer of the good. This, together with the decreasing use and limited efficacy of *mancipatio* in a vast economy, leads some authors to think the Roman publicity was ineffective (e.g., Nicholas 1962: 104). However, this critique may have been unwarranted because, for existing rights to be protected under *usucapio*, possession only needs to inform affected rightholders with sufficient time for them to take action. And owners can always make

---

introducing land registration that allows possessors to file their claims, which, if unchallenged, become conclusive after a certain period (Arruñada 2003b).

[22] With the only exception of goods stolen or taken by force. It must be kept in mind, however, that Romans defined possession narrowly to exclude those who hold on behalf of the owner – borrowers, depositees, hirers, lessees – so that landlords held possession even while their tenants held what modern writers refer to as "detention" (Nicholas 1962: 112–15).

[23] In fact, for the Roman case, it has been argued that *mancipatio* was retained longer for land, at least until the fifth century, because it did not require the presence of the parties on the spot (Buckland 1912: 73). However, it is likely that the *mancipatio* term appearing in later Roman documents really means conveyance (Nicholas 1962: 117).

their possession public if, foreseeing a possible sale, they want to convince future acquirers that they will be protected by the *usucapio* of the seller.

It is consistent with this argument that the time for *usucapio* increased when the information provided by publicity might have taken longer to process. In Rome, *usucapio* of provincial land by *longi temporis praescriptio* took ten or twenty years when parties were or were not in the same district. It also took longer in the last centuries of the Empire, when the possibility of multiple adverse rights probably arose because of the less peaceful environment. At the time of Justinian, three years were required for *usucapio* of movables; and *longi temporis praescriptio* became the only *usucapio* for land (Nicholas 1962: 128).

4.3. The exercise of possessory detention as a source of publicity in real property

For land and other capital goods, many deliveries of possession are not intended to facilitate transfers of ownership but to facilitate productive specialization, by separating ownership and productive use. Unlike movables, land is not meant to be traded by the detentor, who is usually a farmer, not a merchant. In contrast to merchants, who are interested in diluting their in rem right, landowners prefer keeping their property as fully in rem ownership. Therefore, the use of physical possession (mere detention) as the basis for establishing ownership is a poor solution for most capital goods, such as land. Relying on detention to establish ownership would make it easier for detentors to fraudulently use their position to acquire ownership for themselves or to convey owners' rights to third parties. In such cases, owners would often end up holding a mere in personam right, against the detentor committing the fraud. Understandably, under such conditions, owners would be reluctant to cede detention, for fear of losing their property.

In contrast to the limitations of possession to inform on ownership or at least on the lack of in rem rights that may be burdening ownership, simple detention may provide reliable information on single individual rights. This may be used by the legal system to protect these rights in rem based on such information. For example, some modern legal systems enforce residential lessees' rights in rem (whatever the formal definition of these rights) even when such leases remain out of the public record. One can infer that, for such "overriding interests," the law assumes that acquirers can obtain enough information by inspecting the land. This solution is not necessarily efficient, especially now that a growing number of investors cross borders and may want to acquire without ever seeing their purchases. In fact, these interests have often been enacted almost surreptitiously through consumer or housing regulations, without formally asserting the in rem nature of the rights, and, at least until the recent economic crisis, there was a tendency to eliminate their in rem protection (as the English Land Registration Act did in 2002).

Considering the three areas I have just analyzed, when land titling mechanisms rely on possession, an element of independent publicity is present, as proposed by the publicity hypothesis and its corollary: public delivery of possession as part of conveyancing ceremonies, public exercise of possession within the process of acquisitive prescription, and public exercise of possessory rights leading to these possessory rights being enforced in rem against acquirers.

5. The informational value of documentary possession

The limitations of conveyancing ceremonies and the exercise of possession to inform interested parties lead to complementary and alternative solutions with a common characteristic: reliance on a symbolic expression of property rights. These symbols can take three different forms: they can be fixed to the asset, embodied in the contractual documents kept by some of the parties or incorporated in a parties-independent public register.

The practice of physically marking assets illustrates the limitations of possession when multiple rights exist on the same asset, as it is perhaps the simplest way of publicizing hidden abstract in rem rights. This explains why it has been used extensively for announcing ownership in the absence of possession, as with valuable movables such as livestock, automobiles, computers and books. It has also even been used for spouses, with wedding rings being only a pale remnant of the variety of devices traditionally used to "give notice" of marital status. In classical Athens, it was also used to disclose security interests in land: a slab, known as *horos*, was posted on the parcel, to be removed only by releasing the encumbrance (Finley 1952). This system was one of the first to make an hypotheca possible – namely, the use of land as collateral without temporarily transferring ownership or possession to the lender. Similarly, posting of notices and advertisements was also used to claim land in the US West (Anderson and Hill 2002: 500). All these systems have serious limitations because it is difficult to make the brand indelible. More relevantly, they often rely on public registries of either persons or brands – for example, even cattlemen in the US West had to rely on government intervention to make cattle branding effective.[24]

5.1. The use of the chain of title deeds in real property

As we have discussed, conveyances in classical Rome became more private as *mancipatio* ceased to be required and *traditio* became less visible. Eventually, "in the late Roman law, as in developed English law, a conveyance was often, like a contract, nothing more than a document drawn up between the parties" (Nicholas 1962: 104). As mentioned by Nicholas, a similar process took place in medieval England, with delivery of deeds replacing delivery of land (Kolbert and Mackay 1977: 238–39).

The difficulties incurred when possession has to cope with multiple rights in rem can be alleviated by embodying abstract rights, such as ownership and liens, and even complementary consents in the conveying contracts,[25] which then form a series or "chain" of title documents or deeds ("chain of deeds"). The content of the deeds provides the relevant evidence of ownership and all other rights embodied in them, and title experts can examine the history of transactions going back to a "root of title." This should allow ownership to be separated from control (that is, possession in the sense of detention) without posing the risk that possessors may supplant owners. Similarly, the chain of deeds can also be used to enforce a security, by pledging the deeds with the lender, a practice found in Mesopotamia during the second millennium BCE (Silver 1995: 123–24).

But relying on the chain of deeds is also problematic. Above all, new possibilities for destruction, error and fraudulent conveyance appear. In medieval England, "the security of conveyances executed by feoffment accompanied by charter was a continuous source of worry to landowners, for both theft of charters and forgery of them were common" (Simpson 1986: 121). Centuries later, the most egregious cases were perhaps those involving counterdeeds, well described for centuries in modern continental literature (e.g., Alemán 1604; Balzac 1830). Even without forgeries or fraud, the system often gave rise to multiple chains of title, which left

---

[24] See, e.g., Anderson and Hill (2004: 139–41 and 149–51) on the evolution and regulations of the branding of cattle in the US West.

[25] This solution has also been used for a long time. For example, in the Demotic titles used in Ptolemaic Egypt between 650 and 30 BC, the consent of affected rightholders (usually the wife and coheirs of the vendor) was stated in a specific clause (Manning 1995: 254–55).

prospective acquirers facing a serious risk: they might find the title of the seller in his chain of deeds, acquire and eventually be defeated by the title of an unknown claimant based on an alternative chain of deeds. Title deeds may be even less effective than possession in reducing the asymmetry of acquirers, as possession is observable but adverse chains of title remain hidden to the acquirer, who can only examine the chain of deeds offered to him by the seller. This risk is also run by mortgagees, who may find out that their collateral is not owned by the mortgagor or is subject to a previous mortgage. In addition, pledging the titles with the lender poses similar difficulties to the Roman *fiducia* or English medieval *mortgage*: it subjects the debtor to the lender's moral hazards (for example, the lender could impede a sale or even fraudulently sell) and causes switching costs that make mortgage subrogation difficult. Nor does it lend support easily to the possibility of contracting second mortgages with different lenders.

Despite these difficulties, transactions on land in England heavily relied on the chain of deeds up until the last decades of the twentieth century. Typically, possession was used in conjunction with the chain of deeds to prove ownership, and mortgages were formalized by pledging the deeds with the lender (Sparkes 1999: 76–77, 479–82).[26] The potential flaws of the system were palliated by having conveyancing services provided by professionals. It seems natural to impose stricter requirements on the production of deeds when their effects are stronger, and guaranteeing professionals' quality provides a ready argument for restraining entry into the profession and regulating its practices. This seems to have happened in England from the very beginning.[27] Whatever

---

[26] There is also some evidence in the Roman Digest that real securities might have been reinforced by pledging the deeds with the creditor (Scaevola D. 13.7.43).

[27] Holdsworth (1927: 153) explains how the interest of lawyers was already behind the Statute of Uses in 1535. At the time, they impeded the enactment of a "well-considered scheme for the registration of conveyances" and then evaded the Statute of Enrolments by relying on subterfuge: a bargain and sale for a term of years followed by a release (153–59). The results were "a secret method of conveyance ... [and] large amount of complication in the law... making dealings in land expensive, because the whole history of the property must, on the occasion of each purchase, be critically examined by an expert" (165). Conveyance by bargain and sale for a term of years followed by a common law release was the general mode of conveyance until the nineteenth century (292). The conveyancing profession thereafter became a tight monopoly, as lawyers practicing conveyancing became specialists. "At the beginning of the nineteenth century, an intimate knowledge of the law of real property was almost confined to a comparatively small number of eminent conveyancers; and that the majority of lawyers – barristers as well as judges – depended for their information upon the opinion and writings of these conveyancers ... It is not

the effects on the quality of service, this will usually entail costs in terms of monopolization and technological delay.

5.2. Effective titling documents: negotiable instruments and powers of attorney

In general, multiple rights are hard to implement reliably through the chain of deeds. The absence of multiple rights is precisely what makes documentary formalization viable for powers of attorney and negotiable instruments, such as bills of exchange.

Negotiable instruments, such as promissory notes and bills of exchange, and those governed by similar rules (securities, letters of credit, bills of lading, and IOUs) also facilitate impersonal market transactions: assigning rights in such a way that the third party's information asymmetry becomes irrelevant. In general, the third party who acquires a credit formalized in this type of instrument is safe against defenses that the debtor (who acts as the "principal" in my framework) could plead against the "agent." For example, in bills of exchange and promissory notes, the obligation to pay is separated from the underlying transaction, such as the sale for which the bill was issued, unless the instrument returns to the agent. Therefore, a third party who has acquired the instrument in good faith has an unconditional right to be paid by the maker, even if the maker has a valid defense against the original payee (Méndez González 2007).

This is achieved without making the originative contract – that is, the instrument – public. Principals' commitment to the originative contract is ensured by a simpler solution: transferring possession of the instrument, once the principal has signed it, first to the agent and then, when the agent cedes it, to the third party. Consequently, the principal cannot cheat the third party by manipulating it. This solution, despite lacking publicity, is viable because the instrument involves only one obligatory right (that of being paid). Therefore, there are none of the usual difficulties arising from the existence of multiple in rem rights on the same asset as, for instance, with mortgages, when pledging the deeds with the lender. Nor are there several third parties who might be interested in possessing the instrument to protect their rights, with potentially damaging consequences for all others. (Note that, consistent with the legal nature of the

---

surprising to find that, from the beginning of the eighteenth century onwards, the practice and opinions of these conveyancers have been appealed to as the best evidence of the existing state of the law upon many questions connected with the land law" (299).

right involved, such instruments are used for personal transactions safeguarded by knowledge of the debtor's solvency). Significantly, modern forms of secured finance that allow multiple rights on the same movable assets (including accounts receivable) and thus need to prioritize such rights rely on registries, such as the one established by Article 9 of UCC on secured transactions.[28]

Similarly, despite the privacy maintained in documentary proxies and the dependent relationship of the authenticators, representation of individuals and legal persons is based largely on documentary proxies in which representation figures in a document but there is neither notoriety nor the need for registration, with the principal's commitment being ensured by similar means to those used for bills of exchange. On the one hand, the third party checks the proxy and retains, if not the proxy, at least documentary and often (at least in civil law countries) authenticated evidence. On the other hand, a revoked proxy continues to commit the grantor toward good faith third parties, as it is understood to generate an appearance of representation that third parties can trust. This efficacy of revoked proxies avoids the main risk for the third party, that of opportunistic behavior by the principal, who may renege on the agent's act if such reneging suits him. In the terms used above, when granting a proxy, the principal accepts being committed by the agent not only during the validity of the proxy but also afterward, until the power is taken back. Therefore, here again, the viability of this documentary solution depends on the existence of a single right (that of acting in representation of the principal). Revocation poses a problem that is to some degree equivalent to dispossession for a bill holder. But the solution is simpler than what is required for the latter, because of the personal nature of representation, in contrast to the real nature of the relation between the holder and the bill.

However, the efficacy of revoked proxies only transfers the risk to the grantor. In particular, the grantor is in a difficult position if, after revoking the proxy, the agent does not give it back. In such cases, it will be hard for the grantor to destroy the appearance of representation power that the proxy may still give to innocent third parties, which may harm the grantor. Avoiding such consequences may be easier for special proxies that authorize representation in a single transaction. This helps to explain why registration is often required of powers of attorney for general representation (those in which proxies remain in force after

---

[28] See Baird and Jackson (1983), as well as Kötz (1992: 96–97) for an international comparison.

being used) and organic representation of companies. In addition to saving costs in repeated uses of proxies, registration provides a reliable way of revoking them. Without registration, grantors would tend to rely less on proxies, hindering specialization.

Overall, the difficulties faced by powers of attorney and negotiable instruments are of a different order of magnitude than those suffered by chain of title deeds. This seems related to the fact that both powers of attorney and negotiable instruments involve single rights, where third parties can retain the contractual evidence, preventing possible manipulation of originative contracts by principals. This is consistent with the dilution hypothesis and its corollary, which propose that documentary possession is only effective as a titling solution in the presence of single in rem rights.

References

Alemán, Mateo 1604. *Segunda parte de la vida de Guzmán de Alfarache, atalaya de la vida humana*. Lisbon: Pedro Craasbeck.
Anderson, Terry L., and Hill, Peter J. 2002. "Cowboys and Contracts," *Journal of Legal Studies* 31:S489–S514.
2004. *The Not So Wild, Wild West: Property Rights on the Frontier*. Stanford: Stanford University Press.
Arruñada, Benito 2003a. "Property Enforcement as Organized Consent," *Journal of Law, Economics, and Organization* 19:401–44.
2003b. "Vías de acceso al Registro de la Propiedad: La experiencia española." *Revista Crítica de Derecho Inmobiliario* 79:3271–89.
2012. *Institutional foundations of impersonal exchange: Theory and policy of contractual registries*. Chicago and London: University of Chicago Press.
Forthcoming. "The Institutions of Roman Markets." In Giuseppe Dari-Mattiacci, (ed.), *Roman Law and Economics*, Oxford: Oxford University Press.
Baird, Douglas G., and Jackson, Thomas H. 1983. "Possession and Ownership: An Examination of the Scope of Article 9," *Stanford Law Review* 35:175–212.
1984. "Information, Uncertainty, and the Transfer of Property," *Journal of Legal Studies* 13:299–320.
Balzac, Honoré de 1830. *Gobseck*. Paris: Mame-Delaunay (under the title *Les dangers de l'inconduite*).
Blackstone, W. 1765–1769. *Commentaries on the Laws of England*. Oxford. Clarendon Press.
Buckland, William Warwick 1912. *Elementary Principles of the Roman Private Law*. Cambridge: Cambridge University Press.
Calabresi, Guido and Douglas, Melamed A. 1972. "Property Rules, Liability Rules, and Inalienability: One View of the Cathedral," *Harvard Law Review* 85:1089–128.

Caruso, Peter J., II 2000. "To Buy or Not to Buy: Protecting Yourself from Stolen Art," *Arts Editor*, August (artseditor.com, accessed July 13, 2013).

Coase, Ronald H. 1960. "The Problem of Social Cost," *Journal of Law and Economics* 3:1–44.

Demsetz, Harold 1998. "Property Rights." In Peter Newman (ed.), *The New Palgrave Dictionary of Economics and the Law*, 3:144–55. London: Macmillan.

Diamond, Arthur S. [1951] 1975. *The Evolution of Law and Order*. Westport: Greenwood Press.

Epstein, Richard A. 1998. "Possession." In Peter Newman (ed.), *The New Palgrave Dictionary of Economics and the Law*, 3:62–68. London: Macmillan.

Fernández del Pozo, Luis 2004. *El registro de bienes muebles: Los bienes muebles y la preferencia registral de los derechos inscritos*. Madrid: Marcial Pons.

Gaius 170. *The Institutes of Gaius*. Translation, Edward Poste. Revision, E.A. Whittuck. Oxford: Clarendon Press, 1904.

Hansmann, Henry and Kraakman, Reinier 2002. "Property, Contract, and Verification: The *Numerus Clausus* Problem and the Divisibility of Rights," *Journal of Legal Studies* 31:S373–S420.

Holdsworth, William S. [1927] 1977. *An Historical Introduction to the Land Law*. Aalen: Scientia.

Honoré, Anthony Maurice 1989. "Conveyances of Land and Professional Standards in the Later Empire." In Peter Goodwin Birks, (ed.) *New Perspectives in the Roman Law of Property: Essays for Barry Nicholas*, 137–52. Oxford: Clarendon Press.

Kötz, Hein 1992. "Rights of Third Parties: Third Party Beneficiaries and Assignment." In Arthur von Mehren, (chief ed.) *Contracts in General*, chap. 13. vol. 7 in *International Encyclopedia of Comparative Law*. Tubingen: Mohr Siebeck.

Landes, William M. and Posner, Richard A. 1996. "The Economics of Legal Disputes Over the Ownership of Works of Art and Other Collectibles." In Victor A. Ginsburgh and Pierre-Michel Menger, (eds.) *Economics of the Arts: Selected Essays*, 177–220. Amsterdam: North Holland.

Manning, Joe G. 1995. "Demotic Egyptian Instruments of Transfer as Evidence for Private Ownership of Real Property," *Chicago-Kent Law Review* 71:237–68.

Medina, Barak 2003. "Augmenting the Value of Ownership By Protecting It Only Partially: The 'Market-Overt' Rule Revisited," *Journal of Law, Economics, and Organization* 19:343–72.

Méndez González, Fernando P. 2007. "La inscripción como título valor o el valor de la inscripción como título." *Revista Crítica de Derecho Inmobiliario* 83:2059–164.

Merrill, Thomas W. and Smith, Henry E. 2001a. "What Happened to Property in Law and Economics?" *Yale Law Journal* 111:357–98.

2001b. "The Property/Contract Interface." *Columbia Law Review* 101:773–852.

Merryman, John Henry 2008. "The Good Faith Acquisition of Stolen Art." In John Jackson, Maximo Langer, and Peter Tillers, (eds.) *Crime, Procedure and Evidence in a Comparative Context: Essays in Honour of Professor Mirjan Damaska*, 275–94. Oxford: Hart Publishing.

Meyer, Elizabeth A. 2004. *Legitimacy and Law in the Roman World: Tabulae in Roman Belief and Practice*. Cambridge: Cambridge University Press.

Nicholas, Barry [1962] 2010. *An Introduction to Roman Law*. Oxford: Oxford University Press.

North, Douglass C. 1981. *Structure and Change in Economic History*. New York: Norton.

   1990. *Institutions, Institutional Change and Economic Performance*. Cambridge: Cambridge University Press.

North, Douglass C. and Thomas, Robert P. 1973. *The Rise of the Western World: A New Economic History*. Cambridge: Cambridge University Press.

North, Douglass C., Wallis, John Joseph, and Weingast, Barry R. 2009. *Violence and Social Orders: A Conceptual Framework for Interpreting Recorded Human History*. Cambridge: Cambridge University Press.

Oliver y Esteller, Bienvenido. 1892. *Derecho inmobiliario español: Exposición fundamental y sistemática de la Ley Hipotecaria, vol. 1*. Madrid: Sucesores de Rivadeneyra.

Patault, Anne-Marie 1989. *Introduction historique au droit des biens*. Paris: Presses Universitaires de France.

Rose, Carol M. 1985. "Possession as the Origin of Property," *University of Chicago Law Review* 52:73–88.

Sauveplanne, Jean-Georges 1965. "The Protection of the Bona Fide Purchaser of Corporeal Movables in Comparative Law," *Rabels Zeitschrift* 29:651–93.

Silver, Morris 1995. *Economic Structures of Antiquity, Contributions in Economics and Economic History 159*. Westport: Greenwood Press.

Simpson, Alfred William Brian 1986. *A History of the Land Law*. 2nd rev. edn. Oxford: Clarendon Press.

Smith, Adam [1776] 1981. *An Inquiry into the Nature and Causes of the Wealth of Nations*. Indianapolis: Oxford University Press/Liberty Press.

Steiger, Otto 2006. "Property Economics versus New Institutional Economics: Alternative Foundations of How to Trigger Economic Development," *Journal of Economic Issues* 40:183–208.

Tallon, Denis 1983. "Civil Law and Commercial Law." In Konrad Zweigert, (chief ed.) *Specific Contracts*, chap. 2. vol. 8 in *International Encyclopedia of Comparative Law*. Tubingen: Mohr Siebeck.

Weinberg, Harold R. 1980. "Sales Law, Economics, and the Negotiability of Goods," *Journal of Legal Studies* 9:569–92.

II

Specific issues

9

Possession and licenses: the FCC, weak spectrum rights, and the LightSquared debacle

RICHARD A. EPSTEIN

1. Introduction: possession and ownership, then and now

In this chapter, I examine the complex issues relating to the divided interests in various sorts of property, both old and new. The older forms of property are land, chattels, and animals, all of which were subject to an elaborate body of law that was well developed long before modern technical innovations created the new forms of property. One of these, property rights in the spectrum, is the focus of this chapter. In addressing this theme, I will deal first with some of the consequences that flow from the complex division of property rights in various assets, as they emerge in both private and public law disputes. As will become apparent, it is possible to identify a major, if worrisome, shift in the direction of the regulation of the different forms of property. Historically, the early law of both land and chattels sought to increase the security of possession of the various parties with an interest in the property. In contrast, modern regulatory schemes governing the spectrum often move in the opposite direction, by weakening the protection that property rights enjoy both against private interlopers and government actors, who, not surprisingly, often act in concert with each other.

In Section 2, I give a brief account of how these various interests emerged in early Roman and common law. My exposition will not delve into all the nooks and crannies of the law. Most notably, I exclude discussion of the full set of issues relating to common property on the one hand, and relative title and adverse possession on the other, to concentrate

---

Laurence A. Tisch Professor, New York University School of Law; the Peter and Kirsten Bedford Senior Fellow, The Hoover Institution; and the James Parker Hall Distinguished Service Professor of Law, Emeritus, and Senior Lecturer, University of Chicago. My thanks to Mateo Aceves, University of Chicago Law School class of 2015, as well as Chelsea Plyler and Harry Ritter, New York University School of Law class of 2016, for their valuable research assistance. By way of full disclosure, I consulted with Harbinger Capital on all aspects of this case. The opinions in this article remain my own.

exclusively on two sorts of relationships. I focus first on those relationships between two parties who have divided interests, and second on those between the parties and any external party, either private or public. In so doing, I shall address the relationship between leases and licenses. With these preliminaries in hand, Part 2 addresses certain complications that arise when this framework is applied to some key decisions and doctrines of the Federal Communications Commission (FCC).

In many ways, the motivation for this discussion is the FCC's highly controversial decision to revoke LightSquared's license for the construction of an advanced telecommunications system with the capacity to compete with the two communications giants, Verizon and AT&T. I worked in some detail on the case, and I was struck then by how the weak system of property rights allowed the members of the Global Positioning Systems (GPS) industry, both private and public, to pressure the FCC to cancel licenses. The FCC could not have imposed this action if LightSquared had strong property rights in the spectrum analogous to those given to owners and lessees of land or chattels. Unlike both patents and copyrights, the analogies from land and chattels carry over well to the spectrum, in which it is possible to create exclusive and perpetual property rights. Accordingly, as in other property contexts, the main function of government should be to police interference between neighboring users, rather than acting as a licensor with uncertain but powerful rights to terminate or alter licenses, even after private parties have made major investments in reliance on the validity of earlier private transfers and explicit government agreements. Ironically, the entire ongoing fiasco with LightSquared offers, as will become clear, indirect confirmation of the strengths offered by systems of strong property rights in spectrum, which should in my view serve as a normative model (Free State Foundation 2014).

2. Ownership and possession of land and chattels

One of the central maxims of English law is that possession is the root of title (Epstein 1979: 53). More accurately, the maxim states that possession of real estate is prima facie evidence of title in fee simple, so that the party who takes that possession is assumed to claim the largest possible interest that can be taken in the particular thing. The application of this maxim is clearly a more complex endeavor for land (given its durability and fixed features) than it is for chattels or animals, to which the principle has always applied in one form or another (Gaius 1946: Book II 66–68;

Justinian 1987: Book II, Title I 12–16). One application of the principle is to specify how a given party obtains ownership of each form of property that is regarded, as the Romans put it, as a *res nullius*, or something presently in the state of nature and owned by no one, but capable of private ownership (Gaius 1976: Book II 66; Justinian 1987: Book II, Title I 12). The first possession rule is the only way for a person to acquire ownership of these three classes of objects.

Once ownership is acquired through initial possession, it is necessary to determine what rights the owner gains thereby. With respect to land, the first taker (or indeed any subsequent taker) receives not only the exclusive right of possession, but also the right to use and develop the land (within the confines of the law of nuisance) and to dispose of it either in part or in full to some other person.[1] The simplest disposition is an outright sale or gift whereby the original owner transfers all his property rights to the buyer or donee, who then holds the same bundle of rights against the entire world – including the former owner – that the former own had before the transfer took place. For transactions in land and certain valuable chattels, high levels of formality – ceremonies, deeds, records – are commonly used because they signal to the parties when the transaction is complete and give notice to the rest of the world as to who now owns the property in question.

In most cases, moreover, possession of property is generally taken as (prima facie) proof of ownership, so that the protection of the former ordinarily supplies protection of the latter. Possession as an observable fact is typically easier to prove than title, which depends on a chain of deeds. Accordingly, most legal systems tend to organize a significant fraction of their remedies around possession. This linkage between

---

[1] For example, see *United States v. General Motors*, 323 U.S. 373, 377–378 (1945):

The critical terms are "property," "taken," and "just compensation." It is conceivable that the first was used in its vulgar and untechnical sense of the physical thing with respect to which the citizen exercises rights recognized by law. On the other hand, it may have been employed in a more accurate sense to denote the group of rights inhering in the citizen's relation to the physical thing, as the right to possess, use, and dispose of it. In fact, the construction given the phrase has been the latter. When the sovereign exercises the power of eminent domain, it substitutes itself in relation to the physical thing in question in place of him who formerly bore the relation to that thing, which we denominate ownership. In other words, it deals with what lawyers term the individual's "interest" in the thing in question. That interest may comprise the group of rights for which the shorthand term is "a fee simple" or it may be the interest known as an "estate or tenancy for years," as in the present instance. The constitutional provision is addressed to every sort of interest the citizen may possess. (Footnote omitted.)

possession and ownership starts simply, but it takes only a little time before an elaborate body of law develops to deal with those situations where ownership and possession are imperfectly aligned. Thus, the party who wins, for example, under the older writ of *novel disseisin* (recent dispossession) may be subject to suit by a party who can establish a higher title under the Writ of Right (Maitland 1936).

The situation becomes much more complex in those cases with the creation of divided interests in property, which happens with joint tenancies, trusts, leases, life estates, mortgages, and bailments of personal property[2] (Epstein 2009). In each of these situations, the gains from trade exceed the costs of putting the trade together, so that robust institutions develop each with their own rules that govern the rights and duties of the respective parties.

One central challenge for the law is to locate both ownership and possession in these various divided arrangements. In the unitary case, only the party who was deprived of possession can bring the action to recover the land or chattel. Yet once the property is divided by agreement between two or more persons, it becomes far more difficult to assign the remedy to the party who is in possession of the land or chattel, and this difficulty extends to more modern forms of property including spectrum. Whether we deal with old forms of property rights or new ones, the best approach is to engage in a form of reverse engineering: First, identify the kinds of wrongs that can occur, and then devise sensible set of remedies to deal with them. In practice, disputes with respect to divided interests fall into two classes. The first class deals with disputes between the two parties of any arrangement that creates a divided interest. The second class deals with the possession of the two parties with respect to some third person, whether an interloper or, in many cases, the government, in exercise of its eminent domain or regulatory powers.

In the first class, one problem arises where the party in possession on a short-term arrangement refuses to return it in accordance with the terms of the original deal. Alternatively, the transferee of the land or chattel uses it in a manner that is inconsistent with the terms of the original transfer, committing waste to land or damaging a chattel. Conversely, the transferor of the land or chattel may seek to regain its possession prior to the time for its return specified under the agreement. In dealing with these issues, I have studiously avoided answering the question of

---

[2] See *Coggs* v. *Bernard*, 92 Eng. Rep. 107 (1703).

who is in possession of the thing in question, an issue which has been deeply mooted throughout history (Nicholas 1962: 110–14; Pollock and Wright 1888). Thus with respect to land, it was often said that a lessee did not have possession, or more technically "seisin" of land because he only claimed a term interest in the property and thus did not aspire to become its sole and outright owner (Maitland 1885, 1886, 1888; Holmes 1881: 183–219; Pollock and Maitland 1895: ch. 2). An analogous position has been taken with bailees on the ground that their position is strictly that of "detention" because the bailee intends to hold property only for a limited period, without seeking to acquire outright ownership.

In resolving these disputes between two claimants with partial interests in the same, deciding which party has possession of the thing becomes something of a metaphysical question. In all these cases, the proper allocation of potential loss, damage, or delayed return is one of contract between the parties, to which the usual techniques of contractual interpretation apply. Explicit terms trump terms implied by law unless they are objectionable on grounds of public policy, which is not likely to arise in these standard scenarios. However, with informal arrangements, default terms become critical because they tend to supply the first and last word on risk allocation.

The greater challenge arises in questions dealing with the protection that is afforded to land or chattel when it is taken by a stranger or by the government, neither of whom are bound by any contract at all. At this point, it is often unclear which person or group is entitled to bring the action to recoup the thing or obtain damages for its loss. Nor is it clear that the traditional rule – that the party in possession should have the cause of action – applies sensibly in this case. Instead, the first question is whether both parties may or must join in the action to recover the land or chattel from the stranger. There is in principle no reason to object to joint prosecution of suits by the two parties, especially if they have entered into an agreement that covers the proper disposition of the land, chattel, or cash that is recovered. The basic insight on this point, well developed by Victor Goldberg, Thomas Merrill, and Daniel Unumb (1987), is that clauses of this sort will in fact emerge in those cases where the risk of third party action is large enough to warrant some sort of anticipatory response. That frequently happens with leased property subject to condemnation, but rarely for chattels, where the theft risk is usually small. Whenever these clauses are negotiated, they should be respected as ex ante settlements of future disputes, which eliminates the need to make tricky valuations of partial interests that are uniformly less accurate than valuations of the property as a unitary whole.

Nonetheless, much of the law of property develops in a world without these ex ante agreements, and in these cases, there is a real concern about the potential for duplication of actions. Thus in the Roman law of bailments, the question arises whether the bailor or the bailee should be entitled to maintain the action, and the rule in question often turns on which party has to bear the loss in the event that the recovery does not take place (Gaius 1946: Book II 203–07). Under Roman law, if the bailee will be held responsible for the loss, he retains the action because he must pay for the loss. But if the risk of loss is on the bailor, then the action is assigned to him, and the bailee is released from all liability. In these cases, there are savings in litigation costs that come from the proper assignment of the action. It often follows therefore that the term "possession" is denied to someone who has physical control over a thing if the cause of action belongs elsewhere.

> We are familiar with the saying that, of old, the termor was little more than his landlord's servant or bailiff. Now, it is a very natural thing indeed to say that a servant does not possess his master's lands or goods, though he has sole charge of them. Mr. Justice Holmes, in his lecture on possession, has well remarked how free-handed our old law as of its possessory remedies, how it attributed possession of goods to bailees whom the civilians would not have account possessors: still it drew the line above at the servant who, in his master's house, has custody of his master's goods (Maitland 1885: 335).

There is a great deal packed into a few sentences. First, on the question of bailments it is worth asking why it is "very natural" to say that the servant does *not* possess those things over which he has full charge. The modern approach, which defends the earlier result, rests on a transaction costs explanation. Once the thing is taken, it makes little sense to sue the servant for its recovery, when in the simplest situation that servant has to return the good or its proceeds to the employer at the end of the suit. It is far better for the owner to bring the action to recover the possession of the thing from whoever has taken it, which he cannot do if he is not deemed to have the right to its possession.

Accordingly, on this point, it is important to offer a note of caution about the position taken by Yun-chien Chang (Chapter 4). Chang argues that the overall desire to economize on information costs leads to a simple conception whereby "actual control is the necessary and sufficient" condition for a finding of possession. Of course, one obvious advantage of this rule is that it is often possible to identify who that actual possessor is. But that point is not true in all cases. Thus, things often are taken when they are not in the immediate grasp of anyone. The rule of actual possession does not tell us who is in possession of an object that is lying around on the back porch, and surely, it should not matter whether the party who last placed it there is the servant or the master. The key point in these cases is that the assignment of the cause of action to the owner of the thing and not the servant removes the complications that arise after the item, or damages for its loss, have been recovered, a point that the traditional rule recognizes.

On this view, the term possession suffers from an unavoidable technical overlay, which avoids the awkwardness of having a servant successfully recover the goods after he leaves the employment of his master, who is then required to sue for recovery of either the thing or the proceeds from the tenant. The dispute with the civilians rests on their insistence that the bailee cannot have possession because, as noted, he has no ultimate claim to the goods.

Indeed in one sense the servant's case is only one of many situations in the location of possession is uncertain under an actual possession rule. Notable difficulties also arise in cases where things have been lost on the premises of one party only to be picked up by another, as in the case of a customer who picks up banknotes lost by their owner in the public spaces of a store owned by someone else.[3] Indeed, that choice between competing claimants can arise in any case where there is a conflict between the possessor of the place in which a thing is found and the finder of the thing.[4] In all these marginal cases, the ordinary language approach to possession tends to break down and more ad hoc accounts have to be adopted to fill the gap.

The question of possession also arises in connection with the convoluted historical development of English land law, where again the creation of divided interests complicates the analysis. Historically, the most famous instance involves the termor, which is someone who enters onto the land for a term of years, with the permission of the owner. This case requires more detailed explanation because it oddly presages many of the difficulties that arise in the modern law of licensees in both intellectual property and spectrum.

---

[3] See, e.g., *Bridges v. Hawkesworth*, 21 L.J. (Q.B) 75 (1851).
[4] See generally *Hannah v. Peel*, 1 K.B. 509 (1945), which involved conflict between the owner of a large English house requisitioned by the army and the lance corporal who found a valuable brooch that had been lost in a window crevice. The corporal was awarded the brooch on the authority of *Bridges, Id.*, given that the brooch had never been embedded in the land.

Both Roman and English early law had a very broad conception of the contract for hire, which can cover either an employment relationship or the right to enter and use the land of another under a license-type arrangement. For these purposes, the employment side of the equation drops out of the analysis, but the question of licenses with land raises all sorts of questions hinted at in the last sentence of Maitland's quote.

Given this framework, it is important to see how licensees and leases interact with each other to set the stage for dealing with spectrum issues. Earlier Roman and English law did not regard the lease, no matter what its duration, as an estate in land (Maitland 1936). Rather, there was a personal contract of hire between the lessor and lessee, such that possession did not pass between the two of them, no matter what the duration. These licenses can vary by context. An invitation to a visitor to come to a home for an afternoon tea is a short-term license to one person. A public invitation to allow hundreds of customers into a store or restaurant or movie theater is a short-term commercial license. The standard of care for injury owed the entrant to the commercial premises is higher than that owed to entrants of residential premises. (Epstein 1999: 320–27, 329–31).[5] But for these purposes, the liability issues take a back seat to the conveyancing questions. The usual result of a license relationship is that the licensee has at most an action for damages if the license is revoked. But the licensee does not typically have an action for specific performance against the licensor; nor does the licensee have a right to prevent the sale of the property to a third person; nor does the licensee have a damage action for loss of use against any third person who takes over the property from the landlord.

Accordingly, the tenant could not sue the third party to recover possession – which formally belonged to the landlord. Now this relationship makes little or no sense where there is a single tenant on the premises for a long period. Indeed, in some of these cases, where the party let into property under a license makes permanent improvements to the land, some courts are willing to order the conveyance of the property if it is shown that the licensee did not intend to make a gift of the services or improvements to the other side, which is an instructive qualification of the basic rule.[6] By the same token, it makes a good deal of

---

[5] For discussion of the classifications, see on the English side, *Robert Addie & Sons. (Collieries), Ltd.* v. *Dumbreck*, (1929) A.C. 358 (Scot.), and on the American side, *Rowland* v. *Christian*, 443 P.2d 561 (Cal. 1968).

[6] See, e.g., *Seavey* v. *Drake*, 62 N.H. 3939 (1882) (specific performance when either purchaser or donee make extensive property investments); *Holbrook* v. *Taylor*, 532 S.W2d 763

sense in those cases where there are many roomers or boarders in premises on short-term leases, where the single right of action should belong to the landlord, who is in a far better position to maintain a unified claim against these parties, even if in some sense the roomers are in possession of their rooms. It follows, therefore, that in some cases licensees are the proper plaintiffs while in others they are not. Historically, the definition of possession was often altered to make sure that the party who is in the best position to maintain the cause of action is the party who is put in position to do so, which is well reflected in the short passage from Maitland quoted above.

To put the matter in fuller perspective, it is instructive to trace the evolution of the position of the long-term licensee – the termor – under early common law. The evolution of the common law system of licenses for land strengthened the position of the lessee against both the landlord and third parties. The earlier system, which treated the license as a contract for hire, had limited the tenant to a damage remedy for breach of contract against the landlord if the lease were removed, and possibly one against the landlord to pursue any third party who had forcibly ejected the tenant from the property in question. However, given the instability of the arrangement, the great procedural innovation in the post-medieval period developed, through a series of legal fictions, the action for ejectment, which allowed the former licensee the robust property rights of a lessee against both the landlord and the third parties (Maitland 1936).

There remain today some difficult questions as to whether certain types of contracts should be classified as leases or licenses, which usually depends on whether the parties intend to provide the strong protection that is accorded a licensee and is usually denied when the licensee's operations only involve part of some larger premises that might be sold to a third person. One case that demonstrates the potential trickiness of such determinations is *Macke Co. v. Pizza of Gaithersburg*,[7] in which the pizza restaurant leased vending machines from Virginia Coffee Service Inc., all of whose assets were later bought by The Macke Company. *Macke* turned on the characterization of the original contract between Virginia and Pizza of Gaithersburg: was it a license for the restaurant to use vending machines? Were the machines a concession that the

---

(Ky. 1976) (allowing estoppel when owner stands by when licensee makes extensive expenditures).

[7] *Macke Co. v. Pizza of Gaithersburg*, 270 A.2d 645 (Md. 1970).

restaurant could terminate on assignment? Or was the contract a lease that would bind subsequent parties? The court held that the lease survived assignment, even though the landlord had shown specific reliance in the choice of firms used to service the machines.

In many cases of this sort, the explicit contract between the parties takes an intermediate position that allows the tenant to assign a lease only with the consent of the landlord, which in turn cannot be unreasonably withheld. The logic of this standard provision is that it forestalls the holdout should the value of the property increase, but at the same time allows the landlord to make sure that his or her interest in the premises or the rent is not compromised by the transfer. Within this general framework, the correct resolution of any given case counts as strictly a second-order condition since there is no public policy objection preventing the parties deciding which arrangement to adopt. Greater protection for the lessee translates into greater compensation to the landlord, who then loses the right to make a free and clear conveyance of the property without the consent of the tenant. The property system is allowed to reach an efficient equilibrium.

3. Spectrum rights: property or license

3.1. Broadcast

The issues raised with respect to land also arise with respect to the spectrum, which by definition can only obtain value after technology is in place to allow for its exploitation. The institutional question then arises over the extent to which the traditional rules that accord ownership to the first possessor can apply in this area. On this score, I have long taken the position that the only way to develop a coherent set of rules for new forms of property is through thoughtful extension and comparison with existing forms of property, as for example with patents or copyrights (Epstein 2010: 548–59).

I shall not attempt to defend those propositions here, but I use the point to set up the discussion of the spectrum, where exactly the same kinds of issues arise. Do we have a top-down or a bottom-up system? Do we give strong or weak remedies to holders of spectrum? These questions again implicate the relationships between the parties to any transfer of spectrum, no matter how made, as well as the available protection against third parties. The current statutory framework starts with a top-down system, whose central provision is designed intentionally to keep the ownership of the spectrum in public hands, subject to license.

301. License for radio communication or transmission of energy

It is the purpose of this chapter, among other things, to maintain the control of the United States over all the channels of radio transmission; and to provide for the use of such channels, but not the ownership thereof, by persons for limited periods of time, under licenses granted by Federal authority, and no such license shall be construed to create any right, beyond the terms, conditions, and periods of the license. 47 U.S.C.A. § 301.

It should be evident from the text of the statute that the license does not confer on the licensee the strong form of possession that bottom-up ownership creates. The last sentence embodies the common principle that use of frequency in any way outside the term of the license will never create any prescriptive right. But for the same reason, the one yawning gap in this provision is its failure to provide a clear statement of what happens if the federal government decides to cut back on the license when the licensee is operating within the scope of the license.

The uneasy and unsatisfactory administrative compromise did not happen by chance. Historically, it was the direct outgrowth of the evolution of the ownership of the spectrum. The initial spectrum allocation arose in the wake of the failure to the nascent radio communication system to assist the H.M.S Titanic when she sunk on her maiden voyage in April 1912 (Ryan 2012: 9). As is so often the case, the initial regulatory decision on allocation, made in ignorance of the many technical and social developments that would follow, has largely charted the historical course for the next 100 years. Thus, the earliest allocation of the spectrum in the United States was by the Radio-Communications Act of 1912,[8] which made a generous initial allocation of the spectrum to the United States Navy, and organized the key spectrum divisions for other types of services, wholly without any knowledge of future intensity of use (Hazlett 1990). This system remains in place today, largely unchanged from the time of its creation.

Fifteen years later that law was followed by the Radio Act of 1927,[9] which addressed the pressing need for spectrum allocation that accompanied the rise of commercial radio, starting with KDKA, which began broadcasting from Pittsburgh in 1920. That system was doubly complicated because broadcast frequencies were allocated in a bottom-up

---

[8] Radio-Communications Act of August 13, 1912 37 Stat. 302, 47 U.S.C. § 51 et seq.
[9] 47 USC §§ 81–119.

fashion by adopting the rule of first possession to the spectrum, a decision that received some legitimacy through a notable Illinois private law decision, *Tribune Co. v. Oak Leaves Broadcast Station*.[10] The system set up two rival property rights systems for broadcast spectrum. In rapid succession, several key lower federal court decisions first denied then Secretary of Commerce Herbert Hoover the power to exclude new stations from the airwaves,[11] and then compounded the problem by refusing to allow the Department of Commerce to regulate power emissions from these radio frequencies.[12] In principle, a set of private actions could be brought to overcome the lower courts' conclusion, but that could only take place if the property rights claimed by the various parties were well defined. But in spectrum cases, any given signal will always interfere to some degree with countless others. Accordingly, the first possession rule cannot work well if it is construed to mean that the first use of a given frequency at any power allows for its continuous use at some greater power. The nature of the resource demanded more front-end social investment in designing a property rights system. The failure to make this investment was widely, and rightly, understood to make property right "chaotic" with uncontrolled entry.

It is important, however, to understand that the defects in this case did not undermine the case for property rights in spectrum any more than a free-for-all in which anyone could occupy whatever land he pleases or emit whatever pollution he wants would undermine a system of property rights in land. Of course, land requires a coherent system of title, which then is backed by the torts of trespass and nuisance. But that lesson was not quite learned with the spectrum, for the 1927 Radio Act did more than end the chaos from physical interference. Instead, in good top-down fashion, it undertook a notorious double switch whereby it first controlled interference, and then allowed the federal government to issue *licenses* to the bandwidth. These licenses were subject to basic government oversight – continued through the Communications Act of 1934 – imposed in the name of the public interest, convenience, and necessity. It is as though the only way to prevent conflicts over land use was to impose not only strong boundary conditions, but also extensive zoning

---

[10] 68 Cong. Rec. 216 (1926) (reprinting an Illinois Circuit Court decision of November 17, 1926).
[11] *Hoover v. Intercity Radio Co.*, 286 F. 1003 (D.C. Cir. 1926).
[12] *United States v. Zenith Radio Corp.* 12 F.2d 614 (N.D. Ill. 1926).

ordinances that specified the particular uses that each party could make of the frequency.

For our purposes, the central concern is with the security of possession and the capacity to deal with issues of title and transfer. In this connection, the system of licenses also produced a sharp deviation from the development that took place with respect to leasehold interests at common law. Although the long-term lease to a single party rose to the level of a fully protected property interest with respect to both the lessor and the outsider, the FCC licenses have taken the law in the opposite direction. Blocking a key dimension of the control that the licensee exerts over the frequency – use limitations, sublease limitations, and eviction limitations – has had unfortunate economic consequences.

The decisive intellectual moment in this historical sequence was an unfortunate peroration by Justice Felix Frankfurter, a stalwart of the progressive tradition, who wrote in *NBC v. United States*[13] that the standard of public interest, convenience, and necessity did "not restrict the Commission merely to supervision of the traffic. It puts upon the Commission the burden of determining the composition of that traffic."[14] Under this command, it is no longer possible to create, either by sale or by gift, strong property rights in fee simple to each frequency owner. Instead, that system is displaced by one that weakens the right of the licensee in several critical dimensions, all of which play a key role in the overall rights of the system. Left unregulated, the spectrum use rights are in many cases worth billions of dollars, but at every point that value is hemmed in by conditions imposed by license that could not be exacted if the system were organized on a bottom-up first possession regime.

One of the most troubling features of the traditional broadcast licenses to which Frankfurter referred was that they were not allocated by auction (which could work with well-defined frequencies), but by an administrative process that in good progressive style asks each application to explain the advantages that its ownership will give to the nation at large. Ronald Coase exposed the defects of this system in his classic article on the Federal Communications Commission (1959). Coase explained that this kind of "comparative hearing" encourages cheap talk on a massive level, since none of the claims needs to be backed with dollars. Moreover, after one year the winner often is allowed to sell the frequency rights to other parties, which helps cut down on the initial inefficiencies, but

---

[13] 319 U.S. 190 (1943).   [14] *Id* at 215–16.

nonetheless still has defects. The new licensee takes the license subject to all the limitations that the FCC imposed on the prior licensee, which necessarily reduces the resource value of that spectrum. The license restriction also means that any revenues derived from the sale go to the first licensee, not the government, which in turn encourages massive investments in preparing these license applications.

The restrictions on successful licensees, moreover, are not trivial. The short time horizons mean that the broadcast frequencies are subject to renewal in public interest type hearings that allow any member of the public at large, including organized interest groups, to complain of the performance of the licensee on any number of grounds. These threats lead licensees to settle these claims in advance of the hearing for either cash or broadcast concessions. This impetus to make informal settlements is unique to regulated environments; it never arises in connection with outright sales, where the outside protestors have no blocking position against the original licensee. To be sure, they can still seek to impose reputational damages on the spectrum owner, just as they could do with respect to any owner of any property. But the scope of those reputational sanctions is far weaker than any potential blocking position. In most cases, therefore, where property rights are strong, the outsider, with the spectrum as with any other asset, must therefore bid for whatever advantage it hopes to acquire. It is as though the landowner has to buy off all persons who wish to camp on his premises, instead of requiring each potential licensee to purchase approval from the owner.

In a world of zero transaction costs, the differences between these two positions would not matter because all such disputes could be resolved instantly to the perfect satisfaction of all. But in a positive transaction world, the great advantage of the common law system with its right to exclude is that it reduces by orders of magnitude the transaction costs needed to reach the efficient distribution of rights for the competing parties. To be sure, the administrative state represents an awkward middle position between the two extremes. There are no outsiders who can use the frequency as of right, for all such complainants must present some credible claim to the FCC to advance their interest. Therefore, the number of claimants is finite, but the cost to deal with them individually and sequentially is still quite high.

To find out whether these negotiations for spectrum licenses under the FCC serve any useful purpose, it is also necessary to see what other restrictions might come into play. Those who object to these negotiations generally complain that their interests are underrepresented, either on the frequency or in a particular market. Ironically, the very structure of the FCC makes that difficulty more acute than it should be. In the important decision *Cosmopolitan Broadcasting Corporation v. FCC*,[15] Cosmopolitan sought to accommodate the diverse interests of its listeners by subdividing its frequencies into smaller hour time slots that then could be dedicated to broadcasts in specific languages targeted toward particular groups. The use of this strategy allows small or fringe groups to enter the marketplace by acquiring time slots, which they can afford, instead of entire stations, which they cannot. This action is surely open to an owner under the traditional rules that allow for both assignments and subleases of all or part of the frequency. But they are not allowed under licenses, which impose a specific duty on the part of the licensee to make principled decisions on spectrum allocation. The case is a perfect exemplar of the dangers associated with the standard defense of the administrative state, so often associated with the work of James Landis: that a combination of political participation and professional expertise can outperform a market, which depends on secure property rights for its successful operation.

3.2. *Broadband regulation*

The difficulty with the government's licensing system is not confined to broadcast, but also extends to modern broadband regulation. Thus on individual use rights, the license becomes critical because government allocates a given frequency to a given class of use, the licensee is not allowed unilaterally to switch it to some alternative use. At this point the intensity of use in certain bands – such as mobile phones – is literally a thousand-fold more intensive than the intensity of use in other bands, such as for local police departments (Hazlett 2005: 248). This rigidity is inconsistent with any common law system of property rights but is all too consistent with zoning regimes, which received their constitutional blessing in 1926.[16] That same year saw the publication of a revised version of the Standard State Zoning Enabling Act, promulgated by a federal advisory commission on the issue convened by none other than Herbert Hoover in his role as Secretary of Commerce.[17] The federal government

---

[15] 581 F.2d 917 (D.C. Cir. 1978).
[16] See, e.g., *Euclid v. Ambler Realty Co.*, 272 U.S. 365 (1926).
[17] The relevant documents can be found at the website of the American Planning Association, www.planning.org/growingsmart/enablingacts.html.

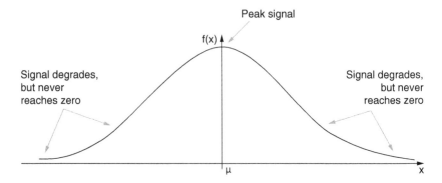

Figure 9.1: Normal distribution of frequencies

used this form because at the time it was widely understood that zoning issues were local matters outside the scope of the federal government under its commerce power, so that this advisory system was a way to exert federal influence on what was then a state system.

It seems perfectly clear that both zoning laws and FCC licenses represented a public unwillingness to rely solely on the nuisance law to police harmful interactions between neighboring property owners (Epstein 1979: 80).[18] Nuisance law offers strong protection against major physical interferences, subject only to a live-and-let-live rule dealing with reciprocal low-level interferences, where the rule on average leaves all parties better off than before. This rule has obvious impacts for the spectrum, where a signal causes interference as it moves out from its designated frequency. If the legal rule for spectrum interference sets the permissible amounts at zero, there could be only a single broadcast signal over the entire spectrum. But set a suitable signal to noise ratio, and large number of frequencies can coexist on a given band. The basic set-up looks like this (Figure 9.1).

Notice that this diagram exhibits a normal distribution of frequencies, but contains no explicit frequency designations. As with all normal distributions, it is possible to change the variance without destroying its two essential properties. First, the area under curve always equals one, which necessarily covers the outcome in every state of the world. Second, the basic symmetry of the arrangement is preserved regardless of the height of the peak. The lack of measurable units, however, is important

---

[18] The key case on live-and-let-live is *Bamford v. Turnley*, 122 Eng. Rep. 25 (Ex. 1862).

for an intensely practical reason. Set any particular signal to noise ratio, and the narrower the variance, the more broadcast signals can be accommodated in any particular band. Those sharper peaks are in fact the product of technological improvements, at which point using statutory licenses to set bandwidth for any particular activity acts as an unnecessary constraint on the license that destroys its value. This is in other words a classic case in which so long as the perimeter of rights in others is respected, there is no reason to impose extrinsic restraints on how property is used. In making this claim, it is also critical to note that the full body of regulatory takings in land – those that leave the landowner in undisturbed possession of the property – impose the same kind of allocative losses, which the live-and-let-live rule avoids in both contexts.[19]

The second key restraint in the nuisance case has to do with lateral support of the land of one by the land of another. Essentially the basic rule prohibits knocking down land up to the border so that the neighbor's land falls in. There are qualifications in the case of improvements, including that one landowner is not entitled to raise the scope of the support easement by building on land close to the boundary line. In dealing with frequencies, the issue of support has no literal parallel, but the question of using adjacent frequencies seeking to gain bandwidth is one that cannot entirely be ignored. Indeed, the multi-dimensional LightSquared case brings this issue to the fore. The weak protection of spectrum property rights leads to proposals whereby frequency owners will back off from their own boundary lines to accommodate trespassing behavior by other parties against whom there is no effective legal remedy.[20]

A similar element arises in connection with the third piece of the nuisance regime: the stout rejection of the "coming to the nuisance" defense, under which the party who creates high levels of noise or other invasive behavior against a neighbor who has not utilized his property is entitled to continue that use even after development takes place on the other plot (Coase 1960: 23–25).[21] The doctrine is often attacked on the ground that the first user should receive some kind of protection under the law, given that the second party to arrive on the scene is able to modify its land use deployment to take into account the preexisting patterns of use (Baxter and Altree 1972). But the weakness of this critique

---

[19] For the leading case, see *Penn Central Transportation Co. v. City of New York*, 438 U.S. 104 (1978).
[20] See infra at page 25 bottom.
[21] For the leading case, see *Sturges v. Bridgman*, 11 Ch D 852 (1879).

is that it ignores the incentives on the first party to begin his activity too soon. It is a mistake to allow early unilateral action by one party on his or her own property to increase that party's rights over a neighbor. It sets up a race to start premature development both to protect the usual bundle of common law rights and to expand those rights vis-à-vis neighbors. The coming to the nuisance rule means that a person need not actively protect rights before development in order to protect them once development takes place. So the first developer gets the benefit of uncontested interim use, such that – and the point was explicit in *Sturges* – the statute of limitations only starts to run when the actual incompatibility arises. This rule makes perfectly good sense for spectrum interferences as well, so that any spillover effects from early spectrum use do not gain any benefits from the conflict that eventually arises.

4. The LightSquared debacle

It is important to see how these rules dealing with the protection of property play out in the spectrum context. These disputes do not arise today with respect to broadcast frequencies, all of which easily fit into their assigned frequencies, which are too large for their stated ends. However, the issue does arise in connection with broadband frequencies, which are dedicated for the transmission of huge amounts of data. There bandwidth is always at a premium. Over the past four years, the catalogue of mistakes set out in the previous section are illustrated by what has been termed the "LightSquared Debacle" (Hazlett and Skorup 2013: 5).[22] The immediate dispute over the use of licensed FCC spectrum started when Harbinger Capital (for whom I have consulted on the many issues raised in this case) received a valuable spectrum license on March 26, 2010 from the FCC permitting the development of two bands of spectrum purchased by Harbinger from various parties over a period of about six years.[23] The spectrum that it purchased had been acquired

---

[22] Kang, Cecilia. "FCC treading lightly after LightSquared debacle," *Washington Post*, February 15, 2012. www.washingtonpost.com/business/economy/fcc-treading-lightly-after-lightsquared-debacle/2012/02/15/gIQAv60cGR_story.html.

[23] The account that follows is drawn from the complaint in *Harbinger Capital Partners LLC v. Trimble Navigation Limited* (filed August 9, 2013 in the Southern District for New York, case no. 1:213cv05543). For some aspects of this acquisition activity, see Hazlett and Skorup (2013: 16) who describe Harbinger's extensive dealings prior to 2010 with other carriers including Inmarsat, to which LightSquared had paid about $490 million by 2012.

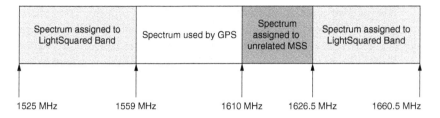

Figure 9.2: Distribution of spectrum in the "LightSquared debacle"

without consideration in prior transactions with the FCC. The distribution of the spectrum looks as follows (Figure 9.2):

The original license was not an outright transfer of spectrum that would allow Harbinger to use it as it saw fit. Rather, the license was made expressly conditional on a covenant by Harbinger that it spend around $14 billion to build out a national 4G (fourth generation wireless) network that by 2015 would reach about 90 percent of the American public, and which would serve as a new entrant to compete with the massive wireless networks owned by such large carriers as AT&T and Verizon. The FCC stated, "Using its terrestrial network, Harbinger proposes to provide service to at least 100 million people in the United States by the end of 2012 with an increase to at least 260 million people in the United States by the end of 2015." Toward that end, the FCC plan required Harbinger to build out its network so that it could operate *without regard to satellite coverage.*

In a series of complex corporate transactions, the new spectrum ended up in a new company known as LightSquared to which Harbinger contributed $2 billion in cash and securities. LightSquared also assumed, with the blessing of the FCC, the financial obligations that Harbinger had taken on itself in the construction of the network. The overall plan had been developed in close collaboration with the FCC, with public hearings and other proceedings, in which the GPS companies, who used their adjacent spectrum for both civil and military aviation as well as other purposes, actively participated, as did the Department of Defense. In reliance on the original arrangement, LightSquared entered into extensive collaborations with Sprint and Nokia. It launched a state-of-the-art satellite at a cost of approximately $1 billion, and took steps to secure a customer base consisting largely of major companies that could then subdivide that spectrum space for their own branded networks, such as BestBuy, to distribute to their own consumers.

One of Harbinger's major achievements was that its coordinated acquisitions allowed it to unify under common ownership the two blue bands, which previously had been held in far smaller chunks by a variety of parties. Once Harbinger acquired and unified these bands, it transferred them to LightSquared Corporation for an extensive development plan that both allowed and required it to enter into major transactions with potential development partners – Sprint and Nokia – a range of suppliers, and do extensive financing of about $2 billion on the project.

In order to make this system work, LightSquared needed to use the spectrum to operate a terrestrial system that started with extensive ground stations supplemented by satellite mobile communications. The spectrum it acquired originally had been designated for mobile satellite service (direct mobile to satellite communication). In the initial agreement, it was understood that LightSquared would deploy an unlimited number of ground stations to beam signals to satellites under what was called "ancillary" terrestrial use, in conjunction with the mobile uses for which the L-Band – the band that LightSquared owned – was licensed following a 2005 FCC rule.[24] At that time, there were no objections of receiver overload.[25] The term "ancillary" normally carries the meaning of secondary, but in this context that definition does not capture the original design of the LightSquared system, where, as the original March 2010 order made clear, the heavy lifting was to come from the terrestrial power, a plan which carried FCC approval. That situation was clarified later in the Handset Waiver the FCC issued on November 18, 2010, which made it clear that LightSquared did not have to use its initial mobile satellite service component in setting up a system if its leasing partners found greater flexibility in a terrestrial-only system.[26] The expedited waiver was granted because the change, if necessary at all, did not impose any additional burdens on the GPS carriers in the adjacent spectrum. It was simply a matter of increasing useful output within the approved envelope, without increasing externalities on adjacent GPS band, which qualifies as the prototypical Pareto improvement.

---

[24] *See* Joint Written Statement of Julius Knapp and Mindel De La Torre, before the House Oversight and Investments Subcommittee, Energy and Commerce, "The LightSquared Network: An Investigation of FCC's Role," September 21, 2012 at 7–8 available at http://democrats.energycommerce.house.gov/sites/default/files/image_uploads/Knapp.De%20La%20Torre.Testimony.pdf (noting the removal in 2005 of all numerical limits on the number of territorial base stations).

[25] *Id.* at 9–10 noting that these objections were first raised only in September 2010.

[26] *Id.*

One issue throughout this process was the potential issues with the so-called Out-of-Band-Emission (OOBE). These emissions are in the spectrum the equivalent of an invasive nuisance to an adjacent property owner (de Vries 2013).[27] The Telecommunications Act defines "harmful interference" as "any emission, radiation or induction that endangers the functioning of a radio navigation service or of other safety services or seriously degrades, obstructs or repeatedly interrupts a radiocommunications service operating in accordance with this chapter."[28] The general conditions of operation contain the key provision that "operation of an intentional, unintentional, or incidental radiator is subject to the conditions that no harmful interference is caused and that interference must be accepted that may be caused by the operation of an authorized radio station."[29] The clear implication is that receivers must be adjusted to deal with authorized frequency emissions. These provisions shape the interaction between emitters and receivers not only for radio broadcasts, but also across the board. Thus in its order of February 5, 2005, the FCC stated, "we do not regulate the susceptibility of receivers to interference from transmissions on nearby frequencies. Rather, we rely on the marketplace – manufacturers and service providers ... In addition, we generally do not limit one party's ability to use the spectrum based on another party's choice regarding receiver susceptibility."[30] There was thus in place prior to the Harbinger purchase of March 2010 a well-organized and consistent set of rights. Within that framework, LightSquared had worked in active collaboration with its GPS neighbors to overcome all the difficulties associated with OOBE emissions, which are subject to these explicit FCC prohibitions.

Of far greater concern in this matter was the activity of the GPS carriers that required the use of LightSquared's L-Band spectrum with respect to Out-Of-Band-Reception (OOBR), which occurs when a signal receiver – say, a GPS unit – fails to limit its reception solely to its designated band. One of the essential features of the overall GPS system was that it worked best when it received signals *outside* its own band, specifically, over the bandwidth that the FCC assigned to LightSquared

---

[27] de Vries recommends the use of minimum claim thresholds before receivers can protest emissions. However, he offers no explanation as to why the current rule that bars all such protests is inefficient.
[28] 47 U.S.C. § 15.3(m).
[29] 54 Fed. Regs. 17714, April 25, 1989, as amended at 75 Fed. Reg. 63031, October 13, 2010.
[30] See Harbinger complaint ¶ 118, quoting the FCC Order.

and its predecessor companies. As long as that spectrum lay relatively unused, the GPS carriers could use their OOBR in the LightSquared spectrum. But once the activity inside the LightSquared band increased, that capacity to receive signals was effectively compromised, which resulted in "interference" between the two systems.

It is at this point that the disjunction between the strong property rights and the FCC licensing system started to matter. Assume for the moment that the strong property rights system is in place. In that scenario, once LightSquared starts to use its frequencies, it need not be troubled by the diminution in value to the GPS on the adjacent system. Consistent with the coming to the nuisance doctrine, LightSquared does not forfeit it user rights in order to make sure that someone else could use its frequency. Indeed, to the extent that the GPS users block LightSquared use of its own frequency, they lay themselves open to both a tort action for the wrongful interference and a potential restitution action for the benefit received from its use of LightSquared frequencies.[31]

The basic point was not lost on the FCC, for in its internal documents, later released, Mindel De La Torre, Chief of the FCC International Bureau, explained the situation: GPS "has been driving in the left lane with impunity, but now that it looks like the left lane might actually have traffic in it, the GPS community is yelling bloody murder."[32] Within a traditional property rights approach, it becomes both possible and necessary to distinguish between the OOBE and the OOBR, because the GPS is entitled to protection only against the former, not against the latter. So the question then arises if in fact LightSquared has the full right to use its frequency, what happens next? One possibility is that the parties will engage in a voluntary transaction in which the GPS interests buy out the LightSquared interest, which they could do if the GPS in fact had greater use value for this spectrum band than LightSquared. If it were thought that there was some risk of holdout potential, the United States could condemn the spectrum that LightSquared has assembled for an amount equal to its highest and best use, which in this instance is for the build-out of its own terrestrial network. The government can then obtain reimbursement from the GPS community for the benefit conferred on it. But both of these alternatives will not be used if, as is the case in reality, the L-Band was worth more to LightSquared than to the GPS interests (Hazlett and Skorup 2013). That hypothetical result would vindicate one

---

[31] For the analogy to mining rights, see *Phillips v. Homfray*, 52 Ch. D. 401 (1883).
[32] Mindel de la Torre, email August 4, 2011, quoted in Harbinger complaint.

of the great functions of the takings system: it stops inefficient takeovers by imposing the same payment requirement for government use of eminent domain power as voluntary purchases.

Once the eminent domain purchase is aborted, under extant FCC guidelines, the GPS companies would have taken cheaper and cost effective steps by upgrading either their transmitters or receivers to eliminate the OOBR that resulted in the so-called interference with its own band, which was 50 percent larger than the adjacent LightSquared band. That result is consistent with FCC policy not to inspect receivers, leaving those questions for the companies to handle for themselves. At this point, moreover, the GPS companies have no incentive to exaggerate the costs of the adjustment because those overstatements will not create any effective claim against LightSquared. They still have to pay LightSquared for its lost value. Under this process, there is no need for any public inquiry to determine how effective these particular changes can be. The point of a strong property system, with its possessory remedies, is that it places effective discipline on both GPS carriers and the United States government. All that is necessary to keep this result is to treat the license as though it were a strong property interest once LightSquared had acted in reliance upon that license to upgrade and organize its own system, which is similar to the protection afforded an entrant into real estate who has entered that property under a license.

The situation, however, goes in the exact opposite direction once the license granted by the FCC is treated as revocable at will, without payment of compensation. Whether that can be done is a difficult legal question that has yet to be formally resolved in this case, but there has been some argument that the FCC statute gives no protection to a party in the LightSquared position. I think that this position has to be wrong as a matter of first principle, but for the purposes of this article, it is quite clear that neither the FCC nor the GPS companies acted on that assumption. Instead, they adopted in this context very fuzzy definitions of interference that ignored the basic regulatory framework set out above, and thus rendered it irrelevant who owned the frequency. In the view of the FCC, the property rights fell into the background, as the parties simply looked at two factors: who got there first, and whether the GPS found great value in its use of the system.

At this point, it was just a matter of time before the entire edifice came tumbling down. The first step in the demise was found in an order of January 26, 2011 whereby the FCC decided that LightSquared was only entitled to a "conditional waiver" of its handset rule that allowed for the independent deployment of its Ancillary Terrestrial Service, so that the overload issue (which had been resolved in March 2010) was now open for re-examination. LightSquared was required to participate in a workgroup with the GPS community to see whether there was any potential interference with GPS operations under the overbroad definition of that term. The clear message is that the interference from the incompatible uses is now the responsibility of the licensee of that frequency, and not of anyone else. Under these circumstances, all the incentives now switch, for it is in the interest of the GPS carriers to find serious interference with operations, which (unsurprisingly) they did. Thus in its letter of January 11, 2011, the government announced its concern for the possible interference with reception on LightSquared's L-Band, with an enclosed letter of December 28, 2010 requesting the FCC to "defer action." This would require a rule-making proceeding "to allow for the development of a robust public record and adequate interference analysis and mitigation options to protect GPS" and other federal activities that take place on that band.[33] On February 14, 2012, the day that the FCC suspended the LightSquared license, the US Department of Commerce communicated to Julius Genachowski, then FCC chairman, as follows: "Based on the NTIAS's [National Telecommunications and Information Administration][34] independent evaluation of the testing and analysis performed over the last several months, we concluded that LightSquared's proposed mobile broadband network will impact GPS services and there is no practical way to mitigate the potential interference at this time." The letter noted that matters could change in the future, but that at the very least the efforts to mitigate these losses were sufficiently complex that "the scheduled deployment" of the LightSquared system had to be postponed. All of the factual allegations could be contested, but not in a timeframe that could undo the damage to LightSquared (and the attendant social losses) from these events.

At this point, the economic and institutional incentives are clear. The GPS group now owes no money for its use of the LightSquared spectrum,

---

[33] Letter of Danny Price (Department of Defense).
[34] Letter from Lawrence E. Strickling, Assistant Secretary for Communications and Information, U.S. Department of Commerce, February 14, 2012, available at, www.ntia.doc.gov/files/ntia/publications/lightsquared_letter_to_chairman_genachowski_-_feb_14_2012.pdf (NTIA is responsible for coordinating spectrum use for the military and other government agencies).

so why should it bother to invest any substantial funds to deal with this issue? Now that the property rights had been effectively flipped, moreover, it was no surprise that LightSquared in the effort to deploy its network offered (unsuccessfully) to pull back from the boundary, by using only the lower portion of its L-Band, which was further away from the GPS band (Hazlett and Skorup 2013). It also offered to replace for up to $50 million all of the GPS units with newer models that did not depend on use of the L-Band. But that offer was rejected as well. Once again, there is no incentive to pay for any upgrade if your entitlement to other people's property is locked in as of right.

The position got only worse when toward the end of 2012 the GPS industry's lobbyists got a special bill through Congress that prevented the FCC from lifting the suspension until two onerous conditions were satisfied.[35] The first of these kept the ban in place "until the Commission has resolved concerns of widespread harmful interference by such commercial terrestrial operations to covered GPS devices." It then further required that any report be widely available for notice and comment procedures, after which an account of the matter had to be made available to a number of Congressional committees, all of which were intended to tie the hands of the FCC so that it could not reverse its decision unilaterally. Thus, social losses stemming from LightSquared's loss of spectrum rights are far higher than the gains to GPS from the use of the LightSquared spectrum.[36]

Following these developments LightSquared's entire business plan unraveled, and the company was forced to file for bankruptcy on May 14, 2012, which in turn has led to an epic struggle between LightSquared and its various creditors over the effort to reorganize the company. One key element of that process is the value assigned to the L-Band, subject as it is to the FCC order. LightSquared is solvent if the order is

---

[35] National Defense Authorization Act for Fiscal Year 2012, PL 112-81, December 31, 2011, 125 Stat 1298.

[36] For discussion, see Hazlett and Skorup (2013: 11):
> The best publicly available information, however, supports the claim that the decision to kill the LTE network was – by orders of magnitude – a net loser for society. LightSquared estimated that its network using 40 MHz L Band would generate about $120 billion (present value) in consumer surplus. One could dismiss these projections as biased, except that independent valuations of mobile radio spectrum in the USA yield higher forecasts – about $200 billion in social welfare (consumer and producer surplus). These benefits from permitting LTE dominate the cost of fixing whatever problems were alleged to occur with GPS receivers, estimated at about $10 billion by the opponents themselves.

removed, but in deep financial trouble if it is not. Therefore, the exercise of administrative discretion in the FCC necessarily clouds the entire reorganization. But even if that spectrum is released for use, the equipment put into place is no longer of any real value, and potential customers have made other arrangements for their spectrum needs, which further slows down its sensible deployment. It is hard to figure out the overall social losses that derive from these actions, but they are surely in the billions of dollars. The damage already done is nearly impossible to revert because the stickiness of political markets makes it impossible for any renegotiation of the FCC order among the various parties. It is pointless to trace in this context the ebbs and flows of the litigation wars in bankruptcy court before Judge Shelley Chapman, as LightSquared struggles to emerge from bankruptcy under a deal that divides the business between Harbinger and the creditors.[37] That division matters less from the social point of view than the massive destruction of value that ensued. Hazlett and Skorup (2013: 13) hit some of the key issues when they lament the complex administrative process that led to the suspension of the LightSquared licenses, which they attributed to the fact that "the L Band was not owned by LightSquared, which owns only licenses authorizing particular activities." From this fact they concluded that the dominant "public interest, convenience or necessity" gives LightSquared little chance to challenge this decision under the standard "arbitrary and capricious standard of administrative law," under which "it has no claim for a violation of its property rights in radio spectrum." From this proposition they conclude that the primary source of this resource misallocation "is the creation of a regulatory commons" that blocks the needed reallocation of property rights.

With respect, this analysis is not quite right, for it misses several key points that may be resolved going forward. First, the FCC licensing system did not create a regulatory commons in this instance. There was clear allocation of frequencies, and there were regulations on the books that imposed strong sanctions against physical interference. The rules in question also leave open the possibility of private rights of action in these cases, including the suit that Harbinger filed against the GPS companies for concealment and nondisclosure by the GPS group of its intention to

---

[37] For an update of the ongoing bankruptcy proceedings from May 9, 2014, see Kary, Tiffany "Falcone's LightSquared Bankruptcy Plan Rejected as 'Shell Game.'" *Bloomberg News*, May 9, 2014. www.businessweek.com/news/2014-05-08/lightsquared-judge-says-bankruptcy-exit-plan-can-t-be-confirmed.

block the deployment of the spectrum. In addition, the situation against the FCC is more complex also because the Harbinger claim is not brought under some legislative provision, but rests on a claim of breach of contract of the original license that was not justified by its intention to protect the GPS interests. It is quite clear that the use of the license arrangements embolden the FCC to engage in these actions. However, it would be most unwise in this setting to revert to the rules that held that a long-term licensee that has made massive investment expenditures should hold, as did the termor of medieval times, only a precarious interest that leaves it with no protection against the actions of third parties or those of the government. In this instance, the simplest way to achieve the right result is to hold that LightSquared was in possession of the designated frequency in ways that offer full protection against both its government licensor and its private opponents. Indeed, if anything, the acceptance of this legal position is critical, for any regime of weak property rights is far more perilous when government actors are on the scene than when they are not. Moreover, so long as property rights in the administrative state remain precarious, we can expect a repetition of these sorry events. The land paradigms should carry over to a situation where they could have eliminated massive litigation and senseless social loss.

In conclusion, it is ironic that the development of new technologies allows governments to repeat the errors that were corrected after extensive activity with respect to land and chattels. There is nothing distinctive about the spectrum that makes inappropriate the same system of rights that is used for land and chattels. The frequencies in question permit their efficient indefinite use. Spectrum is more like trade names and trademarks than it is like patents or copyrights, both of which work efficiently only if the property right is of limited duration. The nuisance law that applies to land can be carried over with little difficulty to protect the various possessory interests, without invoking a hopelessly broad definition of interference, which treats the victim of a tort as though it were the wrongdoer. The division of unitary interests in land or chattels is easily achievable by voluntary contract, at which point the law could follow the earlier patterns, which allow the transacting parties to determine the optimal division of rights while allowing each party to have protection against the harmful invasions wrought by others. Following these rules makes LightSquared an easy case, instead of the protracted and pointless struggle it has turned out to be. The property response to technological change often is the intelligent carryover of traditional systems of rights to the new area. That this has not been done for the spectrum and the social losses that Coase identified with the administrative system of weak entitlements remains all too true today.

References

Baxter, William and Altree, Lillian 1972. "Legal Aspects of Airport Noise," *Journal of Law and Economics* 15:1–113.

Coase, Ronald H. 1959. "The Federal Communications Commissions," *Journal of Law and Economics* 2:1–40.

    1960. "The Problem of Social Cost," *Journal of Law and Economics* 3:1–44.

de Vries, J. Pierre. 2013. "Optimizing receiver performance using harm claim thresholds, Telecommunications Policy," *Telecommunications Policy* http://dx.doi.org/10.1016/j.telpol.2013.04.008i.

Epstein, Richard A. 1979a, Nuisance Law: Corrective Justice and Its Utilitarian Constraints, *Journal of Legal Studies* 8:49–102.

    1979b. "Possession as the Root of Title," *Georgia Law Review* 13:1221–44.

    1999. *Torts*. New York, NY: Aspen.

    2009. "The Many Faces of Fault in Contract Law: Or How to Do Economics Right, without Really Trying," *Michigan Law Review* 107:1461–77.

    2010. "The Disintegration of Intellectual Property? A Classical Liberal Response to Premature Obituary," *Stanford Law Review* 62:455–521.

Free State Foundation Scholars Respond to the House Committee on Energy and Commerce's First White Paper, "Modernizing the Communications Act" Committee on Energy and Commerce, U.S. House of Representatives, (2014), available at http://freestatefoundation.org/images/Response_to_Questions_in_the_First_White_Paper_013114.pdf.

Gaius. Trans. de Zulueta, Francis 1946. *Institutes*. Oxford: The Clarendon Press.

Goldberg, Victor P., Merrill, Thomas W. and Unumb, Daniel 1987. "Bargaining in the Shadow of Eminent Domain; Valuing and Apportioning Condemnation Awards," *U.C.L.A. Law Review* 34:1083–1138.

Hazlett, Thomas W. 1990. "The Rationality of U.S. Regulation of the Broadcast Spectrum," *Journal of Law and Economics* 33:133–76.

    2005. "Spectrum Tragedies," *Yale Journal on Regulation* 22:242–74.

Hazlett, Thomas W., and Brent Skorup 2013. "Tragedy of the Regulatory Commons: LightSquared and the Missing Spectrum Rights," working paper forthcoming in *Duke Law and Technology Review*.

Holmes, Oliver Wendell 1881. *The Common Law*. Cambridge, MA: Little, Brown & Co.

Landis, James M. 1938. *The Administrative Process*. New Haven, CT: Yale University Press.

Maitland, Frederic W. 1885. "The Seisin of Chattels," *Law Quarterly Review* 1:324–41.

    1886. "The Mystery of Seisin," *Law Quarterly Review* 2:481–96.

1888. "The Beatitude of Seisin," *Law Quarterly Review* 4:24–39.
1936. *The Forms of Action At Common Law* A.H. Chaytor and W.J. Whittaker (eds.) Cambridge University Press.
Merrill, Thomas W., and Smith, Henry E. 2000. "Optimal Standardization in the Law of Property: The Numerus Clausus Principle," *Yale Law Journal* 110:1–70.
Nicholas, Barry 1962. *An Introduction to Roman Law*. Oxford: Clarendon Press.
Pollock, Frederick, and Maitland, Frederic W. 1895. *History of English Law*. Cambridge University Press.
Pollock, Frederick, and Wright, Robert S. 1888. *Possession in the Common Law*. Oxford: Clarendon Press.
Ryan, Patrick S. 2012. "The Itu and the Internet's Titanic Moment," *Stanford Technology Law Review* 8:7–10.

10

Jurisdiction, choice of law, and property

DANIEL KLERMAN

1. Introduction

Jurisdiction and choice of law in property disputes have been remarkably stable. While personal jurisdiction and choice of law for torts, contracts, and other areas of the law have changed dramatically, the revolutions in these areas have had little effect on property disputes, especially those involving land (Hay et al. 2010: 1230; Stern 2014). For the most part, the state in which the property is located has exclusive jurisdiction over disputes about the property, and that state's law will be applied to the dispute.[1] While there has been some criticism of this "situs rule," and some have called the exclusive jurisdiction of a state over real property the "land taboo" (Note 1938: 1051; Hancock 1967), the same rules that applied in the nineteenth century continue to apply today in most cases.[2]

This chapter uses new economic theories of adjudicative jurisdiction[3] and choice of law to analyze property disputes, with particular emphasis

---

Charles L. and Ramona I. Hilliard Professor of Law and History, USC Law School. The author thanks Scott Altman, Avi Bell, Patrick Borchers, Michael Hoffheimer, Daniel Kelly, Kevin Klermont, Erin O'Hara O'Connor, Henry Smith, James Stern, and participants in the 5th Law and Economic Analysis Conference, Academica Sinica, Taiwan, for comments and suggestions.

[1] This chapter will use the term "state" to refer both to independent countries (such as France or Japan) as well as to US states (such as Massachusetts or California).

[2] One notable exception is succession, where, in a number of countries, the law of the decedent's last domicile controls all aspects of the probate, even if there is real property in another state. Other exceptions have been created for personal property, especially liens. The author thanks Patrick Borchers and Michael Hoffheimer for pointing out these exceptions.

[3] Adjudicative jurisdiction is the authority of the courts of a state to determine a legal dispute. In most situations, personal jurisdiction and adjudicative jurisdiction are synonyms. On the other hand, some authors do not use the term "personal jurisdiction" when the issue is jurisdiction to adjudicate a dispute that is "in rem." For this reason, this chapter will not use the term "personal jurisdiction" when talking about jurisdiction to adjudicate property disputes, and instead will use "adjudicative jurisdiction" or simply "jurisdiction."

on disputes involving possession. In many instances, for example disputes regarding the acquisition of water rights, this new analysis provides fresh reasons to support existing rules. In other areas, for example adverse possession of stolen art, economic analysis supports rules not currently applied by most courts, such as application of the law of the place where an owner with undisputed title last possessed the property.

This chapter's conclusion that the situs rule is largely correct is similar to that reached by James Stern (Stern 2014). Nevertheless, his analysis is different. Whereas Stern emphasizes the way the situs rule facilitates uniformity, the analysis here focuses on individual behavior and on legislative and judicial incentives to develop efficient law. Stern's article contrasts sharply with Bell and Parchomovsky (2005), "Of Property and Federalism." Bell and Parchomovsky argue that, in most cases, parties should be able to choose the property law they prefer, rather than being forced to follow the law of the place the property is located. The tension between Bell and Parchomosky's article and this chapter is more apparent than real. Bell and Parchomovsky focus on doctrines, such as co-tenancies and easements, that govern rights among small groups of people, all of whom would need to consent to the choice of foreign law to govern their rights. In contrast, this chapter focuses on rules that affect third parties – future acquirers of water rights and unknown prior owners of stolen art. Even Bell and Parchomovsky concede that parties should not be able to choose applicable law in circumstances such as these where there are significant externalities.

Section 2 of this chapter deals with choice of law. Section 2.1 explains the economic approach to choice of law. This approach focuses on the effect of choice of law rules on primary behavior (such as whether to acquire a piece of land or where to sell a work of art) and on the incentive of judges and legislators to make efficient or inefficient law. The ideal choice of law rule gives judges and legislators incentives to make laws that give individuals incentives to act efficiently. Bad choice of law rules give judges and legislators incentives to make laws that inefficiently redistribute wealth to citizens of their states and give individuals and corporations incentives to take actions that reduce social welfare.

Section 2.2 applies this approach to the acquisition of water rights. Traditional territorial rules are generally efficient. They give states incentives to make efficient rules that maximize the value of water resources. In addition, they ensure that land to which water rights attach goes to the persons or entities that are likely to make best use of the land and attendant water, regardless of the residence or citizenship of the potential possessors of those rights. In contrast, under choice of law rules that would make water rights dependent on the residence of the right's holder, land to which water attached would go to residents of states with the most aggressive water law, rather than to those who might make the best use of the land and water. Furthermore, such choice of law rules might encourage some states to formulate rules that gave their residents advantages in acquiring rights in other states, even if those rules reduced overall welfare.

Section 2.3 shows how similar reasoning supports the traditional, territorial rule in most disputes relating to real property, including adverse possession. It also shows how similar reasoning supports the traditional rule in disputes about the acquisition of rights to wild animals.

Section 2.4 turns to stolen art. When the owner (or his or her descendants) tries to reclaim stolen art from a bona fide purchaser, choice of law can make an enormous difference, because some states give the bona fide purchaser strong rights (usually through the doctrine of adverse possession) while others limit the operation of adverse possession. Most courts currently apply the law of the state where the stolen art was sold to the bona fide purchaser. As some commentators have pointed out, this rule encourages art thieves to sell their loot in jurisdictions whose laws favor bona fide purchasers. In addition, this rule gives states incentives to make their laws favorable to bona fide purchasers, because doing so attracts art business to their state. In contrast, a choice of law rule that applied the law of the last place of undisputed ownership would give thieves no incentive to sell in a place with more favorable law. In addition, it would give states incentives to develop law that reaches an efficient balance between protecting property from theft and encouraging a vigorous (legitimate) art market.

Section 3 addresses jurisdiction. Section 3.1 explains the economic approach to adjudicative jurisdiction. That approach focuses on two factors: litigation costs and quality of law. The ideal jurisdictional rule minimizes litigation costs and gives judges and legislators incentives to choose efficient choice of law rules and to reduce bias in adjudication. In contrast, bad jurisdictional rules increase litigation costs. They also give judges and legislators incentives to tolerate or facilitate biased adjudication. Finally, bad jurisdictional rules encourage judges and legislators to choose choice of law rules that inefficiently redistribute wealth to in-state residents.

Section 3.2 applies the economic analysis of jurisdiction to disputes about water rights. Litigation in the courts of the state in which the water would be acquired usually minimizes litigation costs, because at least one party is usually from that state and witnesses are likely to be from that state. In addition, because owners want high prices for land (because eventually they know they are likely to sell), and because most owners are residents of the state where the property is located, a state has an incentive to maximize the value of land in the state. Since water rights are usually attached to land, this gives the state where the relevant land is located an incentive to allocate water rights efficiently through a choice of law rule that mandates application of its own law, and through efficient substantive law and fair adjudication. In contrast, if the state in which an out-of-state claimant resided had jurisdiction over the dispute, litigation costs would be higher and that state would have an incentive to adopt rules and institutions that favored its own residents, because the costs of the resulting inefficiency would mostly be borne by residents of other states.

Section 3.3 shows that similar reasoning favors jurisdiction in the state where the property is located in most disputes related to real property and in disputes related to the acquisition of rights to wild animals.

Section 3.4 addresses jurisdiction in disputes over stolen art and suggests that there is no clear-cut answer to what would be the most efficient forum. Nevertheless, in many cases the courts of the place where the art last was undisputedly owned is a good candidate. Witnesses relating to the alleged theft are likely to be there. In addition, the claimant or his or her descendants may still live there. That state also has an incentive to be unbiased. If neither claimant still lives there, it is neutral. Even if the claimant and his or her descendants still live there, the state has some incentive to be even handed, because those who live there and own art want a vigorous market for that art, and adjudication biased against bona fide foreign purchasers would undermine that market.

2. Choice of law

2.1. Economic analysis of choice of law

There are two dominant approaches to choice of law: the traditional approach and interest analysis. The traditional approach was dominant in the United States. until the 1960s and remains influential in other parts of the world. For the most part, the traditional approach is territorial, so applicable law is the law of the place where a relevant event took place or relevant property is located. Therefore, in tort cases, the traditional approach applies the law of the place where the injury was suffered.

In property disputes, applicable law is usually the law of the place where the property is located. For the most part, the traditional approach is composed of a multitude of rules that attempt to set out clearly the law to be applied in all situations (American Law Institute 1934).

Starting in the 1950s, American academics pioneered a choice of law approach based primarily on the analysis of the interests of relevant states, and starting in the 1960s this approach was adopted by most courts. Therefore, for example, if there were a car accident in Canada that injured two New Yorkers, New York might be the only state with an interest in resolving the case, so New York law would apply. Or, if Canada's interest were acknowledged, New York's interest might be judged more important, again leading to application of New York law. Although there are many variations of interest analysis – including Brainerd Currie's original approach, comparative impairment, New York's approach, and the Restatement Second (which is a hybrid of many approaches) (Symeonides 2006) – the differences are not relevant here. In general, interest analysis makes applicable law much more dependent on the residence of the parties than the traditional approach, which was based more on the location of property or important events. In addition, interest analysis tends to eschew bright line rules in favor of case-by-case adjudication (Symeonides 2006: 11–43).

There is no single economic approach to choice of law. The earliest economic analysis was William Baxter's 1963 comparative impairment theory, which was a variant of interest analysis. More recent economic analyses have focused on individual welfare rather than state interests, and that will be the approach adopted in this chapter. Modern economic approaches focus on incentives for efficient primary behavior and incentives for the creation of efficient substantive law.[4]

Some economic approaches to choice of law generally take substantive law as a given and seek to find the choice of law rule that will result in application of the substantive law that is most efficient for the dispute. For example, in torts, Posner (2011) has argued that the state where an accident takes place usually has a "comparative regulatory advantage" and therefore its law is likely to be most efficient and should be applied. More generally, the goal of choice of law should be to find "which state's law makes the best fit with the circumstances of the dispute" (Posner 2011: 807). In the international tort context, Jack Goldsmith and Alan

---

[4] Bruce Hay (1992) takes the further step of asking what choice of law rules states will have an incentive to choose.

Sykes emphasize the way in which bad choice of law rules can distort parties' incentives (Goldsmith and Sykes 2007; Sykes 2008). For example, if more stringent US tort law applies to torts committed by US companies in Nigeria, while Nigerian law applies to Nigerian or French companies in Nigeria, then US companies will be at a competitive disadvantage in Nigeria. Even if American companies possessed superior technology or were more efficient in other ways, the more stringent laws applied to them would force them out of the market.

Other scholars take a step back and ask how choice of law rules affect the creation of substantive law. Some rules give states incentives to develop efficient law, while others encourage wasteful redistribution. In the contractual context, O'Hara and Ribstein (2000, 2009) argue that, in most circumstances, honoring contractual choice of law clauses will allow parties to choose the most efficient law for their relationship and that doing so will encourage states to generate efficient law. McConnell (1988) focused his analysis on product liability and showed that the traditional rule, which allows victims to sue where they are injured, encourages pro-plaintiff law, because states can enrich their residents by awarding high damages. While in-state residents get the benefits of those damages, the cost is likely to be passed on to consumers in all states. As a result, high damages redistribute wealth from out-of-state consumers and corporations to in-state residents. In contrast, he argued that applying the law of the place of sale would encourage efficient law. Because manufacturers could adjust prices to reflect liability exposure, there is little or no potential for interstate wealth distribution. As a result, legislators and courts would have incentives to create efficient law, because in-state citizens would both get the benefits of higher liability and pay the cost.[5] Guzman (2002) generalized McConnell's approach and applied it to a variety of regulatory situations. For example, he argued that if courts apply the law of the place where the injurious action took place,[6] states will under-regulate because they will take into account the costs of regulation (which will be borne almost exclusively locally), but will not fully consider the benefits of regulation (which will accrue in

---

[5] See critique in Hay (1992).
[6] Guzman (2002: 909) calls this "territoriality," but this chapter will reserve that term for the traditional approach. Under the traditional approach, as exemplified by the First Restatement of Choice of Law, the law governing a tort is usually the place where harm occurs, not the place where the harm-causing action takes place. Under Guzman's nomenclature, the traditional approach would involve extra-territorial application of law.

part to citizens of other states). Conversely, applying the law of the place of injury will result in over-regulation, because a state in which victims but not the injurer resides will get the benefits of more stringent regulation, but bear only some of its costs.[7]

2.2. Choice of law and water rights

There are two main legal regimes governing rights to water from streams and rivers.[8] Under the riparian system, persons[9] owning land adjacent to a river can use a reasonable amount of water. Under the prior appropriation system, the first person to use a particular amount of water acquires the right to use that amount of water indefinitely. Both systems are currently overlaid with a substantial regulatory regime, both for environmental protection and, under the prior appropriation system, to prevent disputes about whose use was prior and how much water the prior user is entitled to. Nevertheless, for simplicity, this section will assume less complex versions of the riparian and prior use regimes, without their more recent regulatory overlays. Although under the prior appropriation system water rights can technically be acquired by persons who do not own land adjacent to the river or stream, this chapter will assume that acquisition, whether under the riparian or the prior acquisition system, is by a person owning land adjacent to the river or stream, because otherwise the person acquiring the water would ordinarily be a trespasser.[10]

The law of the state where the land from which the water was drawn is located universally governs water rights. Although that rule has not been subjected to economic analysis, it makes sense from an economic point of view.

Under Posner's approach, the state in which the river or stream is located has a comparative regulatory advantage, and its law is most likely to be efficient for water uses in its territory. For example, Carol Rose has argued that the riparian system is more efficient when water use is nonconsumptive (for example, for waterpower), whereas the prior use system is more efficient when use is consumptive (for example, for

---

[7] Guzman (2002: 906) calls such a choice of law regime "extra-territoriality," but, as explained in the prior footnote, this chapter avoids that term.
[8] For water law generally, see Tarlock (2013).
[9] This chapter will use the term "person" to refer to natural persons, corporations, and other entities that can own land or operate a business.
[10] Acquisition by a nonlandowner is particular relevant when the land is public or when the owner of mineral rights uses water (Tarlock 2013: 5: 26–27).

mining). Thus, in the nineteenth century, eastern US states adopted the riparian rule, while western states adopted the prior acquisition rule (Rose 1990). Applying the law of the place where the water is drawn thus usually ensures application of the law that is efficient for that place.

Applying a territorial rule – that is, applying the law of the state where the relevant land is located – also makes sense under Jack Goldsmith's and Alan Sykes' approach, because it assures that all who might use water in a particular location will ordinarily be governed by the same legal regime. As a result, the person (or corporation) who will put the water to its most productive use will be the one to acquire the rights. For example, suppose water is needed to mine minerals on a piece of property adjacent to a stream. If one person has superior mining technology or more efficient management, it would be willing to pay more for the land if it were sold on the open market. Even if a less efficient producer currently owned the land, the more efficient miner should be able to offer the current owner a price that would induce the current owner to sell.

On the other hand, suppose water law were determined by the citizenship or residence of the person acquiring the rights.[11] Suppose further that the amount of water allowed by the riparian regime would not be sufficient to operate the mine, but that the amount of water allowed by the prior acquisition system would be, and that the more efficient producer resides in a riparian state, while other potential producers reside in prior acquisition states. In this situation, the less efficient producers will land up operating the mine. If the relevant property were sold on the open market, the efficient owner from the riparian state wouldn't even bid, because it would not be able to secure sufficient water to operate the mine. Similarly, if the current owner were a less efficient miner, then the more efficient miner would not be able to offer an attractive price to buy out the less efficient miner.

Of course, if the situation described in the prior paragraph really occurred, clever businessmen and lawyers would probably find ways around the inefficiency, as Coase would predict. Perhaps the efficient miner, if an individual, would establish residence in a prior acquisition state. Or the efficient miner, if a corporation would reincorporate or establish its primary place of business in a prior acquisition state.

---

[11] Such a result might occur under interest analysis, because under interest analysis rights are often dependent on the residence or domicile of the disputant. Nevertheless, even under interest analysis, courts are likely to decide that the state in which the relevant water and land is located has the sole or dominant interest and apply that state's law.

Or, perhaps the efficient miner would purchase the water rights from an owner who resided a prior acquisition state. For example, if the current owner were a less efficient miner, the efficient miner might not buy the land, but rather might buy the right to mine and the right to use the water, while leaving the inefficient miner as the owner of the land with the right to appropriate the water. Of course, whether the law of relevant states would respect the water rights acquired in this way is a question that (fortunately) has never had to be answered. In any case, all of these solutions involve transactions costs. Therefore, even if a nonterritorial allocation of water rights didn't result in inefficient use of the water, it would result in unnecessary transactions costs, which are themselves a type of inefficiency. Furthermore, the additional transactions costs are likely to block some beneficial uses of the water.

A nonterritorial approach to water rights would cause other inefficiencies as well. Whether water rights are governed by one legal regime or another affects not just the development of the land at issue, but also all downstream users. That is, water law is fundamentally concerned with managing externalities (Smith 2008). The riparian and prior acquisition regimes manage those externalities differently, but the efficiency of either system is impaired when some users can opt into the other legal regime. For example, suppose all current users of a given river are governed by the prior acquisition system and, under that system, no water is available for further appropriation. If a new user were governed by the riparian system, it could use a reasonable amount of water, even though that would reduce the amount of water available to downstream users, thus potentially impairing more productive uses of the water.[12]

---

[12] Of course, it is possible that allowing the identity of the landowner to change the legal regime could increase efficiency in particular cases. For example, suppose, in a prior acquisition state, Y is downstream and has a right to a large amount of water, but uses it inefficiently. Suppose further that X is upstream and has a right to little water, but would use the water efficiently, if he had more. Ordinarily, X and Y would be expected to bargain to reallocate some of Y's water rights to X. Because X would use the water more productively, X and Y should be able to reach a mutually beneficial agreement. Nevertheless, bargaining might breakdown, or legal impediments might block the sale, or Y might not be willing to sell X the water rights he needs. In this situation, it would be efficiency enhancing if X could sell his land to someone, Z, who lives in a riparian state and who could pursue the same efficient use as X planned. Nevertheless, while efficiency would be enhanced under these particular facts, it would make terrible policy to allow purchase to change the legal regime for two reasons. First, this is a setting of low transactions costs, so X and Y should ordinarily be able to bargain to the efficient solution, and second, nothing guarantees that Z will use the water any more efficiently than Y. It might be profitable for Z to buy the land even if he were to planning to use the water less efficiently than Y. The

Andrew Guzman's approach looks at the incentives states have to develop efficient water law in the first place. For example, it was suggested above that an application of Posner's comparative regulatory advantage approach would result in efficient law, because states have incentives to develop law appropriate for the geography and water uses prevalent in their state. This argument is strongest when rivers and streams are located wholly within one state. When, as is common, rivers border or flow through several states, Guzman's approach, which emphasizes the strategic interaction between states, suggests that a territorial approach may not lead to efficiency. When a river is bordered by more than one state, the state whose residents are in a position to acquire a disproportionate share of the rights first has an inefficient incentive to adopt the prior acquisition system, even if riparian rights would be more efficient overall. Conversely, a state whose residents had lost the race to acquire water rights would favor the riparian system, because that would allow its residents to make reasonable use of the water, even if doing so interfered with water rights acquired by residents of other states under the prior acquisition system. In the situation where multiple states have an interest in a given water or stream, no choice of law rule gives states incentives to develop efficient law.

Although incentives to adopt efficient water law are therefore not perfect under the territorial approach, they may be good enough. Whether the territorial approach actually causes states to adopt inefficient water law depends on three factors: the proportion of rivers and streams that are wholly within a state, whether states could develop different water regimes for rivers wholly within a state and those that are shared, and cooperation between states. If nearly all usable rivers and streams were wholly within a state, and if a state were constrained to develop uniform water law,[13] the state would have an incentive to develop efficient water law. While inefficient water law might aid its residents in acquiring water from rivers shared with other states, the cost in inefficient water use for wholly local streams and rivers would be too

---

argument in this footnote is similar to one of the economic arguments for laws against theft. It is true that a thief may sometimes value a piece of property more than the current owner. However, it is usually better to encourage the potential thief to buy the property from the current owner rather than steal it, because if theft were allowed more generally, most thefts would involve situations where the thief valued the property less than the current owner.

[13] An attempt to apply different law to interstate versus intrastate rivers might be a violation of the Commerce Clause of the US Constitution.

great. On the other hand, if a state were allowed to vary its laws, it could adopt efficient water law for wholly internal waters, but apply the legal regime that favored its residents to rivers shared with other states. Fortunately, since the number of affected states is small (perhaps only two), they will often be able to reach an efficient solution through negotiation. That solution might involve both states coordinating on a single choice of law rule for water drawn from shared rivers, or it might involve allocating water quotas to each state. On the other hand, one should not underestimate the danger that negotiations will break down and inefficient water use will result. For this reason, in the United States, the federal government has the power to allocate water between states and to resolve interstate disputes about water.

2.3. Choice of law and most other property disputes

Economic analysis suggests that most other property disputes are properly governed by the territorial approach. For example, the law of the state in which the land is located appropriately governs rules about adverse possession of land. If the rules varied with the residence of the adverse possessor, there would be an incentive for adverse possessors to transfer their possession to residents of states with shorter statutes of limitations. In addition, states that wanted to give their citizens an advantage in adverse possession disputes might inefficiently shorten their statutes of limitations, although that seems unlikely, because of the inefficiency doing so would cause for locals in disputes with their neighbors.

Similarly, the right to acquire wild animals is best determined by the law of the place where the animal is captured rather than by the residence of the hunter. The state in which the hunting takes place is in the best position to decide the efficient time at which rights are established, whether that be pursuit, nonmortal wounding, mortal wounding, or physical possession. In addition, if different hunters in the same location could acquire rights at different points in time, those governed by the law that awarded rights at an earlier point in time would have a potentially inefficient (and unsporting) advantage. Furthermore, since hunters will not always know the residence of other hunters or the laws of other states, the danger of disputes among hunters is greater when different laws apply. Thomas Merrill and Henry Smith (2010: 20–21) have also pointed out that one function of the law in this context is to give hunters notice that a claim is being asserted and thus to prevent wasted time and resources. If different hunters are operating under different legal regimes and, as is plausible, they cannot or do not know the law applicable to the other hunters, this notice function would be vitiated and inefficient use of time and resources would ensue. Finally, states with little hunting but whose residents like to hunt elsewhere would have incentives to create law that inefficiently granted rights at an earlier point in time so that their residents could out-compete hunters in other states.

2.4. Choice of law and stolen property

So far, the economic analysis in this paper has provided a new explanation for the territorial rules that most courts already apply to property disputes. Nevertheless, economic analysis does not always favor territorial rules. As this section will explain, in the context of stolen property, particularly stolen art, the territorial rule may be inefficient, at least as it is usually interpreted.[14]

Although theft is common, litigation about choice of law regarding stolen goods is infrequent, except when the stolen good is art. Because of its high value, some stolen art is worth litigating about. It is also worthwhile for thieves to take into account different local laws when deciding where to sell their art. For these reasons, although much of what is said here would apply to any stolen property, analysis will focus on high-value, stolen art.

Disputes about choice of law and stolen art typically arise when art has been stolen and then sold to a bona fide purchaser. When the owner or his/her descendants discover who now possesses the art, the resulting lawsuit must weigh the rights of the claimant and bona fide purchaser. Such disputes are difficult, because both parties seem blameless. Different states have widely divergent laws applicable to such situations (Reyhan 2001). Some strongly favor the bona fide purchaser and give that person full rights upon purchase. Most determine such disputes through adverse possession. Even though the bona fide purchaser does not immediately acquire any greater rights than the thief, after the statutory time period has passed, the purchaser gains full ownership. Even among states that determine such disputes through adverse possession, the rules vary dramatically. The time necessary to acquire ownership varies. Some states require the adverse possessor to possess in good faith, while others

[14] For more discussion of stolen art, see Chapter 8.

do not, and even those states that require good faith vary in what good faith requires. In addition, states differ about when the adverse possession clock starts. Traditionally, the clock starts when the purchaser purchases the property. Nevertheless, in recent years, that rule has been thought unfair because the original owner and her descendants often have no way of knowing who the current possessor is, especially if the possessor keeps the art in his or her private collection. As a result, many states now "toll" the statute of limitations either until the identity of the current possessor is known or even until the time the claimant makes a demand upon the current possessor and that demand is refused. When the artwork was stolen, sold, or possessed in states with different laws relating to stolen art, difficult choice of law issues arise.

Although one might have thought that the traditional territorial approach would select the law of the state where the art is located at the time of the lawsuit, this is not the case. Instead, most states apply the law of the state where the work was sold, because property transactions are generally governed by the law of the place the transaction took place (Reyhan 2001: 1012–13).

It is widely understood that applying the law of the place of sale results in law that is favorable to the purchaser for two reasons. First, the seller can choose the place of sale. As a result, a sophisticated seller of a high-value work of stolen art can strategically choose to sell in a place with laws that are protective of purchasers (Fincham 2008: 129; Frey 2012: 1069). Second, art sales are lucrative to intermediaries, such as art dealers, appraisers, and shippers. As a result, states have an interest in encouraging art sales within their borders, just as they have an interest in encouraging manufacturers to locate factories in their territory. Since sellers strategically choose their venues, and since purchasers prefer to buy where their interests will be protected, states that want to attract art business have an incentive to choose laws that protect buyers.[15] Although most states are likely to ignore such incentives and base their laws on

---

[15] There may be two countervailing forces. First, states may not want to be havens for stolen art, perhaps because they perceive that the trade in stolen art has negative externalities, such as encouraging other kinds of crime or immoral behavior. In addition, laws that protect true owners may allow sellers with good title to signal the strength of their title. Only those with good title might chose to sell in places with laws favoring original owners over good faith purchasers. Nevertheless, it seems unlikely that, under the law-of-the-place-of-sale rule, the potential for signaling would give states an incentive to have laws less protective of good-faith purchasers. Signaling only works if original-owner protective laws would impose higher expected costs on sellers with bad title than on those with good

principles of justice rather than on what best serves the interest of art intermediaries, it only takes one or two strategic states to have a big effect on the art market. For example, Switzerland had laws that were relatively favorable to purchasers and was thus able to garner a disproportionate share of the art trade (Kunitz 2001: 533–40). In 2001, Switzerland was the fifth largest art market in the world (Weber 2006).

A pro-purchaser bias has consequences that are not just distributional. Bias is likely to impair efficiency as well. Most obviously, a pro-purchaser bias increases transactions cost by encouraging buyers and sellers to transact in Switzerland or other purchaser-protective jurisdictions rather than more convenient or lower-cost venues. More fundamentally, efficiency requires a delicate balance between owner protection (which discourages theft) and purchaser protection (which lowers the costs of transacting). Such a balance is unlikely to be reached in a place that puts excessive weight on purchaser protection in order to attract art business. Similarly, good laws regarding stolen property give owners efficient incentives to pursue and publicize the theft, and give potential purchasers efficient incentives to research the provenance of art they are buying (Landes and Posner 1996; Schwartz and Scott 2011). When states skew the rights in favor or purchasers, they give purchasers insufficient incentive to research their purchases.

A better rule would be to apply the law of the place where the art was last owned by an undisputed owner (Symeonides 2005). For example, if a work of art indisputably was owned by an English resident, allegedly stolen in England, sold in Switzerland, currently possessed by a New Yorker, and claimed by descendants of the English owner currently residing in California, English law would apply to the dispute

---

title, which suggests two limitations on the signaling argument. First, the argument only works if sellers provide a warranty of title, because otherwise sellers would bear no cost if the work turned out to be stolen. If the seller bears no cost regardless of whether it has good or bad title, sale in a place with laws more protective of original owners would provide no signal. Second, signaling information about the strength of title would only be valuable if litigation were likely to take place in a forum that would apply laws more protective of original owners, but not certain to take place there. If litigation in a forum that would apply more original-owner protective laws is unlikely, then signaling the strength of title would not be valuable, because the good-faith purchaser could be fully protected by the laws of the place of sale. On the other hand, if litigation in a forum that would apply laws more protective of original owners were certain, then selling in a place with laws protective of original owners would send no signal, because the law of the place of sale would be irrelevant. The author thanks Erin O'Hara O'Connor for encouraging him to think about these countervailing forces.

between the California claimants and New York possessors. The place where the art last was undisputedly owned has the proper incentives to devise efficient law, because owners of art have an interest both in protecting their art from thieves and in assuring a thriving art market. Although it may seem paradoxical, even owners whose claims are undisputedly legitimate have an incentive to favor some protection of bona fide purchasers of stolen art, because owners are likely someday to want to sell their art. Some protection for bona fide purchasers is probably necessary for a thriving art market.

By linking choice of law to the last place of undisputed ownership, this choice of law rule eliminates the incentive of states to fashion law that is excessively pro-purchaser in order to attract art business. Since the place of sale would have no effect on the applicable law, states with pro-purchaser rules would have no advantage in attracting out-of-state art sales.

An interesting issue is whether applicable law should be current law or the law as it existed at the time the work was allegedly stolen. Good arguments can be made that it makes more sense to apply the law of the time when the work was allegedly stolen. Circumstances that affect the efficient balance between owner protection and purchaser protection may have changed over time (such as the existence of registries of stolen art), and the law at the time the object was allegedly stolen is more likely to have been appropriate for that time. For similar reasons, if the law-of-the-place-of-last-undisputed-ownership rule were applied to cultural property, as some have proposed (Fincham 2008), it would make sense to apply the law of the time when the property was taken out of its original country. Otherwise, states, such as Greece, which claim large amounts of cultural property in foreign hands, would have an incentive to create protective rules, which would then apply retroactively to transfers that were legitimate at the time they occurred.

While the rule suggested here might generally work well, there are some circumstances where it would need to be modified. For example, suppose the work was last undisputedly owned by a German Jew in the 1930s and taken by the German government. It would certainly be inappropriate to apply the law of Nazi Germany to the confiscation. The above discussion of incentives for states to create efficient law assumes that a state values and protects the interests of all its citizens equally. That is a reasonable assumption in many contexts, but certainly not for Nazi Germany. In this situation, it is not clear what law should apply. A plausible candidate would be the law of modern Germany. Still, the connection of modern Germany to the dispute is, in some respects, no greater than the connection of some other random state, such as Thailand. Nevertheless, there is no reason to think that modern German law would be biased in favor of purchasers, so applying modern German law could be efficient.

An alternative to applying the law of the place of last undisputed ownership would be to apply the law of the place where the claimant resides. This may be almost as good. In most circumstances, such a state will have far more art owners than claimants of allegedly stolen art. As a result, the state will have little or no incentive to design rules that favor claimants over current possessors. On the other hand, one might be concerned about a rogue state – perhaps North Korea or Venezuela – where residents owned relatively little art, but that might deliberately tilt its laws in a pro-claimant direction in order to allow its residents to successfully litigate weak or even false claims. Similarly, one might be concerned that those claiming stolen art would move to favorable jurisdictions. While that might seem far-fetched, its practicality depends on how valuable the art is and on how long a residency period would be needed. Even today, students move to establish residency in order to get lower in-state tuition, and it used to be common for couples to move to Nevada or other states with lax divorce laws in order to end unhappy marriages. Similar reasoning suggests that, while applying the law of the place where the defendant resides or the art is currently located is likely to be fine in most cases, it might cause some states to become havens for stolen art and might cause some owners of stolen art to move to such havens.

3. Jurisdiction

3.1. Economic analysis of jurisdiction

Adjudicative jurisdiction traditionally has been allocated to the state or states with the power to enforce a judgment. Therefore, for example, jurisdiction is always proper in the place where an individual resides or is a citizen or the state where a corporation is incorporated or has its principal place of business. For the same reason, jurisdiction in real property disputes usually has been vested in the state in which the property is located. Starting in the twentieth century, with the expansion of interstate business, these rules were loosened, and individuals and businesses became subject to jurisdiction wherever they did business or performed other activities. In the United States, the constitutional test for determining whether a defendant's activities can subject it to jurisdiction in a particular state is whether the defendant "purposeful availed itself" of the benefits of the forum.

The economic analysis of adjudicative jurisdiction is relatively new. Most economic analysis focuses on litigation costs. For example, both Richard Posner (2011: 904) and Geoffrey Miller (2013, 2014) defend existing jurisdictional rules on the ground that they usually select a forum where litigation costs are likely to be the lowest (or at least constrict the plaintiff to choosing among fora with relatively low litigation costs). In general, litigation that takes place close to the plaintiff's and/or defendant's usual residence or principal place of business, and/or close to the residence of witnesses, will have lower costs. Dustin Buehler (2012) argues that is also necessary to take into account the cost of litigating jurisdictional issues and that the law could be made more efficient by loosening the constitutional constraints that can make jurisdictional disputes in the United States so complicated.

This chapter's author adds another dimension to the economic analysis of jurisdiction. As in the economic analysis of choice of law, one should also take into account the way jurisdictional rules may give judges and legislators incentives to develop efficient or inefficient rules and institutions (Klerman 2012, 2014). Bad jurisdictional rules give states incentives to develop rules and institutions that transfer wealth from out-of-state residents to residents of the forum. For example, if the jurisdictional rule were that plaintiffs always sued in their home state, all cases would involve in-state plaintiffs, while some would involve out-of-state defendants. As a result, state judges and legislators could redistribute wealth from out-of-state defendants to forum residents by tilting procedure, choice of law, or substantive law in a pro-plaintiff direction. They could have a similarly inefficient redistributive effect by tolerating or encouraging adjudication by jurors or trial judges that was biased against nonresidents. Conversely, a jurisdictional rule that required litigation in the defendant's home state would encourage rules and adjudication that were biased against out-of-state plaintiffs. These redistributive tendencies, however, may be tempered when parties can avoid states with biased courts. So, for example, a state would not want to be biased against out-of-state corporations that located factories in the state, because the state would not want to discourage other companies from locating in state, nor would it want to give the companies currently operating in the state an incentive to leave. For this reason, the purposeful availment requirement currently applied in the United States may promote efficient adjudication.

Rules that give plaintiffs too much leeway in the choice of forum also have a pernicious effect on state incentives to develop efficient laws and institutions. Although such rules are often criticized as encouraging forum shopping, the reason forum shopping is problematic is not usually well specified. The approach advocated here suggests that the problem with forum shopping is that it encourages "forum selling." If judges or legislators in even a few jurisdictions want to increase local revenue to lawyers and others who profit from litigation, they have an incentive to tilt the law in a pro-plaintiff way, since plaintiffs generally choose the forum.

In addition, one should consider the possible effect of jurisdictional rules on the location of economic activity. Bad jurisdictional rules may encourage parties to locate their activities in inefficient locations that protect them from liability.

3.2. Jurisdiction in water rights cases

The economic analysis of jurisdiction usually favors jurisdiction in the place where the water is drawn. That state's courts are likely to be able to adjudicate the dispute at lowest cost to all relevant parties. In most water disputes, at least one party is likely to reside near the disputed water, and often both will. Similarly, witnesses are likely to be from the neighborhood. In addition, since, as discussed earlier, local law is likely to apply, local judges can more cheaply adjudicate the dispute because they are already likely to be familiar with local water law. Adjudication in the courts of the state where the water is drawn is also a relatively easy rule to apply, so it reduces the cost of disputing jurisdiction.

Adjudication in the place where the water is drawn also gives salutary incentives to judges and legislators to create efficient rules and procedures. First, since it unambiguously identifies a single forum, it eliminates forum shopping and thus the pro-plaintiff bias of forum selling. In addition, the state where the water is drawn has an incentive to adjudicate fairly, even if one of the parties is out-of-state and one is in state. One might think that that judges and jurors could redistribute wealth by favoring in-state residents, but this would be short sighted. If a state got a reputation for being biased against out-of-state litigants in water cases, out-of-state businesses that relied on water rights – such as mining companies or agricultural businesses – would be less likely to locate in state, thus reducing employment and overall economic activity. In addition, discrimination against out-of-state parties would reduce foreign demand for land adjacent to rivers and streams. This would reduce the prices such land would fetch on the open market. Legal rules or adjudicative institutions that discriminated against out-of-state parties would thus harm all who owned land adjacent to streams and rivers. Of course, there may be countervailing interests in favor of such bias. In-state mining and agricultural firms that compete with out-of-state firms might favor bias in order to limit competition. Similarly, in-state residents who do not currently own riparian land but hope to purchase in the future might benefit from bias, because it would drive down the price of the land they hope to buy. Nevertheless, state residents overall would benefit from unbiased rules and adjudication.

Courts in the state where the water is drawn also have incentives to choose efficient choice of law and substantive legal rules. As argued above, the efficient choice of law rule in water disputes is to apply the law of the place where the water is drawn. If the forum is also the state where the water is drawn, it has many reasons to choose that choice of law rule. First, it is more likely to be familiar with that rule, so choosing it saves judicial time. In addition, in-state judges can best ensure application of efficient substantive law if local judges and legislators who know local conditions and care about local citizens make the applicable substantive law. Thus, forum state judges can best advance the welfare of their state's citizens by choosing to apply local law to water disputes.

In contrast, allowing jurisdiction in other states could have deleterious effects. For example, if an out-of-state claimant could get jurisdiction in its home state, that state would have little incentive not to be biased in favor of the in-state party. If it were biased in cases in which the in-state party was claiming out-of-state rights (but not in cases where an out-of-state party was claiming in-state rights), that would not give businesses any reason to avoid establishing mining or agricultural activities in the forum state. Similarly, the value of forum state riparian properties would be unaffected. Finally, out-of-state judges would have little incentive to apply efficient choice of law rules, because the law of the place where the water was drawn would require additional time to learn and might favor the out-of-state party.

An exception to the rule of adjudication in the place where the water is drawn might be appropriate when both of the disputing parties resided the same state and that state was the state where the water is drawn. In that situation, litigation costs might be lower if litigation took place in the state where both resided. Witnesses might incur additional expenses traveling to the forum, and the judge might need extra time to learn foreign water law. Nevertheless, the savings in litigation costs to the in-state parties would probably be larger than the increase in costs to witnesses and judges. In addition, if all parties reside in the forum, there is no reason to fear bias against an out-of-state party.

Nevertheless, there are three reasons to prefer adjudication in the state where the water is drawn, even if all parties to the litigation are from a different state. First, as noted, water rights involve significant externalities, because adjudication of water rights affects not only the disputing parties, but also all who are downstream. There is thus a danger that a court in a state other than the place where the water is located might take insufficient account of the interests of downstream owners not directly represented in the litigation. Second, even if judges in the place of common residence tried to apply the correct choice of law and substantive rules, they are more likely to make mistakes, because they are less familiar with law of the state where the water is located. Third, if the plaintiff were allowed to choose between litigation in its home state or the state where the water was drawn, that would introduce the danger of forum shopping and thus forum selling. With only two fora to choose from, the danger of forum selling is not very large, but it is still best avoided.

3.3. Jurisdiction in most other property disputes

The analysis in the prior subsection also provides reasons to require adjudication in the place where the property is located in most other kinds of property disputes. Litigation in that forum is likely both to reduce litigation costs and to result in adjudication in a forum with at least some incentive to adjudicate fairly.

For example, in hunting cases, at least one party and most witnesses are likely to be from the state where the wild animal was captured, so that state will probably have the lowest litigation costs. In addition, judges in that state have some incentive to adjudicate fairly, because in state residents – including hotel owners, restaurant owners, and rental car agencies – generally benefit when outsiders visit to hunt. In contrast, adjudication in the out-of-state hunter's state would likely increase costs and give judges no incentive to adjudicate fairly.

Cases involving adverse possession of land are also likely to be adjudicated more cheaply in the place where the land is located. In addition, those courts have some reason not to be biased against an out-of-state absentee owner whose land is being occupied by an in-state adverse possessor. If a state got a reputation for being biased against out-of-state absentee owners, out-of-state parties would be less likely to buy land in state, which would reduce the price of all real estate in the state.

3.4. *Jurisdiction in disputes about stolen property*

Determining the most efficient forum for disputes about stolen property (and stolen art in particular) presents a stark choice between fora that minimize litigation costs and fora that are likely to be less biased.

In most cases, the forum where litigation costs will be lowest is likely to be either where the claimant resides or where the current possessor resides. While witnesses are likely to be from elsewhere, most litigation costs are incurred by the parties, so costs can be minimized if at least one of them doesn't have to travel. A judge in such a forum may have to learn the law of another jurisdiction, but learning the law is not that time consuming.

Unfortunately, unless both claimant and possessor live in the same state, the courts of one of the two parties are likely to be biased in favor of the local party. Even more dangerously, if jurisdiction was based on where the claimant resided, claimants of particularly valuable art might move to states that were known to be particularly pro-resident. Similarly, although perhaps less plausibly, if jurisdiction were based on where the possessor resided, possessors might move to jurisdictions that were known to be biased in favor of resident or sell their works to those in such jurisdictions. In fact, persons in such jurisdictions would be able to bid more in the art market, and so would likely purchase a disproportionate share of high-value art. Even worse, states that were interested in attracting wealthy art owners might deliberately encourage pro-resident adjudicatory bias to attract wealthy (but unscrupulous) art owners and claimants. As noted above, most states would almost certainly resist (or even fail to notice) the temptation to contort their justice systems for this purpose. Nevertheless, even if only one or two jurisdictions did so, it could have a large effect on the art market.

For this reason, from a prevention of bias perspective, the best forum is the same as the choice of law solution – the place where the art last was undisputedly owned. Especially when neither claimant currently resides in that state, it has no reason to be biased. In addition, because the forum would be unaffected by the claimant or possessor changing his or her residence, one need not be concerned about strategic moves or sales or about states distorting their laws in order to attract wealthy but unscrupulous art owners or claimants. In addition, even when one party was from the forum and the other was not, this forum would have some incentive not to be biased. For example, if the claimant were from the forum while the current possessor was not, the state would not want a reputation for being biased in favor of the claimant, because that would make purchases from current owners of art in the forum less secure and would thus reduce prices. For similar reasons, bias in favor of in-state possessors could result in lower prices to current owners in the forum, because foreign purchasers would anticipate less protection if the work were stolen and then purchased by a local bona fide purchaser.

Choosing the most efficient forum therefore requires balancing litigation costs (which favor adjudication in the place where the claimant or possessor currently resides) and the danger of biased adjudication (which favors adjudication in the place of last undisputed ownership). Resolution of this issue therefore requires an empirical inquiry into these two factors. Thus, even though the data are not currently available that would be necessary to identify the efficient forum, economic analysis can be helpful in identifying the empirical questions that need to be resolved.

One potential problem with jurisdiction in the place of last undisputed ownership is that that state may not have the power to enforce its judgment. Enforcement would not be a problem if suit were in a US state, but the work of art was in another US state, because the Full Faith and Credit Clause of the US Constitution generally requires states to enforce sister state judgments. Enforcement would similarly be unproblematic in the international context where treaties or statutes provided for enforcement. In other situations, jurisdiction in the state of last undisputed ownership would be impractical, unless the work of art was also currently present in that jurisdiction. If the state where the art is currently located does not, as a matter of comity or treaty obligation, enforce foreign judgments, it might be necessary for the claimant to sue in that state, even though it might be biased in favor of the defendant.

Conclusion

Economic analysis of choice of law and jurisdiction largely confirms the wisdom of current law and practice. It is usually efficient to litigate disputes about property in the courts of the state where the property is located, and it is usually efficient to apply the law of that same state.

Nevertheless, in cases involving stolen art (and perhaps other situations), other rules may be superior in giving states incentives to create efficient law and to create fair adjudicative institutions.

References

American Law Institute 1934. *Restatement of the Law of Conflict of Laws*. St. Paul, Minn. American Law Institute Publishers.

Baxter, William 1963. "Choice of Law and the Federal System," *Stanford Law Review* 16:1–42.

Bell, Abraham and Parchomovsky, Gideon 2005. "Of Property and Federalism," *Yale Law Journal* 115:72–115.

Buehler, Dustin 2012. "Jurisdictional Incentives," *George Mason Law Review* 20:105–55.

Fincham, Derek 2008. "How Adopting the *Lex Originis* Rule Can Impede the Flow of Illicit Cultural Property," *Columbia Journal of Law and the Arts* 32:111–50.

Frey, Laurie 2012. "*Bakalar v. Vavra* and the Art of Conflicts Analysis in New York Framing a Choice of Law Approach for Moveable Property," *Columbia Law Review* 112:1055–95.

Goldsmith, Jack L. and Sykes, Alan O. 2007. "*Lex Loci Delictus* and Global Economic Welfare: *Spinozzi v. Itt Sheraton Corp.*," *Harvard Law Review* 120:1137–47.

Guzman, Andrew T. 2002. "Choice of Law: New Foundations," *Georgetown Law Journal* 90:883–940.

Hancock, Moffat 1967. "Conceptual Devises for Avoiding the Land Taboo in Conflict of Laws: The Disadvantages of Disingenuousness," *Stanford Law Review* 1:1–40.

Hay, Bruce 1992. "Conflicts of Law and State Competition in the Product Liability System," *Georgetown Law Journal* 80:617–52.

Hay, Peter, Borchers, Patrick J., Symeonides, Symeon and Scoles, Eugene F. 2010. *Conflict of Laws*. St. Paul, MN: West.

Klerman, Daniel 2012. "Personal Jurisdiction and Product Liability," *Southern California Law Review* 85:1551–96.

   2014. "Rethinking Personal Jurisdiction," Forthcoming in *Journal of Legal Analysis*.

Kunitz, Michele 2001. "Switzerland and the International Trade in Art and Antiquities," *Northwestern Journal of International Law and Business* 21:519–42.

Landes, William and Posner, Richard A. 1996. "The Economics of Legal Disputes over the Ownership of Works of Art and Other Collectibles." In *Economics of the Arts: Selected Essays*. V.A.P.M.M. Ginsburgh, (ed.) 177–219.

Merrill, Thomas and Smith, Henry 2010. *Oxford Introduction to Us Law: Property*. Oxford University Press.

Miller, Geoffrey 2013. "A New Procedure for State Court Personal Jurisdiction," *NYU Public Law and Legal Theory Working Paper.*
   2014. "In Search of the Most Adequate Forum: State Court Personal Jurisdiction," *Stanford Journal of Complex Litigation* 1:1–39.
Note 1938. "Choice of Law for Land Transactions," *Columbia Law Review* 38:1049–59.
O'Hara, Erin A. and Ribstein, Larry E. 2000. "From Politics to Efficiency in Choice of Law," *University of Chicago Law Review* 67:1151–1232.
   2009. *The Law Market.* Oxford University Press.
Posner, Richard A. 2011. *Economic Analysis of Law.* New York: Aspen Publishers.
Reyhan, Patricia. Y. 2001. "A Chaotic Palette: Conflict of Laws in Litigation between Original Owners and Good-Faith Purchasers of Stolen Art," *Duke Law Journal* 50:955–1043.
Rose, Carol. M. 1990. "Energy and Efficiency in the Realignment of Common-Law Water Rights," *Journal of Legal Studies* 19:261–96.
Schwartz, Alan and Scott, Robert E. 2011. "Rethinking the Laws of Good Faith Purchase," *Columbia Law Review* 111:1332–84.
Smith, Henry 2008. "Governing Water: The Semicommons of Fluid Property Rights," *Arizona Law Review* 50:445–78.
Stern, James 2014. "Property, Exclusivity, and Jurisdiction," *Virginia Law Review* 100 (forthcoming).
Sykes, Alan O. 2008. "Transnational Forum Shopping as a Trade and Investment Issue," *Journal of Legal Studies* 37:339–78.
Symeonides, Symeon 2005. "A Choice-of-Law Rule for Conflicts Involving Stolen Cultural Property," *Vanderbilt Journal of Transnational Law* 38:1177–98.
   2006. *The American Choice-of-Law Revolution: Past, Present and Future.* Leiden; Boston: Martinus Nijhoff Publishers.
Tarlock, A. Dan 2013. *Law of Water Rights and Resources.* Westlaw (online).
Weber, Marc 2006. "New Swiss Law on Cultural Property," *International Journal of Cultural Property* 13:99–113.

11

Small property, adverse possession, and optional law

SHITONG QIAO

1. Introduction

"How to deal with these illegal buildings"? I frequently was asked in my interviews with government officials in Shenzhen, a Chinese city in which almost half of the buildings were built illegally. To demolish them has proved to be a mission impossible; to legalize them would encourage more illegal buildings. This binary choice seems difficult. People in China call these illegal buildings small-property houses (*xiaochanquan*) because their property rights are "smaller" (weaker) than those on the formal housing market, which have "big" property rights protected by the government (Yu 2009). The complication is that the small-property problem is a multiple period, multi-person game rather than a one-period, two-party game. In a pure one-period, two-party game, compromise is often a better strategy than conflict between both parties. In the real world, the government does not want to compromise with an individual owner due to concerns about the consequences in the future: it would encourage other owners to develop their land illegally, and even this particular owner to develop this particular plot illegally again in the future.

This logic also explains why most countries do not allow adverse possession against the government. However, adverse possession against the government does *de facto* exist all over the world and a simple "law

---

Assistant professor, University of Hong Kong Faculty of Law; J.S.D. Candidate, Yale Law School. I thank Yun-chien Chang for bringing to my attention the optional law literature and thorough comments on a previous draft; Bob Ellickson and Susan Rose-Ackerman for extremely helpful guidance, discussions, and suggestions; Jie Yang for a midnight conversation that helped straighten out my thinking; Benito Arruñada, Daniel Klerman, Daphna Lewinsohn-Zamir, Thomas Merrill, Jer-Shenq Shieh, Zhiqiang Wang, Xiaohong Xu, Tian Yan, Taisu Zhang, and participants at the 5th Law and Economic Analysis Conference (Taipei) and the 24th Annual Meeting of the American Law and Economics Association for helpful comments. I dedicate this work to Carol Pang for her invaluable company and support. All errors are my own.

enforcement" strategy does not work (Weiner 2003). Adverse possession is a useful framework for thinking about the small-property problem. Traditionally, our thinking about adverse possession is who should have the title – the adverse possessor or the original owner? This is also consistent with our understanding of the structure of legal entitlements before Calabresi and Melamed published their landmark piece "Property Rule, Liability Rule, and Inalienability: One View of the Cathedral" in 1972, in which they developed a framework ("cathedral") of legal entitlements and in particular introduced the concept of liability rules. In 1985, Thomas Merrill suggested protecting an original owner's property in adverse possession with liability rules. Since then, the cathedral of legal entitlements has been further refurbished and expanded. In particular, Ian Ayres (1998, 2005) and his coauthors (Ayres and Balkin 1996; Ayres and Talley 1995) have reconceptualized liability rules with option theory: there are both "call option" liability rules and "put option" liability rules. This chapter frames the Chinese small-property problem as adverse possession against the government in light of this expanded cathedral of legal entitlements. My argument is that the allocation of initial options matters at least as much as the allocation of initial entitlements and that options should be granted to parties that have the best information to make decisions. In the small-property case, these are the individual owners of small-property houses.

Section 2 of this chapter discusses the basics of Chinese small-property. Section 3 frames the case as an adverse possession question, applies Ayres' structure of legal entitlements to analyze adverse possession, and introduces his best-chooser principle to resolve the small-property problem. Section 4 discusses Shenzhen government's policies in addressing small-property houses, categorizes them into six rules of legal entitlements, and compares their effects. Section 5 concludes and considers the role of options in resolving the tension between informal property rights and formal property law in developing countries.

2. Challenging property law through small property

2.1. Chinese rural land law

The current property regime in rural China is a tri-party model: the village collective exercises ownership; individual households enjoy use rights; and the government monopolizes the rural-urban land conversion. In other words, the right to develop rural land belongs to the state.

2.1.1 The collective's ownership

Article 10 of the Chinese Constitution says that rural land is owned collectively except for that owned by the state. This stipulation is confirmed by Article 8 of the 2004 Land Administration Law (hereinafter "LAL") and Article 59 of the 2007 Chinese Property Law. Both laws designate the villagers' committee, the villagers' group, or corresponding collective economic organizations as the body empowered to exercise the collective ownership and manage the collectively owned land.

The most important aspect of collective ownership is the right to contract rural land to individual households. Most of the time, the villagers' committee or villagers' group represents the collective in exercising ownership. Chinese farmers refer to both institutions as "the collective," to distinguish it from "the state."

2.1.2 Farmers' use right to rural land

Article 8 of the Chinese Constitution institutes the Household Responsibility System (hereinafter "HRS") as the basic rural property institution. The 2007 Chinese Property Law reaffirms this stipulation. Under HRS, the collective should contract collectively owned land to individual households. Individual households as contractors of rural land are free to use the contracted land for agriculture. The contract term has been legally fixed at thirty years, which can be extended. There are comprehensive measures to protect rural households' contract rights. After contracting the land to individual households, the collective has very little right to intervene in the farmers' use of the contracted land. At the same time, there are many restrictions on households transferring their use rights. First, they have to get the agreement of the collective; second, they cannot change the agricultural use of the land; third, members of the same collective enjoy priority in buying transferred rights to contracted land.

Besides engaging in agricultural activities, farmers need shelter for their families. Each household of the collective is eligible for and can only get one piece of rural residential land for free to build a house. Rural land is supposed to be used only by farmers for agricultural use and other daily operations. Article 63 of LAL explicitly prohibits alienation of rural land use rights for non-agricultural use. In particular, urban residents are not allowed to buy rural houses or rural residential land. This prohibition has been resoundingly affirmed in various government ordinances.

2.1.3 State monopoly on rural-urban land conversion

Urban land is state-owned, and rural land is collectively owned. This distinction between rural and urban land is fixed in Article 10 of Chinese Constitution. Preservation of agricultural land is one of the Chinese land administration regime's most important goals. As a result, rural land can be used only for agriculture and several other limited purposes, including building residential houses, public facilities, public interest projects and township-and-village enterprises.

Rural-urban land conversion can be legally achieved only through requisition by the state. Section I, Article 43 of the 2004 LAL further states, "any unit or individual that needs to use land for construction must apply for the use of state-owned land in accordance with law." This clause makes the private transfer of rural land-use rights for non-rural use impossible according to law. Moreover, Section II of Article 43 reiterates that state-owned land in Section I includes both state-owned land and land that the state has requisitioned, which effectively means that rural land can be used for construction only after requisition. Although there have been strict restrictions on the state requisition of rural land, such as the approval procedure and requirement of public interest, these restrictions are not effective. The huge demand for urban housing and other urban uses means that in reality these legal rules are either ignored or relaxed. For example, the requirement of public interest rarely precludes local governments in China from requisitioning rural land for industrial or commercial development.

The government alienates the use rights to state-owned land in two ways: free allocation (in several limited situations) and onerous conveyance. Together, allocation and conveyance constitute the "primary market" for urban land use rights. The initial and subsequent non-government holders of land-use rights may further transfer them within certain limits. These further land transactions constitute the "secondary market" for urban land use rights.

2.2. Small-property rights

The distinction between rural and urban land in China has not insulated the rural land regime from the booming urban real estate market. The boom in China's urban real estate market began in 1998, when the central government decided to replace its earlier inefficient housing allocation system with a housing market. According to official statistics, from 1998 to 2007 the annual nationwide sales of residential houses grew ten times (State Bureau of Statistics 2008). The increasing demand for land promoted Chinese farmers to develop and transfer their land illegally, breaking the state monopoly of land development despite the legal prohibition.

Farmers living in the rural areas near big cities often have great incentives to transfer their houses to urban residents who cannot afford a house in the urban area. Although they cannot sell houses at prices comparable to those on the formal market due to the illegality of the transfer, the profit is much higher than that from farming the land. According to the Chinese Ministry of Land and Resources, by 2007, Chinese farmers had built over 6.6 billion square meters of houses in evasion of the legal prohibition on private rural land development and transfer, resulting in a huge market of illegal houses. By way of comparison, in 2007, the total floor space of housing sold on the legal housing market was 0.76 billion square meters (China Net 2008).

2.3. Shenzhen

Shenzhen, a city in the southern part of Southern China's Guangdong Province, situated immediately north of Hong Kong, has been the symbolic heart of the Chinese economic reform. In 1980, Deng Xiaoping, the then-supreme leader of China, designated Shenzhen, then known as Bao'an, an agricultural county of approximately 300,000 farmers, as a "special economic zone" (SEZ) to pilot market-oriented reforms. Since the establishment of the SEZ, Shenzhen has undergone a miracle of economic growth and urbanization. From 1979 to 2010, the annual average growth rate of Gross Domestic Product ("GDP") in Shenzhen was 25.3 percent (Shenzhen Statistics Bureau and NBS Survey Office in Shenzhen 2011: 5). Shenzhen ranked fourth in GDP and first in GDP per capita among mainland Chinese cities in 2009 (Le 2010: 16). The population of Shenzhen has grown from 314,100, of whom 312,600 had local *hukou* (household registration) in 1979 to 10,372,000 in 2010, of whom only 2,510,300 had local *hukou* (Shenzhen Statistics Bureau and NBS Survey Office in Shenzhen 2011: 4).

The rapid urbanization of Shenzhen has been accompanied by land requisition by the government and resistance by farmers. Three decades ago, most of the land in Shenzhen was rural and collectively owned by the farmers of the respective villages. State-owned land was a bit more than three square kilometers in Shenzhen in 1980. The villages used to be located on the outskirts of the city, but with the expansion of the city, farmland formerly cultivated by the villagers was requisitioned by the government whereas the village housing plots were preserved due to the high social and economic costs to compensate the villagers for their lost buildings. These villages are now called intra-city villages (*chengzhongcun*) as they are now surrounded by urban constructions, sometimes even skyscrapers. Today all the land of more than 1,900 square kilometers in Shenzhen has been declared urbanized and thus nominally nationalized by the city government (Feng 2006). But farmers still exercised *de facto* control over 300 square kilometers of the original rural land, among which 131 square kilometers of land have been developed to 379,400 buildings, totaling 405 million square meters and composing 49.27 percent of the total floor space of Shenzhen (Shenzhen City Government 2010; Qiao 2013, 2015). Shenzhen is the city with the highest ratio of small-property houses, making it the capital of small-property houses in China.[1]

The 300 square kilometers of illegal land pose a big challenge to the Shenzhen government. Legally the land is state-owned and should be managed by the Shenzhen government; but in fact it is used illegally by villagers and other related parties. Buildings on the illegal land house most of the eight million migrant workers in Shenzhen and serve as rented housing, restaurants, factories, private schools, commercial centers and others. Illegal land development has played an indispensable role in the economic miracle of Shenzhen. The vitality of the intra-city villages of illegal buildings is widely recognized. However, the illegality of the land has limited its uses. On one hand, actual users, mostly farmers and their business partners cannot make full use of the land, which would only be possible if the land is legally approved for development by the government. On the other hand, neither can the Shenzhen government make any use of it without the agreement of the actual users. Since 2009, the Shenzhen government has failed to provide enough land for legal development. In 2009, the Shenzhen government only supplied 16.2 square kilometers of land, about 57 percent of its original land supply plan; in 2010, the Shenzhen government supplied 16.46 square kilometers, about 61 percent of its plan. (Shenzhen City Government 2010). There is little land that the Shenzhen government can supply except for the 300 square kilometers of land illegally used by small-property buildings. Due to the high economic and social costs of demolishing the illegal buildings, the

---

[1] In Beijing, the ratio of small property houses to the total stock is 20 percent and in Xi'An 30 percent.

Shenzhen government cannot make use of the land that has been declared urbanized and nationalized but still under the control of farmers.

3. Framing the question: adverse possession in Ayres' cathedral

3.1. The concept: from possession of things to possession of rights

Adverse possession is a method by which someone, without the owner's permission, acquires a new root of title to property already owned. The adverse possessor acquires title in this fashion by possessing the property until the statute of limitations for the relevant action by the title owner to recover possession has run out (Merrill and Smith 2010: 34). American law often requires that possession must be exclusive, open and notorious, actual, continuous, and adverse under a claim of right (Merrill and Smith 2010: 35).

The concept of adverse possession can be extended beyond the possession of things. For example, the revival of research on adverse possession in the 1980s was attributed partly to a decision of the California Supreme Court, *Warsaw* v. *Chicago Metallic Ceilings, Inc.*, which was about prescriptive easement (Merrill 1985). Prescription is "the effect of lapse of time in creating or extinguishing property interests" (Ackerman and Johnson 1996: 86). It is based on the theory that if "one makes non-permissive use of another's land, and the landowner fails to prevent such use, such acquiescence is conclusive evidence that the user is rightful" (Ackerman and Johnson 1996: 86). A prescriptive easement is created "by such use of land, for the period of prescription, as would be privileged if an easement existed, provided its use is (1) adverse, and (2) for the period of prescription, continuous and uninterrupted" (Ackerman and Johnson 1996: 86–7).

Merrill (1985: 1124 fn 11) calls prescriptive easement a first cousin of adverse possession. Prescriptive easement and adverse possession are different in that the former involves nonpossessory use of property, which ripens into an easement, and the latter possession of property, which ripens into a fee simple. Though the non-possessory nature of an easement generally means that the continuity and exclusivity elements must be interpreted differently, the same legal requirements apply to both adverse possession and prescriptive easements. Scholars often do not distinguish too sharply between the rules of legal entitlements under adverse possession and prescriptive easement. Probably due to the more significant position of adverse possession in property law, the discussions of "the effect of lapse of time in creating or extinguishing property interests" are discussed more often under the framework of adverse possession.

In essence, rural land is collectively owned, but the right to develop, a crucial stick of property rights, has been detached from collective ownership of rural land and added onto state property rights. Individual villagers and village collectives have the legal rights to possess their village land, but no legal rights to develop the land. Thus, small property rights are the result of adverse possession of the government's rights to develop rural land. It is not exactly a prescriptive easement as defined in either American law or Chinese law. However, it is prescription, that is, prescriptive acquisition of incorporeal interests (Ackerman and Johnson 1996: 87–8). If we could discuss prescriptive easement under the framework of adverse possession, it is also proper to discuss the small-property case under the same framework. Both cases have to deal with the tension between the *de facto* possession and the *de jure* rights and to resolve whether *de facto* possession could lead to *de jure* rights with the lapse of time.

3.2. Property rule, liability rule and adverse possession

As Calabresi and Melamed (1972: 1090–92) write, the first issue which must be faced by any legal system is one we call the problem of "entitlement." Whenever a state is presented with the conflicting interests of two or more people, or two or more groups of people, it must decide which side to favor. Moreover, the state must decide not only which side wins but also the kind of protection to grant. Calabresi and Melamed (1972) define three types of entitlements: entitlements protected by property rules, entitlements protected by liability rules, and inalienable entitlements. An entitlement is protected by a property rule to the extent that someone who wishes to remove the entitlement from its holder must buy it from him in a voluntary transaction in which the seller agrees upon the value of the entitlement. Property rules protect entitlements by deterring nonconsensual takings. Whenever someone may destroy the initial entitlement if he is willing to pay an objectively determined value for it, the entitlement is protected by a liability rule. Liability rules protect entitlements by compensating the entitlement holder if such takings do occur (Ayres 2005: 5).

Applied to adverse possession disputes, the state can choose among four different rules.

Table 1: *Calabresi and Melamed's two-by-two box applied to adverse possession (For a similar table, see Ayres 2005: 14)*

	Method of Protection	
Initial Entitlement	Property Rule	Liability Rule
Original Owner ("OO")	Rule 1	Rule 2
Adverse Possessor ("AP")	Rule 3	Rule 4

Rule 1: the state prohibits adverse possession – OO has the title, which cannot be taken nonconsensually.

Rule 2: OO has the title, but AP can take it by paying compensation.

Rule 3: the state grants title to AP without requirements of compensation to OO.

Rule 4: the state grants title to AP, but OO can take the title back by compensating AP.

The Calabresi and Melamed categorization has dominated the discussions of legal entitlements – scholars have discussed different aspects of these rules, tried to expand their contents and even invented new rules. Among many others, Ayres (2005: 5–15) significantly expanded the content of liability rules by introducing option theory into this field. Options are defined by identifying who has the option, whether the option is to buy (a call) or to sell (a put), and the price of exercising the option. A call option is an option to buy. The option holder can force a sale at the exercise price even if the seller does not want to sell. According to Ayres, traditional liability rules give potential takers a call option to take. A liability rule gives at least one party an option to take an entitlement nonconsensually and pay the entitlement owner some exercise price. Once the traditional liability rules were reconceived as granting a potential taker a call option, it became almost inevitable to think about put-option rules. A put option is an option to sell. While call options give the option holder the choice of whether to pay a non-negotiated amount, put options give the option holder the choice of whether to be paid a non-negotiated amount. Call options when exercised give rise to "forced sales;" put options give rise to "forced purchases."

Applied to adverse possession disputes again, the possibility of put options suggests two additional rules:

Rule 5: the state grants title to AP, but also gives AP the option of waiving his title in return for compensation from OO.

Rule 6: OO not only can keep his title, but also has the option to give up his title and receive compensation from AP.

Incorporating the possibility of "put-option" rules, the structure of legal entitlements in adverse possession is as following:

Table 2: *Ayres' two-by-three box applied to adverse possession (for similar tables, see Ayres 2005: 16; Chang 2015 forthcoming)*

Initial Entitlement	Method of Protection		
	Property Rule	Liability Rule Call Option	Liability Rule Put Option
OO	Rule 1	Rule 2	Rule 6
AP	Rule 3	Rule 4	Rule 5

According to the distribution of asset and options, the structure of legal entitlements in adverse possession can be depicted as following:

Table 3: *Ayres' (2005: 17) Table of claims applied to adverse possession*

	OO's Claim	AP's Claim
Rule 1	Asset	0
Rule 2	Asset-Call	Call
Rule 3	0	Asset
Rule 4	Call	Asset-Call
Rule 5	−Put	Asset + Put
Rule 6	Asset + Put	−Put

3.3. *The best-chooser principle*

How to allocate legal entitlements efficiently? Ayres' optional law theory tells us that: "Liability rules delegate allocational authority – allocational options – to privately informed disputants. The delegation effect gives us strong reasons to believe that liability rules do a better job than property rules in harnessing the private information of disputants" (Ayres 2005: 183).

In the small-property case, the government knows its own needs and valuation of the right to develop; individual small-property owners have the information of their illegal real estate. The government has double roles in this case: one as a disputant and potential entitlement holder; the other as a policy maker, which can decide who decides, and does not have to decide the final allocation of entitlements. Thus, the policy-maker in this case has complete information about one disputant – the government – but has not enough information about numerous small-property houses and their owners' valuation of them, which is more speculative than that of the government.

As Ayres (2005: 45) writes in the American law context: "When the court is choosing between a litigant whose value is commonly known and another litigant whose value is not, the litigant with the known value is never the efficient chooser because he has no private information to bring to the allocative table."

In this case, the government's information is known to itself as a policy maker; what it does not have in making a policy is the information of numerous individuals. Thus, the government is not the efficient chooser in this case. Small-property owners should be the efficient choosers because they can bring their private information to the allocative table.

Krier and Schwab (1995) have argued that less-numerous parties are more efficient choosers than more-numerous parties because of the collective-action problem. As Ayres (2005: 31) has correctly pointed out, Krier and Schwab focus too narrowly on numerosity as the exclusive determinant of which side will be the more efficient chooser. As discussed previously, information is still a crucial element in deciding which party is the more efficient chooser. Moreover, the cost of overcoming the collective-action problem of numerous parties also varies according to the specific institutional and social contexts. As Ostrom (1990), Ellickson (1993) and many others have proved both theoretically and empirically, the collective action problem can be overcome if the numerous parties constitute a close-knit community or has a well-functioning decision-making mechanism, as shown in the *Caiwuwei* case in the following part.

Ayres (2005: 44) makes another point: "The litigant with the more speculative valuation will tend to be the more efficient chooser because he has greater informational advantage." This also applies to the small-property case. Individual valuation is more speculative to the market than government's valuation of land development. The number of individuals amplifies the government's information disadvantage. It is impossible for the government to have precise information about each individual's valuation of his or her particular small-property houses; or even to set an average valuation.

The third point is about the problem of multiple takings. As recognized by Ayres (2005: 125), liability rules might induce disputing parties to engage in a protracted series of destructive takings of the same entitlement from one another, and multiple takers to threaten taking. Epstein (1997: 844–45) argues that Ayres' optional theory only applies to two parties playing a one-period game, and that traditional property rules work better when many parties play the game over many periods. Epstein correctly points out that "in all real world settings, the legal rules must work over many periods and must be resistant not only to the machinations of the two parties to the original dispute, but also to third parties who might come in." Epstein (1996) supports his critique with a real world case – whether the government is entitled to decree without paying compensation that owners are not allowed to develop their land if that development will interfere with the survival of endangered species. In this specific case, Epstein (1997: 844–45) argues:

> The rule that denies the owner compensation could induce him to destroy valuable habitat lest his lands be frozen by government action. A decision to allow the government to designate land as habitat makes renegotiation of property rights impossible. The owner who buys back the rights faces the risk that a second designation will result in another loss of these rights to the government.

Small-property development and its legalization is a multi-period and multi-party game. There is a concern similar to Epstein's, but in the opposite direction: The Shenzhen government is worried that legalizing the existing illegal buildings would encourage further illegal development of rural land, not only on the land of existing small-property buildings, but also on the land that small-property buildings have not been built. Over time, small-property buildings have grown from two floors to four floors, to six floors, and to over eight floors or higher today; the number of illegal buildings and the land area they cover also have exploded.

Epstein's worry about the abuse of government power should be left to the political process, as it is in most land use regulation practices (Ellickson and Been 2005: 46). We should consider not only the possibility of multiple takings, but also which party is more capable of multiple takings in specific case settings. In the situation of land use regulation, such as in my small-property case and in Epstein's habitat preservation case, it is one government dealing with numerous individuals, who not only have the information advantage, but also the advantage of overall control through their daily possession and operation of a specific plot against the government. These individuals are more capable of using the land according to their will, even when the law prohibits a particular land use, than the government' law-enforcement capability.

Let's think about Epstein's habitat preservation case: even if the government pays compensation to a landowner, it cannot prevent numerous landowners from developing their land for more valuable uses than habitat preservation. A better strategy would be the government designating some land as habitat-preservation land, but giving options to the landowners to buy their land development rights back. The government can set the quota and price of the land development rights according to its need for habitat preservation. These legal options would allow individual landowners to incorporate the environmental value into their consideration of land use, and push them to use land legally (and often more valuably) rather than illegally (and less valuably).

Going back to the small-property case in Shenzhen, the reality has proved that individuals are much more capable than the government in deciding the use of a particular plot. Huge numbers of small-property houses make the situation even more difficult to deal with. Granting legal titles to the existing small-property houses would not only encourage individuals who have not used their land illegally to do so; it also would encourage further illegal use of the land by individuals granted the legal titles. It is exactly a multi-period, multi-party game as depicted by Epstein. However, we need to investigate the real-world specifics to decide which party is more capable of multiple takings of a specific plot. It turns out in cases of one government versus numerous individuals, it is often the individuals that are more capable of multiple takings. The same as in Epstein's habitat preservation situation, the party that is more capable of multiple takings is the more efficient chooser.

In summary, the best chooser should be the party that has private information unknown to the policy-maker, with the more speculative valuation, and is more capable of multiple takings. As shown in the following part, it is the numerous owners of small-property houses in my case.

4. Structuring legal entitlements for small property

As early as in 1982, the Shenzhen government tried to make a feasible plan to deal with the illegal rural houses (SZ Govt. [1982] 1). In the past years, the Shenzhen government has tried five of the six rules under Ayres' optional law framework, the efficiency of which thus could be tested in this case. I analyze and discuss the results of these Shenzhen government's efforts. The only missing rule in the Shenzhen government policies, Rule 5, is actually applicable to a certain group of cases. I discuss the theoretical application of Rule 5 to these cases.

4.1. Rule 1

Content: Only the government is entitled to develop rural land; adverse development of rural land is prohibited and deterred through legal enforcement.

The Shenzhen government's initial response to the illegal development of rural land was to enforce the legal prohibition on rural land development and to demolish the illegal buildings, which turned out to be a huge task. From 1980s to the mid-1990s, the Shenzhen government promulgated a series of regulations to deal with the illegal development of rural land. However, compared to the widespread illegal development of rural land, the government's enforcement power seemed to be limited. When daily legal enforcement did not work, the Shenzhen government tried campaign-style legal enforcement, which means concentrating government resources in a fixed period to demolish illegal buildings and to punish people who violated the legal prohibition with a hope of deterring further violations. This was not successful and the number of illegal buildings has continued to increase as time went by. As land available for development became less and less, the Shenzhen government's tolerance of illegal rural land development became lower and lower.

In 1999, the Standing Committee of the People's Congress of Shenzhen made a decision to monitor and punish illegal rural land development. It made a comprehensive plan to deter illegal rural land development, including:

- The Department of Planning and Land should strictly monitor and punish illegal rural land development;
- The Department of Housing Renting should not issue permits to illegal buildings and should seriously punish the renting of illegal housing;
- The Department of Business Administration should not issue licenses to businesses located in illegal buildings and should suspend the licenses of businesses operating in illegal buildings;
- The Department of Construction Administration should not issue permits to illegal rural land development and should punish construction companies that participate in illegal rural land development;

- The Department of Public Security should punish and deter activities held in illegal buildings;
- The Departments of Electricity, Water and Gas should not supply electricity, water, or gas to buildings without legal approval documents.

In 2004, the Shenzhen government established a small leadership team headed by the mayor and consisting of the heads of relevant government departments, and a discipline team to supervise government officials to ensure that they fulfill their responsibilities in dealing with illegal rural land development. In 2009, the Shenzhen government established a new Department of Land Use Monitoring ("DLUM"), which has branches in all fifty-seven subdistricts of Shenzhen (Shenzhen Land Use Monitoring 2012).

According to a senior government official of Shenzhen, each street-level unit of the Department of Land Use Monitoring has to spend six to ten million RMB each year to monitor illegal rural land development and demolish illegal buildings. A typical demolition of illegal buildings involves dozens of government employees, including construction workers who are responsible for demolition and police officers who maintain order during the demolition (Fu 2007). The huge expense of demolition has become unaffordable to the government. In March 2013, the local People's Congress published a draft of Regulation of Land Use Monitoring, which required the owners of illegal building to pay the demolition fees. In order to do that, the DLUM could take the owners' properties, such as automobiles, legal real estate, and bank savings as lien (Peng 2013).

The crackdown was ineffective. Even the small leadership team, the specialized legal enforcement organ, and the supporting legal measures have not deterred illegal rural land development. From 1999 to 2010, the number of illegal buildings has grown from 221, 600 to 348, 400 (Shenzhen City Government 2010: 26).

These legal enforcement measures not only triggered widespread corruption, but also increased social conflicts. In my interviews with journalists, rural land investors, and retired government officials, it was widely acknowledged that many government employees bought apartments and even villas developed on the rural land. Villagers intentionally get government employees involved in the business. Selling part of their real estate to government employees is a strategy used in many cases of rural real estate development. Generally, a village head would approach a government official and tell him that their village has a plot or dozens of apartments for sale, and he can pay whatever price he likes. A Chinese

Central TV (hereafter "CCTV") report also testified to this fact. In a CCTV reporter's undercover investigation of a rural building of residential apartments, the reporter was told by both villagers and house brokers that about forty employees of the district government agency of land administration had bought apartments in the building (Li 2009).

At each level of government (street/subdistrict, district, and municipal), there is a division responsible for the enforcement of land laws and the demolishment of the illegal buildings. There are many publicly reported cases of the corruption in this division of the government (Du and Wan 2009). In reflecting upon its failure to stop rural real estate development, the Shenzhen city government also acknowledged corruption as an important reason. Villagers told me that payment to government officials is part of their investment. There are prices by the floors of the building. For example, in one village I investigated, the price is 6,000 RMB per floor. In a reported case, an accounting note prepared by a land developer revealed that the cost of development included a land use fee of 15.3 million and "other fees" of 5 million paid to government officials (Chen 2013). According to China Securities Daily, about one-third of the profits of the informal housing market fall into the hands of government officials in charge of enforcing land and housing laws (Du and Wan 2009).

In cases where "other fees" are not paid or where the legal prohibition has to be enforced due to political pressure from the city level, social conflicts might occur. Under this risk, each demolition is a battle between the government and villagers, which frequently results in bloody conflicts. Here is a typical case from Shenzhen:

> Hundreds of fully equipped legal enforcement officers assembled in a village to demolish illegal rural buildings. Several miles away, the traffic police blocked the road to stop "irrelevant parties" entering the village. Nevertheless, when the big machines began to demolish the illegal buildings, desperate villagers climbed onto the roof of the buildings and threw stones at the legal enforcement officers. The conflict resulted in five policemen and more villagers hurt
>
> (Fu 2007).

On the villagers' side, the legal enforcement did bring uncertainty to their *de facto* property and brought great loss to them from each successful demolition of illegal buildings. In 2012, the Shenzhen government took 7,093 legal enforcement actions and demolished illegal buildings totaling 1.39 million square meters (Zhou and Liu 2013). In a case the Shenzhen government flags as a model of legal enforcement, a mall for automobile sales was demolished without any violence. Twenty-three car companies had salerooms in this mall, which employed more than 1,900 people. The annual sales revenue of the mall was more than six billion RMB. Unfortunately, the building was illegal and it was demolished. The government demolished it with a wide mobilization of government resources, including one working team for each automobile saleroom (Zhou and Liu 2013). Obviously, this method of legal enforcement cannot be widely reproduced. Additionally, the demolition incurred huge economic losses, not to say other costs that might be caused by the demoralized possessors (Ellickson 1986) or the bribes they paid to evade the legal enforcement.

Finally, organized violence emerged in this illegal world to reduce demolition and social conflicts. For example, in 2012 the Shenzhen City Court adjudicated the case of the so-called biggest mafia in the history of Shenzhen. In this case, the main business of the gang was illegal rural land development. It exercised huge influence in the governance of many villages within a sub-district of Shenzhen through bribing government officials of the sub-district government and violence against villagers. This is definitely neither the best nor the most efficient order.

4.2. Rule 3

Content: The government grants legal titles to adversely developed buildings without demanding compensation.

In the United States, an adverse possessor can acquire title by possessing the property until the statute of limitations for the title owner to recover possession has run. Chinese law does not recognize the rights of adverse possession.[2] But that does not mean there is no adverse possession in reality. Actually, the tension between *de facto* possession and the *de jure* rights is particularly acute in the rapidly changing China, as we could see from the small-property case in Shenzhen. The Shenzhen government officials do consider seriously granting titles to adverse possessors. But they worry that such a measure would encourage further adverse possession. This worry has proved to be well founded.

Rule 3 means the AP gets title without paying for it after satisfying several conditions. The Shenzhen government tried this kind of policy in

---

[2] In the legislative process of the Property Law, many Chinese scholars suggested incorporating acquisitive prescription into the law, which is very similar to adverse possession. At the end, acquisitive prescription was not included in the Property Law, in opposition to the consensus among Chinese mainstream scholars. (See Chang 2012).

dealing with small-property real estate. In 1993, in the first regulation that recognized illegal rural land development as a serious problem, the Shenzhen government made a policy that houses built before 1986 could be registered without paying any fines (SZ Govt. [1993] 426). For houses built after 1986, the Shenzhen government cannot afford to grant all of them legal titles. Instead, the Shenzhen government said that it recognized indigenous villagers' rights to have their own residential houses. This meant the legal entitlement to a house on a 80-square-meters plot, with a total floor area of 240 square meters in 1986 (SZ Govt. [1982]185) and to a house on a 120-square-meters plot, with a total floor area of 480 square meters in 2001 (SZ Cong. S.C. [2001]33).

Meanwhile, to respond to some villagers' claim that they did not have a chance to build their own houses because of the Shenzhen government's harsh deterrent of illegal rural land development, the Shenzhen government promulgated a policy in 2006 to issue permits to villagers to build a house if they had not already built one (SZ Govt. [2006]105).

This free-titling policy greatly encouraged illegal rural land development. First, villagers devoted substantial resources to obtaining a permit to build a house, regardless of whether they had already built one. Getting a permit sometimes depended on how a "household" was defined. One household could be divided into two households just to get the benefits from the "one household, one house" policy. Many resources were spent on lobbying and bribing government officials with authority to issue such permits. Once villagers obtained such permits, almost no villager built only 480 square meters. Rather, 1000 square meters (eight to ten floors) was the average (Sun 2010; Xie 2010). Some villagers even made fake permits to post at construction sites. It was difficult to distinguish between the fake permits and the real ones. Thus, this policy has significantly increased the monitoring cost of the government. Not only did it take more time to identify construction projects with fake permits, but it also was costly to deter the construction of the extra floors beyond the legal permits. Moreover, with a hope of getting legal titles, villagers devoted time and money to building houses, which they would not have done without this policy. To strengthen their claim of rights under this policy, they also tended to build houses very rapidly – the rate was one floor per two days at the cost of safety and quality. Construction workers built twenty-four hours a day without adequate safety precautions and some were hurt or even killed in accidents (Shen 2009).

Second, many people viewed this and other policies that provide mechanisms for villagers to legalize their illegal real estate as a signal that the government was unable to enforce harsh demolition rules and would have to grant legal titles to all the illegal buildings. Villagers responded with more illegal rural land development to secure their claims of rights in the possible situation of free-titling-for-all. This was the main reason that each time the Shenzhen government initiated a campaign to deal with illegal buildings, there was a burst of illegal rural land development (Interview Transcript II 2012: 637, 648). As time passed, the government was more likely to recognize the historical illegal buildings and to seek to deter future illegal rural land development. For villagers, this gave them an incentive to develop adversely as much and as quickly as possible for fear of losing the chance in the future and in anticipation of receiving legal titles for their developments.

In Shenzhen, the free-titling policy has been limited to the "one household, one house" policy and several other very limited situations. In addition to encouraging illegal rural land development, the Shenzhen government gained very little revenue from this policy.

4.3. Rule 6

Content: The government not only has a monopoly of rural land development, but also has the option of giving up its monopoly and receiving compensation from the adverse developers.

If neither property rule works out, one should consider liability rules. Liability rules under the Calabresi and Melamed framework are actually call-option liability rules. Surprisingly, the liability rule that the Shenzhen government has used most was a put-option liability rule: Rule 6, according to which the government not only can keep its title, but also has an option to transfer its title to villagers, without the villagers' consent, in exchange for compensation.[3] This might be simply because the government was accustomed to a top-down approach and control.

---

[3] Chang (2015 forthcoming) argues that the Ayresian Rule 6 is not a put, as it is premised on the condition that a dispute has happened. He further argues that the contract/in personam nature of options make it incompatible with the in rem nature of property rights. Whether property rights are in personam or in rem rights is an open question. A short response is that whenever we examine a property dispute, it is a relationship between certain parties, and thus in personam relations. Property rights are defined to avoid and resolve disputes. Both property rules and liability rules are rules of protecting a legal entitlement, that is, rules that define available remedies whenever a violation of a legal entitlement happens, and not rules that grant extra in rem rights to an entitlement holder. Thus, put-option liability rule is not supposed to grant a property holder rights to force a

Early in 1988, the Shenzhen government promulgated a policy of allowing villagers to keep their illegal houses after paying fines, which were calculated according to the area of the illegally developed real estate. Each household has right to develop 80 square meters; but beyond that, the more they developed, the higher the fines they had to pay (SZ Govt. [1998] 253). In 1993, an owner of an illegal building could get a legal title after paying RMB 100 per square meter if the building was for industrial use and RMB 500 if for commercial use. Even nonvillagers who bought the illegal houses could get legal titles after paying some amount of money (SZ Govt. [1993]426).

In 2001, recognizing the reality that almost half of the houses in the city were illegal, the standing committee of the Shenzhen People's Congress promulgated a detailed decree to legalize most of the illegal buildings. Except for those in serious conflict with the city planning system, such as blocking a main road, the Shenzhen government intended to grant titles to most of the illegal buildings if their owners paid fines and land-use fees. The standards of fines and fees were again set according to owners' identities and the total areas of the buildings. It was a comprehensive plan, and it was supposed that legal title for each illegal building would have a price after calculation according to that plan. Owners of illegal buildings were required to apply for legal titles from the government within one year of the decree's promulgation, giving the Shenzhen government information on illegal buildings within its jurisdiction (SZ Cong. S.C. [2001]33; SZ Cong. S.C. [2001]34).

This did not work out well. It was not until 2010 that the Shenzhen government obtained the first detailed report on illegal buildings, which acknowledged that the 2001 legalization plan had not been well received despite the government's major efforts. From 2002 to 2010, among the 221, 600 illegal buildings built before 1999, only 57,400 were granted legal titles. In addition, by 2010, the total number of illegal buildings had increased to 348, 400 and kept growing day-by-day (Shenzhen City Government 2010: 289). There were other owners of illegal buildings who applied for legalization but who eventually declined to pay the fines and fees.

---

random person to purchase his property. In this sense, I do not see put-option liability rules fundamentally different from property rules or call-option liability rules. Also regarding Chang's critique that a real-world example of Rule 5 "is hard to come by," Section 4.6 of this chapter argues that Rule 5 could provide a better solution than direct condemnation to Jingui villagers who have been unable to make use of their illegal buildings due to the environmental regulation in Shenzhen.

In 2009, the government thought it might have set the prices too high and made the procedures too complicated. The People's Congress of Shenzhen promulgated another decision to legalize the increasing number of illegal buildings with more willingness to compromise (SZ Cong. S.C. [2009]101). Article I of the decision says that the government should respect history (*zunzhong lishi*), an indication of its respect for the rights of owners of the illegal buildings. This time the government tried to set lower prices and to make the procedures more convenient. This decision also required that a detailed plan should be made within one year. However, such a plan was not promulgated until December 30, 2013, which adopted both Rule 1 and Rule 6 to deal with small-property houses (SZ Govt. [2013]261). The Shenzhen government has decided to test this plan in several selected intra-city villages before fully implementing it, which would encourage villages not selected to develop further their land illegally.

This plan will not resolve the conundrum with which the Shenzhen government has been confronted. The information cost is too high for the government to enforce the put-option liability rule. It has to accumulate all the information on all illegal building within its jurisdiction, which is actually impossible. First, physical information might be the easier part: the location, height and floor areas are not difficult to collect; however, the history, quality and other invisible characteristics of the illegal buildings are actually very costly to collect. What's more complicated are the social and economic relations of the illegal buildings: who owns them? Who should get the legal title? What is worse, even with all the qualities of a building fixed and its owner identified, it is hard to know how much the owner values it. The cost of strategic bargaining could be prohibitively high, in particular when the government exercised its put option and thus had no opportunity to know the owner's evaluation. The complicated titling procedure makes the situation worse. For owners of illegal buildings, the complicated procedures imposed high information costs to them and fostered distrust of the government, both of which might prevent them from even thinking about whether the fees and fines charged by the government are reasonable or not. Several government officials told me that the fees and fines for a particular group of villagers were actually not high at all. Villagers in this particular group told me that they did not understand the government policies and that their friends had told them that the government would charge a lot of money for granting titles to their buildings. The amounts of both sides differed by a hundredfold.

In summary, there might be a price that both the government and adverse possessors would accept for legalization of the illegal buildings. But the government's put option is too costly to exercise. To make sure that the price was set right, the government had to design complicated rules, which in turn caused great information costs to villagers.

4.4. Rule 2

Content: The right to develop rural land belongs to the government, but adverse developers can get legal titles to their adversely developed buildings by paying compensation.

The most successful and promising solution has been the application of Rule 2. The government has the title, but adverse possessors can take it by paying compensation. This rule gradually emerged in numerous village redevelopment projects of Shenzhen. Originally in redeveloping the intracity villages where the illegal rural land development was prevalent, the Shenzhen government insisted that only legally developed land could be redeveloped and only legally built houses could be compensated, which turned out to be infeasible. It is clear to both the government, the villagers and other market participants that village redevelopment would bring them substantial profits. Slowly the government relaxed the requirements of legality. Whether the demolished buildings were legal or illegal fell to the wayside when one could build a modern neighborhood or a luxurious commercial center at the same location. In the end the government set its standard: if a redevelopment project can supply 20 percent of its land to the government for free and develop another 12 percent of land for public roads and other public facilities, the government would approve the project without considering whether the old buildings were illegal or legal (National School of Development 2013: 33).

It is essentially a call-option liability rule. The government has the title, but the village can pay the fixed price, that is, 32 percent of its land, to the government for legal rights to develop the remaining land. It is an option villagers can choose if they find it profitable. (They can choose not to exercise the option if they find it unprofitable.) The government needs to do very little. Villagers best know the value of their land. The cost of getting such information is much lower for them than for the government. This rule differs from the government's put-option liability rule in several aspects. First, this decentralized approach leaves the decision to villagers, who are more attuned to opportunities in the market, in addition to their better knowledge of the real estate under their control. Second, titling becomes a continuous process under this rule. Thus, villagers can decide whether to exercise their call option based on real market opportunities, rather than a theoretical prediction that legal titles would increase the value of their real estate. This flexibility in timing can even counteract the negative effects of the government's potential bad pricing – the price of exercising the call option might be too high for villagers one year, but with new market opportunities and increasing prices of real estate, the villagers might exercise their options anytime in the future. Villagers do not have this advantage when the government exercises its put option. The government could also choose the timing of exercising its put option, but without knowing the villagers' information, it is more difficult to choose the right time than it is for villagers, who have both their own information and the government's. Thus, Rule 2 leaves the decision to the party with better information.

Reality has proved that Rule 2 is the most effective one. In 2011, among the newly developed 3.8 million square meters of houses on the formal market of Shenzhen, 1.5 million square meters came from village redevelopment. Compared with the reluctant responses to other legalization plans, villagers have very actively applied for village redevelopment. From 2009 to 2012, there have been 342 such projects, involving 30 square kilometers of the illegally developed land (National School of Development 2013: 33). In the following, I present an example.

Caiwuwei is a village in the central area of Shenzhen. Villagers developed its land illegally, relying on the rent from the illegal buildings for their livelihood. Life was quite good for them because of the strong rental market. Many middle- to low-income people, including factory workers, restaurant waitresses, and even white-collar company employees, rented apartments in this village because of the convenient location and the lower rents and living expenses in the village. Most villagers did not see any necessity of applying for legal titles to their buildings from the government, which, in turn, did not want the instability risk from demolishing a village where thousands of people lived.

But everybody saw the wide gap between the rental price of apartments within the village and legal apartments one block away from the village. There was huge capital embedded in this village. After the government set the standards of village redevelopment, village leaders began to think about the possibility of awakening this sleeping capital. Land developers also came to tell villagers how much money they could make from the proposed redevelopment.

The project demolished illegal buildings of about 150,000 square meters and built a 100-floor skyscraper on the plot of 45,000 square meters. The total area of saleable floors of the building was 480,000 square meters, one-third of which were used to compensate the owners of the illegal buildings. (A few villagers chose compensation in cash, which turned out to be a big mistake.) Owners of the illegal buildings received the same size of apartments after the village redevelopment. However, the value of this real estate was about ten times higher, making many villagers millionaires or even billionaires. The government received revenue of 200 million RMB and well-built public roads, parks, and schools in the neighborhood. The land developer, which spent over six billion RMB redeveloping this village, got about 300,000 square meters of commercial real estate worth at least 15 billion RMB (National School of Development 2013: 72).

Not all village redevelopment can bring such a dramatic change. However, the advantage of Rule 2 is that it greatly reduces the information costs required to make it possible. Moreover, since the option is at the hands of villagers, it cannot make the situation worse – status quo is the baseline.

4.5. Rule 4

Content: The government grants legal titles to the adversely developed buildings, but has an option to take these buildings so long as it compensates their owners.

Another option that the government tried was to requisition illegal buildings with compensation to the owners. In the past five years, the Chinese central government has required local governments to build some amount of public housing for low-income population. The Shenzhen government did not have enough land to build public housing required by the central government. At the same time, most low-income people in Shenzhen lived in the small-property houses. The Shenzhen government found that rather than developing extra houses, requisitioning small-property houses might be a better solution.

Zhongmin Garden was a small-property building built by villagers and outside land developers in violation of the governmental prohibition of rural land development. The total floor area was 74,352 square meters. The Shenzhen government requisitioned it at the price of 3,642 RMB per square meters, which was about one-third of the average price of legal buildings in the surrounding area. The Shenzhen government made a comprehensive examination of the quality of the building and found that it was safe. The reason was that it was designed by qualified construction designers and built by qualified construction companies, as most small-property high-rises were. The price was a bit higher than the construction cost and thus the developer and villagers could still make a small profit (Interview Transcript II 2012: 11–12).

This single case was successful. However, it is unclear how widely it could be replicated. As the number of cases increases, the costs to the government of finding proper buildings and requisitioning them would increase rapidly. Setting a proper price is also a key issue, the failure of which would be more disastrous than Rule 6. There would be social conflicts if the government insisted on requisitioning the illegal houses with too little compensation. The costs of information and bargaining to set the proper price could be high. Moreover, the Shenzhen government could not afford to purchase about 400 million square meters of illegal buildings and might not even need so much public housing at all. At the end, the purpose of "requisitioning small-property buildings for public housing" is dubious. If small-property buildings were good for public housing and indeed served as homes to low-income population through the small-property market, why should the government intervene?

4.6. Rule 5

Content: The government not only grants legal titles to adversely developed buildings, but also gives their owners an option of selling their buildings in return for compensation from the government.

Under Rule 5, villagers would not only have the legal title, but also an option to waive their titles in return for government compensation. The Shenzhen government has not taken such a rule in dealing with the illegal rural land development in its history, but this rule could be very helpful in dealing with a special category of illegal buildings in Shenzhen.

Jingui Village is located close to the water sources of the city. It is about 13 square kilometers and has about 1,200 villagers. In 2004, the Shenzhen government delineated ecological control lines and the whole village is within these control lines. There were 408 illegal buildings with the total floor area of 125,000 square meters and total land area of 64,700 square meters. The Shenzhen government could not afford to demolish these buildings because they were shelters and factories on which villagers relied for living. On the other hand, the villagers could not make full use of these illegal buildings or even make necessary maintenance and repairs due to environmental regulations. These illegal buildings were in quite poor states. In contrast to villagers in other parts of Shenzhen who have become rich from illegal rural land development, Jingui villagers are poor (Interview Transcript 2012: 418–21). Jingui village is not alone. In 2006, the total land area of illegal buildings within the ecology control lines was 31.76 square kilometers, about 500 times of that of Jingui village (Liu 2010).

Some have proposed ecological compensation to involved villagers. Similar to the discussions on regulatory compensation in the United States, the proposed ecological compensation would be a huge financial burden on the government. Moreover, the value of these buildings and land has not dropped to zero. Not all of them can be used for industry or commerce. It would be hard to decide on the standards of compensation. Instead, Rule 5 is a good choice here. The Shenzhen government should not only grant legal titles to the villagers' illegal buildings; it also should give them an option to sell those buildings to the government at a fixed price. With all values in consideration (efficiency, aesthetics, quietness, and so forth), villagers should have the freedom to choose whether to sell their buildings to the government or not. As distributional fairness is a main concern behind this rule, the government does not have to set prices high, and it should set them at reasonable levels to help villagers maintain an average standard of living.

Conclusion: an optional law approach to informal property rights

The tension between legal entitlements and *de facto* possession is prevalent in developing countries (e.g., Trebilcock and Veel 2008; Fitzpatrick 2006). How to revive dead capital has been a hot topic in developmental economics in the past decades (e.g., De Soto 1989, 2000; Di Taranto 2012). Scholars have argued about whether to formalize the informal property rights but we do not understand well how to incorporate the informal property rights into the formal legal system. In De Soto's (2000) words, how to "root the law in the social contracts"? The conflicts between formal law and informal property rights are essentially those between *de facto* possessors and *de jure* owners. Adverse possession provides a feasible mechanism to integrate informal property claims to the formal system, and avoids the shock of a top-down centralized rearrangement of property rights.

More importantly, by applying Ayres's framework of legal entitlements to the particular area of adverse possession, this case study shows that there are actually more choices for structuring the legal entitlements than simply deciding whether to grant a title to the original owner or the possessor (see King 2003; Field 2003). The essential idea is that the government should decide who decides, rather than deciding the final allocation of resources. Options, rather than titles, should be granted to individual adverse possessors as they are more numerous and more capable of multiple takings than one government, and have both private information unknown to the government and the more speculative valuation of the land than the government.

This case study is also further evidence for the relevance of Ayres' optional law theory to real-world policy making. It does not investigate the property/liability rule debate comprehensively, but it does provide examples in which liability rules are more efficient than property rules.

References

Ackerman, William G., and Johnson, Shane T. 1996. "Outlaws of the Past: A Western Perspective on Prescription and Adverse Possession," *Land & Water Law Review* 31:79–112.

Ayres, Ian 2005. *Optional Law: The Structure of Legal Entitlements*. University of Chicago Press.

Ayres, Ian, and Balkin, Jack M. 1996. "Legal Entitlements as Auctions: Property Rules, Liability Rules, and Beyond," *Yale Law Journal* 106:703–50.

Ayres, Ian, and Eric Talley 1995. "Solomonic Bargaining: Dividing A Legal Entitlement to Facilitate Coasean Trade," *Yale Law Journal* 104:1027–1117.

Calabresi, Guido, and Melamed, A. Douglas 1972. "Property Rules, Liability Rules, and Inalienability: One View of the Cathedral," *Harvard Law Review* 85:1089–1128.

Chang, Yun-chien 2015 forthcoming, "Optional Law in Property: A Theoretical Critique," New York University Journal of Law and Liberty, available at SSRN: http://ssrn.com/abstract=2351651.

2012. "Property Law with Chinese Characteristics: An Economic and Comparative Analysis," *Brigham-Kanner Property Rights Conference Journal* 1:345–72.

Chen, Feng April 14, 2006. "Secret of 50 Times of the Land Price," *Huaxia Daily*, at A12.

Chen, Xiaoying May 10, 2013. "Chawei Fee: Toll for Illegal Buildings," *Huaxia Daily*, available at http://house.hexun.com/2013-05-10/154000572_1.html (last accessed September 15, 2013).

China Net 2008. "Small-Property Houses total 6.6 Billion Square Meters, almost the same amount of Legal Housing Transactions within a Decade," www.china.com.cn/info/txt/2008-11/17/content_16779899.htm (last accessed May 6, 2014).

China News 2010. "Ministry of Land and Resources Emphasized to Clear Small Property House and Golf Court This Year," http://politics.people.com.cn/GB/1027/10895913.html (last accessed February 27, 2010).

De Soto, Hernando 1989. *The Other Path*. New York: Harper & Row
   2000. *The Mystery of Capital: Why Capitalism Triumphs in the West and Fails Everywhere Else*. New York: Basic books.

Di Taranto, Giuseppe 2012. "Towards a Renewed Development Theory: Hernando De Soto and Institutionalist Contractualism," *Journal of European Economic History* 41:81–99.

Du, Yawen, and Wan, Jing August 21, 2009. "Billions of Hot Money Bet on the Legalization of Small-Property Houses,"*China Securities Daily*, available at http://biz.xinmin.cn/rehouse/2009/08/21/2410786_6.html (last accessed February 15, 2013).

Ellickson, Robert C. 1986. "Adverse Possession and Perpetuities Law: Two Dents in the Libertarian Model of Property Rights," *Washington University Law Quarterly* 64:723–37.
   1993. "Property in Land," *Yale Law Journal* 102:1315–1400.

Epstein, Richard A. 1996. "Babbitt v Sweet Home Chapters of Oregon: The Law and Economics of Habitat Preservation," *Supreme Court Economic Review* 32:1–57.
   1997. "Protecting Property with Legal Remedies: A Common Sense Reply to Professor Ayres," *Valparaiso University Law Review* 32:833–53.

Feng, Jie 2006. "Two Decades of Land Administration in Shenzhen," *Shenzhen SEZ Daily*, June 22, 2006: A1.

Field, Erica 2003. "Property Rights, Community Public Goods, and Household Time Allocation in Urban Squatter Communities: Evidence from Peru," *William and Mary Law Review* 45:837–87.

Fitzpatrick, Daniel 2006. "Evolution and Chaos in Property Rights Systems: The Third World Tragedy of Contested Access," *Yale Law Journal* 115:996–1048.

Fu, Ke January 23, 2007. "Many Police Got Hurt in Demolition of Private Houses," *Southern Metropolitan Daily*, available at http://news.sina.com.cn/c/l/2007-01-23/115112115150.shtml (last accessed December 9, 2009).

Galiani, Sebastian, and Schargrodsky, Ernesto 2010. "Property Rights for the Poor: Effects of Land Titling," *Journal of Public Economics* 94:700–29.

Interview Transcript II 2012, on file with the author.

King, Winter 2003. "Illegal Settlements and the Impact of Titling Programs," *Harvard International Law Journal* 44:433–71.

Krier, James E., and Schwab, Stewart J. 1995. "Property Rules and Liability Rules: The Cathedral in another Light," *New York University Law Review* 70:440–83.
Le, Zheng (ed.) 2010. *The Path of Shenzhen*. Shenzhen: Haitian Press.
Li, Jie June 13, 2009. "Shenzhen Land Developers Issue Certificates of Small-Property Houses," CCTV Economics Half an Hour, available at http://finance.sina.com.cn/china/dfjj/20090613/22346345587.shtml.
Liu, Fang October 25, 2010. "Bargaining about the Ecological Lines in Shenzhen," *China Youth Daily*, available at http://zqb.cyol.com/content/2010-10/25/content_3432311.htm (last accessed September 15, 2013).
Merrill, Thomas W. 1985. "Property Rules, Liability Rules and Adverse Possession," *Northwestern University Law Review* 79:1122–54.
National School of Development 2013. *Report on Land Reform in Shenzhen*, on file with the author.
Ostrom, Elinor 1990. *Governing the Commons: The Evolution of Institutions for Collective Action*. Cambridge University Press.
Peng, Yan March 12, 2013. "New Regulations Require Owners of Illegal Buildings to Pay for the Demolition Expenses," *Shenzhen Commercial Daily*, available at www.ceosz.cn/SzNews/SzYw/SzNews_20130312093619_166233_2.html (last accessed May 6, 2014).
Qiao, Shitong 2013. "Planting Houses in Shenzhen: A Real Estate Market without Legal Titles," *Canadian Journal of Law and Society*, available at http://papers.ssrn.com/sol3/papers.cfm?abstract_id=2391012.
  2015 forthcoming. "Small Property, Big Market: A Focal Point Explanation," *American Journal of Comparative Law* 63, available at http://papers.ssrn.com/sol3/papers.cfm?abstract_id=2399675.
Shen, Wenfeng November 1, 2011. "Some Communities Rush to Build Houses Illegally for Sale," *Shenzhen Evening Newspaper*, available at http://news.dayoo.com/shenzhen/200911/01/73553_100291041_4.htm (last accessed September 15, 2013).
Sun, Zhongchun October 18, 2010. "Street Office Applied for License to Build Small-Property Houses," *Shenzhen Evening Newspaper*, available at http://szhome.oeeee.com/a/20101018/316592_2.html. (last accessed September 15, 2013).
Shenzhen City Government 2010. Investigation Report on Illegal Buildings in Shenzhen, on file with the author.
  1982a. Stipulations on Strictly Prohibiting Private and Non-Planning Housing Building within the Special Economic Zone (March 29, 1982, SZ Govt. [1982] 1).
  1982b. Temporal Regulations on Rural Collective Members' Use of Land for Housing Construction(September 17, 1982, SZ Govt. [1982] 185).
  1988. Stipulations on Illegal Land Development and Land Registration (January 1, 1988, SZ Govt. [1988] 253).
  1993. Stipulations on Property Rights of Historical Real Estate Problem(November 9, 1993, SZ Govt. [1993] 426).

2006. Temporal Stipulations on Indigenous Villagers' Construction of Non-Business Residential Houses (June 19, 2006, SZ Govt. [2006] 105).

2013. Experimental Implementation of the Decision on Dealing with Historical Illegal Buildings in Rural Urbanization (December 30, 2013, SZ Govt. [2013] 261).

Shenzhen People's Congress Standing Committee 2001a. Stipulations on Historical Illegal Residential Buildings (October 17, 2001, SZ Cong. S.C. [2001] 33).

2001b. Stipulations on Historical Illegal Business Buildings (October 17, 2001, SZ Cong. S.C. [2001] 34).

2009. Decision on Dealing with Historical Illegal Buildings in Rural Urbanization (May 21, 2009, SZ Cong S.C. [2009] 101).

Shenzhen Statistics Bureau and NBS Survey Office in Shenzhen 2011. *Shenzhen Statistical Yearbook 2011*, Beijing: China Statistics Press.

Shenzhen Land Use Monitoring 2009. "Review of the Municipal Policies of Illegal Buildings," available at www.szpls.gov.cn/whkj/xxdy/201203/t20120312_71655.html. (last accessed Dec. 9, 2009).

State Bureau of Statistics 2008. "Economic Review of the Second Quarter of 2008: Market does not Support High Housing Price," http://news.xinhuanet.com/fortune/2008-08/05/content_8974798.htm (last accessed Dec. 10, 2009).

Smith, Henry E., and Merrill, Thomas W. 2010. *The Oxford Introductions to U.S. Law: Property*. Oxford University Press.

Song, Linfei July 4, 2012. "No Special Economic Zone for Legalization of Small-Property Houses," http://theory.people.com.cn/n/2012/0704/c112851-18443279.html (last accessed February 15, 2013).

Wang, Songcai June 22, 2009. "Observation: Sale of Small Property Houses in Defiance of Law, Local Government Facing Inquiry," *China Economic Times*, available at www.chinanews.com.cn/estate/estate-zcpl/news/2009/06-22/1744199.shtml (last accessed May 6, 2014).

Trebilcock, Michael, and Veel, Paul-Erik 2008. "Property Rights and Development: The Contingent Case for Formalization," *University of Pennsylvania Journal of International Law* 30:397–481.

Weiner, Justus Reid 2003. "The Global Epidemic of Illegal Building and Demolitions: Implications for Jerusalem," *Jerusalem Letter*, available at www.jcpa.org/jl/vp498.htm.

Xie, Xiaoguo, et al. February 24, 2010. "Interest Groups Lobby the Mayor of Shenzhen for Illegal Buildings," *Yang Cheng Evening Newspaper*, available at www.fwwwd.com/content/2010-02/24/content_4412896_3.htm (last accessed May 6, 2014).

Yu, Zhong "Why Is Small-Property Small?," *Dushu*, No. 4, 2009.

Zhou, Chang and Genghuai, Liu June 28, 2013. "Punishing Illegal Land Use to Serve Scientific City Development," *Southern Metropolitan Daily*, http://sz.house.sina.com.cn/news/2013-06-28/08263288834.shtml (last accessed May 6, 2014).

12

Title in the shadow of possession

ABRAHAM BELL

1. Introduction

Possession is an important source of rights in property law. Several common maxims reflect this importance (though not with the highest degree of precision). "Possession is the root of title," we are told. "Possession is nine-tenths of the law" (Compare Chapter 2).

In modern property law, possession can be an important source of legal property rights, both as a means of acquiring title, and as its own kind of independent property right. Possession can also support title owners by providing evidence of title where there is no more formal process for proving rights.

A small but significant body of scholarship has sought to justify property law's use of possession as a key to acquiring greater property rights. In his classic article on the question of why property doctrines are so deferential to first possessors, Richard Epstein (1979) posited that first possession is an essential rule in property law primarily because it long has been used, and it provides for rapid dissemination of private property rights. Carol Rose (1985), by contrast, argued that first possession serves as a proxy for the dissemination of information about property claims, and thereby plays a key role in ensuring that claims of title are well known and clear.

This chapter advances an entirely different justification for the importance of possession in property law. The chapter posits that rules of possession are important for maintaining the integrity and importance of a legal property system. Simply put, it is essential for the law to

Professor, University of San Diego School of Law and Bar Ilan University Faculty of Law. This paper was prepared for the Fifth Law and Economic Analysis Conference on issues of possession in property law at Institutum Iurisprudentiae, Academia Sinica (2013) and was presented as well at the 2014 annual conference of the Association for Law, Property and Society at the University of British Columbia. The author thanks Benito Arruñada Yun-chien Chang, Tze-Shiou Chien, Dan Kelly, Dan Klerman, Daphna Lewinsohn-Zamir, Tzu-Yi Lin, Kung-Chung Liu, Thomas Merrill, Gideon Parchomovsky and Shitong Qiao for helpful comments and suggestions.

recognize *de jure* rights that already exist *de facto*, lest the legal system of property lose its salience. *De facto* possession, in many cases, offers nearly all the utility to possessors that they would enjoy if they were *de jure* owners. If the law did not recognize legal rights because of possession, many first possessors would find it advantageous to eschew legal rights, and protect their possessory rights extra-legally. Indeed, in cases where the law denies property rights notwithstanding possession, robust black markets have developed, undermining the goals that led lawmakers to split property rights from possession. Examples of this phenomenon can be found, for instance, in the markets for illegal antiquities and some kinds of natural resources.

First possession rules can have undesirable results. As noted in studies in settings as disparate as the California Gold Rush (Umbeck 1977a; Umbeck 1977b; Zerbe and Anderson 2001; Libecap 2007), patents (Barzel 1968), and modern fisheries (Johnson and Libecap 1982; Leal 2005; Singh, Weninger and Doyle 2006; Libecap 2007), first appropriation rules can lead to destructive races that deplete the underlying resource. Thus, rewarding possession with title is not always the ideal reward for *de facto* possession. This chapter suggests that salvage rewards and similar mechanisms will often be a superior means of easing the transition from *de facto* possession to *de jure* rights.

2. Justifying the importance of possession

At the risk of oversimplification, one can say that property recognizes the power of possessors' rights in three different kinds of ways.

First, possession can become a gateway to title. Many doctrines award title to previously unowned assets based on "first possession." One acquires title to previously unowned wild animals and some natural resources, for instance, by capturing them and reducing them to possession (illustrated by the classic case of *Pierson* v. *Post*, 3 Cai. R. 175, 2 Am. Dec. 264 (N.Y. 1805)). In some cases, possession can even transfer title to assets that are owned by another. For example, the doctrine of adverse possession transfers title from a passive owner to a long-term trespasser because of continuous possession of the asset (subject to the other conditions of adverse possession) (Hovenkamp, Kurtz and Gallanis 2014).

Second, possession can be important for evidentiary reasons. Many traditional doctrines grant a possessor prima facie evidence of title. For instance, the Twyne's case, [1601] 76 ER 809, famously ruled that a gift should be set aside as fraudulent where the donor maintained possession. Possession, in other words, sometimes should be treated as more reliable evidence of the true state of title in the asset than an otherwise valid document attesting to ownership of a nonpossessor.

Third, possession can itself be a form of lesser and informal "title." A possessor, for instance, has the right to maintain suits to recover possession, or to repel trespassers, even in the absence of any formal title. The famous case of *Armory* v. *Delamirie*, [1722] 1 Strange 505, for instance, held that a finder who became the lawful possessor of a piece of jewelry could recover the value of the item from a jeweler when the jeweler accepted a bailment from the finder, even though the finder acknowledged that he had no ownership interest in the jewelry.

The most significant pieces of scholarship on possession focus on the first of these three phenomena: the use of doctrines of possession to allocate title. The idea that "possession is the root of title" has spurred a fascinating scholarly literature. Two major articles by leading modern property scholars advance competing normative theories in justification of doctrines of first possession.

In his celebrated "Possession as the Root of Title," Richard Epstein (1979) explores the normative justification for the common law's allocation of title in property to the first possessor of an unowned item. Epstein's defense is surprisingly qualified. He offers moral reasons to award title to a first possessor, but finds them wanting. Ultimately, Epstein finds that first possession is imperfect and best justified as a time-honored and workable way of awarding title, to which the only real alternative is the less-desirable common ownership by all.

Carol Rose's (1985) account of possession focuses on information. Rose covers much of the same ground as Epstein, but argues that first possession is better justified as a basis of ownership on the grounds that it "amount[s] to something like yelling loudly to all who may be interested." Rose argues that possession generally is accompanied by open assertions of title, and that property law recognizes title based on the best communication of rights where first possession serves as a proxy for that communication. Unfortunately, Rose acknowledges, possession is an imperfect proxy, and the communication of rights is not the sole value to be promoted in rules of property.

Epstein's and Rose's classic articles have not exhausted the field. Much scholarship has focused on the question of when first possession rules can be expected to lead to optimal exploitation of resources. In some cases, it is argued, awarding title to first possessors can lead to wasteful races for assets, or, potentially, excessive exploitation of the resource. In other cases, first possession rules can provide a low-cost rule for allocating title, and prevent overexploitation of the commons.

Dean Lueck (1995) argues that the tradeoff between the good and bad aspects of rules of first possession does not universally lead to a single best outcome, and that every first appropriation rule is vulnerable to some rent dissipation. Lueck identifies a number of factors as crucial to the question of whether and when first possession rules will lead to excessive consumption and rapid dissipation. First, Lueck distinguishes between possession in stock (for example, the right to an entire underground pool of oil) or flow (for example, the right only to that oil from the pool drawn out and captured). Naturally, in some cases, giving possession only to flow encourages excessively rapid extraction of the resource. Second, Lueck points to the importance of capture technology and the heterogeneity of parties seeking to capture the resource. To take an extreme example, if only one person has oil-extracting technology, a rule of first possession of the flow will lead to the same outcome as first possession of the stock or any other rule: the person with the technological advantage will own all the oil and extract it at the optimal speed. Lastly, Lueck notes that other factors, such as the likelihood of capturing influence in the political system, may affect the optimality of one rule or another.

In synthesizing this scholarship, Gary Libecap (2007) commented:

> First-possession has been criticized on fairness grounds because it discriminates against new entrants, and existing holdings may be large ... First-possession also has been criticized for leading to rent dissipation if homogeneous claimants race to establish property rights. But if the parties are heterogeneous with respect to cost and the resulting rights are secure and permanent, then full dissipation will not occur. Moreover, the "winners" of such a race may be the most efficient producers ... There are ... costs with any rights allocation rule and there is no reason to believe that first-possession is more costly than other assignments. Generally, if the transaction costs of subsequent exchange are high, then it makes sense to assign rights to low-cost users with histories of past involvement in the resource.

Recent scholarship has paid much less attention to the other roles possession plays in the law of property. This is due to the decline over the years in the importance of these other possession-related doctrines of property (Epstein 1998).

Douglas Baird and Thomas Jackson (1984), for example, explain that the evidentiary importance of possession has declined as other means of transmitting information about property rights, such as property registries ("filing systems" in the terminology of Baird and Jackson), have proliferated. However, doctrines granting evidentiary weight to possession in title disputes have not disappeared. Baird and Jackson, for instance, recall the rule of *Twyne's Case*, (1601) 76 ER 809, according to which transfers of ownership of chattel unaccompanied by transfers of possession are presumptively fraudulent, and they note that modern law may still make similar presumptions of fraudulent intent when title is transferred without possession.

Likewise, Richard Epstein (1998) observes that while modern rules have reduced the importance of doctrines focused on protecting possession (as opposed to title), they have not disappeared entirely. The law of trespass, for instance, still sounds in possession; a possessor may maintain a trespass suit, notwithstanding the lack of proper title. A bailee still has the right to maintain a suit against a tortfeasor who harms the bailed item, even though the bailor has superior title to the object. Epstein writes that possession has declined in legal importance not due to the disappearance of the relevant legal doctrines, but, rather, because the doctrines are less frequently invoked. Possession still lies at the core of modern private actions sounding in trespass. However, writes Epstein, "private rights of action are not normally needed to maintain the security of possession" today. As well, the procedural niceties dividing the formal causes of action have lost importance to the courts.

Nonetheless, even with the decline of importance of some kinds of legal doctrines of possession, possession continues to maintain a position of prominence in the law of property. And without gainsaying the insights of the scholarly literature on possession to date, more remains to be said in support of the role of possession in property law.

3. Possession as a valuable attribute

To understand why possession is important in property law, it is useful to set aside the law for a moment, and consider the importance of possession outside the law. Possession is and would be important outside the law. In many – perhaps most – contexts, actual possession provides enough for the possessor to enjoy nearly all the benefit of ownership. If someone takes possession of an apple from a tree, he or she can almost realize the full benefit of the apple even in a world without ownership rights. The possessor of the apple can consume it, preserve it, store it, exchange it, and perform any number of other actions. Indeed, if the possessor can find a reliable mechanism for enforcing the promise, the possessor can even temporarily relinquish possession by allowing another to hold the apple, while still expecting to enjoy the benefit of repossessing it afterward.

The importance of possession for one asset is reinforced by the importance of possession for another asset. Possessors often use the security of their possession in one asset to guarantee the security of possession in another. For instance, where the possessor of a home on Blackacre feels secure that her possession of the home is likely not to be breached, she may keep jewelry, art and other valuables locked up inside the home. The locks, both on the home itself, and on any combination safe or other security mechanism within, illustrate the importance the possessor attaches to being able to maintain continued possession, and the degree to which utility in the items is tied to security of possession.

Oftentimes, scholars point to security interests as the quintessential proof of the advantage legal title holds over mere possession (De Soto 2000; Kerekes and Williamson 2008). The argument, popularized by De Soto, is that a person who merely possesses an object without legal title cannot unlock the object's capital potential because she cannot use the object as security for a loan. Undoubtedly, De Soto is right to observe that legal title is valuable, yet even security interests can be based on naked possession. Pledges are security interests based solely on possession (Gilmore 1999), and they play an important part in financing, even today.

Because possession is so valuable, it has social meaning even where there is no legal property to speak of. Children fiercely guard possessions, even without a legal concept of ownership. People guard parking spots, seats at dining tables, and innumerable other items outside the framework of formal property rights. Sometimes, people guard such possession in direct opposition to formal legal rights. Squatters guard their trespassing shacks, and art thieves guard their stolen paintings. In these cases, possession may be the only way the possessors can extract utility. Once art thieves lose possession of their stolen paintings, they are unlikely ever to recover them.

Possession, in other words, is extremely valuable, quite apart from property law. Possession would be a vital part of the property framework, even if the law had not invested importance in it. In a world without legal property rights, actual possession would be guarded fiercely, as it would potentially be the most reliable means of enjoying the benefits we associate with property ownership.

4. Different kinds of property rights

The importance of possession outside the formal bounds of legal property is a key to understanding the reasons why property law must pay heed to possession. To understand this, we should examine the relationship between formal property law and *de facto*, or informal, property rights.

The *actual* ability to enjoy utility from property is not restricted to the *legal* ability to enjoy such utility. Non-owners can realize utility from assets over which they have no legally recognized property rights. A beautiful private garden, for instance, may give enjoyment to passersby or neighbors, even though they have no rights in the garden. So long as the owner receives sufficient utility from the garden by herself and she lacks reasonable means for withholding the benefit from non-paying third parties, there is little reason to worry that she will curtail the positive externalities to others. The utility enjoyed by non-owner beneficiaries can also come in less congenial forms. Thieves, for example, predictably enjoy some unlawful portion of the value of others' formal property. The owner of an apple orchard on a public road can guess that passersby will steal some of the apples. The owner may nevertheless eschew remedial action because the cost of security measures is high while the losses to thievery are low (Barzel 1997).

In fact, the ability to enjoy benefit from assets need not be related at all to any legal private property rights. The open seas, air, and, in some jurisdictions, beachfront and navigable waters may all be excluded from the realm of private property rights, but this does not mean that no one is able to enjoy utility from the assets.

Yoram Barzel (1997) terms the ability to enjoy utility from assets, irrespective of ownership, as "economic property rights." By contrast, he defines the ability to enjoy such utility from assets according to law as "legal property rights." The terminology reflects the fact that the law does not set the practical bounds of a person's ability to enjoy utility in assets.

Barzel's dichotomy highlights a different way of dividing actual property rights: *de facto* and *de jure* rights in property. The difference between *de facto* and *de jure* rights is slightly different than that between economic and legal property rights. Like Barzel's economic property rights, *de facto* property rights are those that can be enjoyed in fact, lawfully or unlawfully. *De jure* property rights, by contrast, are those that are recognized at law. *De jure* property rights might exist without any practical ability to enjoy the rights. For instance, the law may recognize the title of Smith in Blackacre, but Blackacre may be so situated as to defy the ability of Smith or anyone else to obtain utility from the property. Whereas Barzel appears to consider legal property rights a subset of economic property rights, there is no reason to believe that *de jure* rights are necessarily a subset of *de facto* rights. Sadly, there will be cases when the property rights that exist on paper are utterly useless in the real world. Rather, we should consider both *de facto* and *de jure* property rights as describing potential rights in assets, where the two categories may completely overlap, partially overlap, or completely diverge.

If we consider the matter further, we should see that, at any given time, several parallel systems of *de jure* and *de facto* rights may exist. Generally, the systems will overlap, at least in part. For instance, a legal entity may own property and create a set of legal property claims that are valid within the organization, but not without. This will be true even as the outside legal regime sets its own set of rules of property rights. To illustrate the example, consider a kibbutz (an Israeli commune). The kibbutz has its own set of internal property rights within the kibbutz, allocating living space, parking rights, and so on among its members. However, these rights are internal to the kibbutz only. Under Israeli law, the kibbutz is a collective organization that owns all the property and the members own nothing and have only a share in control over the kibbutz. We might say that in this case there are two parallel systems of *de jure* rights, each of which is limited. The kibbutz members' rights are licit and lawfully protected under the terms of the organizational law governing the kibbutz, while the kibbutz's rights as a collective are also licit and protected under the terms of the more general property law within the jurisdiction. The two sets of *de jure* rights are not fully translatable, but no less real for that (Bell and Parchomovsky 2013).

Bell and Parchomovsky (2013) examined the potential costs of translating rights across different property systems. Even if different property systems are fully compatible – that is, where it is possible to find for every right in one system a corresponding right in another that will offer the same protections over the same assets – there are translation costs. Rights in one system must be deciphered for another. Registration of rights might be incomplete or simply different, meaning that it will be costly to obtain information about the different rights. Frequently, the property systems are not fully compatible, meaning that the rights one has under one system cannot be fully enjoyed in another. This, for example, is the case with property rights within kibbutzim.

Possessory rights outside the law can be seen as a type of *de facto* property right that exists in parallel with other property rights systems. *De facto* possessory rights created by possession are valuable for the possessors even without any formal corresponding legal property rights. The value of the *de facto* rights depends on the degree to which the possessor can enjoy the utility of the object based on possession alone as well as the translatability of the rights.

Consider, for instance, a legal regime in which river waters are treated like air; that is, there are no formal property rights in the waters of rivers, even if water is drawn from the river. Anyone who happens upon a river may draw as much water as he or she wants. Even in the absence of any formal legal rights in the water, a possessor can enjoy all or nearly all of the utility in water drawn from the river. The possessor can drink the water, wash with it, and engage in any other consumptive use. The possessor can also transfer the water, and any transferee who considers the delivery more convenient than independently drawing the water will readily pay for transfer of possession. In such a system, the *de facto* property rights have their maximum value, because the possessor can enjoy essentially all the rights she would get with legal title, as well as the ability to transfer the rights to another in free exchange.

5. Lawful and unlawful possession

Not all *de facto* possessory rights are alike. Some such rights are unrecognized by the law, but do not conflict with the law. Other such rights are themselves unlawful. In some cases, the *de facto* rights attach to the same assets to which *de jure* rights attach, but the right holders are different persons.

Consider for instance, possession of a stolen car. There is almost certainly an owner who holds *de jure* title in the car. That owner will also likely be considered to be *de jure* "in possession" of the car for purposes of maintaining various private rights of action to enforce her property rights. At the same time, the thief enjoys *de facto* possession of the car. The thief, and not the owner, can drive the car from place to place. The thief can chop the car into pieces, not the owner. Thus, the owner and the thief simultaneously own contradictory sets of rights. The thief can sell the *de facto* possessory rights on the black market. The owner, in the meantime, even without actual possession, has title to the car and can sell ownership and the right of possession in licit markets, subject, of course, to proper disclosure about the relevant facts concerning the purchase. For simplicity's sake, we can call this kind of case a *de jure-de facto* clash, characterized by the existence of simultaneous lawful and unlawful rights of possession in competing hands.

Other cases present no clash at all. In many cases, the law has little to say about *de facto* property rights because the state has no interest in regulating possession of the item, or, more likely, it has a strong interest in not regulating possession of the item. Such is the case in many localized property systems, that is, nonstandard property regimes that coexist alongside state property regimes (Bell and Parchomovsky 2013). For instance, the state refrains from regulating property rights within the kibbutz, for the most part, because the state wants to preserve the autonomy of the kibbutz and its ability to regulate its internal functioning. Similarly, the United States refrains from regulating possessory rights among members of Native American tribes in certain kinds of tribal property in an effort to preserve what is left of American Indian autonomy and culture. (Clinton 1981). In other cases, state regulation is simply not worth the bother. It is difficult to find the state's interest in regulating as property the number of hotels a player "owns" in a Monopoly board game. In such cases *de facto* possessory rights are best viewed as independent of lawful markets, but not unlawful themselves.

Finally, there are cases where possessory rights exist only in unlawful markets. Consider, for example, a controlled substance for which there is no lawful use and all possession is illegal, such as crack cocaine. Clearly, there can be no licit market for such a drug. Yet, in view of the robustness of markets for recreational forms of drugs such as marijuana, heroin, and ecstasy, it is plain that there might nevertheless be a large, valuable and functioning market for *de facto* possessory rights in such controlled substances.

This plethora of possible relationships between *de facto* rights and licit markets means that there cannot be a single approach to property in the law. Indeed, a number of cases show some confusion in the law of possession when it is clear that the *de facto* possessory rights were obtained by theft, or otherwise illicitly (Helmholz 1985).

However, as the next section shows, there are peculiar problems that develop when unlawful markets form and flourish. These problems are sufficiently strong that they can and should exercise an influence over the formation and shape of property's laws treatment of possession.

6. Black markets

Black markets are markets where goods are traded illegally. The full value of black markets in the world is difficult to measure, but there is little doubt that it is worth billions, and perhaps trillions of dollars (Naylor 2002).

Black markets are not solely comprised of trade in illegal goods; in some cases, the markets involve unlawful services, such as prostitution. Illegal goods, however, constitute a mainstay of the black market. There are flourishing international markets in numerous unlawful goods such as human organs (Ambagtsheer and Weimar 2012), drugs (Thoumi 1995), ivory (Thornton and Currey 1991; Potgeiter 1995), and illegal antiquities (Brodie, Kersel, Luke, and Tubb 2006), to name just a few examples.

Black markets are detrimental to society. Black markets are more than simply arenas for economic transactions that do not enjoy the imprimatur of law. Black markets are necessarily attended by other phenomena. If there are significant law enforcement efforts to block the operation of the black markets, the markets must be accompanied by market participants' efforts to avoid detection. Since the *de facto* rights purchased and sold in the black market will likely not be enforceable in courts, other mechanisms must be developed to protect the illicit property rights. The venues for licit markets will not do, so illicit venues must be cultivated. In some cases, profits from sales must be hidden, so the black market feeds laundering (Schneider 2011).

Additionally, network effects characterize property rights in illicit markets just as much as property rights in licit markets (Kinsella 2006). The rights are more valuable the more widely they are recognized. As black markets grow, the value of the rights traded in them become disproportionately more valuable.

At the extreme, black markets feed an entire economic, social, and political apparatus parallel to the state. Consider illegal drug markets. Criminal organizations manage the markets. They manage disputes by internal mechanisms, using force (sometimes deadly). They invest in other illicit markets, and are able to use their power to muscle into licit markets. In areas where organized crime has made significant headway, such as parts of Afghanistan, southern Italy, or Latin America, illicit trade dominates many markets. Illegal enforcers from organized crime compete with police and the judicial system, and often supplant them entirely. Residents suffer from violence and relative poverty. As the illicit markets grow, both the licit market and the institutions of the state become correspondingly weaker (Fiorentini and Peltzman 1995; Dixit 2004; Levitt and Venkatesh 2000; Varese 2001).

Black markets are attractive where *de facto* possessory rights cannot be traded legally. If cocaine cannot be purchased lawfully at the local pharmacy, consumers of the drug may turn to local criminal drug dealers. The absence of formal legal property rights will not eliminate consumption. For the consumer, the utility from the illicit drug can be fully realized through *de facto* possessory rights. The presence of robust black markets in even a single valuable good, such as cocaine, can therefore be devastating to an entire society (Naylor 2002.). It is important to recall that black markets are not exclusively for goods that almost never can be legally owned, such as some kinds of drugs. Black markets can exist when there are clashes between illicit *de facto* possessory rights and *de jure* property rights as well. Where auto theft is rampant, black markets in stolen automobile parts and automobiles will flourish, notwithstanding the clarity of legal title in the cars and car parts (Fiorentini and Peltzman 1995).

Likewise, clashes of *de facto* and *de jure* rights are not restricted to theft. Consider countries like Israel, where law defines antiquities as property of the state. When landowners dig in their cellar, and uncover an antique coin, they have only one licit choice. They must report the find to the state, and, in exchange, get nothing except the dubious pleasure of watching state officials take away the find. In many situations, the find will lead to even more undesirable outcomes for the landowners, as it will prompt the state to undertake excavations to look for more antiquities (which will similarly belong to the state) (Einhorn 2014). At the same time, the landowners have a very simple and attractive illegal option. Instead of reporting the find, they can keep the *de facto* possessory rights in the coin. If the landowners are antiquities collectors, they can keep the coin and enjoy the utility of adding it to their collection. Alternatively, the landowners can sell the coin in the black market for antiquities, realizing a greater gain than they would have if they had reported the find to the state.

Here, once again, the network effects of illicit property rights play a role. The fewer legal antiquities are available, the more attractive the illegal market becomes to antiquities collectors, all things being held equal. A rule concentrating all ownership in the antiquities in the state feeds the black market, and makes trade in it valuable.

State institutions, of course, are not without recourse when faced with black markets. Law enforcement measures may be taken to wipe out the black market by making transactions in the market too costly. However, experience suggests that such efforts are never completely successful. Notwithstanding vigorous efforts by states, the trade in illegal drugs, illegal antiquities, illegal ivory, and so on continues to flourish (Naylor 2002; Manacorda and Chappell 2011).

7. Preventing black markets in possessory assets

Sometimes, when faced with the possibility of black markets, the wiser course for the state is simply to give legal force to the *de facto* possessory rights that are traded in the black market. While doing so largely gives up on the aims the state hoped to achieve in rendering such informal rights illegal, it also countermands the many undesirable satellite effects of black markets. Of course, in some cases, this is too high a price to pay. Sometimes, the costs of keeping such *de facto* rights illegal are justified by the gains from reducing trade in such rights. But just as surely, in other cases, the wiser course would be to bow to reality and recognize the *de facto* rights.

In fact, at least one of the most prominent uses of possession in the law of property appears to reflect an adoption of just such a strategy. Consider again the allocation of private property rights by first possession. Where the goods so allocated are sufficiently scarce, doctrines of first possession keep title in the items in legal markets, and disputes about such items in courts of law. For instance, if the first person to take possession of an elephant owns elephants and the trade in ivory tusks is legal, the elephants will be no less exposed to danger than if ivory trade is illegal, but at least the other ill effects of black markets will be avoided (Thornton and Currey 1991). Where antiquities belong to the finder, rather than the state, the antiquities will almost certainly make their way to legal markets, rather than black markets, and at least some of their scientific value will be preserved.

If property law did not recognize rights in first possessors, this would not eliminate the possession. It would just eliminate the title that goes with such possession. For the many items where *de facto* possessory rights are sufficient for possessors, the state refusal to recognize possessory rights would simply drive the possessory rights to the black market.

Fear of illicit markets may also explain property doctrines that recognize possession as its own independent kind of property right. If the law refused to grant recognition to the property rights of finders, it would not eliminate the practice of keeping possession of found objects; it would just drive such practices into the black market.

8. Custom as an analogue

It may be that possessory rules are not the only example of the law bending to accommodate what happens extra-legally. One example might be the law's treatment of custom.

In the legal literature, custom is an industry or community practice that is not grounded in law per se, but rather in the common activities of members of the industry or community. In some cases, the law adopts the custom after the fact as a legal standard that must be obeyed. In torts, for instance, a number of cases have defined legally required standards of care not in reference to an abstract standard, but rather, by reference to existing practice in the industry. Epstein (1992) justifies courts' resort to custom on the grounds of cost-effectiveness. He suggests that custom might be seen as a good estimation of the economically efficient standard of care, and one where the industry players can more efficiently determine optimal standards of care with fewer errors and lower costs than in courts. Epstein also notes that sometimes the custom can be seen as an implicit contract from which courts should be wary of varying.

However, an entirely different justification can be adduced for custom. As Ellickson (1991) famously showed, there are cases where custom replaces legal arrangements because of the high costs of learning and enforcing the law. In many settings, the rules followed by society develop from below, to meet the needs of society, in open contradiction to the rules imposed by law. Legal respect for custom in such settings can reflect acceptance of the reality of existing social norms that are impervious to the law, rather than respect for the efficiency of those social norms.

9. Salvage as an alternative

Although respecting possession as a source of rights is a plausible strategy for dealing with the existence of markets for goods that lawmakers would prefer not to be traded, it is not the only possible strategy. There is an alternative means of maintaining the relevance of the licit property system.

To keep the law relevant to the social practices regarding illicit goods, it is not necessary to give full title to possessors. Illicit possession necessarily is limited by potential legal penalties, and the inability to obtain full access to legal markets. As a result, all things being equal, illicit possession is less valuable than full title. A lesser reward than full title may still be sufficient to induce illicit possessors to relinquish their holdings.

In other words, the law need not protect possession as a property right or a source of property rights. It need simply provide sufficient rewards to possessors that bring their *de facto* rights into the legal markets. It can do so by rewarding *de facto* possessors who yield their possession, through the granting of rewards or salvage rights.

The rewards strategy animates a different set of doctrines in property law, such as the English law of treasure trove, which traditionally placed title to the objects defined as treasure trove in the Crown, but under modern law gives rewards to the finder. The Treasure Act 1996 modified the law slightly by requiring finders to offer treasure to a museum, in exchange for a price set by a Treasure Valuation Committee. The result is a reward for possession that is close to the value of full title, accompanied by a legal arrangement for transferring custody

Under admiralty law, similar doctrines obtain in some cases to objects found at sea. For instance, where a salvor rescues distressed property at sea, and the owner has not abandoned the property, courts will order the owner to pay a reward to the salvor (Lipka 1970; Swan 2009). Doctrinally, the salvage reward is based upon the idea that title in the object belongs to someone other than the salvor (the original owner or the Crown, for example), but the salvor has a good claim in restitution for an equitable reimbursement of the salvor's expenses and trouble. Salvage law aims to encourage salvage by rewarding those who rescue objects, while granting title in the rescued object to another, presumably higher value, owner.

Salvage law can only achieve its aims if several conditions are met. It is not enough that there is sufficient value in the rescue of the object to reimburse the salvor. A reward of this magnitude incentivizes rescue of the object, but not transfer of the object to the true owner. An additional condition must be met. The value of illicit possession of the object to the salvor must be lower than the reward and lower than the value to the true owner, such that the salvor will readily relinquish possession in exchange for the salvage reward when the law so requires, while leaving the true owner willing to pay the salvage reward in exchange for possession. What might lead the salvor to enjoy such low value from possession? It might be that the visibility of salvage at sea, together with the unusual nature of objects found in salvage, make it very difficult for a salvor to earn full value of the rescued objects in black markets. The salvor can therefore anticipate a larger profit from the salvage reward than from sale on the black market.

Salvage law might present a promising way of dealing with objects such as illegal antiquities. In these markets too, the state can likely offer a reward of sufficient magnitude to encourage relinquishing possession, and thereby join possession and title in a societally preferred owners, such as a museum. Such rules might be preferable to the more general compromise offered by the rules of first possession.

Conclusion

This chapter reexamined the normative impulse for property law's use of possession as a key to acquiring greater property rights. The chapter argued that in some cases property law recognizes first possession as a source of title in order to maintain the salience of the legal system of property. If the law did not recognize legal rights as a result of first possession, many first possessors would find it advantageous to eschew legal rights and protect their possessory rights extra-legally, as witnessed by the robust extra-legal asset markets that have developed, for instance, in the markets for illegal antiquities and natural resources. However, first possession is often a problematic way to allocate title, and in some cases, salvage rules can provide an alternative that both rewards *de facto* possession and reduces wasteful overexploitation.

References

Ambagtsheer, Frederike and Weimar, Willem. 2012. "A Criminological Perspective: Why Prohibition of Organ Trade Is Not Effective and How the Declaration of Istanbul Can Move Forward," *American Journal of Transplantation* 12:571–75.

Andreano, Ralph and Siegfried, John J. (eds.) 1980. *The Economics of Crime*. New York: Wiley.

Baird, Douglas, and Jackson, Thomas 1984. "Information, Uncertainty, and the Transfer of Property," *Journal of Legal Studies* 13:299–320.

Barzel, Yoram 1968. "Optimal Timing of Innovation," *Review of Economics and Statistics* 50:348–55.

  1997. *Economic Analysis of Property Rights*. 2nd edn. Cambridge University Press.

Bell, Abraham and Parchomovsky, Gideon 2013. "Property Lost in Translation," *University of Chicago Law Review* 80:515–73.

Benson, Bruce L. and Baden, John 1985. "The Political Economy of Governmental Corruption: The Logic of Underground Government," *Journal of Legal Studies* 14:391–410.

Brodie, Neil, Kersel, Morag M., Luke, Christina and Tubb, Kathryn Walker, (eds.) 2006. *Archaeology, Cultural Heritage and the Trade in Antiquities*. Gainesville FL: University Press of Florida.

Clinton, Robert N. 1981. "Isolated in Their Own Country: A Defense of Federal Protection of Indian Autonomy and Self-Government," *Stanford Law Review* 33:979–1068.

De Soto, Hernando 2000. *The Mystery of Capital: Why Capitalism Triumphs in the West and Fails Everywhere Else*. New York: Basic Books.

Dixit, Avinash K. 2004. *Lawlessness and Economics: Alternative Modes of Governance*. Princeton University Press.

Dreher, Axel and Schneider, Friedrich 2010. "Corruption and the Shadow Economy: An Empirical Analysis," *Public Choice*, 144:215–38.

Einhorn, Talia 2014. "Israel," in *Handbook on the Law of Cultural Heritage and International Trade* James A.R. Nafziger and Robert Kirkwood Paterson (eds.) Cheltenham: Edward Elgar Publishing Limited.

Ellickson, Robert C. 1991. *Order Without Law: How Neighbors Settle Disputes*. Cambridge, Massachusetts: Harvard University Press.

Epstein, Richard A. 1979. "Possession as the Root of Title," *Georgia Law Review* 13:1221–43.

  1992. "The Path to the T. J. Hooper: The Theory and History of Custom in the Law of Tort," *The Journal of Legal Studies* 21:1–38.

  1998. "Possession," in *The New Palgrave Dictionary of Economics and the Law*, Peter Newman, (ed.) New York, NY: Stockton, pp. 62–68.

  2002. "The Allocation of the Commons: Parking on Public Roads," *Journal of Legal Studies* 31:S515–44.

Fiorentini, Gianluca and Peltzman, Sam, (eds.) 1995. *The Economics of Organized Crime*. Cambridge, UK and New York: Cambridge University Press.

Gilmore, Grant 1965. *Security Interests in Personal Property*. Boston and Toronto: Little, Brown and Company.

Helmholz, Richard. H. 1985. "Wrongful Possession of Chattels: Hornbook Law and Case Law," *Northwestern University Law Review* 80:1221–43.

Hovencamp, Herbert, Kurtz, Sheldon F. and Gallanis, Thomas P. 2014. *The Law of Property: An Introductory Survey*. 2nd edn. St. Paul, MN: West Publishing.

Johnson, Ronald N. and Libecap, Gary D. 1982. "Contracting Problems and Regulation: The Case of the Fishery," *American Economic Review* 72:1005–22.

Kerekes, Carrie B. and Williamson, Claudia R. 2008. "Unveiling de Soto's Mystery: Property Rights, Capital, and Development," *Journal of Institutional Economics* 4(3):371–87.

Kinsella, David 2006. "The Black Market in Small Arms: Examining a Social Network," *Contemporary Security Policy* 27:100–17.

Lansakara, Francis. 2012. "Maritime Law of Salvage and Adequacy of Laws Protecting the Salvors' Interest," *International Journal on Marine Navigation and Safety of Sea Transportation* 6:431–35.

Leal, Donald R. 2005. *Evolving Property Rights in Marine Fisheries*. Lanham, MD: Rowman and Littlefield.

Levitt, Steven and Venkatesh, Sudhir A. 2000. "An Economic Analysis of a Drug-Selling Gang's Finances," *Quarterly Journal of Economics* 115(3):755–89.

Libecap, Gary D. 2007. "The Assignment of Property Rights on the Western Frontier: Lessons for Contemporary Environmental and Resource Policy," *The Journal of Economic History* 67:257–91.

Lipka, Lawrence J. 1970. "Abandoned Property at Sea: Who Owns the Salvage 'Finds'?" *William and Mary Law Review* 12:97–110.

Lueck, Dean 1995. "The Rule of First Possession and the Design of the Law," *Journal of Law and Economics* 38:393–436.

Manacorda, Stefano and Chappell, Duncan, (eds.) 2011. *Crime in the Art and Antiquities World: Illegal Trafficking in Cultural Property*. New York: Springer.

Naylor, R.T. 2002. *Wages of Crime: Black Markets, Illegal Finance and the Underworld Economy*. Ithaca: Cornell University Press.

Potgeiter, De Wet 1995. *Contraband: South Africa and the International Trade in Ivory and Rhino Horn*. Cape Town: Queillerie.

Rose, Carol M. 1985. "Possession as the Origin of Property," *University of Chicago Law Review* 52:73–88.

Schneider, Friedrich and Enste, Dominik H. 2000. "Shadow Economies: Sizes, Causes and Consequences," *Journal of Economic Perspectives*, 38:77–114.

Schneider, Friedrich, (ed.) 2011. *Handbook on the Shadow Economy*. Cheltenham: Edward Elgar Publishing Limited.

Singh, Rajesh and Weninger, Quinn and Doyle, Matthew 2006. "Fisheries Management With Stock Growth Uncertainty and Costly Capital Adjustment," *Journal of Environmental Economics and Management* 52:582–99.

Swan, Catherine Melissa 2009. "The Restitutionary and Economic Analyses of Salvage Law," *Australian and New Zealand Maritime Law Journal* 23:99–110.

Thornton, Alan and Currey, David 1991. *To Kill an Elephant: The Undercover Investigation into the Illegal Ivory Trade*. London: Doubleday.

Thoumi, Francisco E. 1995. *Political Economy and Illegal Drugs in Colombia*. Boulder, CO: United Nations University Press.

Umbeck, John 1977a. "A Theory of Contract Choice and the California Gold Rush." *Journal of Law and Economics* 20:421–437.

1977b. "The California Gold Rush: A Study of Emerging Property Rights," *Explorations in Economic History* 14:197–226.

Varese, Federico 2001. *The Russian Mafia: Private Protection in a New Market Economy*. Oxford University Press.

Zerbe, Richard O. and Anderson, C. Leigh 2001. "Culture and Fairness in the Development of Institutions in the California Gold Fields," *The Journal of Economic History* 61:114–43.

INDEX

accession, first possession and, 75
acquisition principle, 75
acting like owner
   adverse possession and, 57, 60
   first possession and, 55–56
   in *Lessee of Ewing* v. *Burnet*, 53–54, 56–57
   limitations of, 60–61
   normative claims of, 55–57
   with physical resources, 61
   Pollock on, 48
adjudicative jurisdiction, 266
admiralty law, 334
adverse possession, 53–54
   acting like owner and, 57, 60
   animus domini and, 116
   of art, 277–78
   Ayres' Cathedral theory for, 296–302
   bad faith and, 168
   claim of right and, 57–59
   color of title doctrine, 167
   constructive possession and, 167
   defined, 296
   earning theory and, 168
   entitlements and, 297–98
   as extended possession, 83–84, 296
   forced transfers with, 167–68
   functions of, 36
   as heuristic, 167–68
   in jurisdiction for property disputes, 268, 285–86
   law of, 26, 36–37
   in *Lessee of Ewing* v. *Burnet*, 53–54
   over time, 168
   pedis possessio and, 83–84
   prescriptive easement and, 296–97
   property rule and, 297–99

provenance in, 59
sleeping theory and, 168
of small property, 290–91
statute of limitations for, 167
agency
   possessory rights and, costs of, 184
   under property laws, 210
agent in possession
   under civil codes, 120–22
   under common law, 122–23
   control and, 120–23
Alexander, Gregory, 169
allocation rules, 218
animus domini, 114–15
   adverse possession and, 116
   civil codes and, 116–17
   detention and, 114
   first possession and, 116
   titles and, 115–17
anti-fragmentation rules, 190
art, as property
   adverse possession for, 277–78
   under choice of law, 277–81
   jurisdiction over, in property disputes, 268, 286–87
   in Nazi Germany, 280–81
   place of sale as influence on, 278–79
   pro-purchaser bias, 279
assembly rules, 190–91
auctions, 132–33
audience of potential transactors, 30–31
audience of strangers, 29–30
Austria, civil codes in, 104–5
automobiles. *See* personal property
Ayres, Ian, 291, 296–302

INDEX

bailment, law of, 19, 242
Baird, Douglas, 323–24
Barzel, Yoram, 72, 326
Baxter, William, 270
behavioral studies, for property law
  endowment effect in, 137, 141–42
  expansion of possession in, 133–36
  future applications of, 143
  incomplete data for, legal use of, 137–38
  for legal topics, 128–29
  length of contact as variable in, 139–40
  nonphysical possession and, 130–36
  possession compared to ownership in, 136–37
  for possession effect, 139–42
  with reasoning and analogy, 128
Berra, Yogi, 156
best-chooser principle
  liability rules and, 301
  for small property, 299–302
bills of exchange, 229
black markets, 329–32
  de facto possessory rights in, 330–31
  de jure property rights in, 330–31
  state-sponsored prevention of, 331–32
Blackstone, William, 44–45
broadband regulation, 251–54
  under Standard Zone Enabling Act, 251–52
broadcast licenses. *See* spectrum rights
bundle of rights concept, 109–10
  numerus clausus principle and, 109

call-option liability rule, 311–12
capitalization, division of possessory rights and, 187
Chang, Yun-chien, 11–12, 49, 242
chattel ownership, legal rights of
  bailments and, 242
  divided interests for, 240–41
  under English law, 238–46
  failure to return issues in, 240–41
  government claims against, 241
  spectrum rights compared to, 263

China. *See also* Shenzhen, China; small property
  adversely developed buildings in, 314–15
  civil codes in, 108
  collective ownership of land in, 292
  development of rural land in, 303–6
  farmers' use rights in, for rural land, 292
  free-titling policy in, 306–8
  illegal buildings in, 308–11, 313–14
  Land Administration Law in, 292
  Property Law of 2007 in, 103–4, 292
  Rural Land Law in, 291–93
  rural-urban land conversion in, 293
choice of law, in property disputes. *See also* water rights
  for adverse possession, 276
  for art, 277–81
  comparative impairment theory for, 270
  economic analysis of, 269–72
  First Restatement of, 271
  for stolen property, 277–81
  substantive law and, 270–72
  territoriality in, 271
  traditional approach to, 269–70
  for water rights, 272–76
  for wild animals, 276–77
civil codes, 103–5, 108, 110, 123
  agent in possession under, 120–22
  animus domini and, 116–17
  indirect possession and, 118–19
civil law tradition. *See also specific nations*
  in China, 108
  in France, 103–5, 108
  in Germany, 103–5, 108
  intent to possess under, 107
  in Japan, 104–5, 108
  modular framework for, 69
  noneconomizing cerebral concepts in, 118–23
  ownership under, 103–4
  possession and, 12, 87–88, 103–4
  property laws and, 103–4
  relativity of title under, 84–85
  in South Korea, 104–5, 108

claim of right, 57–59
claims, 45–46
   under General Mining Law, 78
   historical foundation for, 44
   to ownership, 45–46
   provenance of, 44–45
Coase, Ronald, 249–50
collective ownership of land, in China, 292
   under Land Administration Law, 292
   under Property Law of 2007, 103–4, 292
   under Rural Land Law, 291–93
color of title doctrine, 167
commercial exchange, 216–20
   contract rules and, 218–19
   property rules and, 219
   UCC and, 217
The Common Law (Holmes), 114
common law systems
   agent in possession under, 122–23
   finders under, 162–63
   possession in, 12, 87
   relativity of title under, 84–85
   rule of capture in, 156
   shared possession under, 166–67
communication, social possession through, 15–16
Communications Act of 1934, 248–49
constitutum possessorium, 119–20
constructive delivery, 120
constructive possession, 152
   adverse possession and, 167
continuous possession, 117–18
contract for hire, 244
contract rules, 211
   commercial exchange and, 218–19
contracts. *See also* leases
   division of possessory rights through, 185–86
control
   acquisition of titles and, 115–17
   agent in possession and, 120–23
   animus domini and, 115–17
   continuous possession and, 117–18
   information economizing with, 123–24
   ownership and, 17
   possession and, 11–12, 106, 117–18

Cook, Walter Wheeler, 164
Cosmopolitan Broadcasting Corporation v. FCC, 251
Currie, Brainerd, 270
custom, law and, 332–33

Dagan, Hanoch, 169
de facto possession, 12, 41, 44, 80
   extended possession and, 82
   in property theory, 69–70
   salience and, 66
   transference of, 82
de facto possessory rights, 327
   in black markets, 330–31
de facto property rights, 326–27
de jure property rights, 326–27
   in black markets, 330–31
De La Torre, Mindel, 258–59
defense of possession, 19–20
delivery of possession
   for boundary disputes, 222
   publicity in, 221–23
   in real property exchange, 221–23
   titles and, 216
   writ of right and, 221
Demsetz, Harold, 50
Deng Xiaoping, 294
detention
   animus domini and, 114
   in France, 110
   property laws and, 105
development rights, 134
devil's proof. *See probatio diabolica*
doctrine of necessity. *See* necessity, doctrine of
documentary possession, 216
   chain of title deeds and, 227–29
   historical applications of, 226–27
   informational value of, 226–31
   multiple rights and, 229
   negotiable instruments in, 229–31
   powers of attorney and, 229–31
   proxies for, 230–31
   under Statute of Uses, 228–29

Eads v. Brazelton, 52
earning theory, 168

economic property rights, 326
economy of concept theory, 105–6
Eigenbesitzer (person who holds things for herself), 123
endowment effect, 131–33
  in behavioral studies, 137, 141–42
English land law, 238–46
  contract for hire under, 244
  in *Hannah v. Peel*, 243
  historical development of, 243
  long-term licensees under, 245
  tenant rights under, 244–45
entitlements
  adverse possession and, 297–98
  for small property, 302–15
Epstein, Richard, 322, 324
evolutionary game theory, 150–52
exclusion, as right
  possession and, 94
  in possession as heuristic, 154
  possessory rights and, 175
extended possession, 80–85
  adverse possession as, 83–84, 296
  de facto possession and, 82
  first possession as, 82

FCC. *See* Federal Communications Commission
FED statute. *See* Forcible Entry and Detainer statute
Federal Communications Commission (FCC), 249–50
  in *Cosmopolitan Broadcasting Corporation v. FCC*, 251
  LightSquared Debacle and, 254–55, 259–63
finders
  in *Hannah v. Peel*, 162–63
  in heuristic of possession, 161–65
  in *McAvoy v. Medina*, 163–64
  under mislaid rule, 163–64
  property rights for, 161
  rightful owners and, 162–63
first possession, 18, 49–53, 134
  accession and, 75
  acting like owner and, 55–56
  animus domini and, 116
  in *Eads v. Brazelton*, 52

  as extended possession, 82
  fairness of, 323–24
  under *Haslem v. Lackwood*, 52
  heuristic for, 149
  in *Pierson v. Post*, 51, 134–35
  possession law and, 82
  property law and, 104
  in *Ray v. Beacon Hudson Mountain Corp.*, 54
  rule of, 12
  titles and, 322–23
Forcible Entry and Detainer (FED) statute, 40–41
frail possessors, 46–48
France, detention in, 110
Frankfurter, Felix, 249–50
free-titling policy, in China, 306–8
Fremdbesitzer (person who holds things for another), 123
French Civil Code, 103–5, 108
  agent in possession under, 120
  indirect possession under, 118–19

game theory
  evolutionary, 150–52
  hawks and doves, 41–46
  for Hume, 70
Genachowski, Julius, 260
General Mining Law, 78
Geomet Exploration, Limited v. Lucky Mc Uranium Corp., 79
German law
  property laws and, 103–4
  thinghood under, 71
Germany, civil codes in, 103–5, 108, 110, 123
  agent in possession in, 120–22
  indirect possession in, 118–19
Goldberg, Victor, 241
Goldsmith, Jack, 270–71, 273
Guzman, Andrew, 275

Hannah v. Peel, 162–63
  English land law in, 243
Haslem v. Lackwood, 52
hawks and doves, 41–46
  possession heuristic for, 150

heuristic, possession as
　academic literature on, 149–50
　for adverse possession, 167–68
　for animals, 150–51, 157–58
　applications for, 154–68
　court adoption by, 154–55
　deference variable in, 152–53
　doctrine of relative title and, 153–54
　evolution and, 150–52
　for finders, 161–65
　for first possession, 149
　fixes for, 154–68
　hawks and doves and, 150
　for humans, 151–52
　modifications of, in literature, 169
　priority as variable in, 152–54
　problems with, 154–68
　property and, 160, 168–72
　right to exclude, 154
　rule of capture and, 155–60
　rule of increase and, 156
　for shared possession, 165–67
Hirshleifer, Jack, 151
Hobbes, Thomas, 151
Holmes, Oliver Wendell, 11, 114, 142–43
home ownership, 198–99
Hoover, Herbert, 251–52
Heuristics and the Law, 149
Hughes, Charles Evans, 11
Hume, David, 46, 151
　de facto possession for, 69–70
　game theory for, 70
　property theory for, 76
　theories of justice for, 76

illegal buildings, 308–11, 313–14
impersonal exchange theory, 207–12
　See also commercial exchange; real property exchange
in personam possessory right, 110–12
in rem possessory right, 110–12
indirect possession, 118–20
　civil codes and, 118–19
　constitutum possessorium and, 119–20
　constructive delivery and, 120
informal property rights, 315–16

information costs
　audience of strangers and, 29–30
　for division of possessory rights, 189, 194–95
　numerus clausus principle and, 194–95
　of ownership, 10–11, 27–28
　of possession, 9–11, 27–28
intangible possession, 135–36
intellectual property (IP)
　in division of possessory rights, 201
　government allocation of, 201
　possession of, 61
　temporal division of, 181
intention, in possession, 15, 114–15
　animus domini and, 114–15
　in civil law, 107
IP. *See* intellectual property
Italian Civil Code, 103–4

Jackson, Thomas, 323–24
Japan, civil codes in, 104–5, 108
　animus domini and, 116–17
jewelry. *See* personal property
joint finding. *See* shared possession
judges, 41–46
　"possession is nine-tenths of the law" for, 42–46
　property rules applied by, 213
judgment, systems of, 28
jurisdiction, in property disputes
　adjudicative, 266
　for adverse possession, 268, 285–86
　economic analysis of, 281–83
　for stolen art, 268, 286–87
　succession in, 266
　for water rights, 267–69, 283–85
　for wild animals, 285–86
justice, theories of, 76

Kahneman, Daniel, 28
Korean Civil Code, 104–5, 108
Kuhn, Thomas, 149

labor theory, 73
land ownership, legal rights of
　bailments and, 242
　divided interests for, 240–41

under English land law, 238–46
government claims against, 241
livery of seisin and, 34
under Roman Law, 238–46
spectrum rights compared to, 263
Landis, James, 251
law. *See also* Roman Law; *specific laws*
custom and, 332–33
ownership and, 9
possession and, 9, 12, 18–24, 40–41, 49–54, 207–8
settled, 62
social norms as influence on, 47
law of finders, 19
lawful possession, 328–29
leases, 184–85
Lectures on Jurisprudence (Smith, A.), 87
legal possession, 49–54. *See also* adverse possession; first possession
defined, 51–52, 60
in *Eads* v. *Brazelton*, 52
in *Haslem* v. *Lackwood*, 52
in *Pierson* v. *Post*, 51
legal property rights, 326–27
legalized theft, 167–68
Lessee of Ewing v. *Burnet*, 53–54, 56–57
Leuck, Dean, 323
liability rules, 211
best-chooser principle and, 301
call-option, 311–12
for small property, 291
Libecap, Gary, 323
LightSquared Debacle, 254–64
bankruptcy as result of, 261–62
FCC and, 254–55, 259–63
OOBE and, 257
OOBR and, 257–58
under Telecommunications Act, 257
livery of seisin, 34, 221–22. *See also* delivery of possession
Locke, John
conventions for, 151
labor theory for, 73
property theory for, 70–71
lost grant theory, 45

Macke Co. v. *Pizza of Gaithersburg*, 245–46
Maynard Smith, John, 150–51
McAvoy v. *Medina*, 163–64
Merrill, Thomas, 49, 169, 241, 276–77, 291
mislaid rule, 163–64
modularity of possession, 85, 89–93
mortgages
division of possessory rights for, 199–200
as subsidiary possessory right, 109
multiple rights, 229

NBC v. *United States*, 249–50
necessity, doctrine of, 185
nemo dat, principle of, 91
the Netherlands, civil codes in, 104–5
indirect possession under, 118–19
New Institutional Economics, 76, 207
"The New Property" (Reich), 133
nonphysical possession
endowment effect and, 131–33
intangible possession and, 135–36
in property law studies, 130–36
psychological evidence of, 131–33
Nozick, Robert, 44
property theory of, 44, 70–71
nuisance laws, spectrum rights and, 252, 263
nuisance principle, 166
numerus clausus principle, 107
bundle of rights concept and, 109
division of possessory rights and, 176, 186–87, 189
information costs and, 194–95
personal property under, 200–1
verification costs and, 195–96

OOBE. *See* Out-of-Band-Emission
OOBR. *See* Out-of-Band-Reception
opportunism
costs of, 185–86
division of possessory rights and, 184–85
Out-of-Band-Emission (OOBE), 257
Out-of-Band-Reception (OOBR), 257–58

ownership. *See also* property laws; property rights; property theory
   with audience of potential transactors, 30–31
   for audience of strangers, 29–30
   in behavioral studies, 136–37
   broadness of, 24–25
   under civil law, 103–4
   claims to, 45–46
   as concept, 32, 107–8
   control as part of, 17
   cultural meaning of, 17–18
   duration of, 26
   endowment effect and, 137
   establishment of, 10, 25
   fragmentation of, 26–27
   information costs of, 10–11, 27–28
   legal protections for, 9, 20–21
   numerus clausus principle and, 107
   possession as proof of, 239–40
   possession compared to, 11–18, 85–86, 103–4, 136–37
   possession separated from, 207–8, 212
   self-help with, 22–23
   social norms for, 32–34
   societal differences in, 11
   subsidiary rights and, 107
   surrogate explanations for, 23–24
   time-limited, 26
   transfer of, 34–35
   transfer of possession and, 21–22
   under Writ of Right, 221, 240

patents, division of possessory rights and, 201
pedis possessio, doctrine of, 78–79
   adverse possession and, 83–84
   under General Mining Law, 78
   in *Geomet Exploration, Limited* v. *Lucky Mc Uranium Corp.*, 79
person who holds things for another. *See* Fremdbesitzer
person who holds things for herself. *See* Eigenbesitzer

personal property
   division of possessory rights and, 200–1
   under *numerus clausus* principle, 200–1
Pierson v. *Post*, 55, 130–31
   first possession in, 51, 134–35
pledges, 325
Pollock, Frederick, 11, 41, 46
   on acting like owner, 48
Posner, Richard, 161–62
possession. *See also* adverse possession; delivery of possession; first possession; heuristic, possession as; legal possession; non-physical possession; property laws; social possession
   acquisition of titles and, 113–17
   animus domini and, 114
   architecture of, 65–66
   as attribute, 324–25
   with audience of potential transactors, 30–31
   for audience of strangers, 29–30
   in behavioral studies, 136–37
   civil law tradition and, 12, 87–88, 103–4
   claims of, 25–26
   in common law systems, 12, 87
   as concept, 32, 67–68, 106
   constructive, 152
   continuous, 117–18
   control as part of, 11–12, 106, 117–18
   cultural meaning of, 11–16
   de facto, 12, 41, 44, 66
   defense of, 19–20
   deference to, 152–53
   defined, 79
   doctrine of adverse possession, 12
   doctrine of *pedis possessio* and, 78–79
   documentary, 216
   duration of, 26
   in economics, 207–8
   elsewhere pattern for, 90–91
   endowment effect and, 137, 141–42
   exclusion and, 94
   exclusivity of, 27
   expansion of, 133–36

extended, 80–85
as fact, 117–24
FED statute and, 40–41
formalization of, 67
under French Civil Code, 103–4
generalization of, 80
indirect, 118–20
information costs of, 9–11, 27–28
information economizing with, 123–24
intangible, 135–36
intention as part of, 15, 114–15
of IP, 61
under Italian Civil Code, 103–4
justification of, 321–24
under law of bailment, 19, 242
law of finders and, 19
law of security interests and, 35–36
lawful, 328–29
layering principle for, 93–96
legal entitlements and, 315–16
legal protections for, 9, 12, 18–24, 40–41, 49–54, 207–8
in material world, 24–27
modular theory of, 85, 89–93
narrow range of interests in, 25–27
neighbors' view of, 48–49
New Institutional Economics and, 207
noneconomizing cerebral concepts in, 118–23
in organizations, allocation of, 14–15
as origin of property, 324–25
ownership compared to, 11–18, 85–86, 136–37
ownership separated from, 207–8, 212
persistence of, 88
pledges and, 325
as proof of ownership, 239–40
in property law, 18
in property theory, 69–80, 86–88
provenance of, 44
proverbs about, 40–41
as provisional order, 89
in public spaces, 12–14
publicity hypothesis for, 215
recovery of, 19–20

reliance hypotheses for, 212–16
Restatement (First) of Property and, 12
under Roman Law, 11, 22, 79, 224
as root of title (Epstein), 5, 227, 238, 296, 322
roots of, 77
salience and, 66–67
self-help domains for, 112, 141
shared, 165–67
skepticism about, 11
social norms for, 32–34
stability of, 79
as surrogate explanation for ownership, 23–24
under Taiwan Civil Code, 103–4
thinghood and, 71, 81–82, 86
transfer of, 21–22
universal respect for, 9–10
unlawful, 112–13, 328–29
will and, 21, 73
possession effect, 139–42
"possession is nine-tenths of the law," 40–41, 62
judges' response to, 42–46
possessory rights, 108–13. *See also* titles
bundle of rights concept, 109–11
custom and, 332–33
de facto, 327
defined, 175
mortgage as, 109
numerus clausus principle and, 176
in personam, 110–12
in real property exchange, 225–26
registration of, 223–24
in rem, 110–12
under right to exclude, 175
salvage law as alternative to, 333–34
social order influenced by, 111–12
subsidiary, 109
under Treasure Act 1996, 333–34
unlawful possession and, 112–13
possessory rights, division of
agency costs for, 184
anti-fragmentation rules and, 190
applications of, 198–201
bounded rationality as influence on, 187

possessory rights, division of (cont.)
    capitalization and, 187
    through contracts, 185–86
    excessive fragmentation in, 177–78, 186–93
    through formal mechanisms, 185
    functional divisions, 181–82
    for home ownership, 198–99
    incentives for, 186–87
    through informal arrangements, 185
    information costs for, 189, 194–95
    for IP, 201
    through leases, 184–85
    legal mechanisms for, 177, 190–91
    for mortgages, 199–200
    numerus clausus principle and, 176, 186–87, 189
    observability and, 183
    opportunism as influence on, 184–85
    owner incentives for, 177
    for patents, 201
    for personal property, 200–1
    by private parties, 178, 182–91
    for property rights, 179–80, 182–83, 185
    psychological disposition against, 178, 196–98
    by public officials, 178, 189–90
    puzzle for economic thinking and, 191–92
    retransfer of externalities and, 186
    social benefits of, 176–77
    spatial divisions, 180–81
    temporal division of, 181
    theories for, 191–98
    tragedy of anticommons and, 192–93
    transfer rights and, 182
    by type of property, 197–98
    types of divisions, 179–82
    verifiability of, 183
    verification costs for, 189, 195–96
powers of attorney, 229–31
prescriptive easement, 296–97
private parties
    division of possessory rights by, 178, 182–91
    opportunism of, 184–85
probatio diabolica (devil's proof), 111

promissory notes, 229
Property Law of 2007 (People's Republic of China), 103–4, 292
property laws, 11. *See also* behavioral studies, for property law; chattel ownership, legal rights of; land ownership, legal rights of; small property
    agency structure under, 210
    in civil law nations, 103–4
    defense of possession and, 19–20
    detention and, 105
    dual nature of, 20–21
    dual systems of, 29–32
    efficiency analysis of, 135–36
    expansion of, 133–36
    first possession and, 104
    livery of seisin and, 34
    possession compared to ownership under, 136–37
    possession heuristic and, 160, 168–72
    private aspects of, 208
    recovery of possession and, 19–20
    Restatement (First) of Property and, 12
    tort liability and, 20
    transaction costs and, conflict with, 208–12
    transfer of ownership under, 34–35
    under UCC, 20, 217
property rights. *See also* chattel ownership, legal rights of; choice of law, in property disputes; jurisdiction, in property disputes; land ownership, legal rights of; small property; spectrum rights
    architecture of, 65–66
    for audience of potential transactors, 30–31
    for audience of strangers, 29–30
    black markets and, 329–32
    bundle of rights concept and, 109–10
    de facto, 326–27
    de jure, 326–27
    defined, 72–73
    delivery requirements for, 34–35
    division of possessory rights and, 179–80, 182–83, 185

dual systems of, 29–32
economic, 326
for finders, 161
functional divisions of, 181–82
informal, 315–16
involuntary division of, 185
involuntary transfer of, 185
legal, 326–27
livery of seisin and, 34
under New Institutional Economics, 76
personhood and, 197–98
possession heuristic and, 160, 168–72
resource scarcity and, 150
as sociable institution, 53
spatial divisions of, 180–81
temporal division of, 181
transactions over, 72
transfer of, 327–28
types of, 325–28
property rules, 211
adverse possession and, 297–99
commercial exchange and, 219
judicial application of, 213
property theory
architectural aspects in, 95
de facto possession in, 69–70
for Hume, 76
for Locke, 70–71
for Nozick, 44, 70–71
possession and, 69–80, 86–88
provenance
in adverse possession, 59
of claims, 44–45
public spaces, possession of, 12–14
publicity hypothesis, for possession, 215

Radio Act of 1927, 247
Radio-Communications Act of 1912, 247
Ray v. Beacon Hudson Mountain Corp., 54
real property exchange, 220–26
chain of title deeds and, 227–29
delivery of possession in, 221–23
exercise of possession in, 223–25

exercise of possessory detention in, 225–26
under Roman Law, 220
recovery of possession, 19–20
Reich, Charles, 133
relativity of title, 84–85
in possession as heuristic, 153–54
reliance on possession, 212–16
respect, social possession and, 16
Restatement (First) of Property, 12
right to exclude. *See* exclusion, as right
rights. *See specific rights*
riparian system, 272
Roman Law
contract for hire under, 244
exercise of possession under, 223–25
land ownership under, 238–46
possession under, 11, 22, 79, 224
real property exchange under, 220
root of title under, 227
usucapio, 223–25
root of title, 5, 227, 238, 296, 322
Rose, Carol, 15–16, 272, 322
rule of capture, 155–60
extension of, 159–60
legislative regulation with, 158–59
rule of first possession, 12
rule of increase, 156
Rural Land Law (People's Republic of China), 291–93
rural-urban land conversion, in China, 293
Russell v. Hill, 113

salience
de facto possession and, 66
defined, 66–67
thinghood and, 74–75
salvage law, 333–34
admiralty law and, 334
security interests, law of
function of, 35–36
possession and, 35–36
self-help domains, 112, 141
settled law, 62
shared possession
under common law, 166–67
coordination with, 166

shared possession (cont.)
  as heuristic, 165–67
  nuisance principle and, 166
  through tenancy, 166
Shenzhen, China, 294–96
  adversely developed buildings in, 314–15
  development of rural land in, 303–6
  free-titling policy in, 306–8
  illegal buildings, 308–11, 313–14
skepticism, about possession, 11
sleeping theory, 168
small property, 290
  adverse possession of, 290–91
  adversely developed buildings, 314–15
  best-chooser principle for, 299–302
  under call-option liability rule, 311–12
  development of rural land, 303–6
  free-titling policy and, 306–8
  illegal buildings, 308–11, 313–14
  legal entitlements for, 302–15
  liability rules for, 291
  multiple takings and, 301–2
  rights for, 293–94
  under Rural Land Law, 291–93
  in Shenzhen, 294–96
  state compensation for, 311–13
Smith, Adam, 87
  ownership separated from possession for, 207
Smith, Henry, 47, 50, 169, 276
Smoot v. United States, 90
social norms
  law influenced by, 47
  for ownership, 32–34
  for possession, 32–34
social possession
  through communication, 15–16
  intention as part of, 15
  in organizations, 14–15
  in public spaces, 12–14
  respect for possession as part of, 16
spectrum rights, 246–54. *See also* LightSquared Debacle
  broadband regulation and, 251–54
  chattel ownership compared to, 263
  under Communications Act of 1934, 248–49
  in *Cosmopolitan Broadcasting Corporation v. FCC*, 251
  FCC allocation of, 249–50
  land ownership compared to, 263
  in *NBC v. United States*, 249–50
  negotiations for, 250–51
  nuisance laws and, 252, 263
  under Radio Act of 1927, 247
  under Radio-Communications Act of 1912, 247
  restriction of licenses, 250
  security of possession for, 249
  under Standard Zone Enabling Act, 251–52
  under Telecommunications Act, 257
  in *Tribune Co. v. Oak Leaves Broadcast Station*, 247–49
Standard Zone Enabling Act, 251–52
Statute of Uses, 228–29
Stern, James, 267
style, defined, 103
subsidiary possessory rights, 109
subsidiary rights, 107
  mortgage as, 109
Sugden, Robert, 42, 50, 151
  de facto possession for, 69–70
Switzerland, civil codes in, 110
Sykes, Alan, 270–71, 273
System 1, 3, 28, 92–93, 169
System 2, 3, 28, 92–93, 169

Taiwan Civil Code, 103–5, 108, 110
  agent in possession under, 120–22
  animus domini and, 116–17
  indirect possession under, 118–19
Telecommunications Act, 257
tenant rights, 244–45
territorial rule
  in choice of law, for property disputes, 271
  for water rights, 272–73
thinghood
  under German law, 71
  possession and, 71, 81–82, 86
  salience and, 74–75
time-limited ownership, 26

titles. *See also* impersonal exchange theory
  for adversely-developed buildings, 314–15
  animus domini and, 115–17
  chain of title deeds, 227–29
  color of title doctrine, 167
  control and, 115–17
  de facto possessory rights and, 327
  de facto property rights and, 326–27
  de jure property rights and, 326–27
  delivery of possession and, 216
  doctrine of relative title, 84–85, 153–54
  first possession and, 322–23
  free-titling policy, in China, 306–8
  possession and, 113–17
  possessions separated from ownership through, 212
  publicity hypothesis for, 215
  reliance hypotheses with, 212–16
  in Shenzhen, 306–8
tort liability, 20
tragedy of anticommons theory, 192–93
transaction costs, 34, 176, 180, 185, 208–13, 215, 218, 220, 242, 250, 323
transfer rights, 182
Treasure Act 1996, 333–34
Tribune Co. v. Oak Leaves Broadcast Station, 247–49
trust forms, 190
Twyne's Case, 323–24

Uniform Commercial Code (UCC), 20, 217
United States v. General Motors, 239
United States v. One 1985 Cadillac Seville, 43–44
unlawful possession, 112–13, 328–29
  self-help domains and, 112
Unumb, Daniel, 241
usufruct, 111

Van Valkenberg v. Lutz, 59
verification costs, 189
  numerus clausus principle and, 195–96
von Jhering, Rudolf, 114
von Savigny, Friedrich Carl, 114

Warsaw v. Chicago Metallic Ceilings, Inc., 296
water rights
  choice of law for, 272–76
  incentives for efficiency in, 275–76
  jurisdiction over, in property disputes, 267–69, 283–85
  nonterritoriality of, 274
  residence of rights owner as influence on, 273–75
  under riparian system, 272
  territorial rule for, 272–73
wild animals, jurisdiction over, 285–86
will, possession and, 21, 73
Wright, Robert Samuel, 46
Writ of Right, 221, 240

For EU product safety concerns, contact us at Calle de José Abascal, 56–1º,
28003 Madrid, Spain or eugpsr@cambridge.org.

www.ingramcontent.com/pod-product-compliance
Ingram Content Group UK Ltd.
Pitfield, Milton Keynes, MK11 3LW, UK
UKHW020926110825
461507UK00029B/197